SAVAGE DRAGON

GANG WAR

ERIK LARSEN

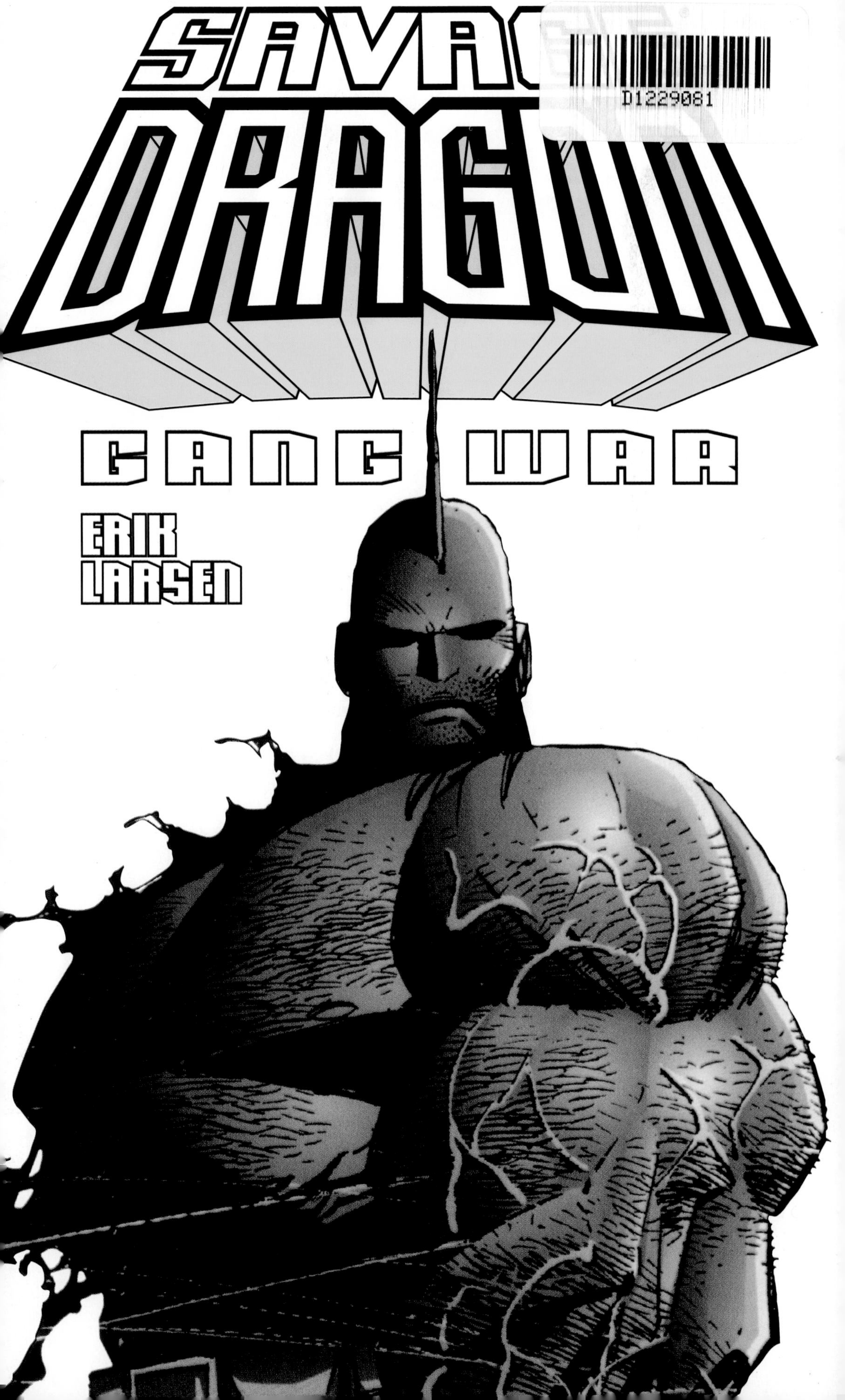

SAVAGE DRAGON

GANG WAR

ERIK LARSEN — Creator • Writer • Penciller • Inker

CHRIS ELIOPOULOS — Letterer

I.H.O.C — Colors
REUBEN RUDE, ABEL MOUTON
ANTONIO KOHL, BILL ZINDEL,
LEA RUDE, STEPHANE KRIESHOK,
ROBERTA TEWES & JOHN ZAIA

QUANTUM COLOR FX — Film Output

JOSH EICHORN — Still wonders why he wasn't picked for that "Who wants to marry a millionaire?" fiasco.

IMAGE COMICS

Jim Valentino	Publisher
Eric Stephenson	Director of Marketing
Brent Braun	Director of Production
Traci Hale	Controller/Foreign Licensing
Brett Evans	Art Director
Allen Hui	Web Developer
Cindie Espinoza	Accounting Assitant
Tim Hegarty	Book Trade Coordinator

DEDICATED TO
Jim Demonakos
& Evan Long

SAVAGE DRAGON VOL. VI: GANG WAR. OCTOBER 2003. SECOND PRINTING. Originally published in single mazazine format as Savage Dragon #22-26. An Image Comics Group title published by Image Comics 1071 Batavia St. Ste. A Orange, CA 92867. Image and its logos are ® and © 2003 Image Comics, Inc. The Savage Dragon® is a registered trademark Erik Larsen 2003. All other related characters are trademark and copyright© Erik Larsen 2003. All rights reserved. Any similarities to persons living or dead is purely coincidental. With the exception of artwork used for review purposes, none of the contents of this publication may be reprinted without the permission of Erik Larsen. Publisher and creators assume no responsibility for unsolicited materials. Printed in Canada.

WWW.IMAGECOMICS.COM

Introduction by Kurt Busiek.

've bought the original Savage Dragon mini-series five times now-once when it came out as the original issues, once when it was collected into a trade paperback, once when I stumbled over the Graphitti hardcover edition in a comics store in Berkeley (Comic Relief; hi Rory), once when it came out on CD-ROM, and once when Erik brought it out as a set of 99-cent issues. And if Erik ever collects the 99-cent version into a book, I'll buy that, too.

And it's all Paul Dini's fault.

See, I have to admit, I didn't much like a lot of Erik's earlier work. I think I first saw his stuff on DNAgents, where I thought it had promise. But I didn't enjoy his run on Doom Patrol, I didn't think he was appropriate for the stories or the general tone of The Punisher, and much as I thought he did a pretty nifty-looking Spider-Man, I wasn't wild about the rest of the book. His Peter Parker, his Mary Jane-when interpreted through Erik's idiosyncratic cartooning style, I didn't think they looked right. I couldn't get past the drawings as drawings, and get into the story.

So when that fateful bunch of artists walked away from Marvel and formed Image Comics, I wasn't planning on trying the Larsen book. I already knew enough to know I wasn't going to like it, right? And what kind of name was "The Savage Dragon"? It sounded dopey, it wasn't by a creator whose work I enjoyed, and it obviously wasn't for me.

And then, either at Wonder Con or the San Diego Con, Paul Dini ran into me and said, "Hey, have you tried this new Savage Dragon book? It's wild. It's funny as hell, and it's a hoot and a half. You've got to try it. Now. They're on sale over there. Go get one." And he wandered off to buttonhole someone else and make them buy the book too, and I figured what the heck, and went and bought one.

And now, Savage Dragon's my favorite straight-ahead superhero book going. So thanks, Paul-I owe you one.

The thing is, Paul was right. Savage Dragon is funny, and it's jam-packed with action, energy, and pound for pound, more goofy-ass super-villains than any other book in the history of comics. It's a great ride. But more-it's obvious from every page, from every line, that this is the book Erik Larsen was born to do.

Everything that put me off about his style before-the exaggerated cartooning, the overstated costume designs, the unrestrained Kirby-by-way-of-Miller-and-Kane graphics-all clicked into something that worked for me, and worked beautifully, from the very first scene in that first issue. Erik wasn't trying to tell someone else's story with his style, or work with someone else's characters-he was creating his own world from the ground up, and everything in that world was of a piece. Everything's bigger in Erik's world, bigger and louder. The heroes, the villains, the women (definitely the women!), but it all belongs that that way. It's the essence of cartooning-Erik has a vision, and he expresses that vision clearly, straightforwardly and entertainingly, without anyone else getting in the way. No inkers modifying his linework, no writers trying to force a different kind of pacing over his storytelling-it's pure Erik, so it all works together.

And it's fun. The action, the adventure, the running around and beating each other up-it's all high-energy, straightforward fun and games, and very enjoyable on that level. But as I read Savage Dragon, issue after issue, I found out that there was something else to it, too, that I liked even more.

The rhythms of the series, the pacing of it all, not just within the individual issues, but across the whole series, is different from most other superhero series. It's not all about the adventures, with the hero's private life as a kind of garnish, wedged in between the action and exposition scenes to keep the fights from all happening at once-it's simply about the hero's life, about his day-to-day existence as he struggles with the business of life, love, work and just getting by. His work simply involves butting heads with giant, superstrong chickens and gorillas with exposed brains, that's all (and his love life involves fiends from hell, possessive girlfriends with lightning powers and starstruck superstrong nutcases, for that matter). He lives in Larsen World, where everything's bigger, louder and wilder-but he's still just doing what any of us do. Getting by, one day at a time, and dealing with whatever life throws at him. What he gets thrown at him is weirder than what we generally deal with, but it's still the same mindset. Deal with it, and keep going.

I can't explain it more clearly than that. I don't know just what it is about Erik's approach, about how he tells his stories, that gives it this quality. I wish I did, because then I'd be able to do it, too, but suffice it to say that there's something different about Savage Dragon, something that, for all the unrealistic, over-the-top, in-your-face outrageousness of it all, makes it all the more real, because there's real emotions and real, human reactions driving the whole thing.

Savage Dragon has heart, and that makes it all the more affecting and involving than most other books, no matter how dizzying the technique or realistic the lighting.

So why did I end up buying that first mini-series five times? Well, there's a story to that, and it actually has something to do with the book you're holding.

I went on for a while, up above, about how distinctive and different Savage Dragon is. That's an approach Erik takes to just about every facet of the book, not just the writing and drawing of each monthly issue. He also takes care to make each package-be it the comic, a book collection, a reprint, whatever-work on its own terms, as a satisfying package. Each book is not simply an archival collection of the stories as they appeared in the comics, but a book, designed to read like a book, as a single narrative.

When collecting the mini-series into book form, Erik rearranged the pages, taking apart the individual issue structures and running it all chronologically. He added a couple of short stories into the mix, and wrote and drew new pages to bridge them all together. And the result is a booklength story that makes no attempt to give the reader exactly what he'd get if he was reading the magazines. Why should it? It's not the magazines-it's a book. And just as writers who used to serialize their novels in magazines would re-edit them into books, Erik does the same with Savage Dragon.

Some people don't like that. Me, I love it.

Erik doesn't do so much rearranging of scenes any more, but he will add pages to bridge a scene, or to expand on something that couldn't fit before-and there are a few examples of that in this book. You won't notice them, though, unless you read the individual issues. Those extra pages aren't about getting readers to buy the book for those few more moments of story, but about making it just as well-crafted a reading experience as a book as it was as a comic.

So I bought the mini-series because Paul Dini made me, and it was terrific.

And I bought the trade paperback because I like books-and I was delighted with the way Erik reworked the package.

And then I found out there was a hardcover, and since I liked the book so much, I "upgraded" to the cooler format.

And then there was a CD-ROM, with all the early issues, plus reprints of the Graphic Fantasy stories and an interview with Erik, and I had to buy that, too. Actually, I bought it because it came as a package with a Savage Dragon screensaver that looked pretty neat, but the damn screensaver didn't work on the Mac. Grumble grumble.

And then Erik put out a 99-cent reprint mini-series of that original material, expanding what was once three issues to five, and once again adding more material to the package, to make them work as what they were. And I bought that, too-and even with all the new stuff, it was less expensive than the original mini-series. How cool is that?

And I'll admit it-if Erik ever collects the expanded reprint mini into a book, I'll get that, too, without even flinching...

Erik's got commitment. He's got dedication. He cares about each and every character, every story, every scene. And he never stops trying new things. If you're a regular reader, you know that already. If this is your first experience with the book, you'll see that on display here-not only in the hundreds of Vicious Circle goons Erik made up for the gangwar sequences (my favorites are the Rumble Brothers, but you'll have your own), but in things like the taxi driver and his overvoice narration; a new technique for Savage Dragon, and one that Erik uses very well.

[See, Erik? I did say something about the actual stories!]

So give yourself up to Larsen World-you're in good hands, and you'll have a great time.

And by way of closing, I'll leave you with a song-the theme song I wrote when I heard there was going to be a Savage Dragon cartoon:

> "Heee's savage, he's a dragon,
> He's the Savage Dragon!
> Crooks he'll whop 'cause he's a cop,
> He's the Savage Draaaaa-gon!"

Okay, okay. I'll stick to my day job. But the real fun starts in a page or two. Go ahead-dive right in.

- Kurt Busiek
December 1999

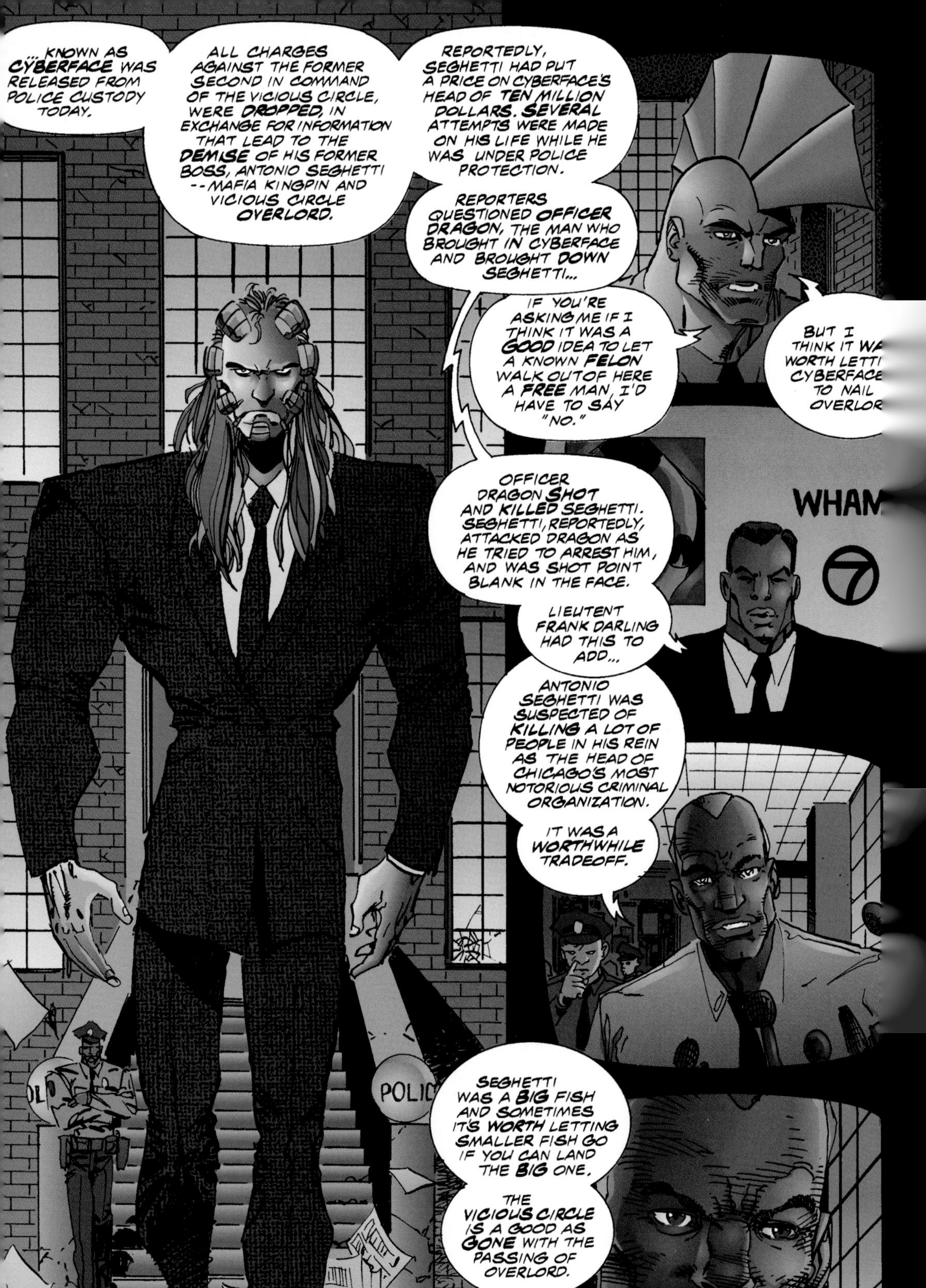

...KNOWN AS CYBERFACE WAS RELEASED FROM POLICE CUSTODY TODAY.
ALL CHARGES AGAINST THE FORMER SECOND IN COMMAND OF THE VICIOUS CIRCLE, WERE DROPPED, IN EXCHANGE FOR INFORMATION THAT LEAD TO THE DEMISE OF HIS FORMER BOSS, ANTONIO SEGHETTI --MAFIA KINGPIN AND VICIOUS CIRCLE OVERLORD.
REPORTEDLY, SEGHETTI HAD PUT A PRICE ON CYBERFACE'S HEAD OF TEN MILLION DOLLARS. SEVERAL ATTEMPTS WERE MADE ON HIS LIFE WHILE HE WAS UNDER POLICE PROTECTION.
REPORTERS QUESTIONED OFFICER DRAGON, THE MAN WHO BROUGHT IN CYBERFACE AND BROUGHT DOWN SEGHETTI...
IF YOU'RE ASKING ME IF I THINK IT WAS A GOOD IDEA TO LET A KNOWN FELON WALK OUT OF HERE A FREE MAN, I'D HAVE TO SAY "NO."
BUT I THINK IT WA WORTH LETTI CYBERFACE TO NAIL OVERLOR
WHAM
7
OFFICER DRAGON SHOT AND KILLED SEGHETTI. SEGHETTI, REPORTEDLY, ATTACKED DRAGON AS HE TRIED TO ARREST HIM, AND WAS SHOT POINT BLANK IN THE FACE.
LIEUTENT FRANK DARLING HAD THIS TO ADD...
ANTONIO SEGHETTI WAS SUSPECTED OF KILLING A LOT OF PEOPLE IN HIS REIN AS THE HEAD OF CHICAGO'S MOST NOTORIOUS CRIMINAL ORGANIZATION.
IT WAS A WORTHWHILE TRADEOFF.
SEGHETTI WAS A BIG FISH AND SOMETIMES IT'S WORTH LETTING SMALLER FISH GO IF YOU CAN LAND THE BIG ONE.
THE VICIOUS CIRCLE IS A GOOD AS GONE WITH THE PASSING OF OVERLORD.
I HOPE THAT CYBERFACE USES HIS FREEDOM WISELY.

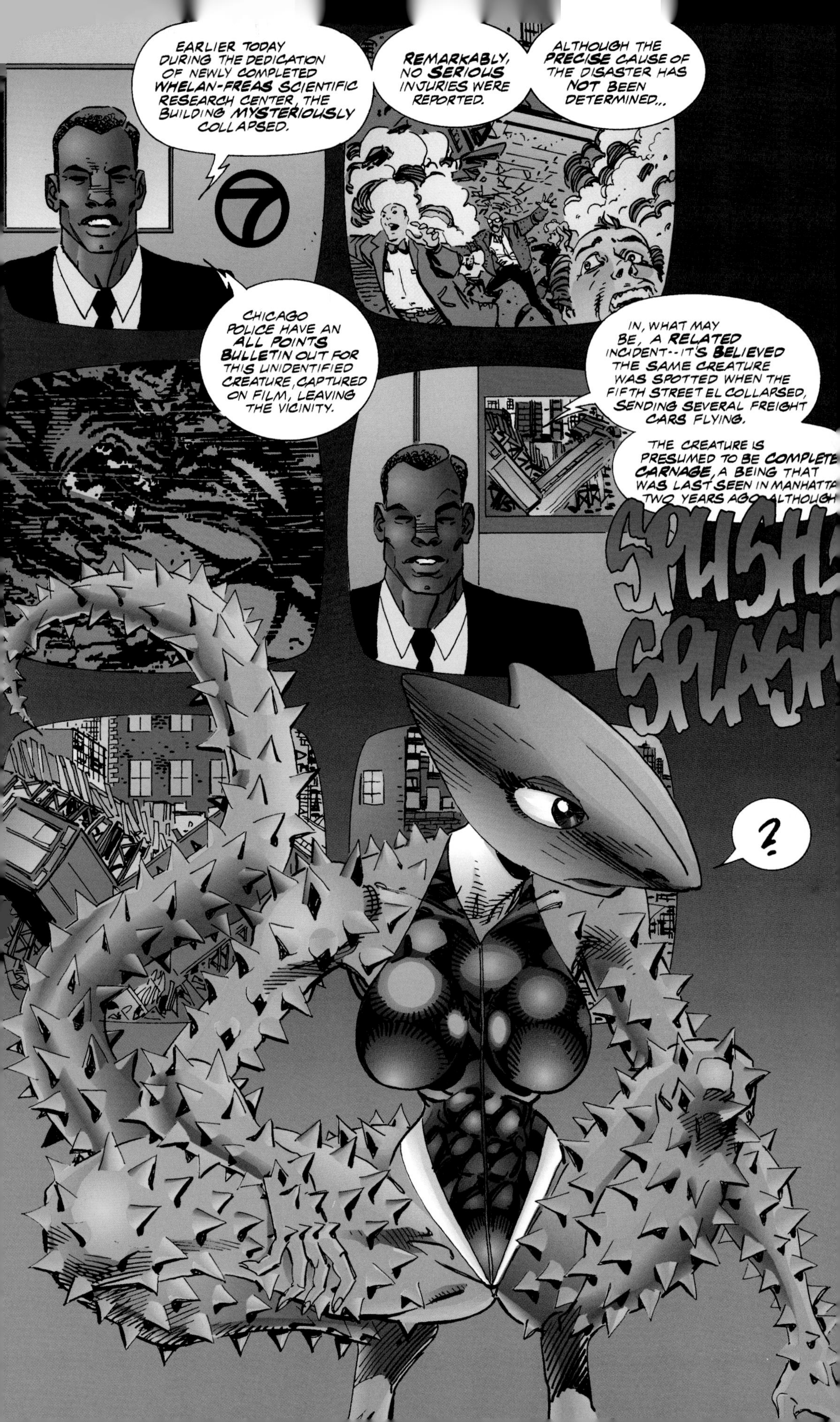
EARLIER TODAY DURING THE DEDICATION OF NEWLY COMPLETED WHELAN-FREAS SCIENTIFIC RESEARCH CENTER, THE BUILDING MYSTERIOUSLY COLLAPSED.
REMARKABLY, NO SERIOUS INJURIES WERE REPORTED.
ALTHOUGH THE PRECISE CAUSE OF THE DISASTER HAS NOT BEEN DETERMINED...
CHICAGO POLICE HAVE AN ALL POINTS BULLETIN OUT FOR THIS UNIDENTIFIED CREATURE, CAPTURED ON FILM, LEAVING THE VICINITY.
IN, WHAT MAY BE, A RELATED INCIDENT--IT'S BELIEVED THE SAME CREATURE WAS SPOTTED WHEN THE FIFTH STREET EL COLLAPSED, SENDING SEVERAL FREIGHT CARS FLYING.
THE CREATURE IS PRESUMED TO BE COMPLETE CARNAGE, A BEING THAT WAS LAST SEEN IN MANHATTA TWO YEARS AGO ALTHOUGH
?

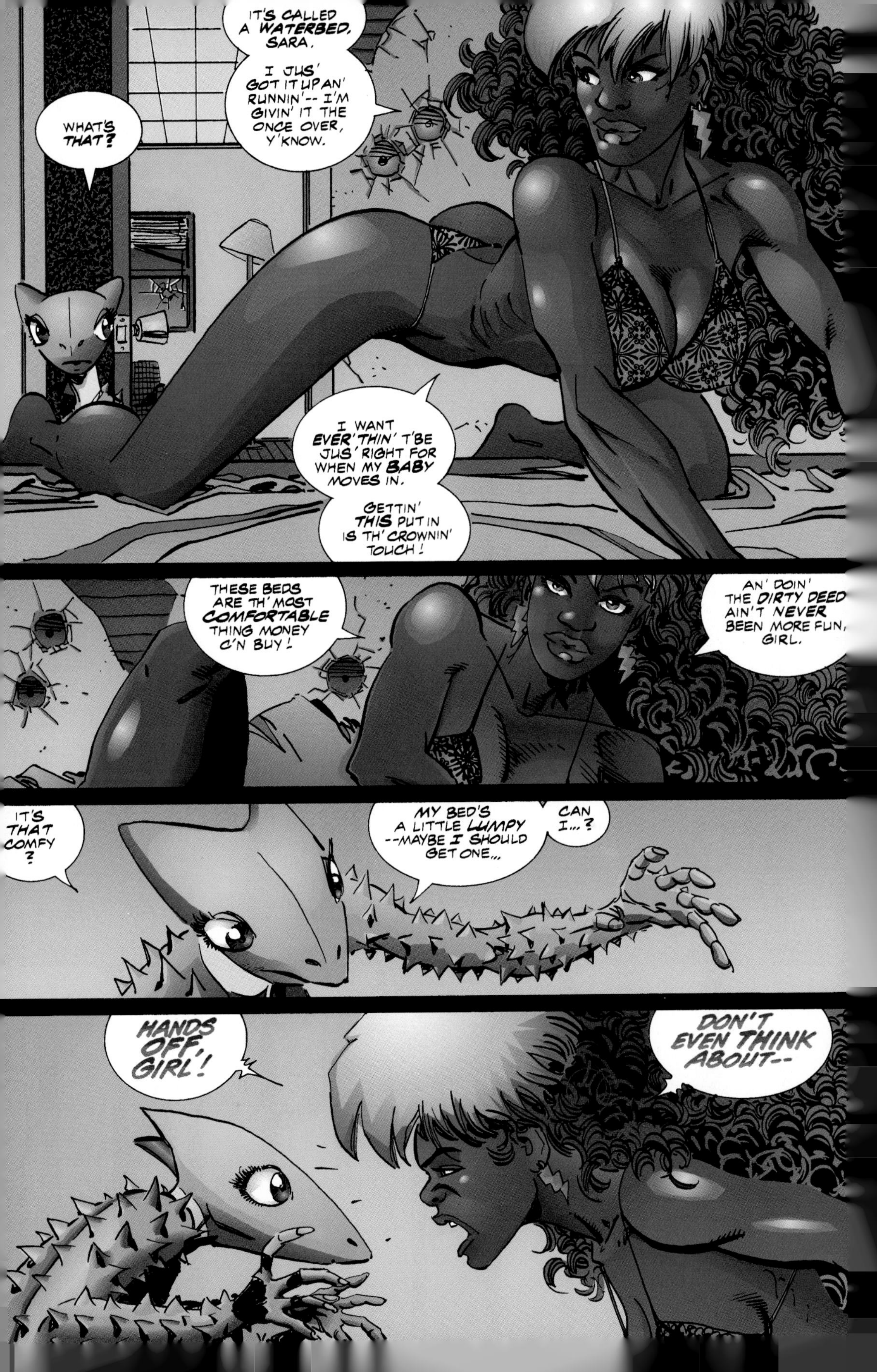
WHAT'S THAT?
IT'S CALLED A WATERBED, SARA.
I JUS' GOT IT UP AN' RUNNIN'-- I'M GIVIN' IT THE ONCE OVER, Y'KNOW.
I WANT EVER'THIN' T'BE JUS' RIGHT FOR WHEN MY BABY MOVES IN.
GETTIN' THIS PUT IN IS TH' CROWNIN' TOUCH!
THESE BEDS ARE TH' MOST COMFORTABLE THING MONEY C'N BUY!
AN' DOIN' THE DIRTY DEED AIN'T NEVER BEEN MORE FUN, GIRL.
IT'S THAT COMFY?
MY BED'S A LITTLE LUMPY --MAYBE I SHOULD GET ONE...
CAN I...?
HANDS OFF, GIRL!
DON'T EVEN THINK ABOUT--

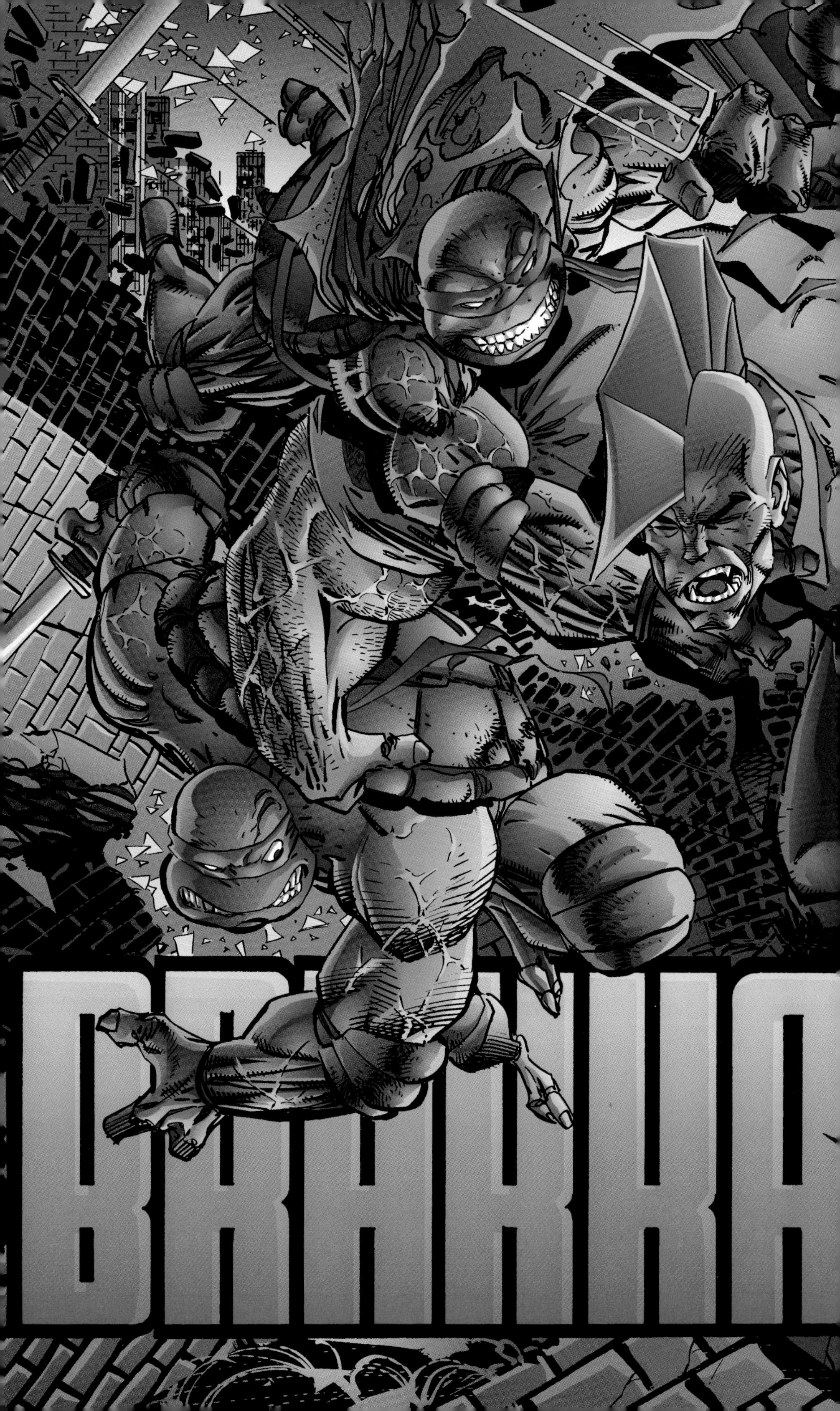

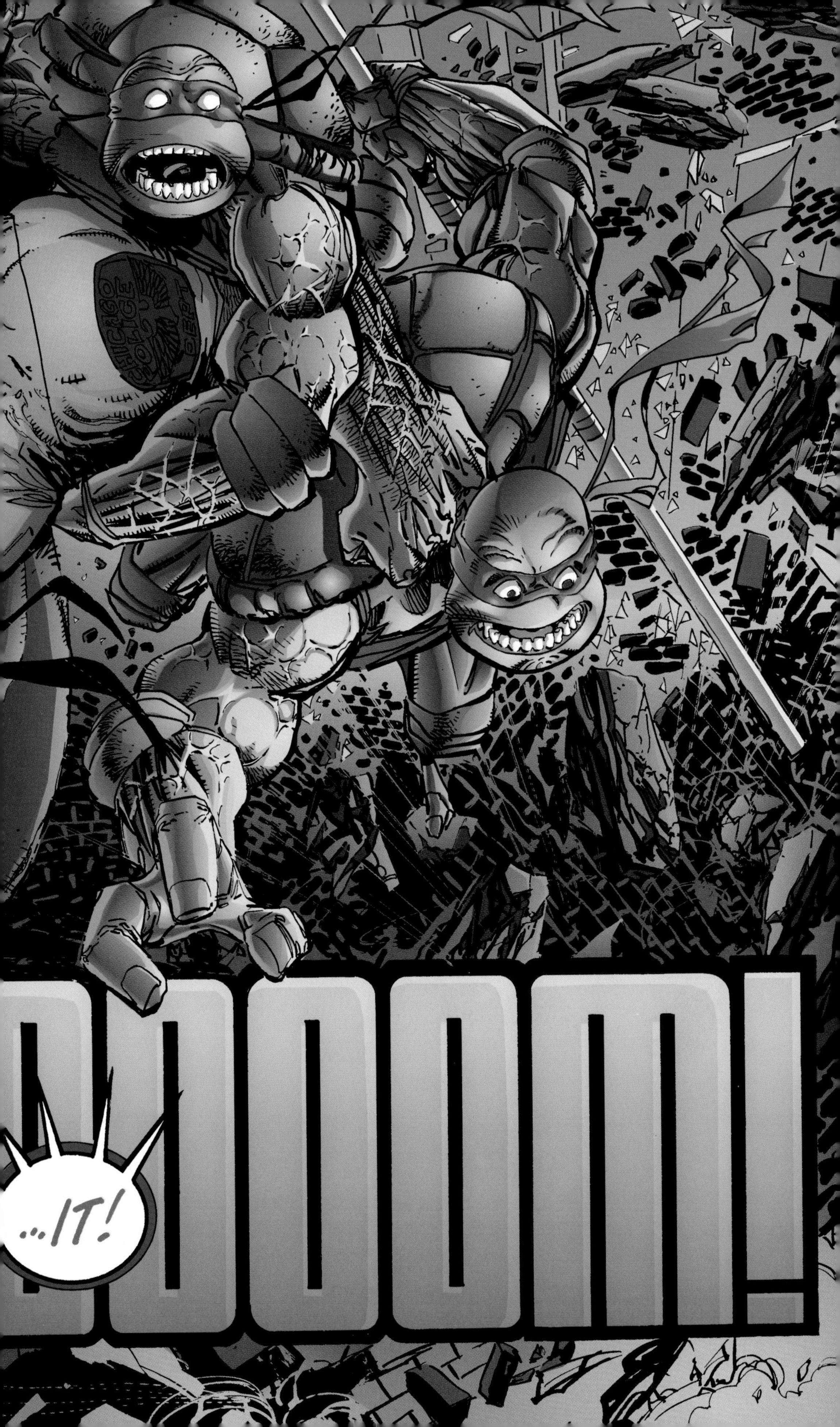
OOOM!
...IT!

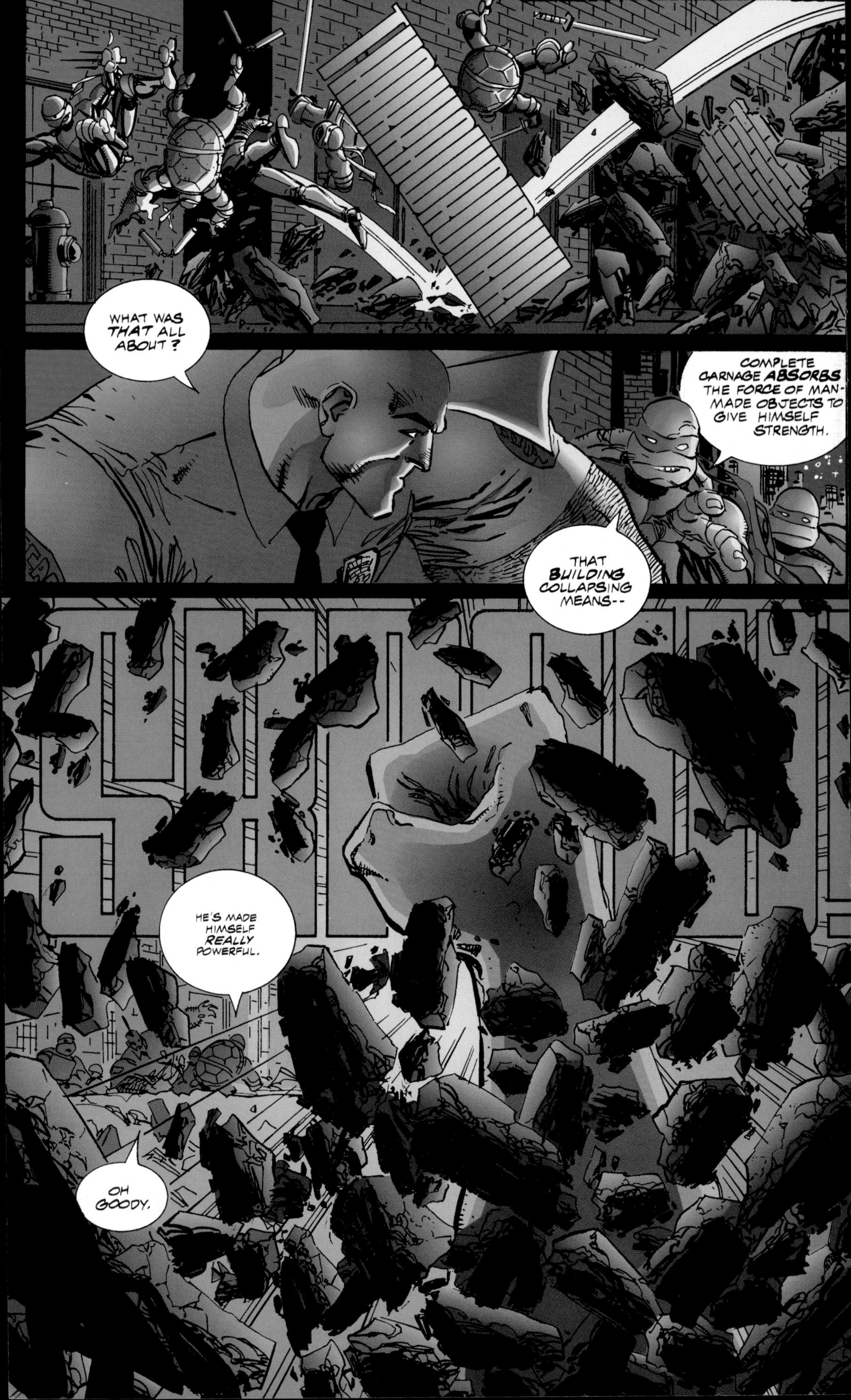
WHAT WAS THAT ALL ABOUT?
COMPLETE CARNAGE ABSORBS THE FORCE OF MAN-MADE OBJECTS TO GIVE HIMSELF STRENGTH.
THAT BUILDING COLLAPSING MEANS--
HE'S MADE HIMSELF REALLY POWERFUL.
OH GOODY.

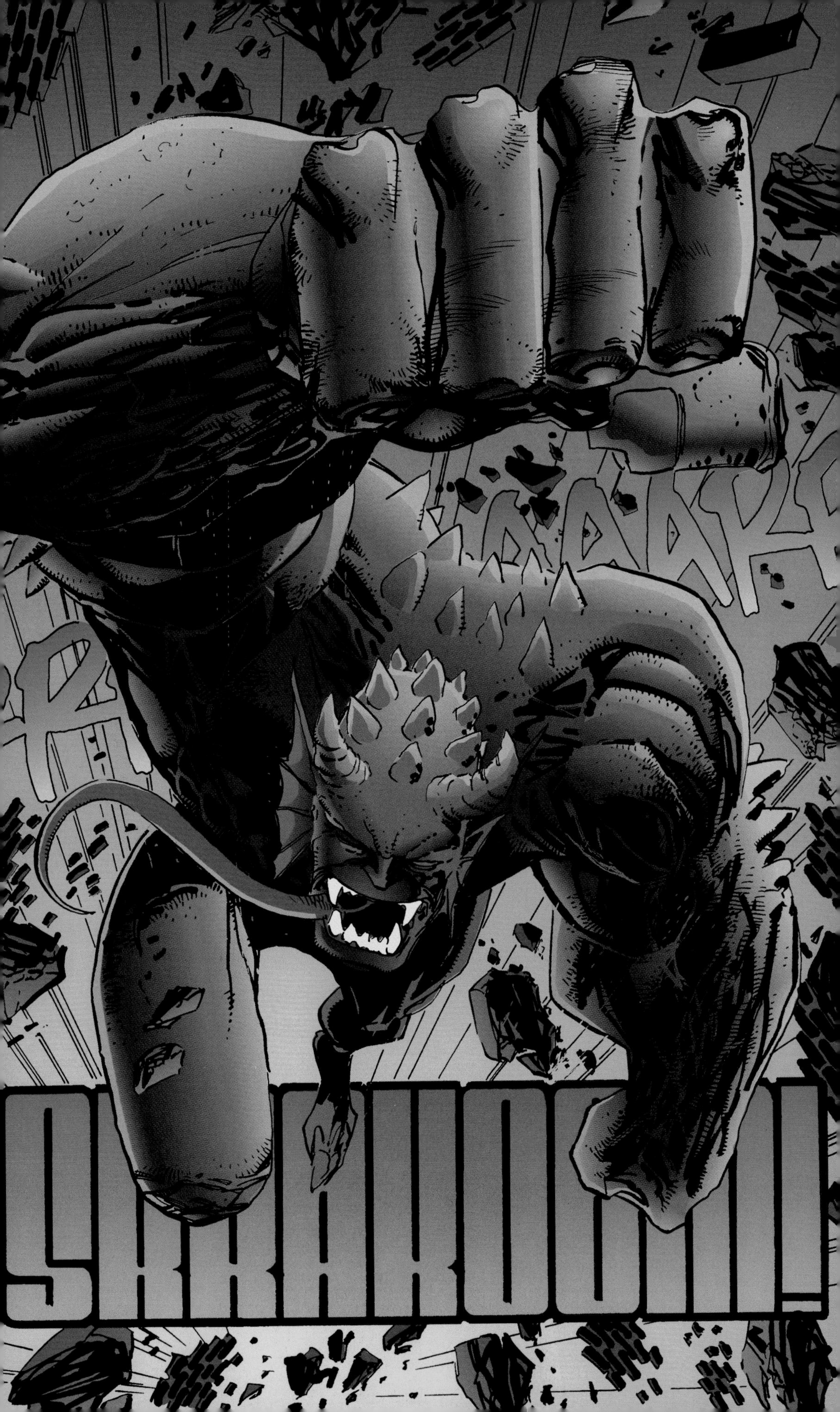
SKRAKOOM!

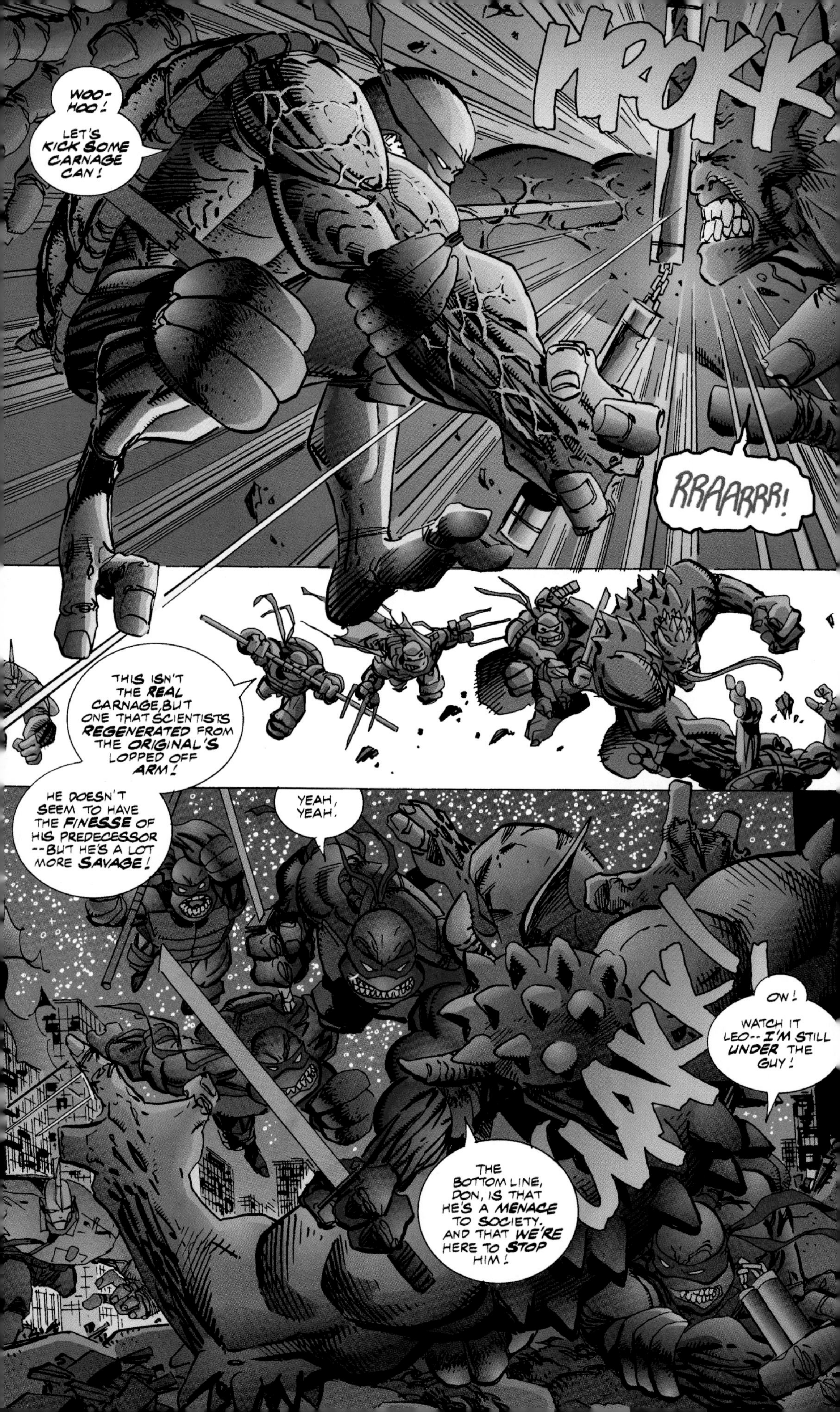

KRAKK
WOO-HOO! LET'S KICK SOME CARNAGE CAN!
RRAARRR!
THIS ISN'T THE REAL CARNAGE, BUT ONE THAT SCIENTISTS REGENERATED FROM THE ORIGINAL'S LOPPED OFF ARM!
HE DOESN'T SEEM TO HAVE THE FINESSE OF HIS PREDECESSOR --BUT HE'S A LOT MORE SAVAGE!
YEAH, YEAH.
OW! WATCH IT LEO-- I'M STILL UNDER THE GUY!
THE BOTTOM LINE, DON, IS THAT HE'S A MENACE TO SOCIETY. AND THAT WE'RE HERE TO STOP HIM!

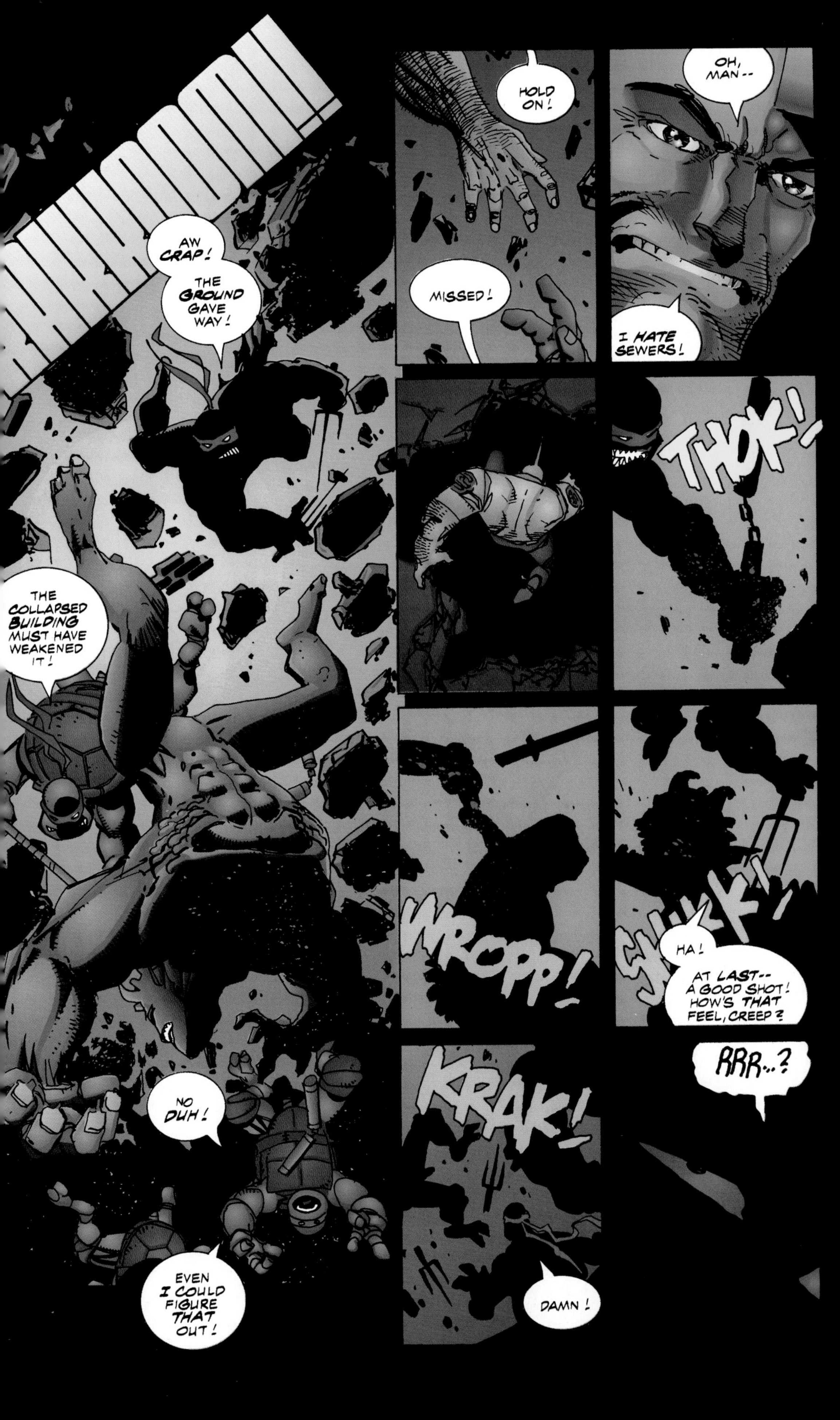
AW CRAP!
THE GROUND GAVE WAY!
THE COLLAPSED BUILDING MUST HAVE WEAKENED IT!
NO DUH!
EVEN I COULD FIGURE THAT OUT!
HOLD ON!
MISSED!
OH, MAN--
I HATE SEWERS!
THOK!
WROPP!
HA!
AT LAST-- A GOOD SHOT! HOW'S THAT FEEL, CREEP?
KRAK!
DAMN!
RRR..?

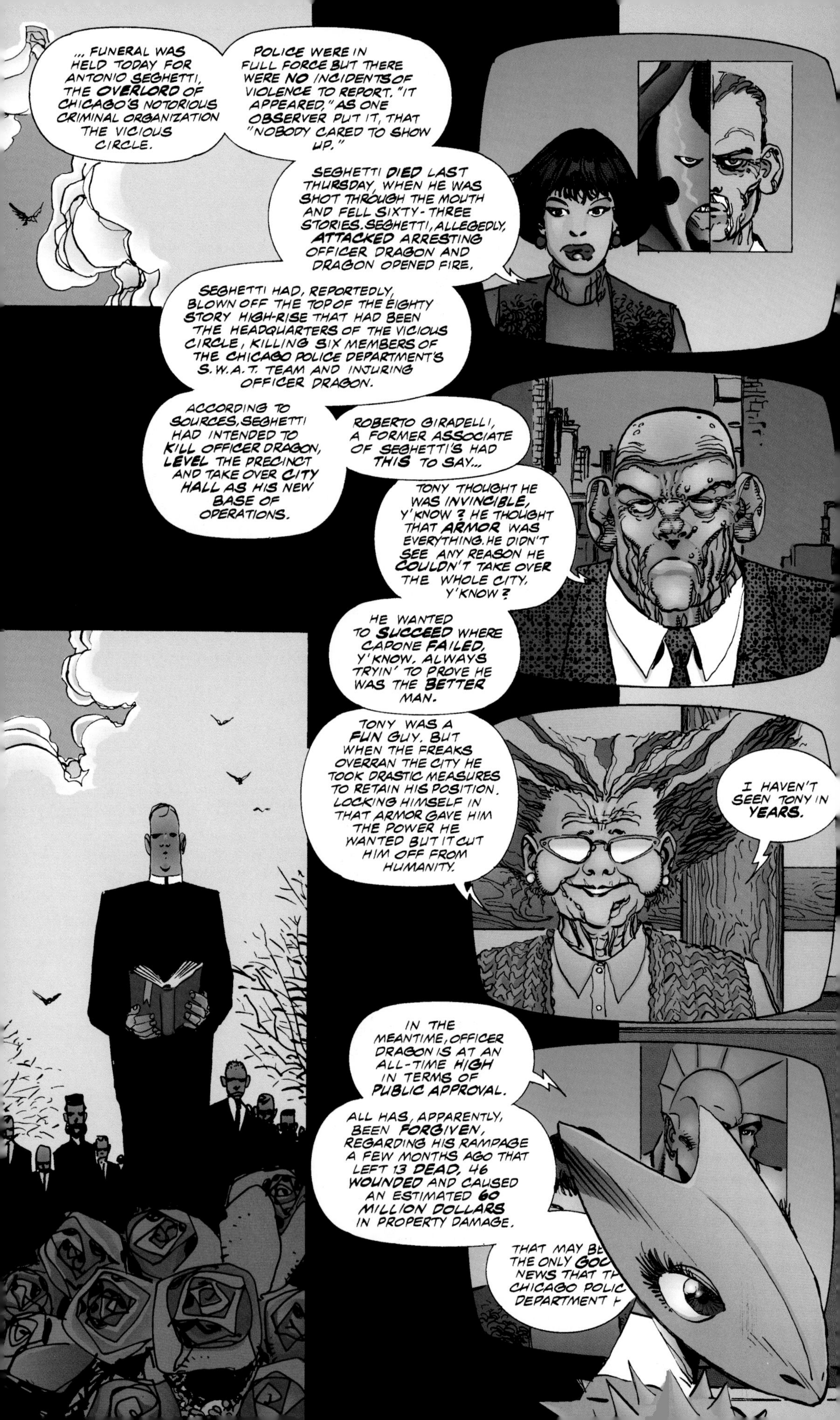
... FUNERAL WAS HELD TODAY FOR ANTONIO SEGHETTI, THE OVERLORD OF CHICAGO'S NOTORIOUS CRIMINAL ORGANIZATION THE VICIOUS CIRCLE.
POLICE WERE IN FULL FORCE BUT THERE WERE NO INCIDENTS OF VIOLENCE TO REPORT. "IT APPEARED," AS ONE OBSERVER PUT IT, THAT "NOBODY CARED TO SHOW UP."
SEGHETTI DIED LAST THURSDAY, WHEN HE WAS SHOT THROUGH THE MOUTH AND FELL SIXTY-THREE STORIES. SEGHETTI, ALLEGEDLY, ATTACKED ARRESTING OFFICER DRAGON AND DRAGON OPENED FIRE.
SEGHETTI HAD, REPORTEDLY, BLOWN OFF THE TOP OF THE EIGHTY STORY HIGH-RISE THAT HAD BEEN THE HEADQUARTERS OF THE VICIOUS CIRCLE, KILLING SIX MEMBERS OF THE CHICAGO POLICE DEPARTMENT'S S.W.A.T. TEAM AND INJURING OFFICER DRAGON.
ACCORDING TO SOURCES, SEGHETTI HAD INTENDED TO KILL OFFICER DRAGON, LEVEL THE PRECINCT AND TAKE OVER CITY HALL AS HIS NEW BASE OF OPERATIONS.
ROBERTO GIRADELLI, A FORMER ASSOCIATE OF SEGHETTI'S HAD THIS TO SAY...
TONY THOUGHT HE WAS INVINCIBLE, Y'KNOW? HE THOUGHT THAT ARMOR WAS EVERYTHING. HE DIDN'T SEE ANY REASON HE COULDN'T TAKE OVER THE WHOLE CITY, Y'KNOW?
HE WANTED TO SUCCEED WHERE CAPONE FAILED, Y'KNOW. ALWAYS TRYIN' TO PROVE HE WAS THE BETTER MAN.
TONY WAS A FUN GUY. BUT WHEN THE FREAKS OVERRAN THE CITY HE TOOK DRASTIC MEASURES TO RETAIN HIS POSITION. LOCKING HIMSELF IN THAT ARMOR GAVE HIM THE POWER HE WANTED BUT IT CUT HIM OFF FROM HUMANITY.
I HAVEN'T SEEN TONY IN YEARS.
IN THE MEANTIME, OFFICER DRAGON IS AT AN ALL-TIME HIGH IN TERMS OF PUBLIC APPROVAL.
ALL HAS, APPARENTLY, BEEN FORGIVEN, REGARDING HIS RAMPAGE A FEW MONTHS AGO THAT LEFT 13 DEAD, 46 WOUNDED AND CAUSED AN ESTIMATED 60 MILLION DOLLARS IN PROPERTY DAMAGE.
THAT MAY BE THE ONLY GOO NEWS THAT TH CHICAGO POLIC DEPARTMENT

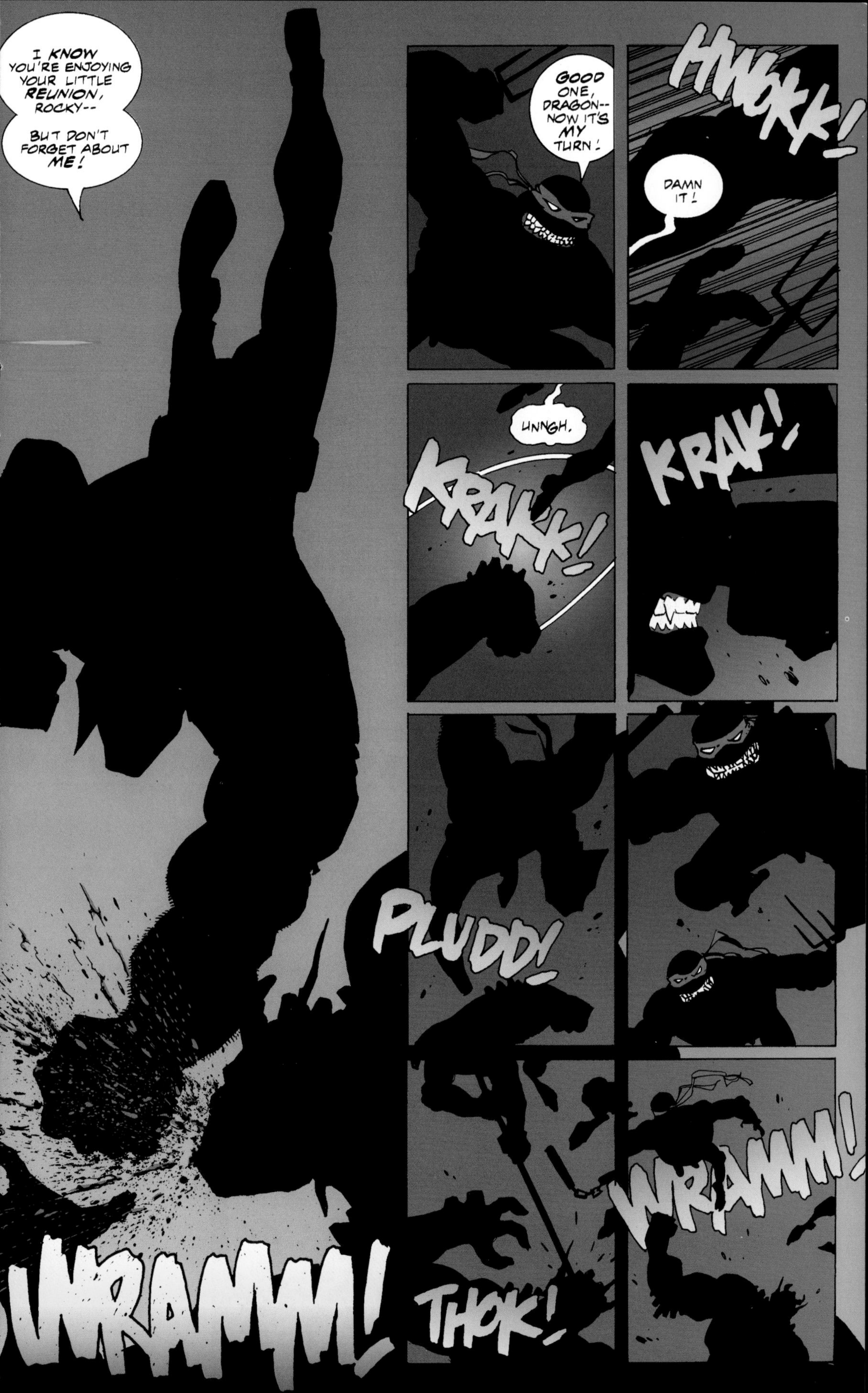
I KNOW YOU'RE ENJOYING YOUR LITTLE REUNION, ROCKY--
BUT DON'T FORGET ABOUT ME!
GOOD ONE, DRAGON-- NOW IT'S MY TURN!
HWOKK!
DAMN IT!
UNNGH.
KRAKK!
KRAK!
PLUDD!
WRAMM!
THOK!
WRAMMM!

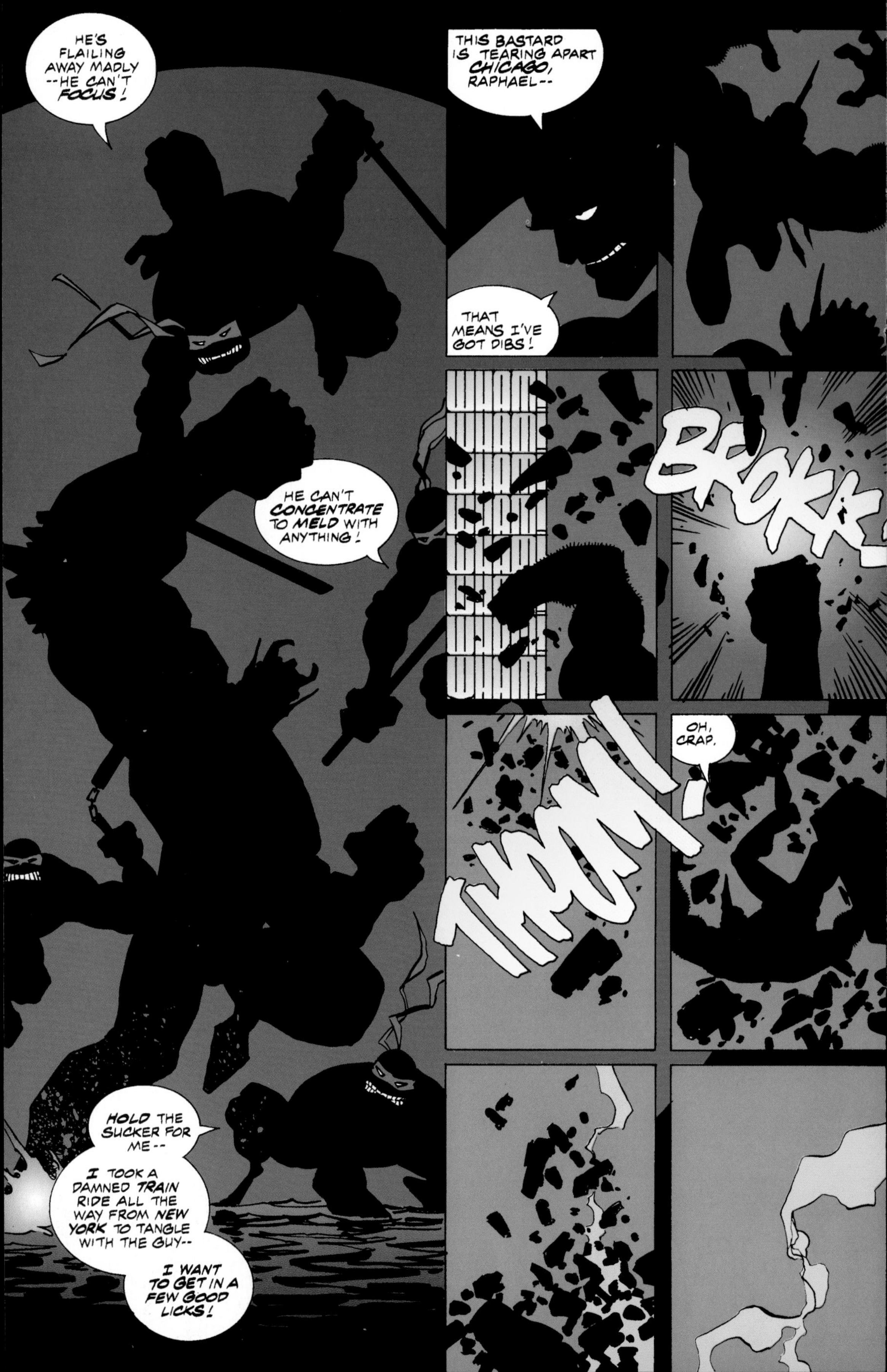
HE'S FLAILING AWAY MADLY --HE CAN'T FOCUS!
HE CAN'T CONCENTRATE TO MELD WITH ANYTHING!
HOLD THE SUCKER FOR ME--
I TOOK A DAMNED TRAIN RIDE ALL THE WAY FROM NEW YORK TO TANGLE WITH THE GUY--
I WANT TO GET IN A FEW GOOD LICKS!
THIS BASTARD IS TEARING APART CHICAGO, RAPHAEL--
THAT MEANS I'VE GOT DIBS!
WHAM! WHAM! WHAM! WHAM! WHAM! WHAM! WHAM! WHAM!
BROKK
THOOM!
OH, CRAP.

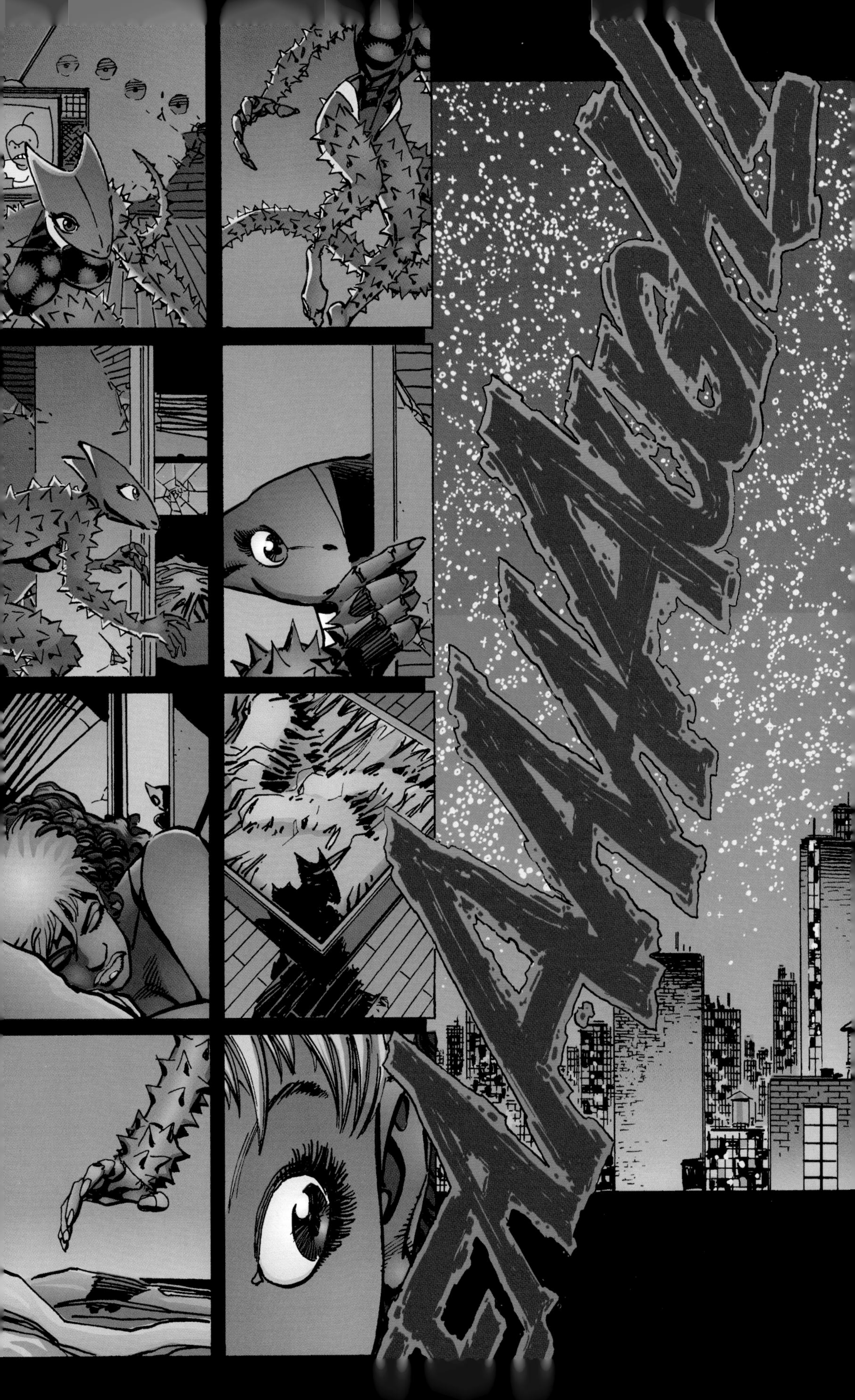

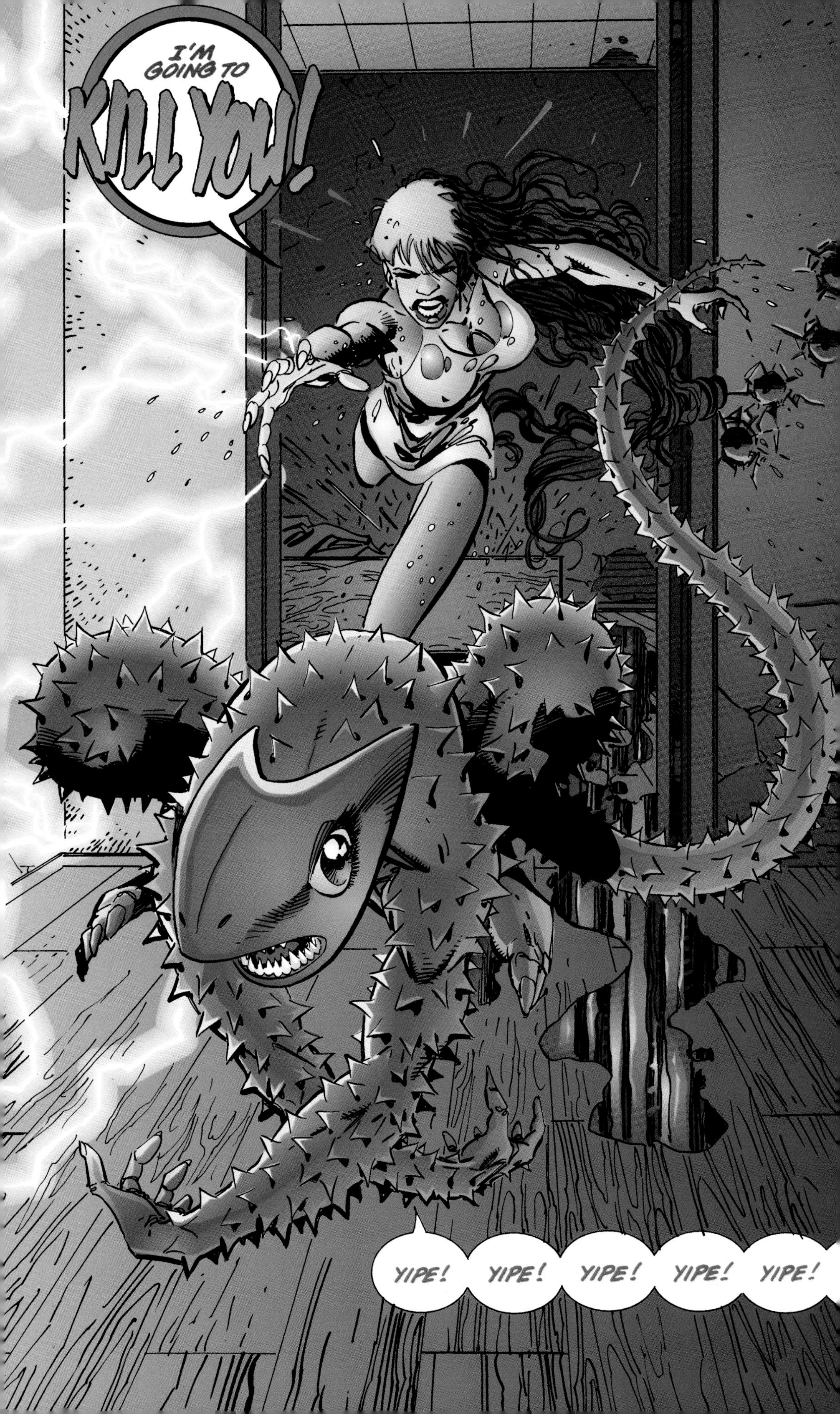
I'M GOING TO KILL YOU!
YIPE! YIPE! YIPE! YIPE! YIPE!

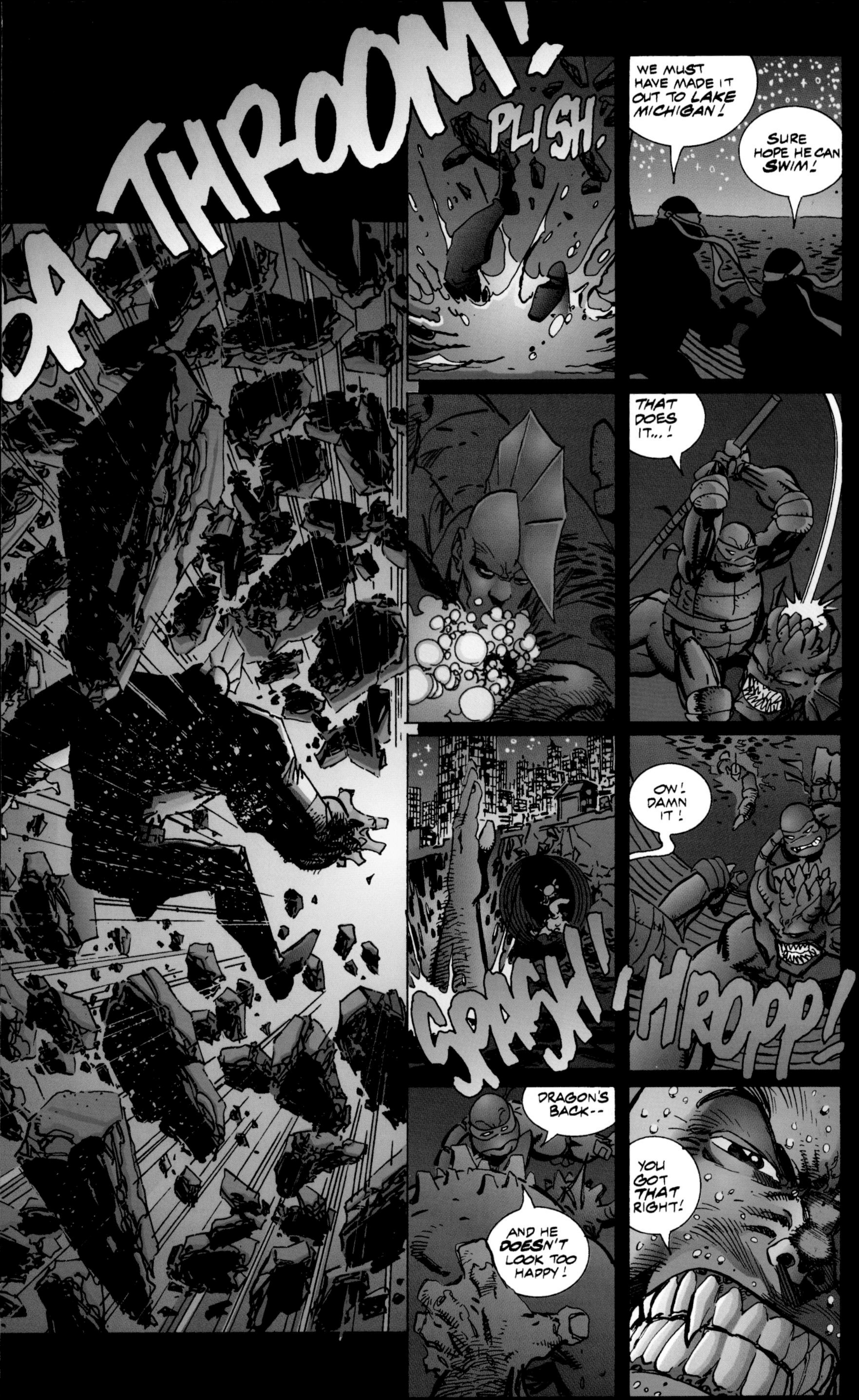
KA-THROOM!
PLISH
WE MUST HAVE MADE IT OUT TO LAKE MICHIGAN!
SURE HOPE HE CAN SWIM!
THAT DOES IT...!
OW! DAMN IT!
CRASH!
HROPP!
DRAGON'S BACK--
AND HE DOESN'T LOOK TOO HAPPY!
YOU GOT THAT RIGHT!

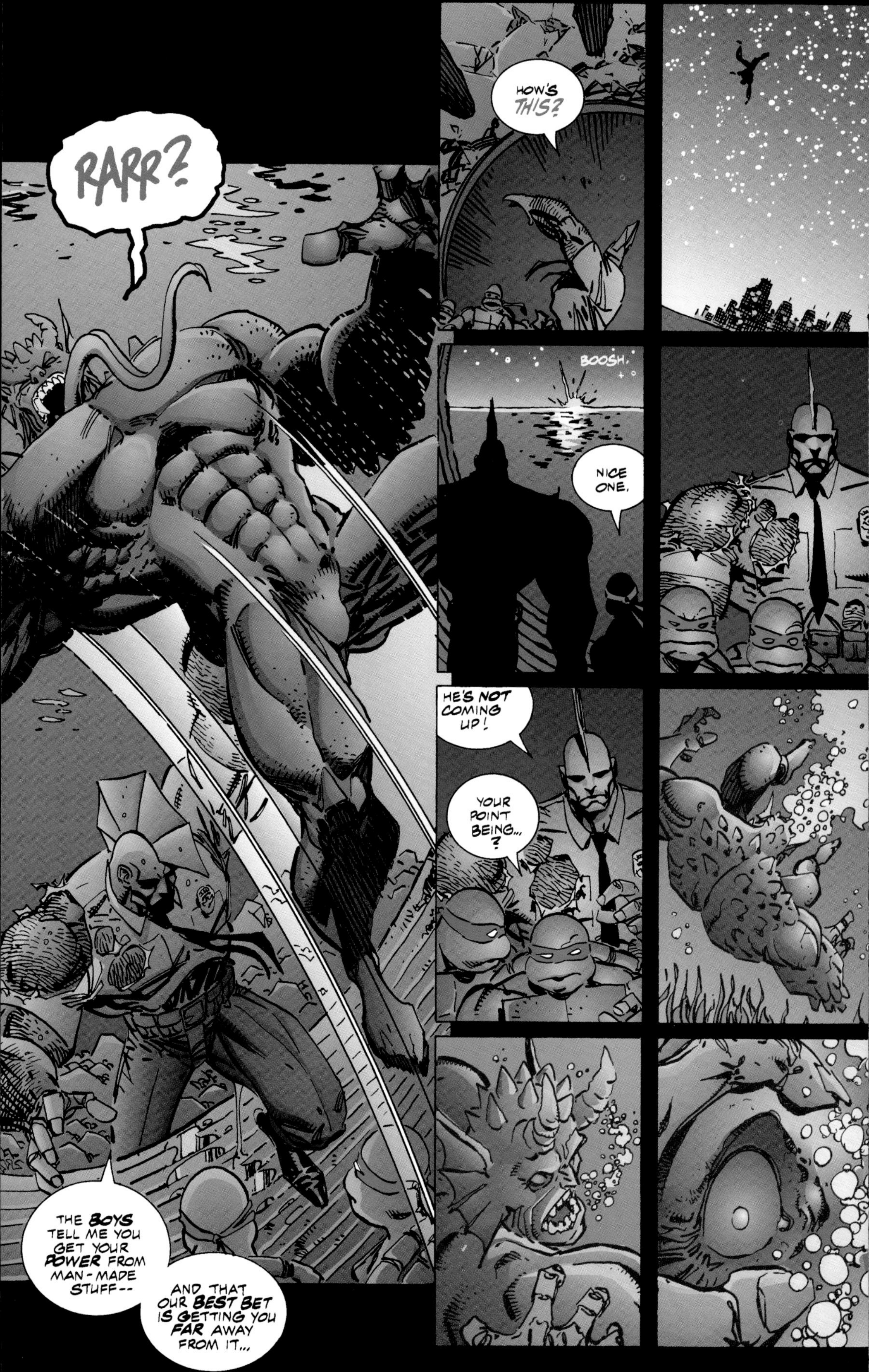
RARR?
THE BOYS TELL ME YOU GET YOUR POWER FROM MAN-MADE STUFF--
AND THAT OUR BEST BET IS GETTING YOU FAR AWAY FROM IT...
HOW'S THIS?
BOOSH
NICE ONE.
HE'S NOT COMING UP!
YOUR POINT BEING...?

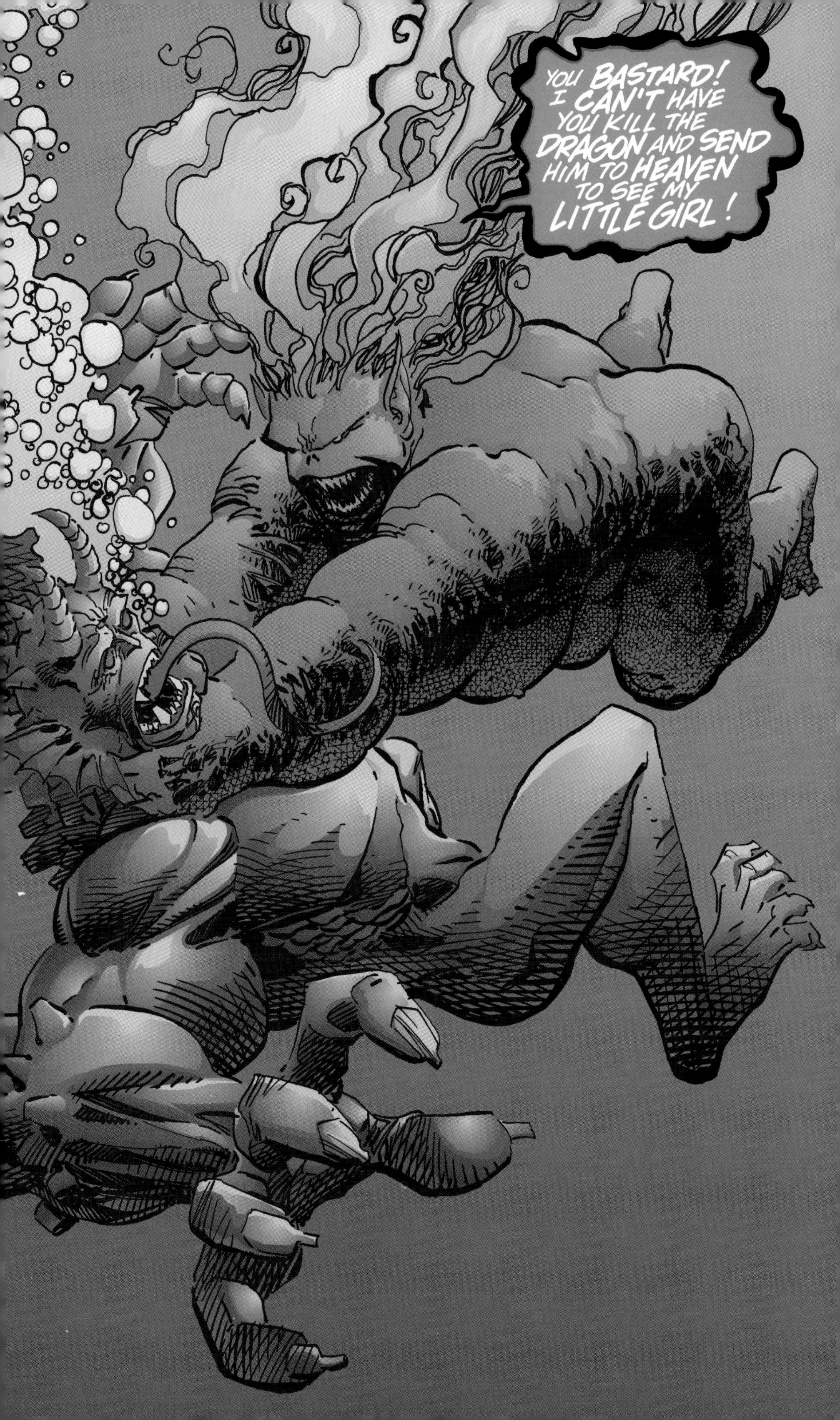
YOU BASTARD! I CAN'T HAVE YOU KILL THE DRAGON AND SEND HIM TO HEAVEN TO SEE MY LITTLE GIRL!

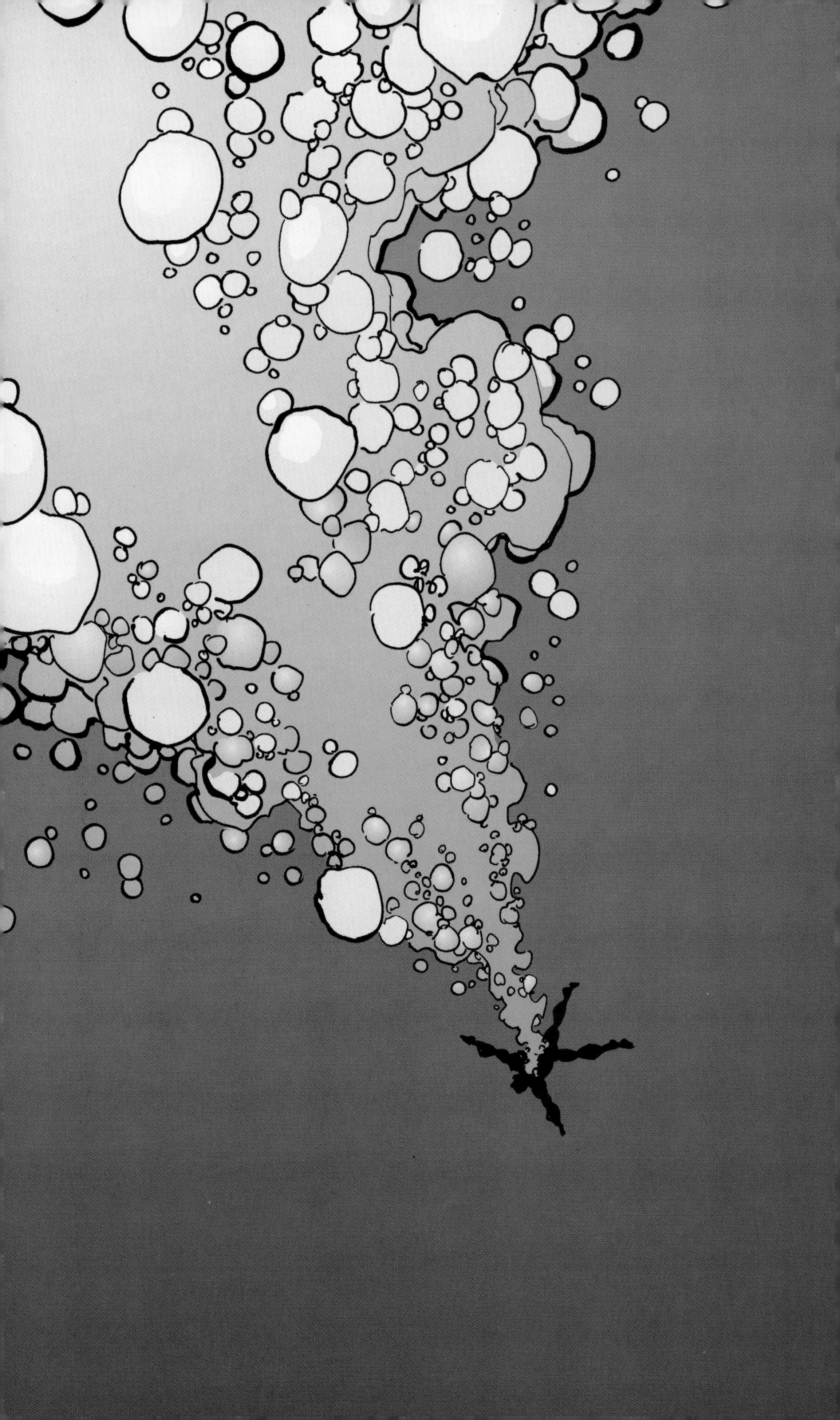

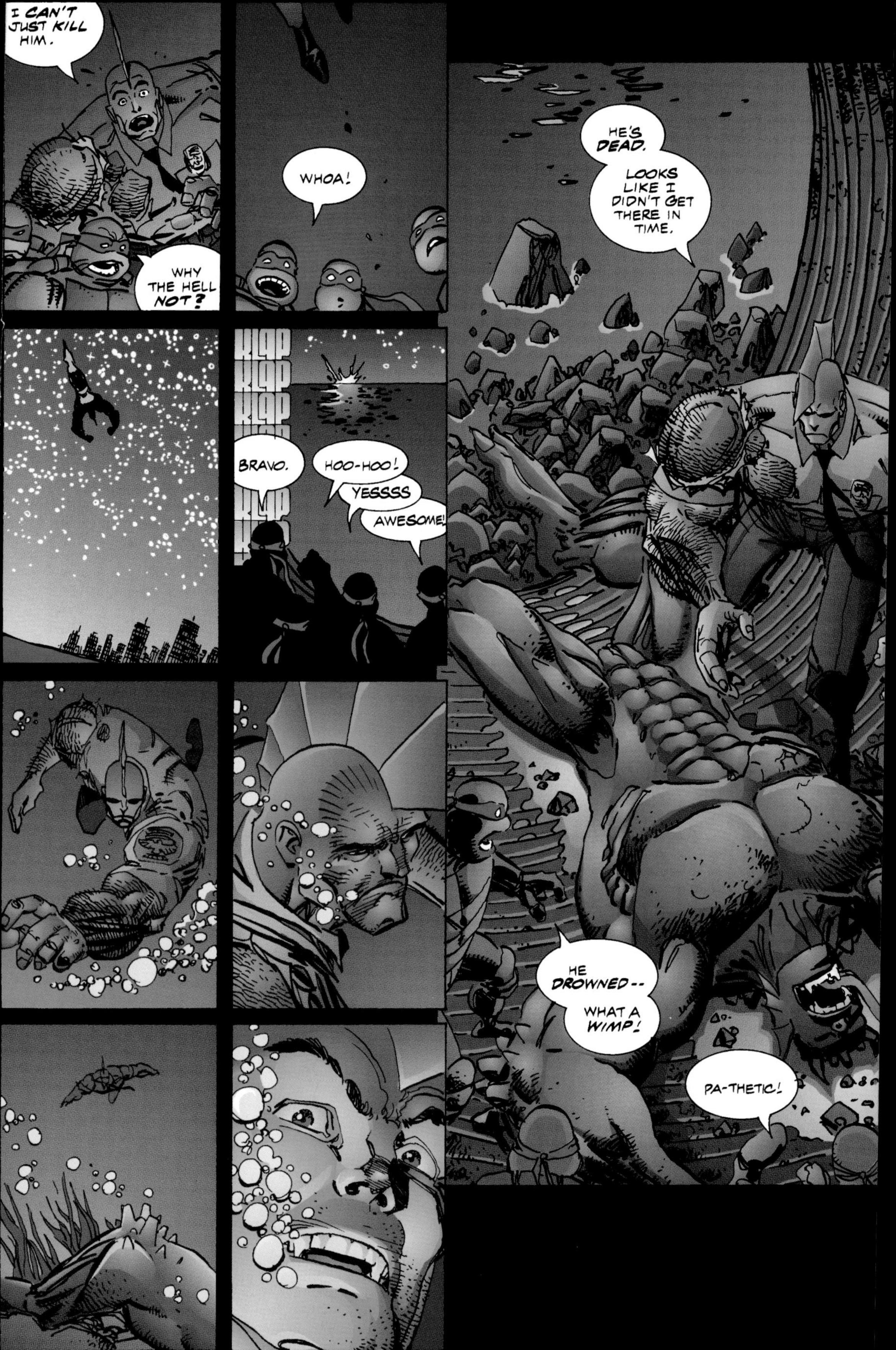
I CAN'T JUST KILL HIM.
WHY THE HELL NOT?
WHOA!
KLAP KLAP KLAP KLAP KLAP
BRAVO.
HOO-HOO!
YESSSS
AWESOME!
HE'S DEAD.
LOOKS LIKE I DIDN'T GET THERE IN TIME.
HE DROWNED--
WHAT A WIMP!
PA-THETIC!

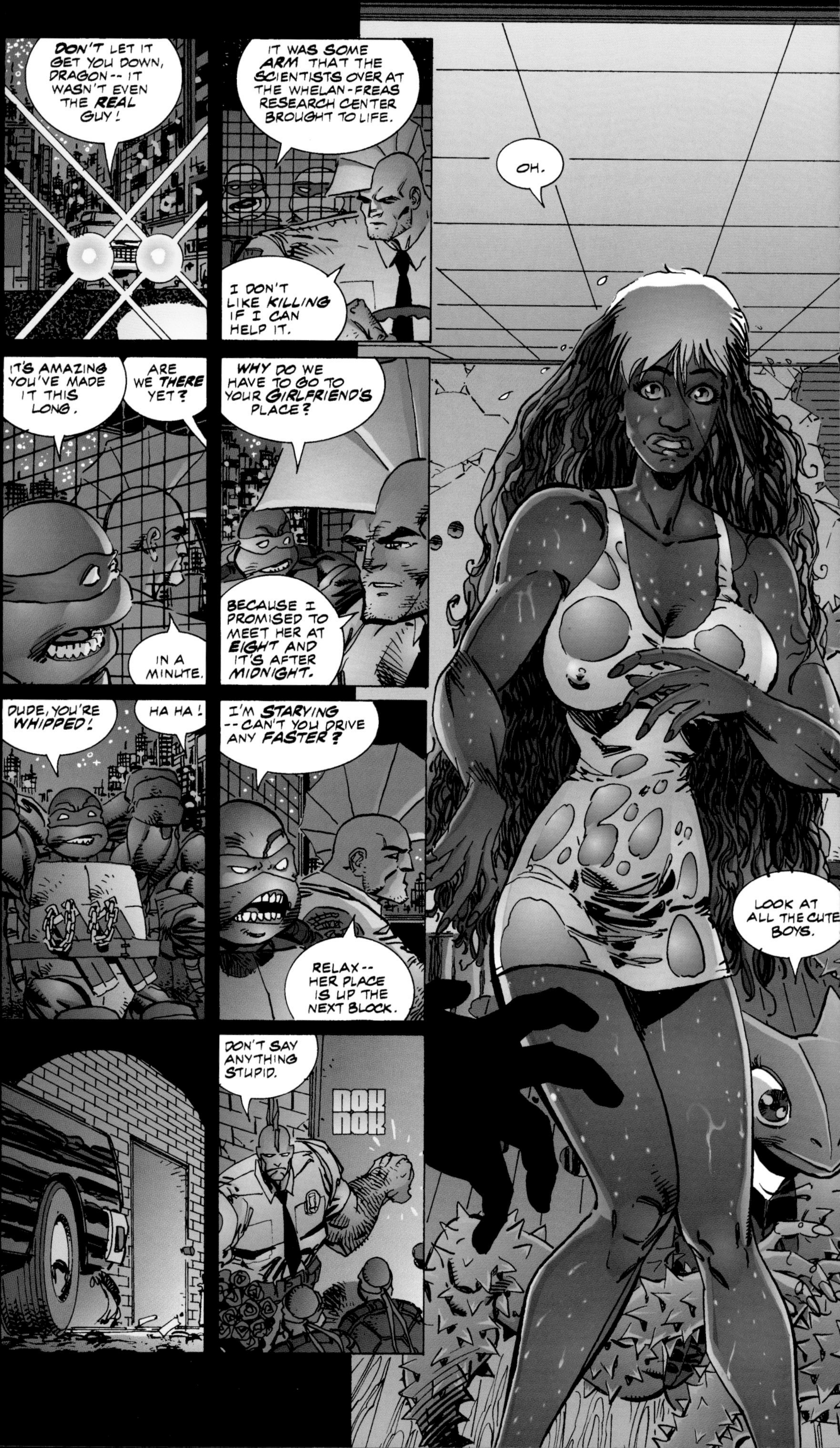
DON'T LET IT GET YOU DOWN, DRAGON -- IT WASN'T EVEN THE REAL GUY!
IT WAS SOME ARM THAT THE SCIENTISTS OVER AT THE WHELAN-FREAS RESEARCH CENTER BROUGHT TO LIFE.
I DON'T LIKE KILLING IF I CAN HELP IT.
IT'S AMAZING YOU'VE MADE IT THIS LONG.
ARE WE THERE YET?
IN A MINUTE.
WHY DO WE HAVE TO GO TO YOUR GIRLFRIEND'S PLACE?
BECAUSE I PROMISED TO MEET HER AT EIGHT AND IT'S AFTER MIDNIGHT.
DUDE, YOU'RE WHIPPED!
HA HA!
I'M STARVING --CAN'T YOU DRIVE ANY FASTER?
RELAX-- HER PLACE IS UP THE NEXT BLOCK.
DON'T SAY ANYTHING STUPID.
NOK NOK
OH.
LOOK AT ALL THE CUTE BOYS.

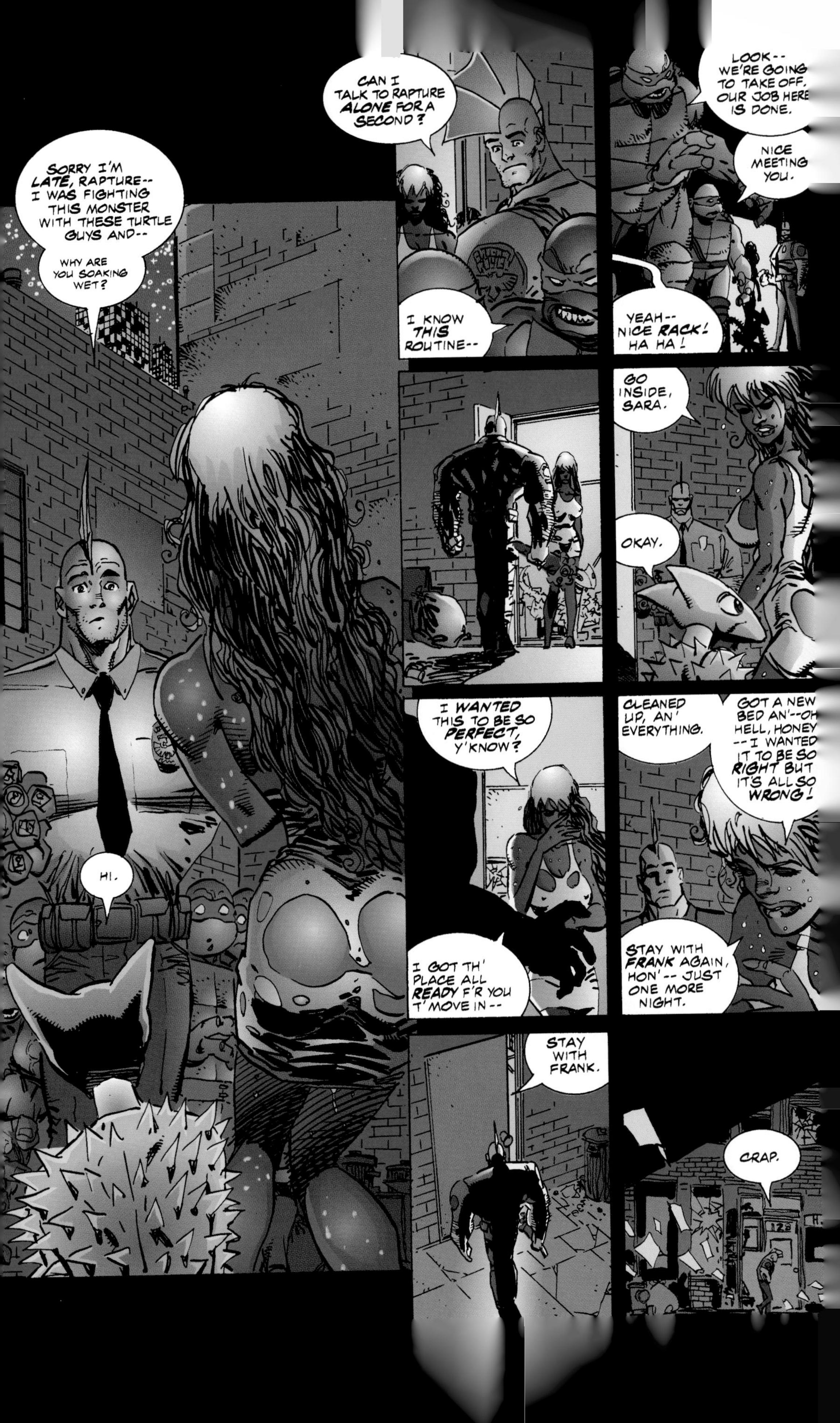
SORRY I'M LATE, RAPTURE-- I WAS FIGHTING THIS MONSTER WITH THESE TURTLE GUYS AND--
WHY ARE YOU SOAKING WET?
HI.
CAN I TALK TO RAPTURE ALONE FOR A SECOND?
I KNOW THIS ROUTINE--
LOOK-- WE'RE GOING TO TAKE OFF. OUR JOB HERE IS DONE.
NICE MEETING YOU.
YEAH-- NICE RACK! HA HA!
GO INSIDE, SARA.
OKAY.
I WANTED THIS TO BE SO PERFECT, Y'KNOW?
I GOT TH' PLACE ALL READY F'R YOU T'MOVE IN--
CLEANED UP, AN' EVERYTHING.
GOT A NEW BED AN'--OH HELL, HONEY --I WANTED IT TO BE SO RIGHT BUT IT'S ALL SO WRONG!
STAY WITH FRANK AGAIN, HON'-- JUST ONE MORE NIGHT.
STAY WITH FRANK.
CRAP.

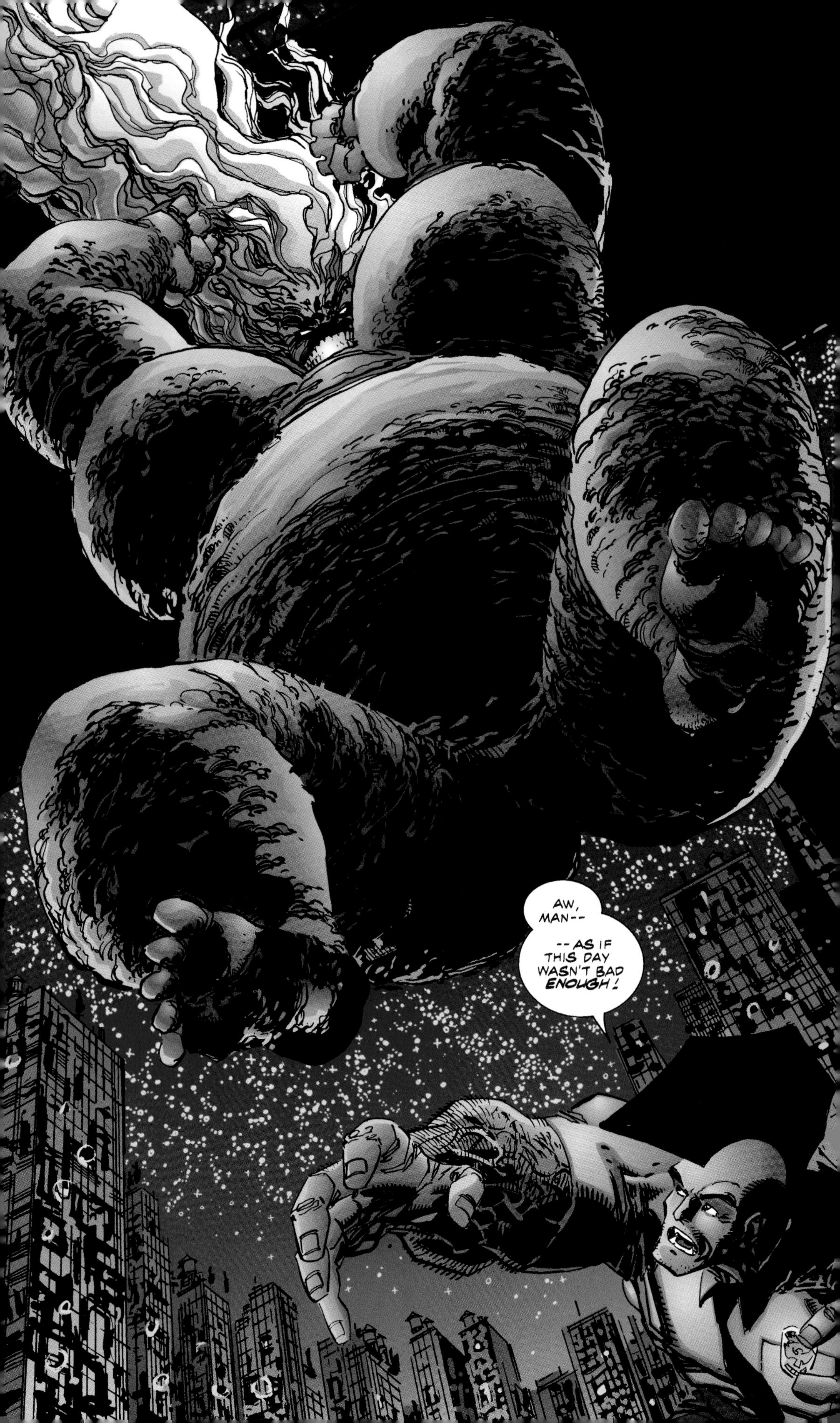
AW, MAN--
--AS IF THIS DAY WASN'T BAD ENOUGH!

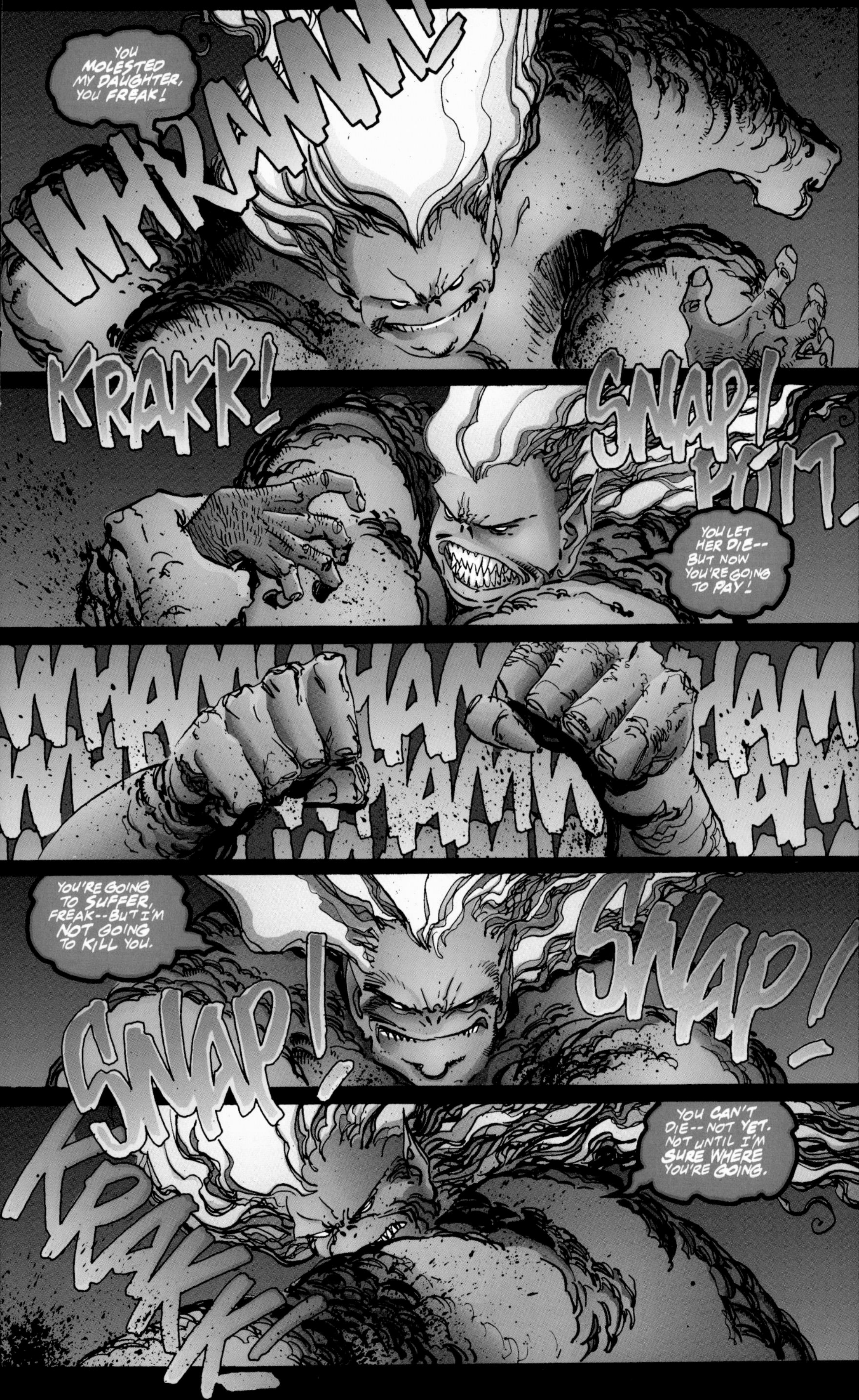
YOU MOLESTED MY DAUGHTER, YOU FREAK!
KRAKK!
SNAP!
YOU LET HER DIE-- BUT NOW YOU'RE GOING TO PAY!
YOU'RE GOING TO SUFFER, FREAK--BUT I'M NOT GOING TO KILL YOU.
SNAP!
SNAP!
YOU CAN'T DIE-- NOT YET. NOT UNTIL I'M SURE WHERE YOU'RE GOING.

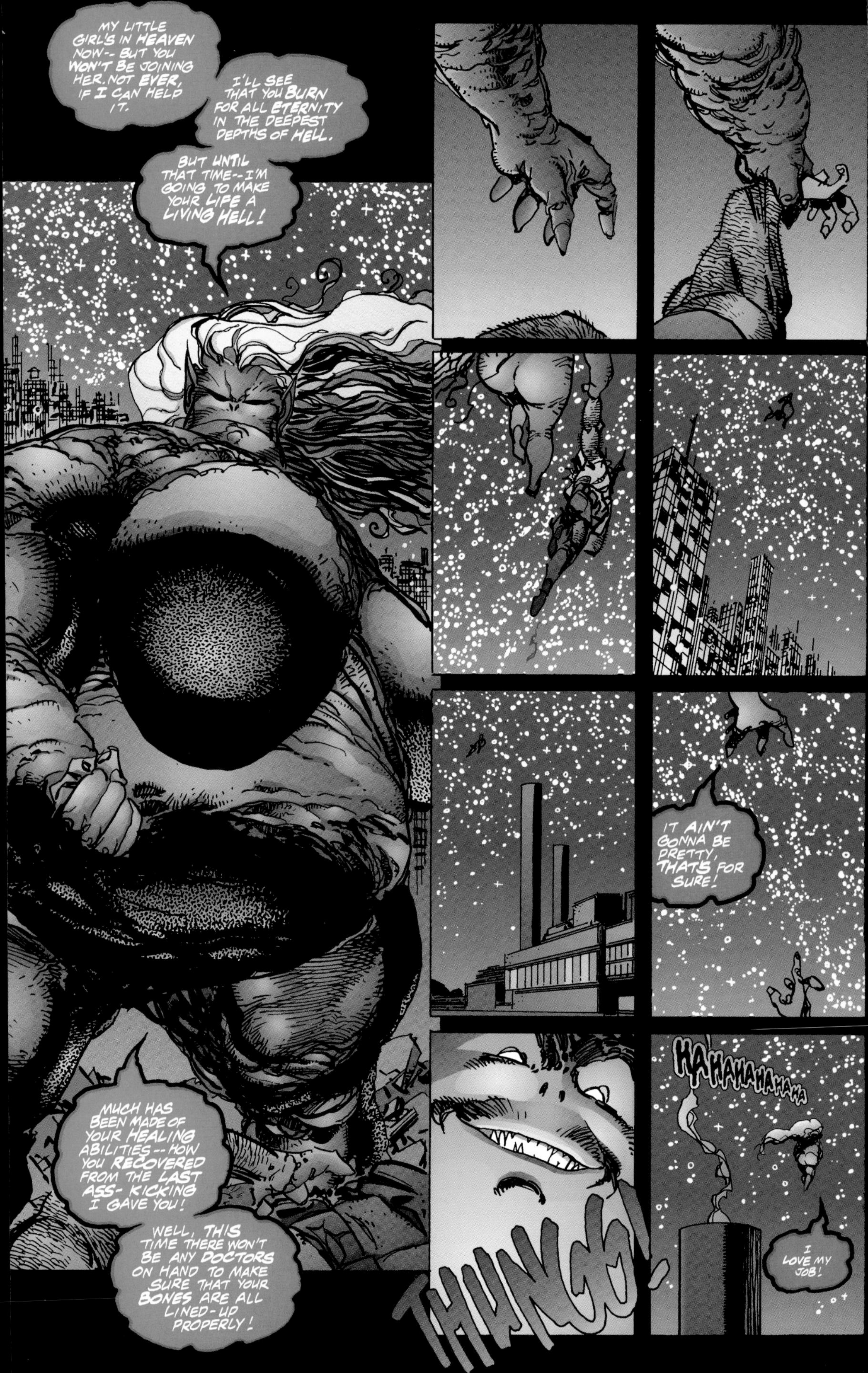
MY LITTLE GIRL'S IN HEAVEN NOW-- BUT YOU WON'T BE JOINING HER. NOT EVER, IF I CAN HELP IT.
I'LL SEE THAT YOU BURN FOR ALL ETERNITY IN THE DEEPEST DEPTHS OF HELL.
BUT UNTIL THAT TIME-- I'M GOING TO MAKE YOUR LIFE A LIVING HELL!
MUCH HAS BEEN MADE OF YOUR HEALING ABILITIES -- HOW YOU RECOVERED FROM THE LAST ASS- KICKING I GAVE YOU!
WELL, THIS TIME THERE WON'T BE ANY DOCTORS ON HAND TO MAKE SURE THAT YOUR BONES ARE ALL LINED-UP PROPERLY!
IT AIN'T GONNA BE PRETTY, THAT'S FOR SURE!
THUNGG!
HAHAHAHAHAHAHA
I LOVE MY JOB!

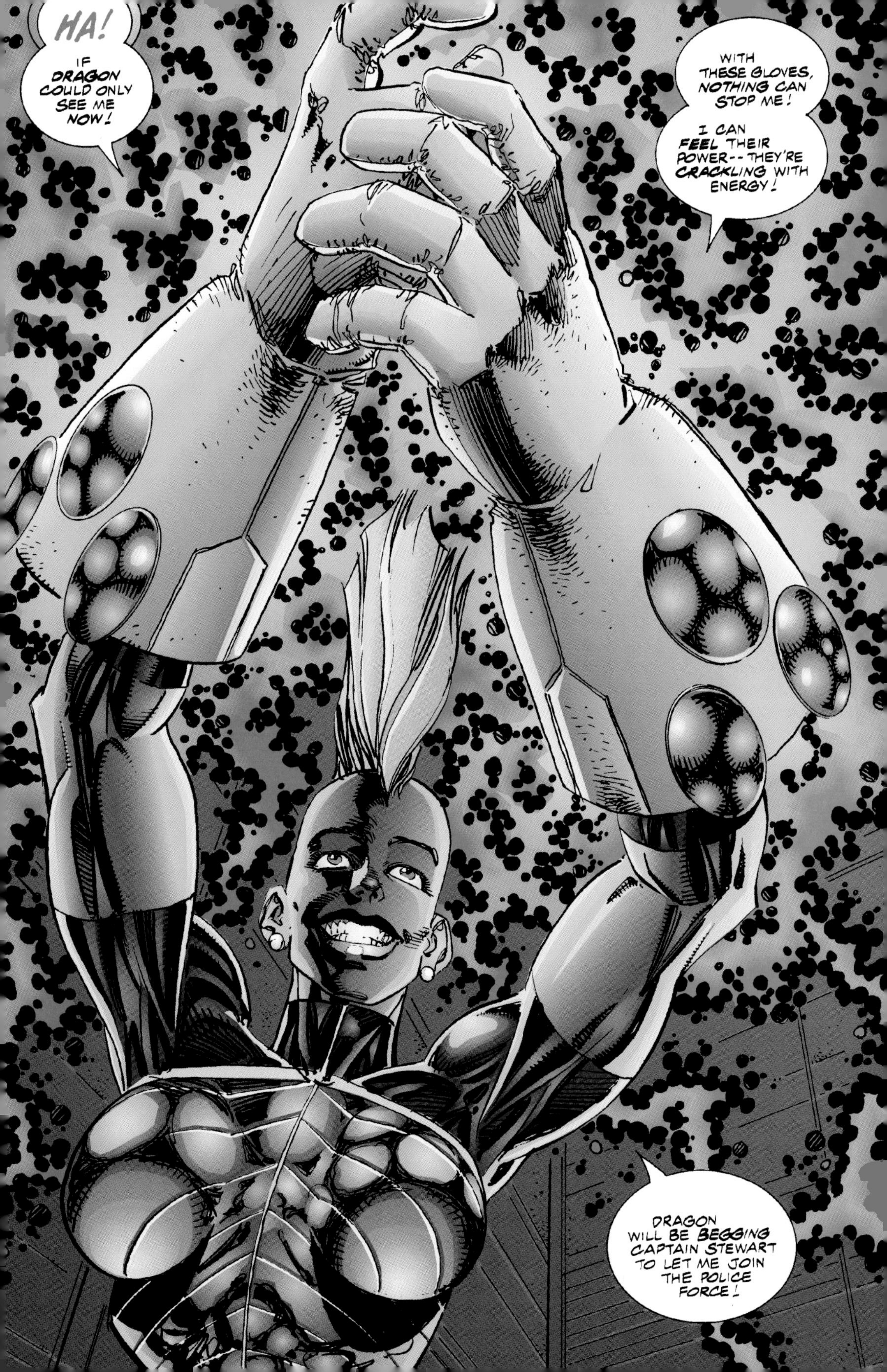
HA!
IF DRAGON COULD ONLY SEE ME NOW!
WITH THESE GLOVES, NOTHING CAN STOP ME!
I CAN FEEL THEIR POWER-- THEY'RE CRACKLING WITH ENERGY!
DRAGON WILL BE BEGGING CAPTAIN STEWART TO LET ME JOIN THE POLICE FORCE!

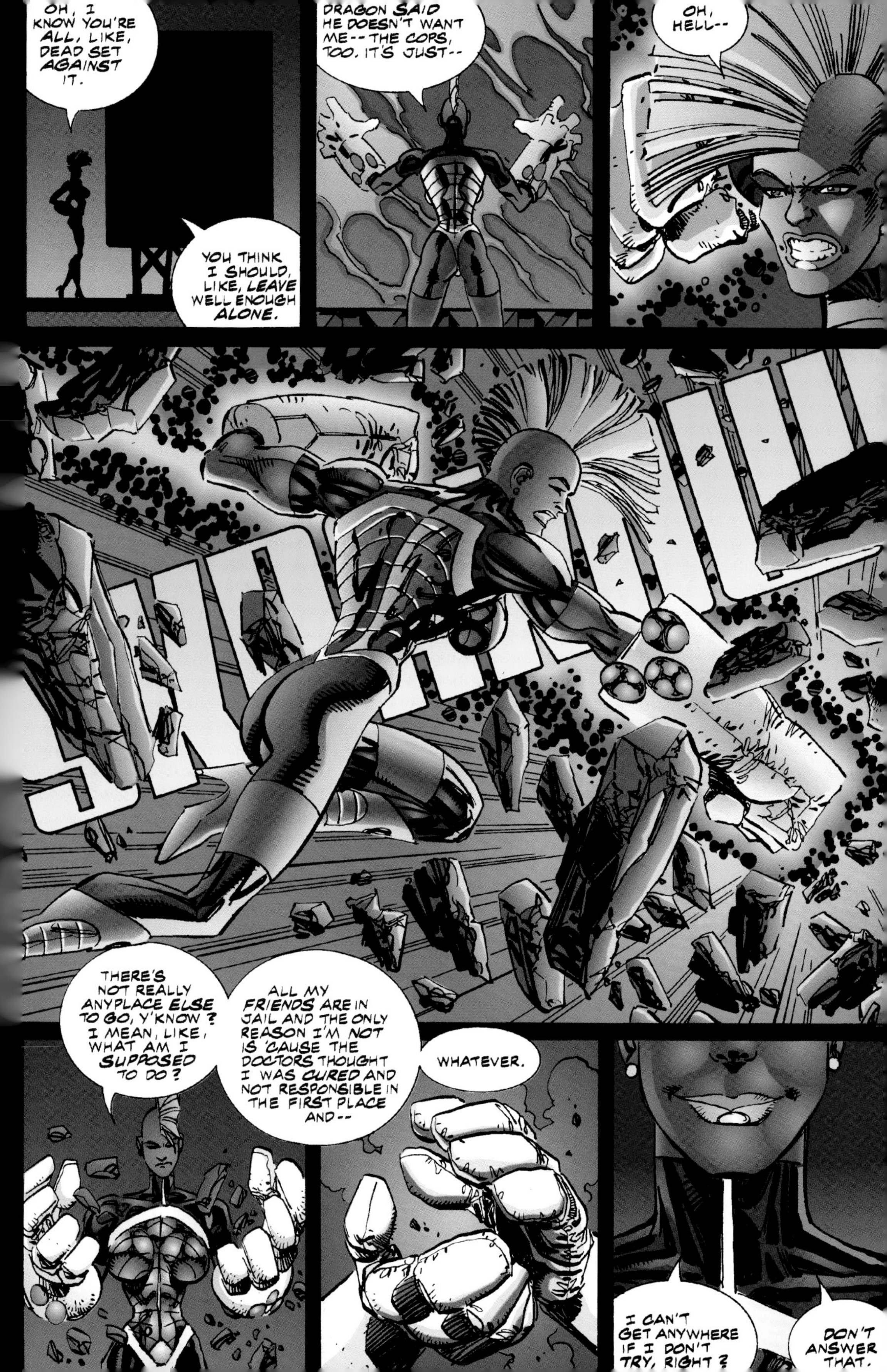
OH, I KNOW YOU'RE ALL, LIKE, DEAD SET AGAINST IT.
YOU THINK I SHOULD, LIKE, LEAVE WELL ENOUGH ALONE.
DRAGON SAID HE DOESN'T WANT ME-- THE CORS, TOO. IT'S JUST--
OH, HELL--
THERE'S NOT REALLY ANYPLACE ELSE TO GO, Y'KNOW? I MEAN, LIKE, WHAT AM I SUPPOSED TO DO?
ALL MY FRIENDS ARE IN JAIL AND THE ONLY REASON I'M NOT IS 'CAUSE THE DOCTORS THOUGHT I WAS CURED AND NOT RESPONSIBLE IN THE FIRST PLACE AND--
WHATEVER.
I CAN'T GET ANYWHERE IF I DON'T TRY, RIGHT?
DON'T ANSWER THAT.

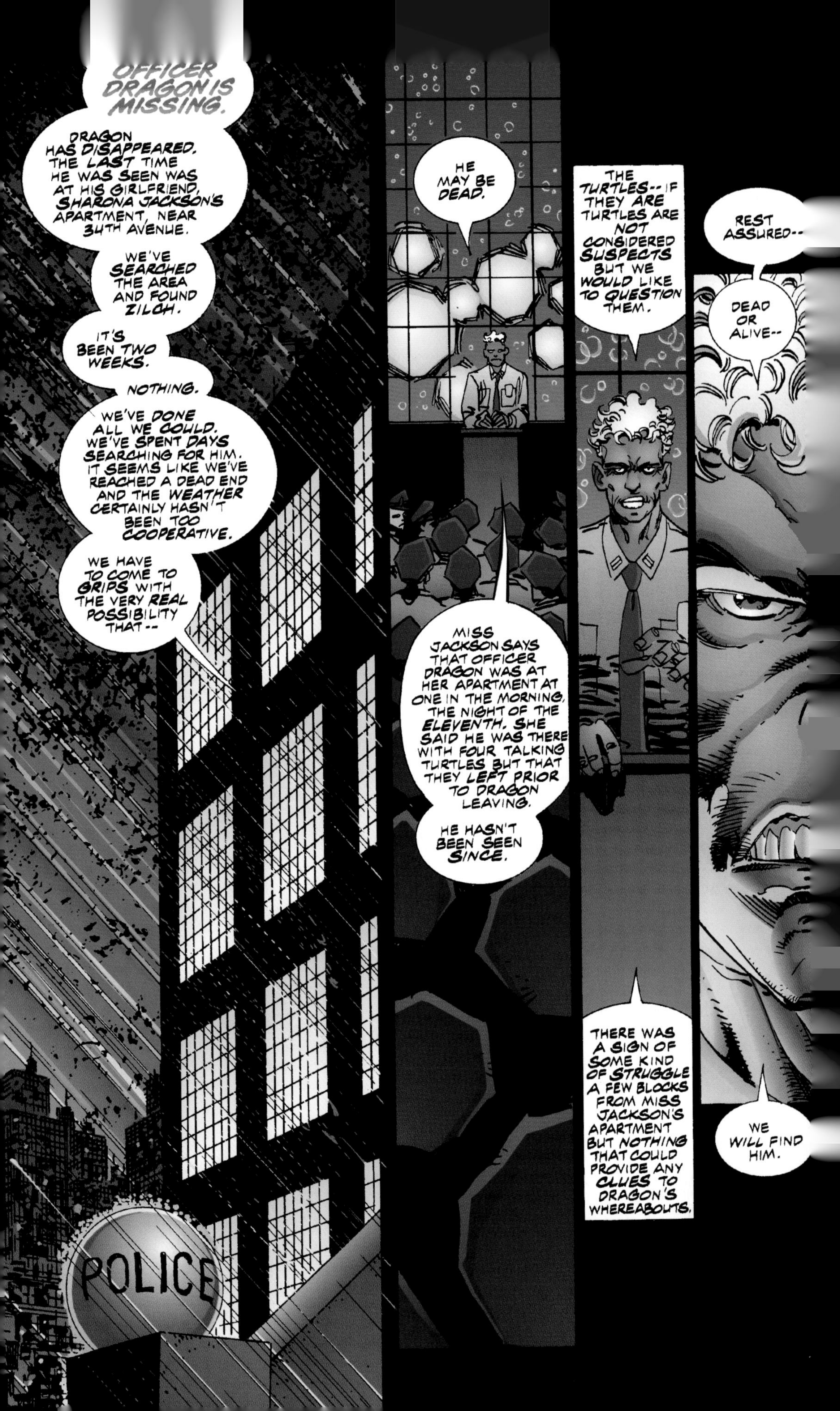

OFFICER DRAGON IS MISSING.
DRAGON HAS DISAPPEARED. THE LAST TIME HE WAS SEEN WAS AT HIS GIRLFRIEND, SHARONA JACKSON'S APARTMENT, NEAR 34TH AVENUE.
WE'VE SEARCHED THE AREA AND FOUND ZILCH.
IT'S BEEN TWO WEEKS.
NOTHING.
WE'VE DONE ALL WE COULD. WE'VE SPENT DAYS SEARCHING FOR HIM. IT SEEMS LIKE WE'VE REACHED A DEAD END AND THE WEATHER CERTAINLY HASN'T BEEN TOO COOPERATIVE.
WE HAVE TO COME TO GRIPS WITH THE VERY REAL POSSIBILITY THAT--
POLICE
HE MAY BE DEAD.
MISS JACKSON SAYS THAT OFFICER DRAGON WAS AT HER APARTMENT AT ONE IN THE MORNING, THE NIGHT OF THE ELEVENTH. SHE SAID HE WAS THERE WITH FOUR TALKING TURTLES BUT THAT THEY LEFT PRIOR TO DRAGON LEAVING.
HE HASN'T BEEN SEEN SINCE.
THE TURTLES-- IF THEY ARE TURTLES ARE NOT CONSIDERED SUSPECTS BUT WE WOULD LIKE TO QUESTION THEM.
THERE WAS A SIGN OF SOME KIND OF STRUGGLE A FEW BLOCKS FROM MISS JACKSON'S APARTMENT BUT NOTHING THAT COULD PROVIDE ANY CLUES TO DRAGON'S WHEREABOUTS.
REST ASSURED--
DEAD OR ALIVE--
WE WILL FIND HIM.

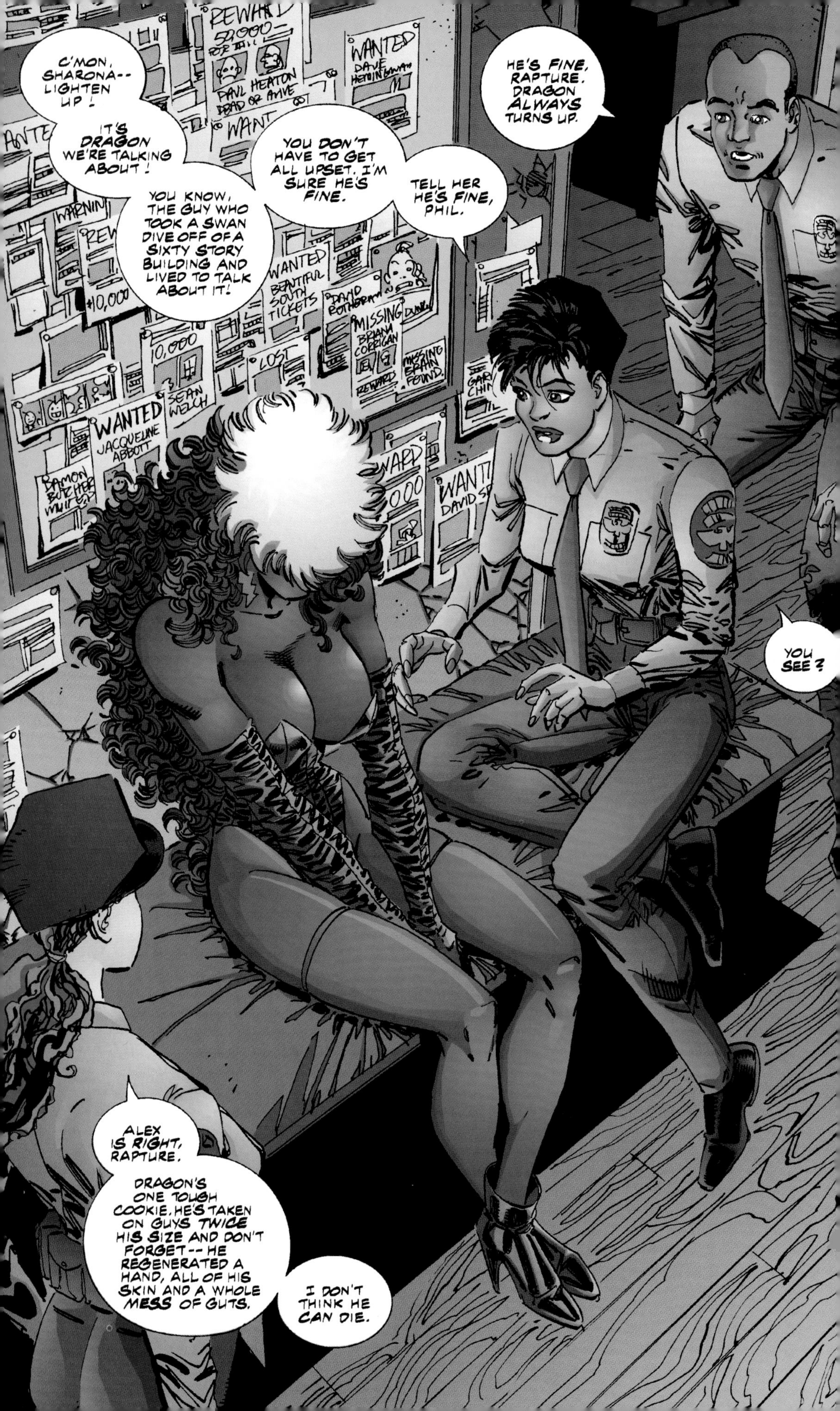
C'MON, SHARONA-- LIGHTEN UP!
IT'S DRAGON WE'RE TALKING ABOUT!
YOU KNOW, THE GUY WHO TOOK A SWAN DIVE OFF OF A SIXTY STORY BUILDING AND LIVED TO TALK ABOUT IT!
YOU DON'T HAVE TO GET ALL UPSET. I'M SURE HE'S FINE.
TELL HER HE'S FINE, PHIL.
HE'S FINE, RAPTURE. DRAGON ALWAYS TURNS UP.
YOU SEE?
ALEX IS RIGHT, RAPTURE.
DRAGON'S ONE TOUGH COOKIE. HE'S TAKEN ON GUYS TWICE HIS SIZE AND DON'T FORGET-- HE REGENERATED A HAND, ALL OF HIS SKIN AND A WHOLE MESS OF GUTS.
I DON'T THINK HE CAN DIE.

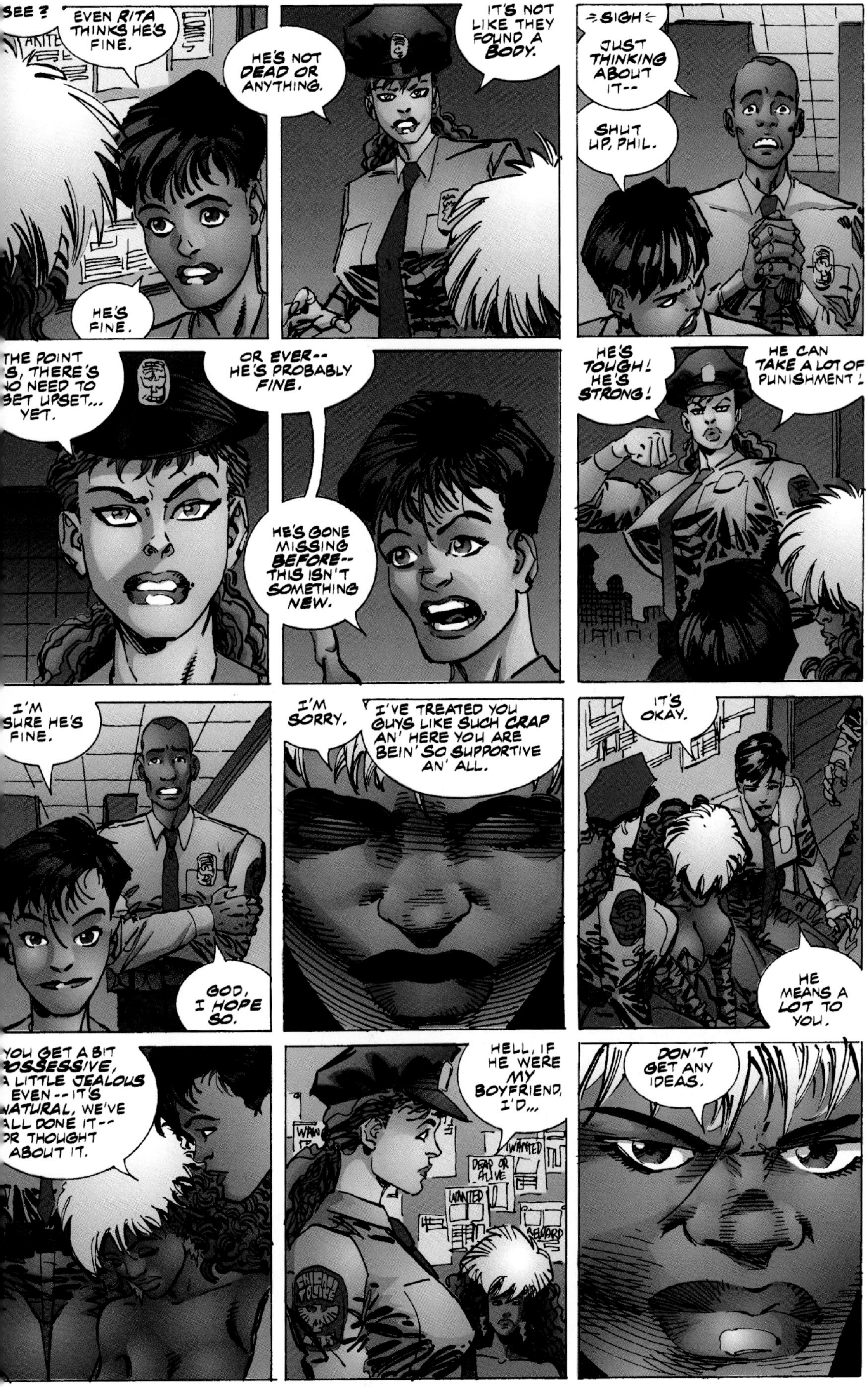
SEE?
EVEN RITA THINKS HE'S FINE.
HE'S FINE.
HE'S NOT DEAD OR ANYTHING.
IT'S NOT LIKE THEY FOUND A BODY.
SIGH
JUST THINKING ABOUT IT--
SHUT UP, PHIL.
THE POINT IS, THERE'S NO NEED TO GET UPSET... YET.
OR EVER-- HE'S PROBABLY FINE.
HE'S GONE MISSING BEFORE-- THIS ISN'T SOMETHING NEW.
HE'S TOUGH! HE'S STRONG!
HE CAN TAKE A LOT OF PUNISHMENT!
I'M SURE HE'S FINE.
GOD, I HOPE SO.
I'M SORRY.
I'VE TREATED YOU GUYS LIKE SUCH CRAP AN' HERE YOU ARE BEIN' SO SUPPORTIVE AN' ALL.
IT'S OKAY.
HE MEANS A LOT TO YOU.
YOU GET A BIT POSSESSIVE, A LITTLE JEALOUS EVEN -- IT'S NATURAL, WE'VE ALL DONE IT-- OR THOUGHT ABOUT IT.
HELL, IF HE WERE MY BOYFRIEND, I'D...
WANTED
DEAD OR ALIVE
WANTED
REWARD
CHICAGO POLICE
DON'T GET ANY IDEAS.

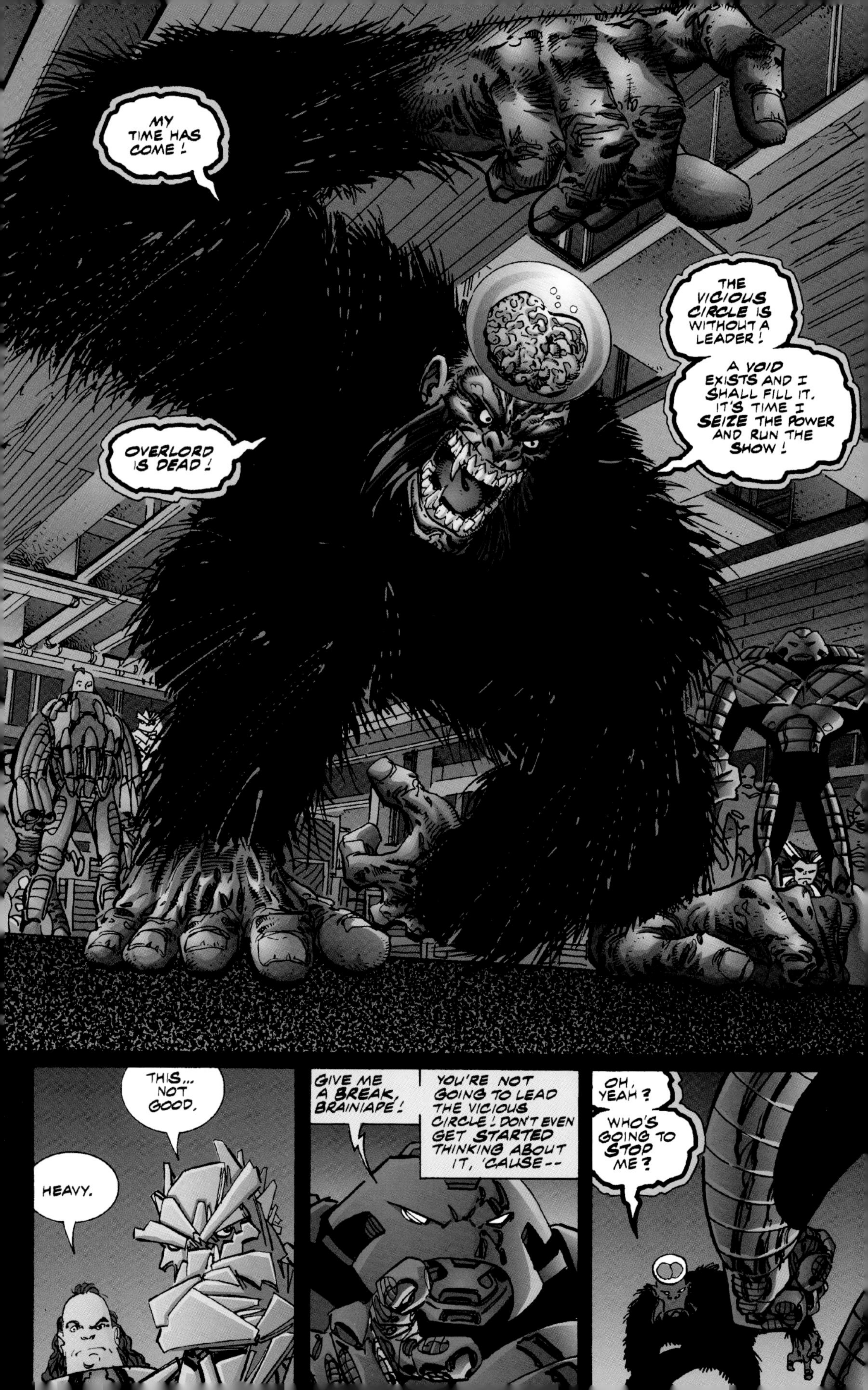
MY TIME HAS COME!
OVERLORD IS DEAD!
THE VICIOUS CIRCLE IS WITHOUT A LEADER!
A VOID EXISTS AND I SHALL FILL IT. IT'S TIME I SEIZE THE POWER AND RUN THE SHOW!
THIS... NOT GOOD.
HEAVY.
GIVE ME A BREAK, BRAINIAPE!
YOU'RE NOT GOING TO LEAD THE VICIOUS CIRCLE! DON'T EVEN GET STARTED THINKING ABOUT IT, 'CAUSE--
OH, YEAH?
WHO'S GOING TO STOP ME?

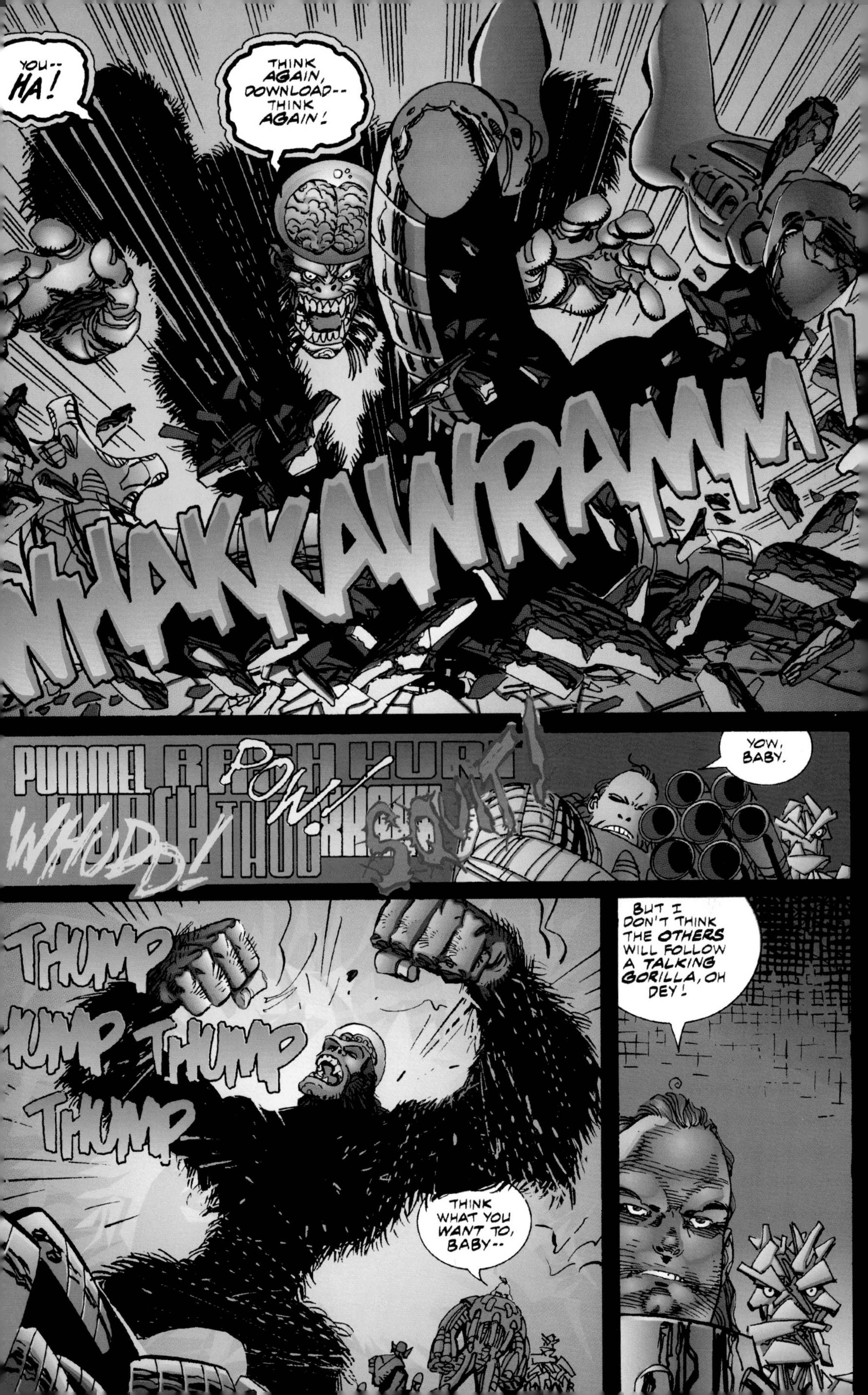
YOU-- HA!
THINK AGAIN, DOWNLOAD-- THINK AGAIN!
WHAKAWRAMM!
PUMMEL
POW!
THUD
WHUDD!
YOW, BABY.
THUMP
THUMP
THUMP
BUT I DON'T THINK THE OTHERS WILL FOLLOW A TALKING GORILLA, OH DEY!
THINK WHAT YOU WANT TO, BABY--

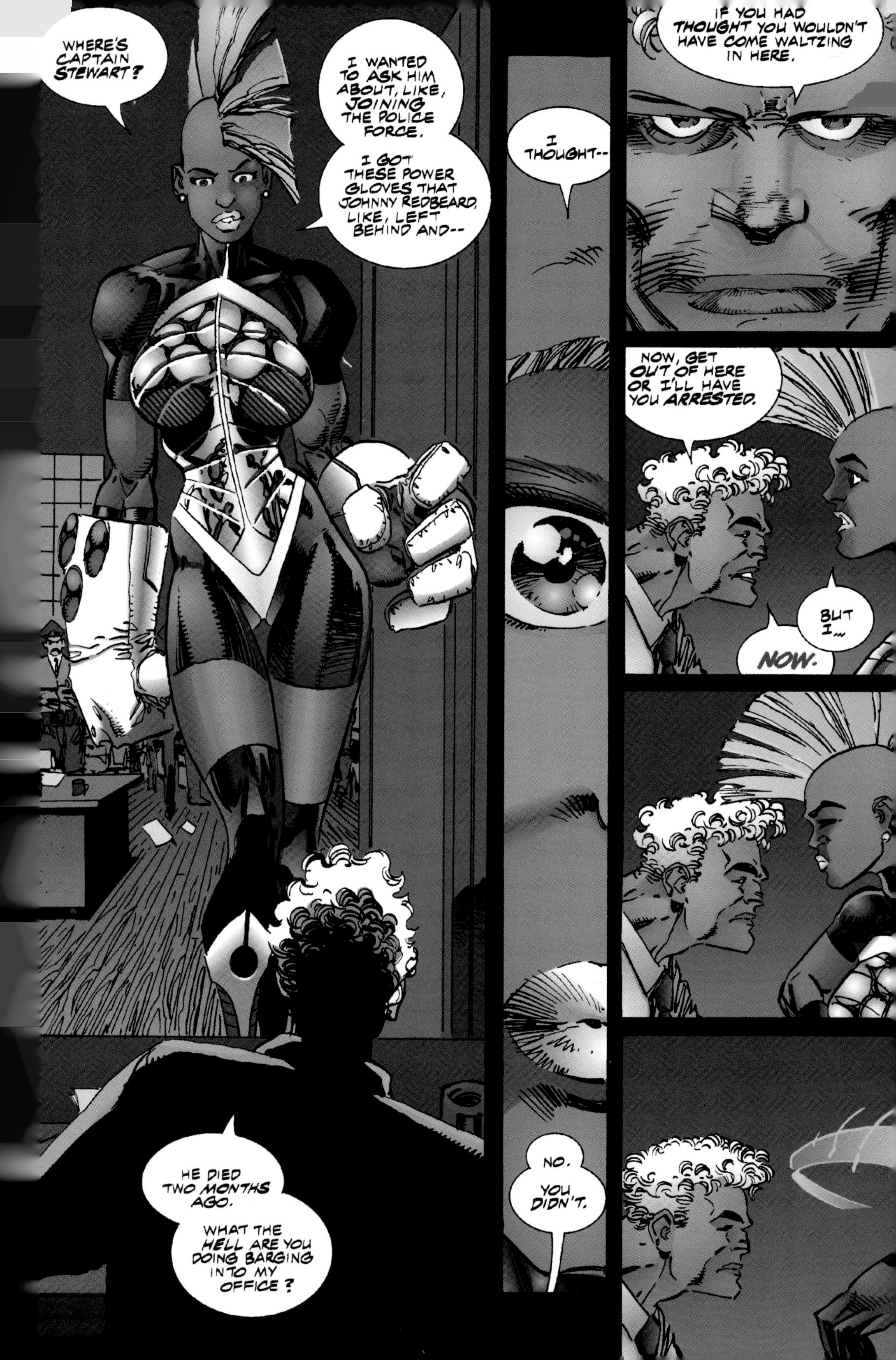
WHERE'S CAPTAIN STEWART?
I WANTED TO ASK HIM ABOUT, LIKE, JOINING THE POLICE FORCE.
I GOT THESE POWER GLOVES THAT JOHNNY REDBEARD, LIKE, LEFT BEHIND AND--
HE DIED TWO MONTHS AGO.
WHAT THE HELL ARE YOU DOING BARGING INTO MY OFFICE?
I THOUGHT--
NO.
YOU DIDN'T.
IF YOU HAD THOUGHT YOU WOULDN'T HAVE COME WALTZING IN HERE.
NOW, GET OUT OF HERE OR I'LL HAVE YOU ARRESTED.
BUT I...
NOW.

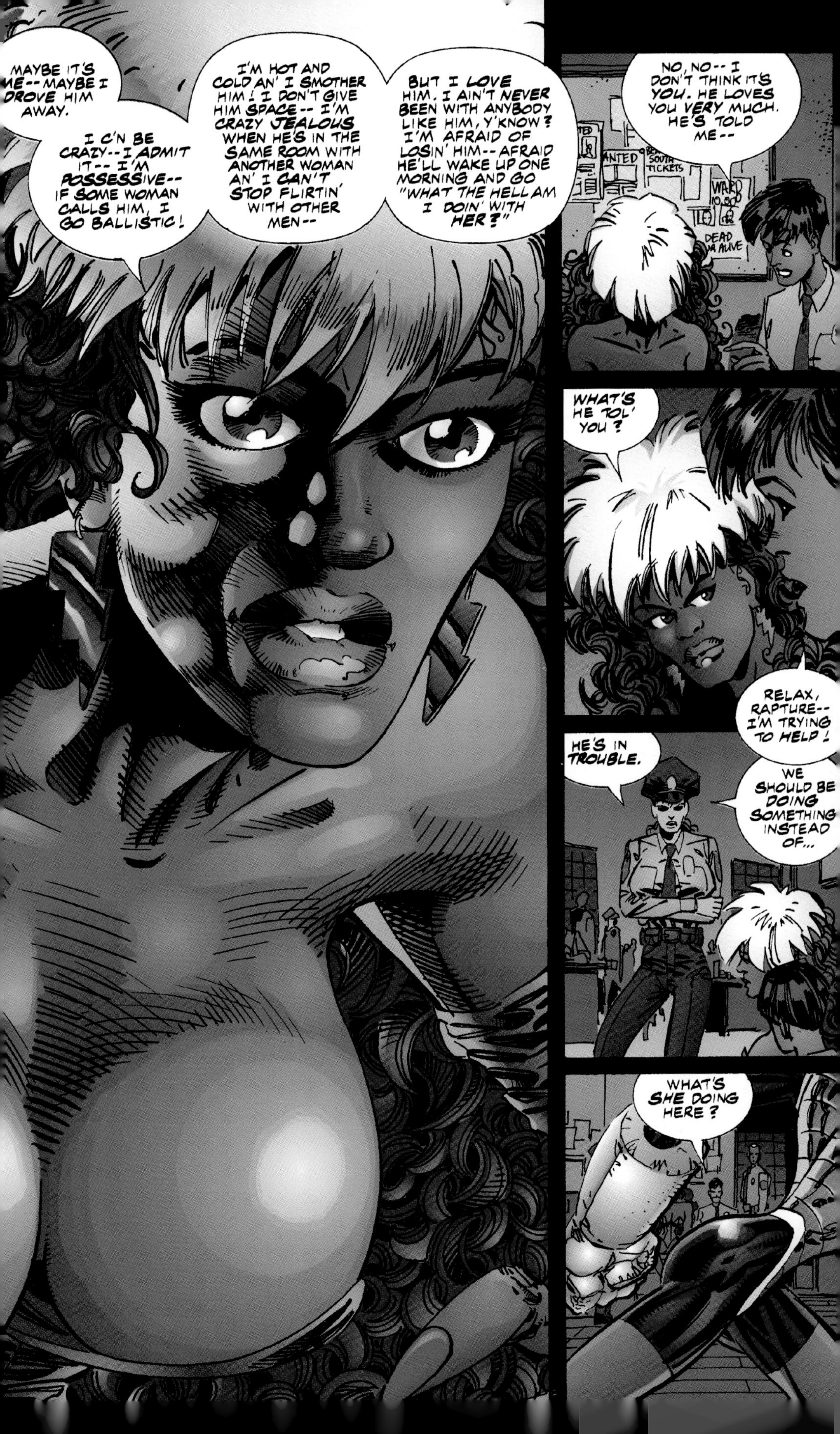
MAYBE IT'S ME-- MAYBE I DROVE HIM AWAY.
I C'N BE CRAZY-- I ADMIT IT-- I'M POSSESSIVE-- IF SOME WOMAN CALLS HIM, I GO BALLISTIC!
I'M HOT AND COLD AN' I SMOTHER HIM! I DON'T GIVE HIM SPACE-- I'M CRAZY JEALOUS WHEN HE'S IN THE SAME ROOM WITH ANOTHER WOMAN AN' I CAN'T STOP FLIRTIN' WITH OTHER MEN--
BUT I LOVE HIM. I AIN'T NEVER BEEN WITH ANYBODY LIKE HIM, Y'KNOW? I'M AFRAID OF LOSIN' HIM-- AFRAID HE'LL WAKE UP ONE MORNING AND GO "WHAT THE HELL AM I DOIN' WITH HER?"
NO, NO-- I DON'T THINK IT'S YOU. HE LOVES YOU VERY MUCH. HE'S TOLD ME--
SOUTH TICKETS
DEAD
WHAT'S HE TOL' YOU?
RELAX, RAPTURE-- I'M TRYING TO HELP!
HE'S IN TROUBLE.
WE SHOULD BE DOING SOMETHING INSTEAD OF...
WHAT'S SHE DOING HERE?

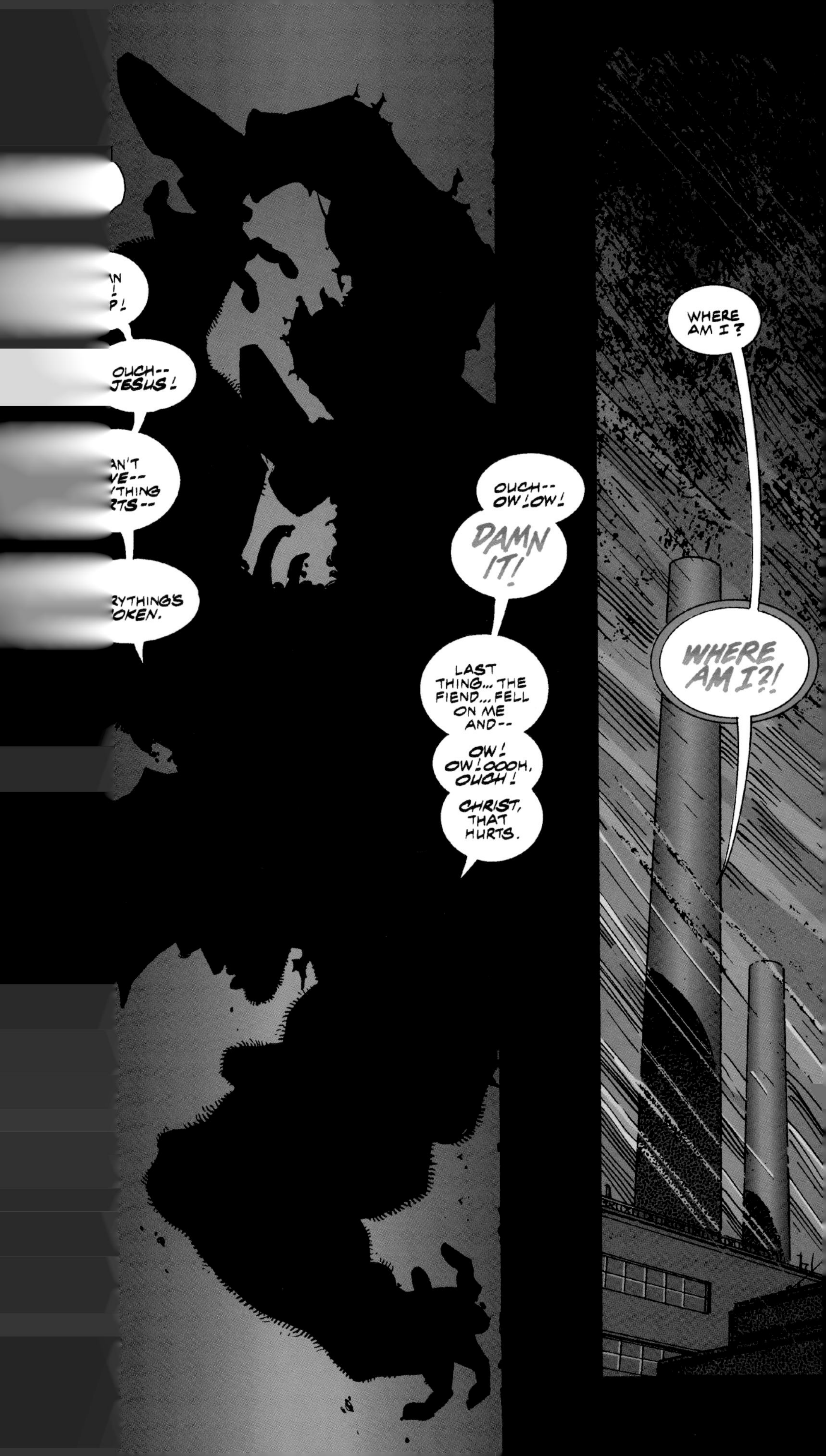

OUCH-- JESUS!
OUCH-- OW! OW!
DAMN IT!
LAST THING... THE FIEND... FELL ON ME AND--
OW! OW! OOOH, OUCH!
CHRIST, THAT HURTS.
WHERE AM I?
WHERE AM I?!

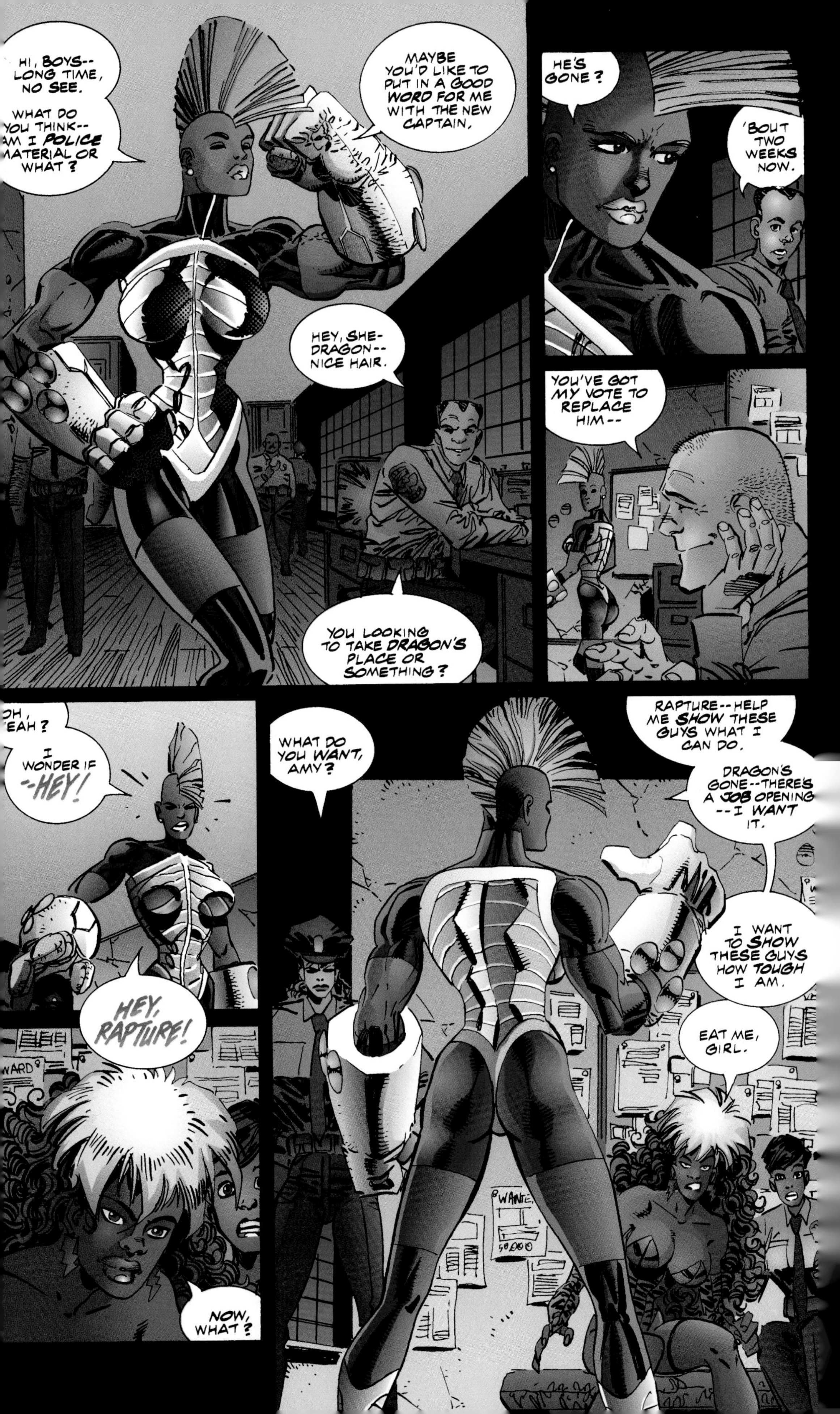
HI, BOYS-- LONG TIME, NO SEE.
WHAT DO YOU THINK-- AM I POLICE MATERIAL OR WHAT?
MAYBE YOU'D LIKE TO PUT IN A GOOD WORD FOR ME WITH THE NEW CAPTAIN.
HEY, SHE-DRAGON-- NICE HAIR.
YOU LOOKING TO TAKE DRAGON'S PLACE OR SOMETHING?
HE'S GONE?
'BOUT TWO WEEKS NOW.
YOU'VE GOT MY VOTE TO REPLACE HIM--
OH, YEAH?
I WONDER IF --HEY!
HEY, RAPTURE!
NOW, WHAT?
WHAT DO YOU WANT, AMY?
RAPTURE--HELP ME SHOW THESE GUYS WHAT I CAN DO.
DRAGON'S GONE--THERE'S A JOB OPENING --I WANT IT.
I WANT TO SHOW THESE GUYS HOW TOUGH I AM.
EAT ME, GIRL.

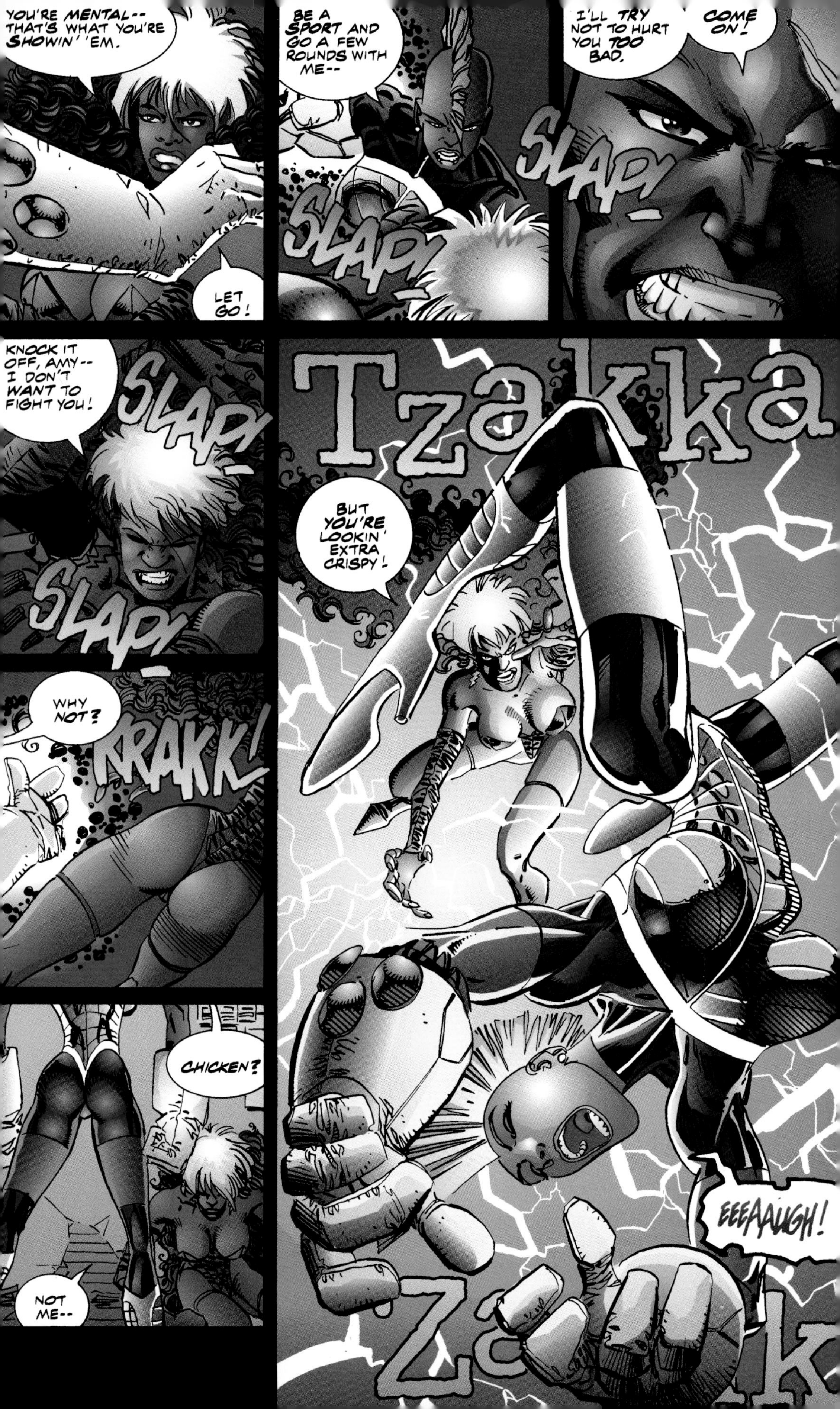

YOU'RE MENTAL-- THAT'S WHAT YOU'RE SHOWIN' 'EM.
LET GO!
BE A SPORT AND GO A FEW ROUNDS WITH ME--
SLAP!
I'LL TRY NOT TO HURT YOU TOO BAD.
COME ON!
SLAP!
KNOCK IT OFF, AMY-- I DON'T WANT TO FIGHT YOU!
SLAP!
SLAP!
WHY NOT?
KRAKK!
CHICKEN?
NOT ME--
Tzakka
BUT YOU'RE LOOKIN' EXTRA CRISPY!
EEEAAUGH!

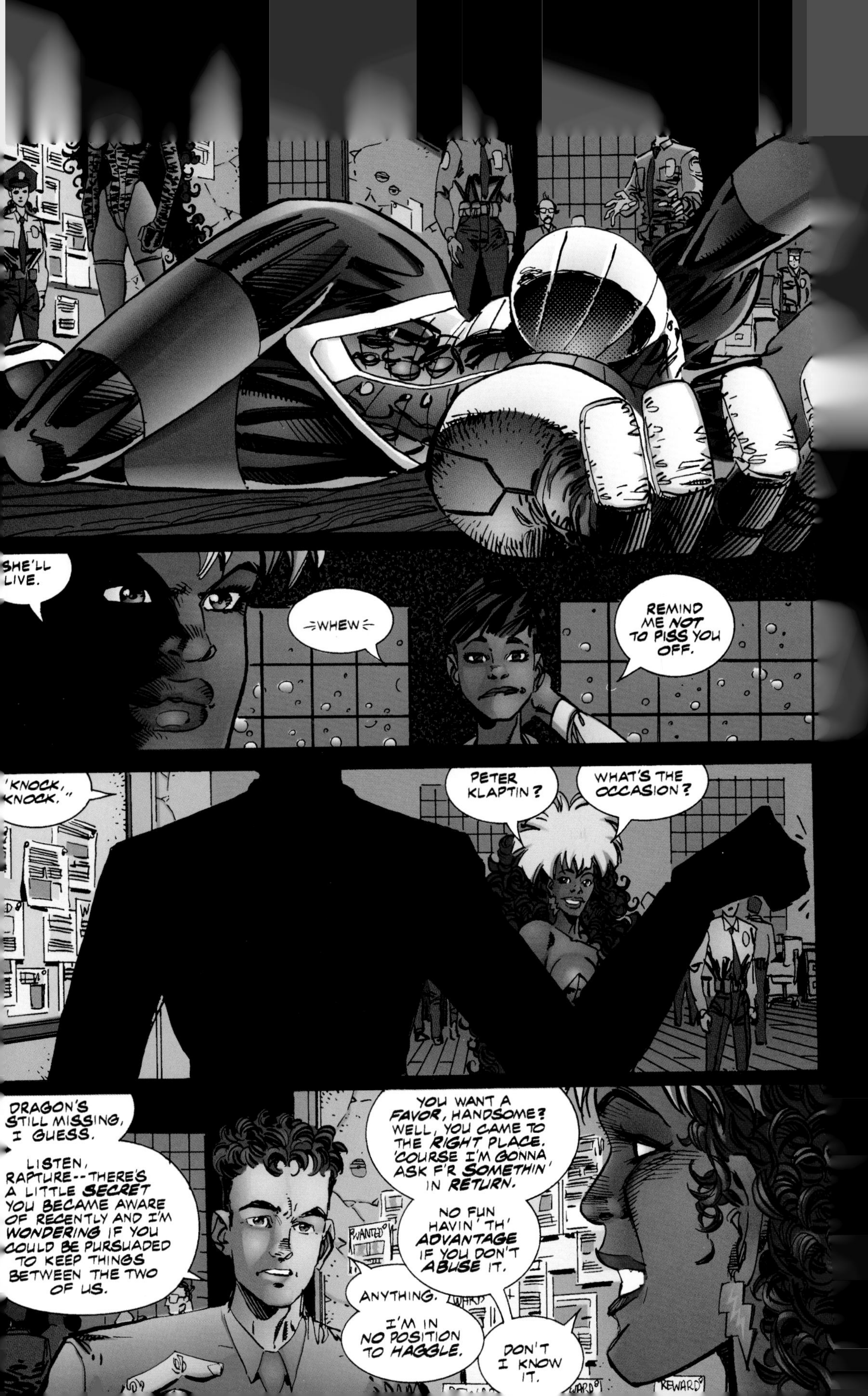
SHE'LL LIVE.
WHEW
REMIND ME NOT TO PISS YOU OFF.
'KNOCK, KNOCK.'
PETER KLAPTIN?
WHAT'S THE OCCASION?
DRAGON'S STILL MISSING, I GUESS.
LISTEN, RAPTURE--THERE'S A LITTLE SECRET YOU BECAME AWARE OF RECENTLY AND I'M WONDERING IF YOU COULD BE PURSUADED TO KEEP THINGS BETWEEN THE TWO OF US.
YOU WANT A FAVOR, HANDSOME? WELL, YOU CAME TO THE RIGHT PLACE. 'COURSE I'M GONNA ASK F'R SOMETHIN' IN RETURN.
NO FUN HAVIN' TH' ADVANTAGE IF YOU DON'T ABUSE IT.
ANYTHING.
I'M IN NO POSITION TO HAGGLE.
DON'T I KNOW IT.
WANTED
REWARD

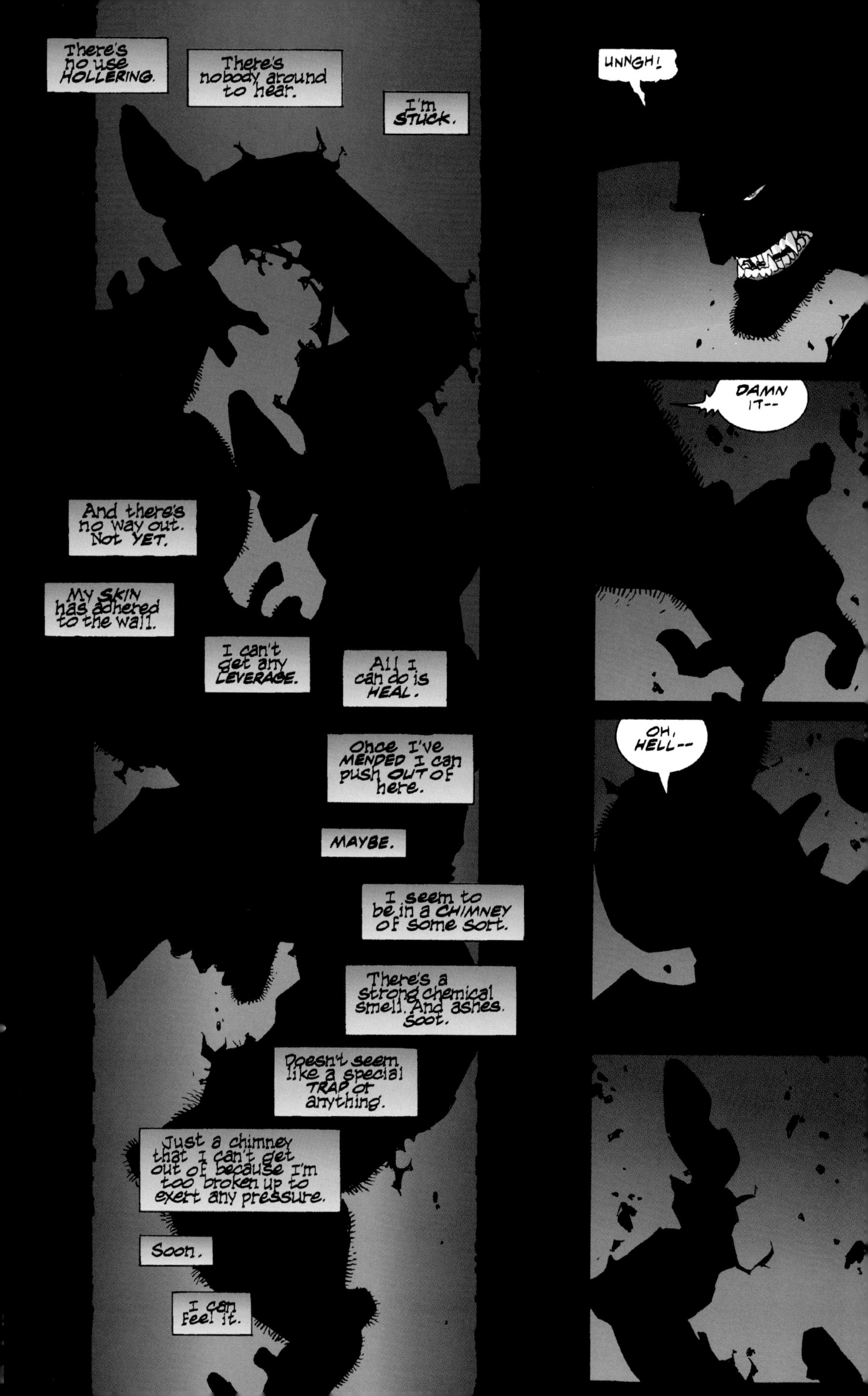
There's no use HOLLERING.
There's nobody around to hear.
I'm STUCK.
And there's no way out. Not YET.
My SKIN has adhered to the wall.
I can't get any LEVERAGE.
All I can do is HEAL.
Once I've MENDED I can push OUT of here.
MAYBE.
I seem to be in a CHIMNEY of some sort.
There's a strong chemical smell. And ashes. Soot.
Doesn't seem like a special TRAP or anything.
Just a chimney that I can't get out of because I'm too broken up to exert any pressure.
Soon.
I can feel it.
UNNGH!
DAMN IT--
OH, HELL--

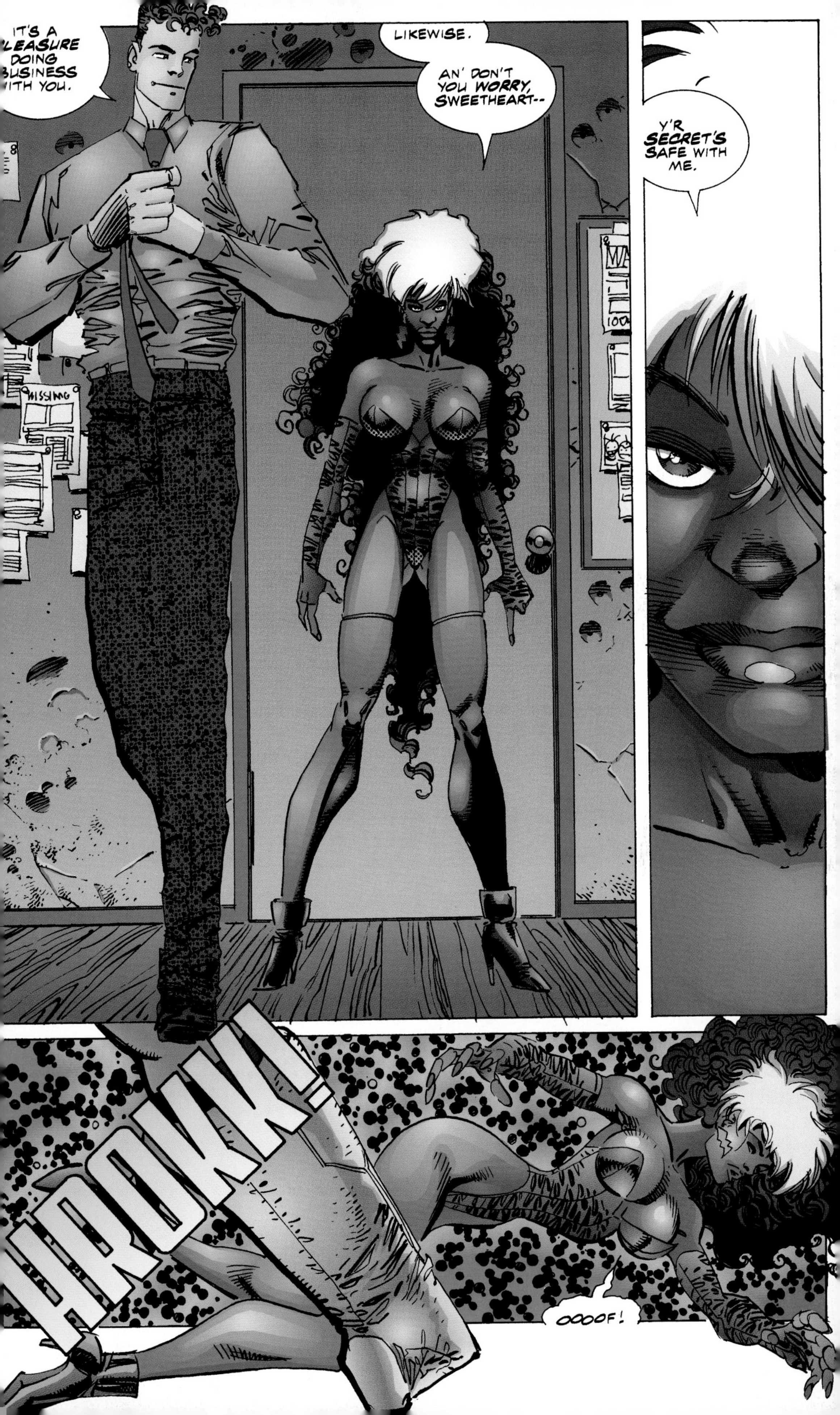

IT'S A PLEASURE DOING BUSINESS WITH YOU.
LIKEWISE.
AN' DON'T YOU WORRY, SWEETHEART--
Y'R SECRET'S SAFE WITH ME.
MISSING
HROKK!
OOOOF!

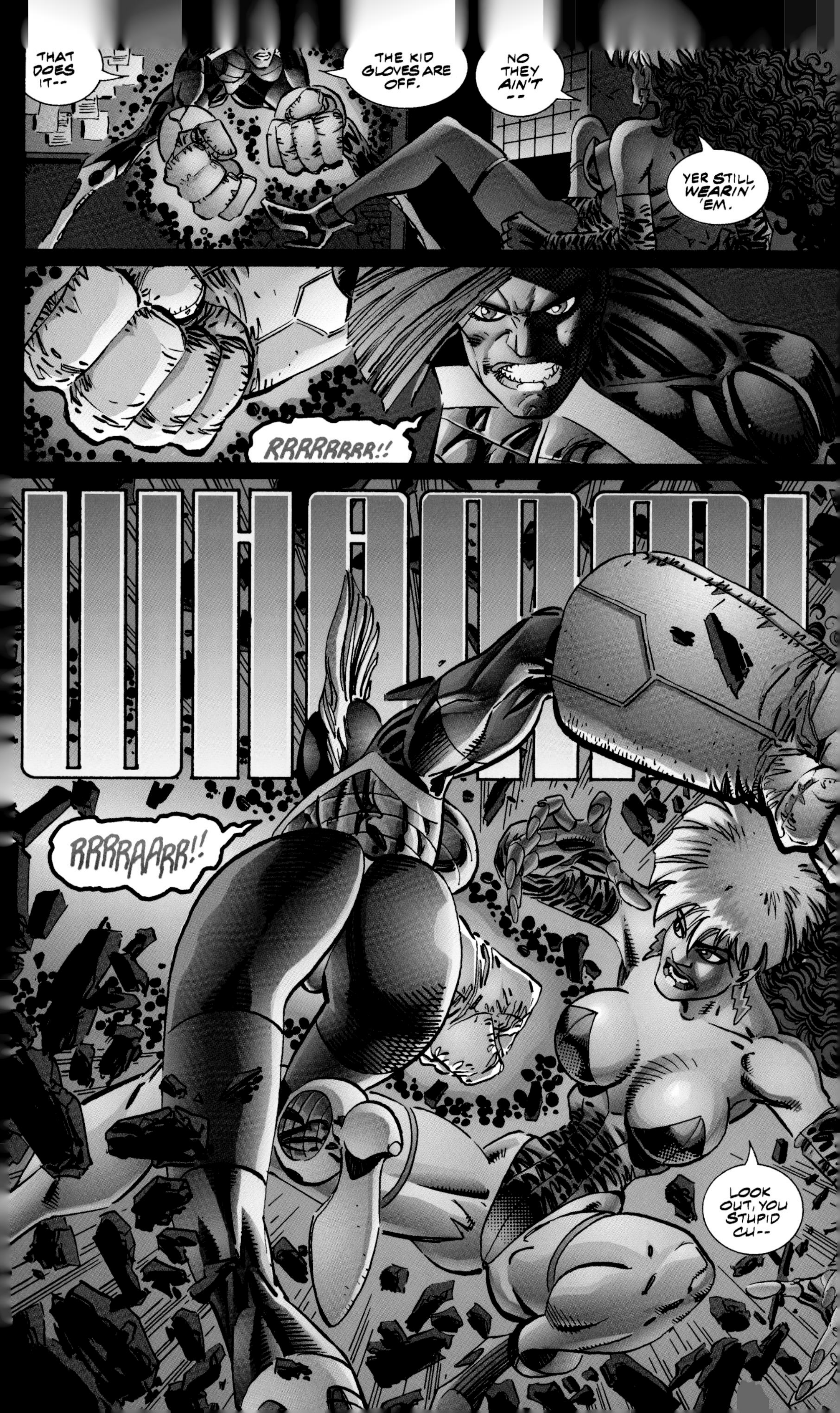
THAT DOES IT--
THE KID GLOVES ARE OFF.
NO THEY AIN'T --
YER STILL WEARIN' 'EM.
RRRRRRRR!!
RRRRAARR!!
LOOK OUT, YOU STUPID CU--

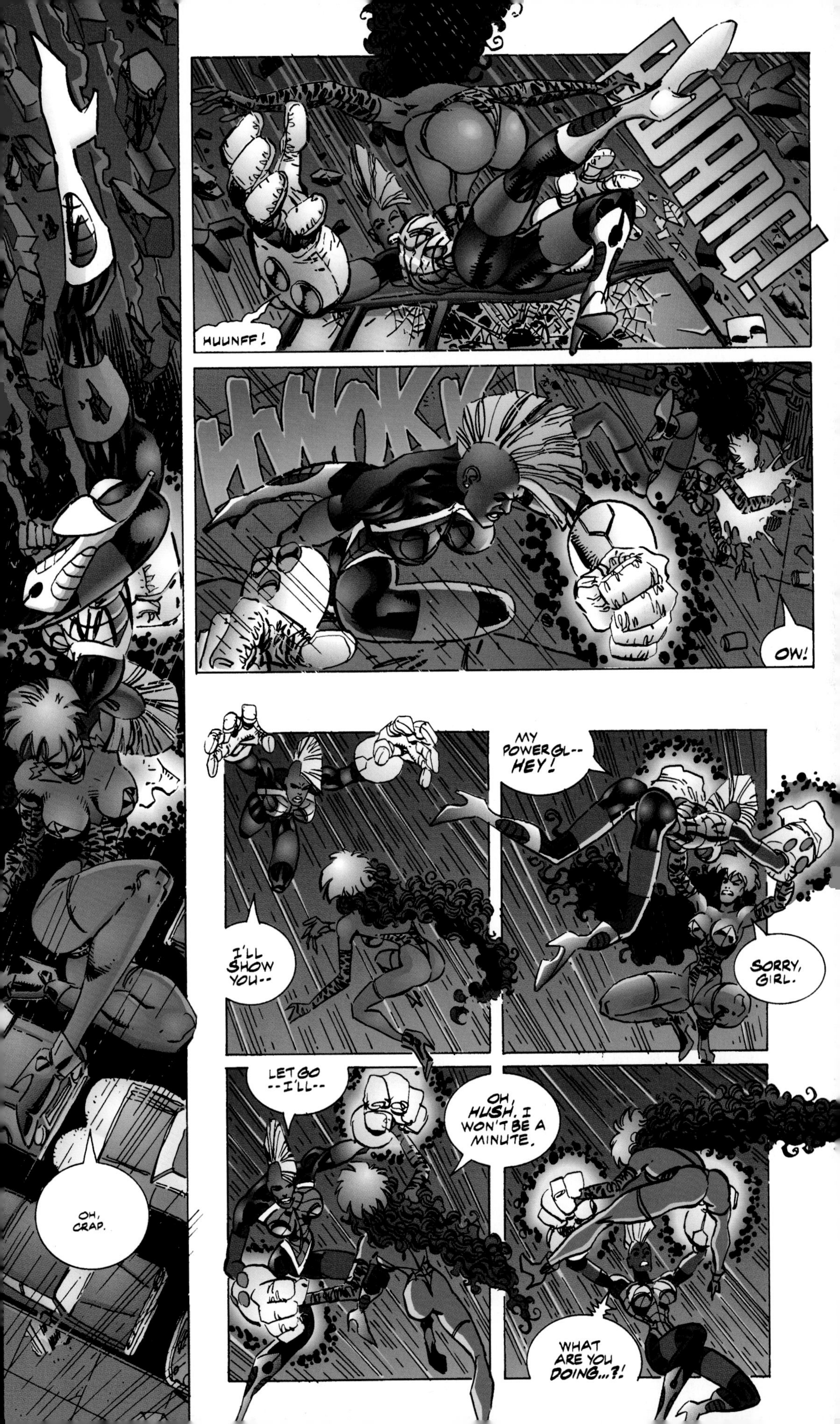
BWANG!
HUUNFF!
KWOK!
OW!
OH, CRAP.
I'LL SHOW YOU--
MY POWERGL-- HEY!
SORRY, GIRL.
LET GO --I'LL--
OH, HUSH. I WON'T BE A MINUTE.
WHAT ARE YOU DOING...?!

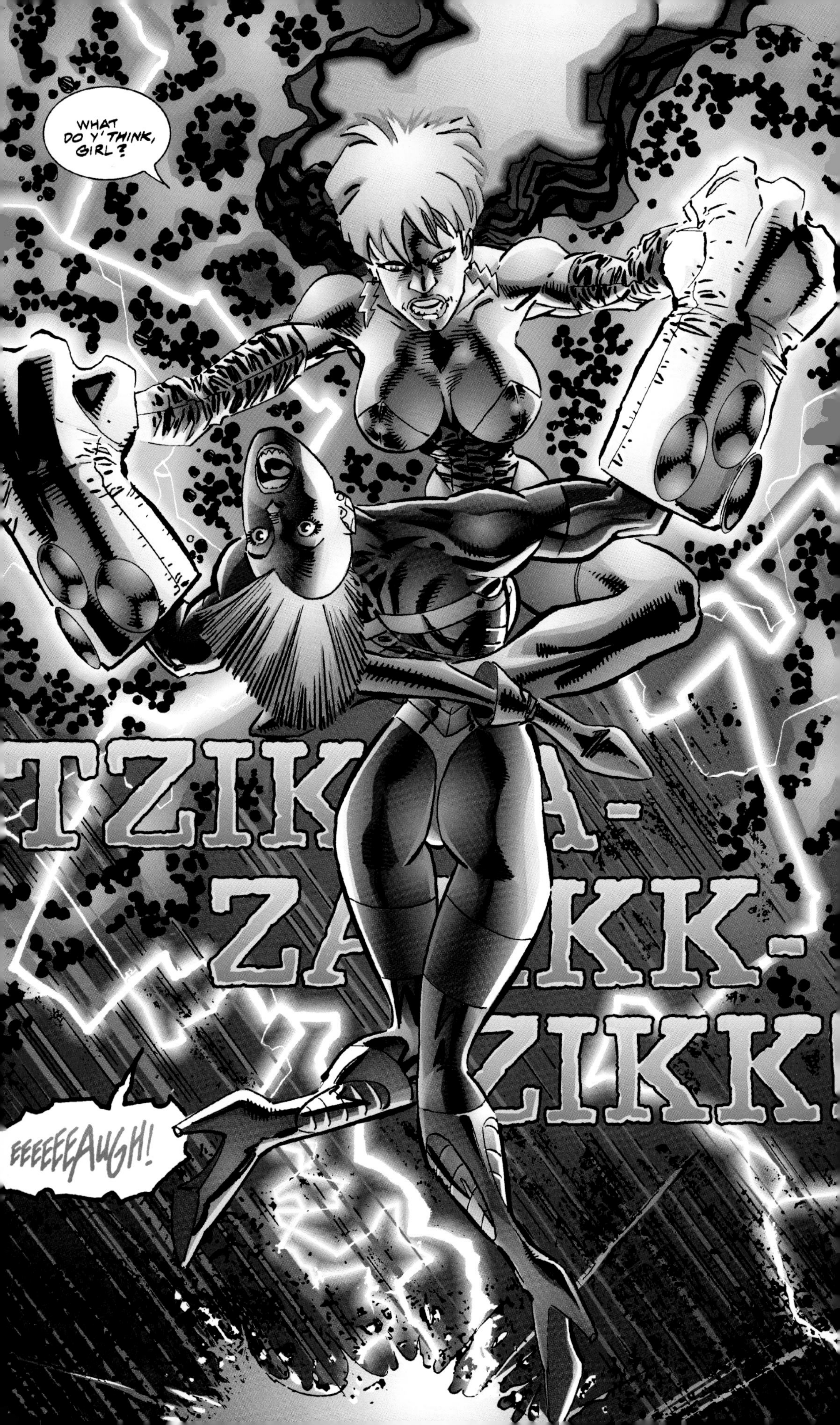
WHAT DO Y'THINK, GIRL?
TZIKKA-ZAKKK-ZIKKK!
EEEEEEEAUGH!

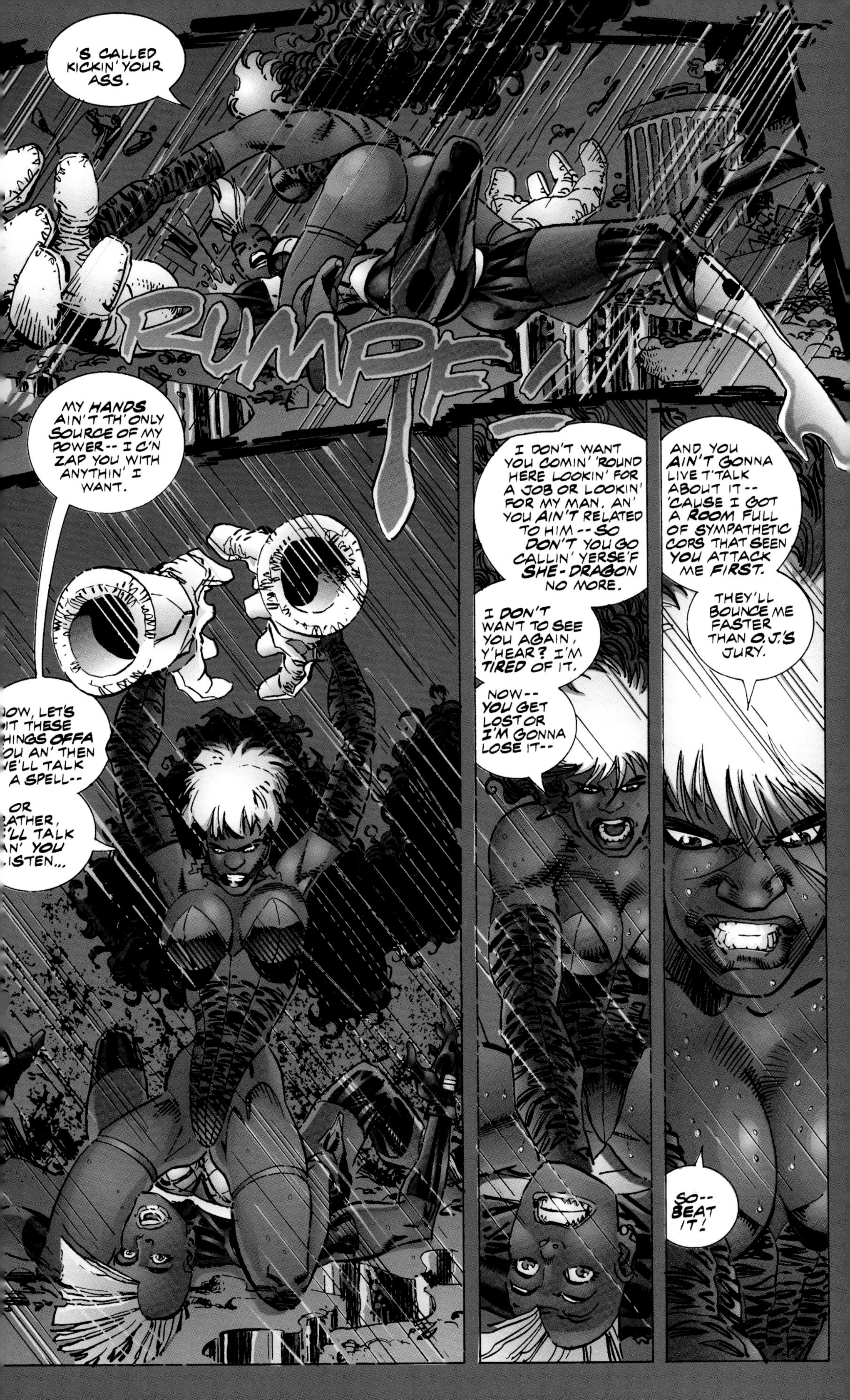

'S CALLED KICKIN' YOUR ASS.
RUMPF--
MY HANDS AIN'T TH' ONLY SOURCE OF MY POWER-- I C'N ZAP YOU WITH ANYTHIN' I WANT.
I DON'T WANT YOU COMIN' 'ROUND HERE LOOKIN' FOR A JOB OR LOOKIN' FOR MY MAN, AN' YOU AIN'T RELATED TO HIM-- SO DON'T YOU GO CALLIN' YERSE'F SHE-DRAGON NO MORE.
I DON'T WANT TO SEE YOU AGAIN, Y'HEAR? I'M TIRED OF IT.
NOW-- YOU GET LOST OR I'M GONNA LOSE IT--
AND YOU AIN'T GONNA LIVE T'TALK ABOUT IT-- 'CAUSE I GOT A ROOM FULL OF SYMPATHETIC COPS THAT SEEN YOU ATTACK ME FIRST.
THEY'LL BOUNCE ME FASTER THAN O.J.'S JURY.
SO-- BEAT IT!

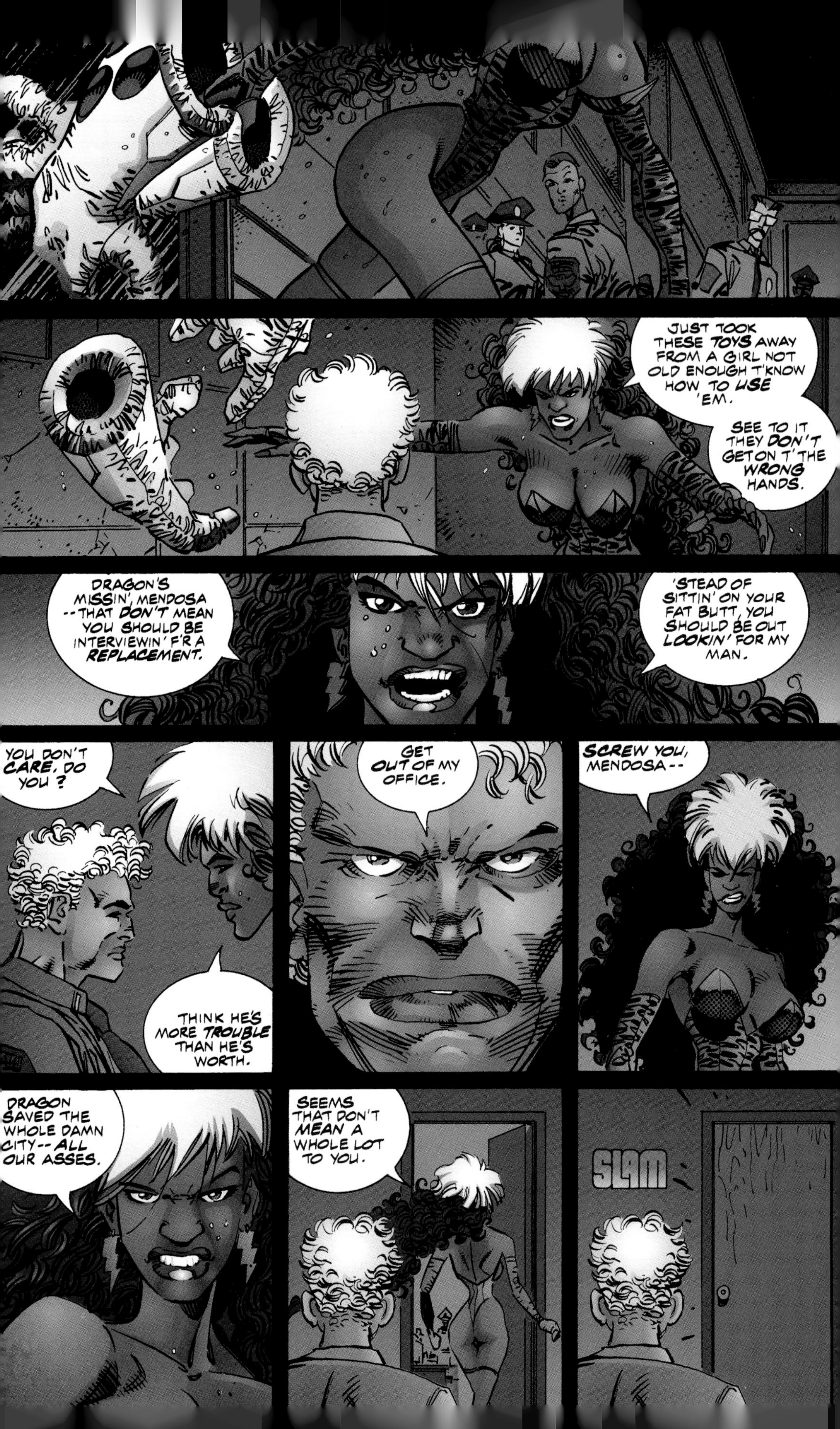
JUST TOOK THESE TOYS AWAY FROM A GIRL NOT OLD ENOUGH T'KNOW HOW TO USE 'EM.
SEE TO IT THEY DON'T GET ON T'THE WRONG HANDS.
DRAGON'S MISSIN', MENDOSA --THAT DON'T MEAN YOU SHOULD BE INTERVIEWIN' F'R A REPLACEMENT.
'STEAD OF SITTIN' ON YOUR FAT BUTT, YOU SHOULD BE OUT LOOKIN' FOR MY MAN.
YOU DON'T CARE, DO YOU ?
THINK HE'S MORE TROUBLE THAN HE'S WORTH.
GET OUT OF MY OFFICE.
SCREW YOU, MENDOSA--
DRAGON SAVED THE WHOLE DAMN CITY-- ALL OUR ASSES.
SEEMS THAT DON'T MEAN A WHOLE LOT TO YOU.
SLAM

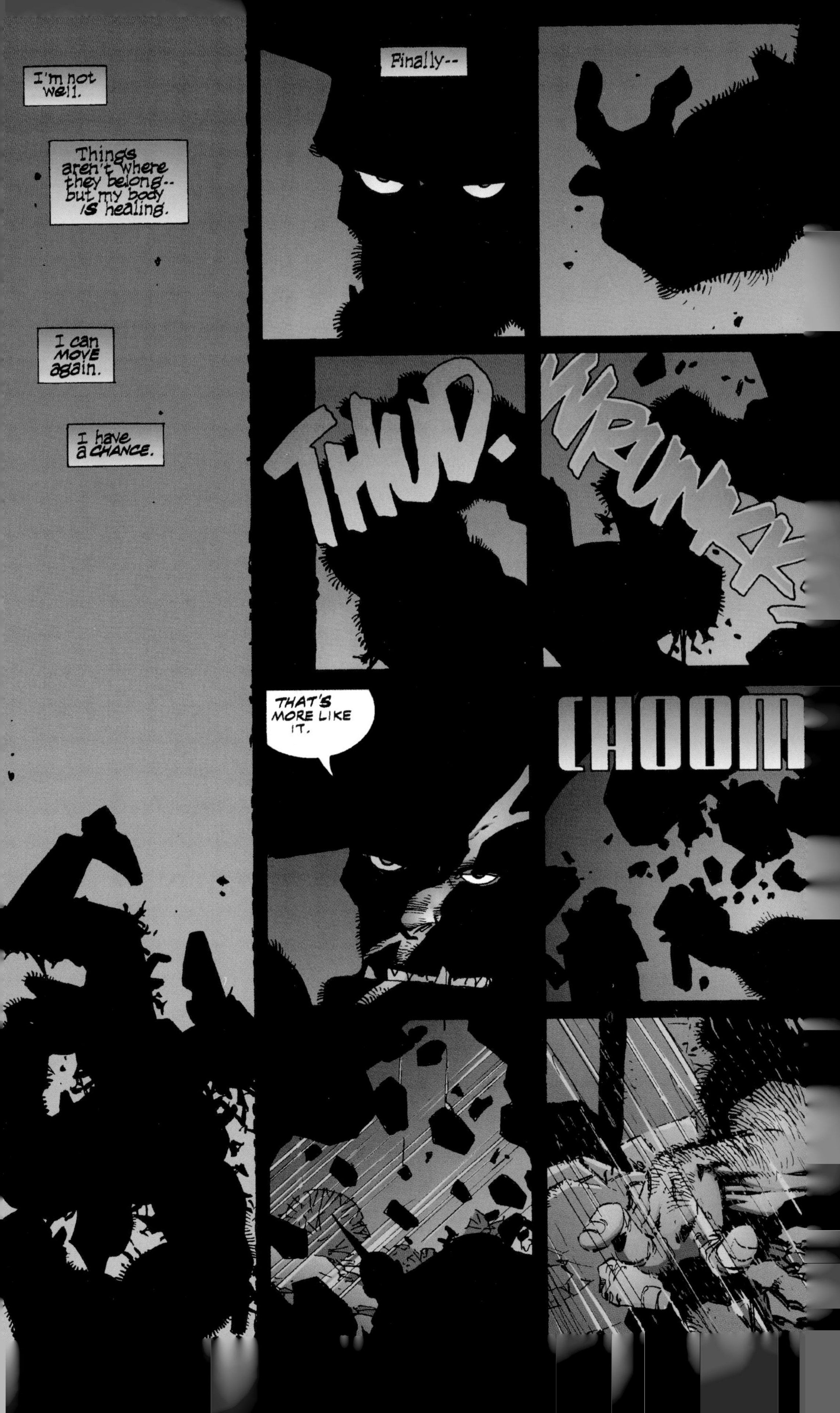
I'm not well.
Things aren't where they belong.. but my body IS healing.
I can MOVE again.
I have a CHANCE.
Finally--
THUD.
WRUNNK
THAT'S MORE LIKE IT.
CHOOM

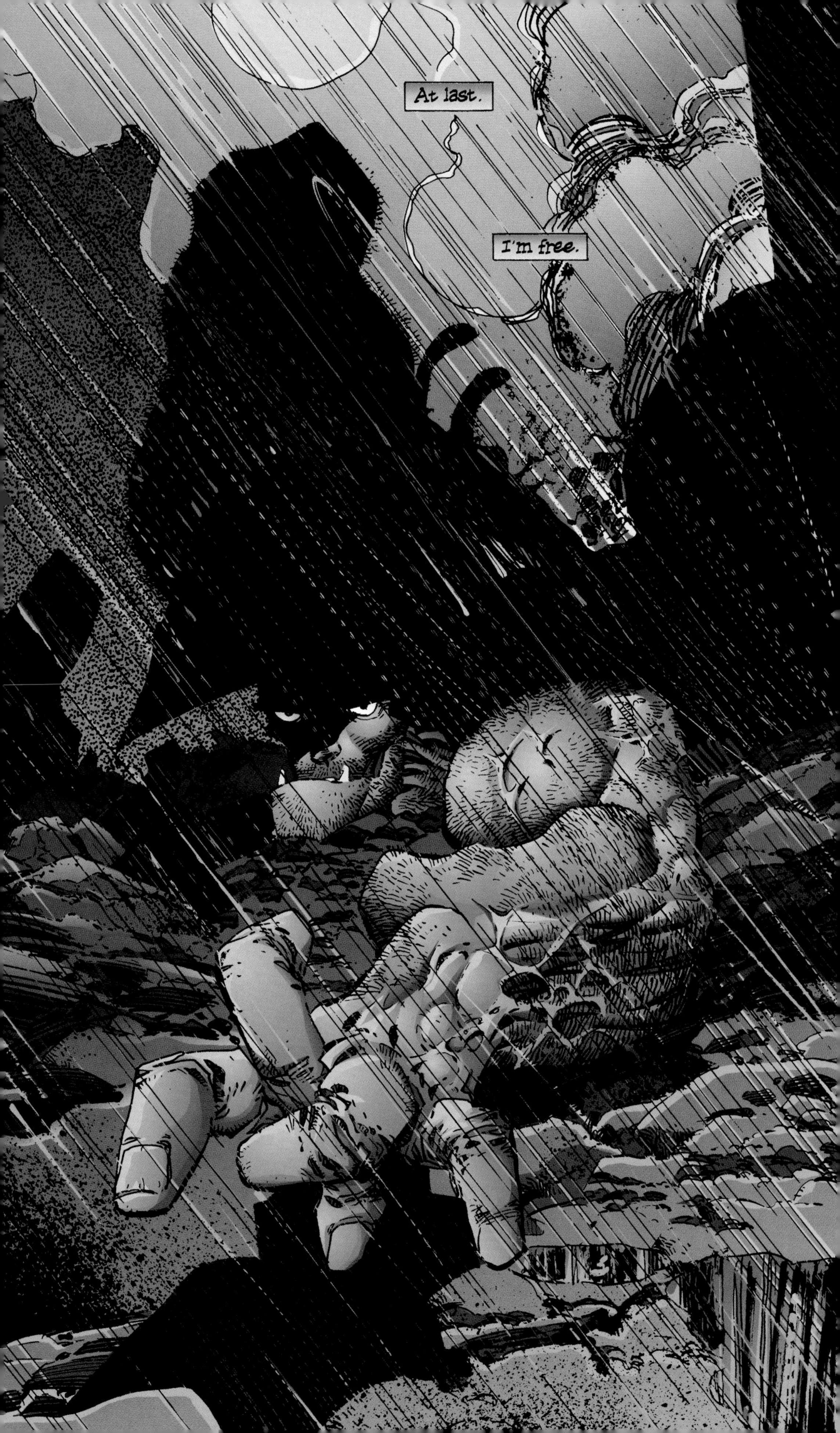
At last.
I'm free.

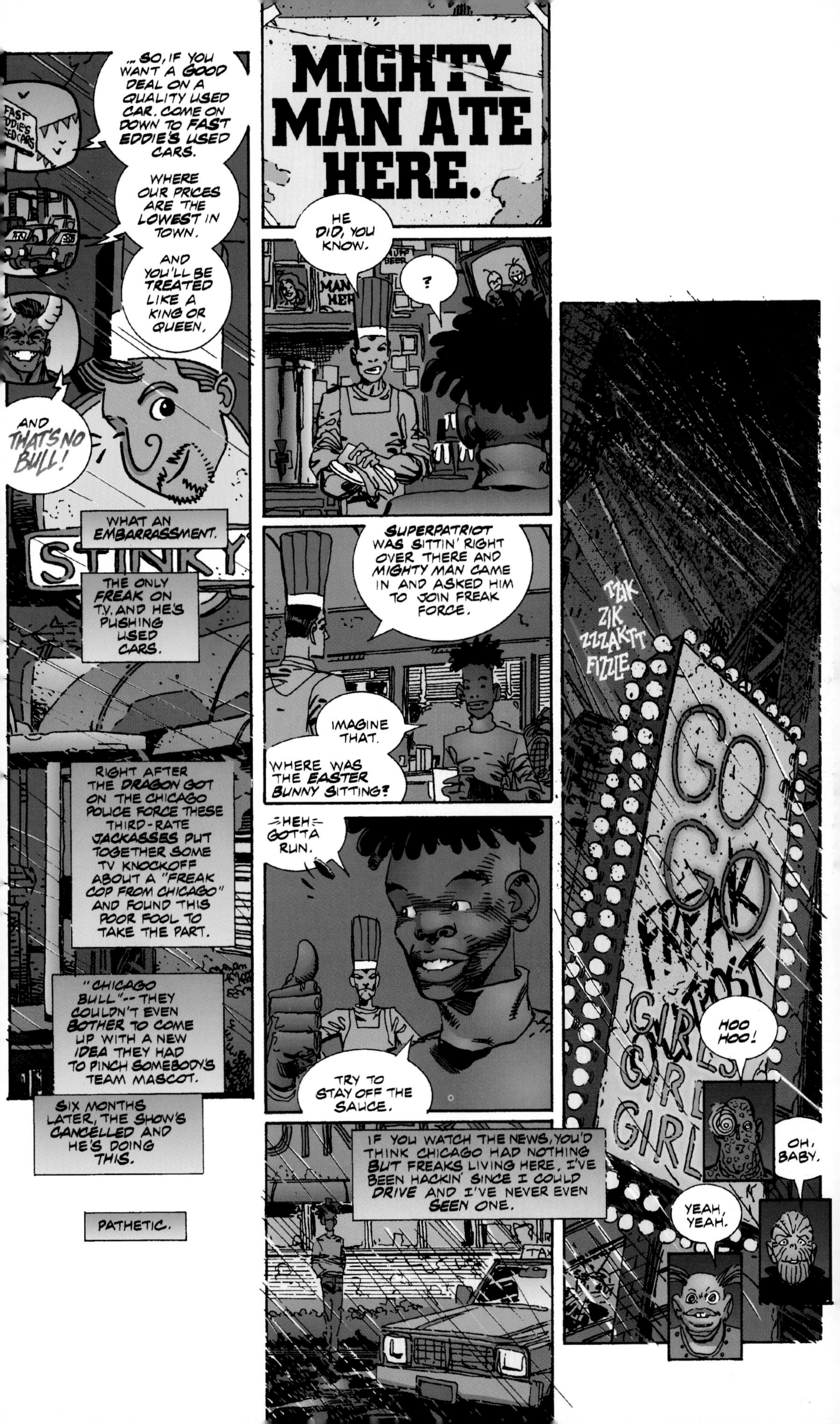

...SO, IF YOU WANT A GOOD DEAL ON A QUALITY USED CAR, COME ON DOWN TO FAST EDDIE'S USED CARS.
FAST EDDIE'S USED CARS
WHERE OUR PRICES ARE THE LOWEST IN TOWN.
AND YOU'LL BE TREATED LIKE A KING OR QUEEN.
AND THAT'S NO BULL!
WHAT AN EMBARRASSMENT.
STINKY
THE ONLY FREAK ON T.V., AND HE'S PUSHING USED CARS.
RIGHT AFTER THE DRAGON GOT ON THE CHICAGO POLICE FORCE THESE THIRD-RATE JACKASSES PUT TOGETHER SOME TV KNOCKOFF ABOUT A "FREAK COP FROM CHICAGO" AND FOUND THIS POOR FOOL TO TAKE THE PART.
"CHICAGO BULL"-- THEY COULDN'T EVEN BOTHER TO COME UP WITH A NEW IDEA THEY HAD TO PINCH SOMEBODY'S TEAM MASCOT.
SIX MONTHS LATER, THE SHOW'S CANCELLED AND HE'S DOING THIS.
PATHETIC.
MIGHTY MAN ATE HERE.
HE DID, YOU KNOW.
?
SUPERPATRIOT WAS SITTIN' RIGHT OVER THERE AND MIGHTY MAN CAME IN AND ASKED HIM TO JOIN FREAK FORCE.
IMAGINE THAT.
WHERE WAS THE EASTER BUNNY SITTING?
-HEH- GOTTA RUN.
TRY TO STAY OFF THE SAUCE.
IF YOU WATCH THE NEWS, YOU'D THINK CHICAGO HAD NOTHING BUT FREAKS LIVING HERE. I'VE BEEN HACKIN' SINCE I COULD DRIVE AND I'VE NEVER EVEN SEEN ONE.
TZIK ZIK ZZZAKTT FIZZLE
GO GO FREAK
GIRLS GIRLS GIRLS
HOO HOO!
OH, BABY.
YEAH, YEAH.

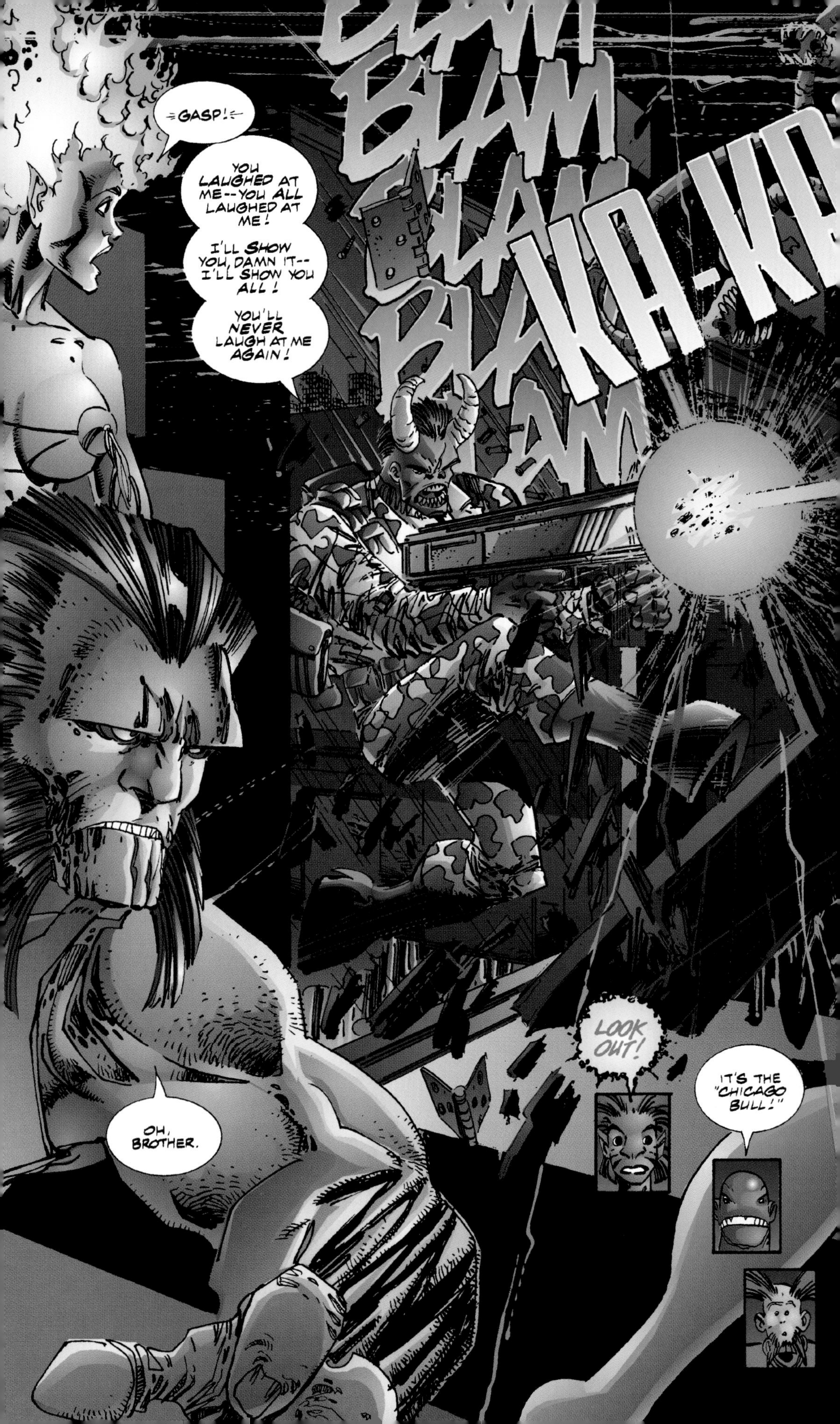
BLAM
BLAM
BLAM
BLAM
KA-KA
GASP!
YOU LAUGHED AT ME--YOU ALL LAUGHED AT ME!
I'LL SHOW YOU, DAMN IT-- I'LL SHOW YOU ALL!
YOU'LL NEVER LAUGH AT ME AGAIN!
OH, BROTHER.
LOOK OUT!
IT'S THE "CHICAGO BULL!"

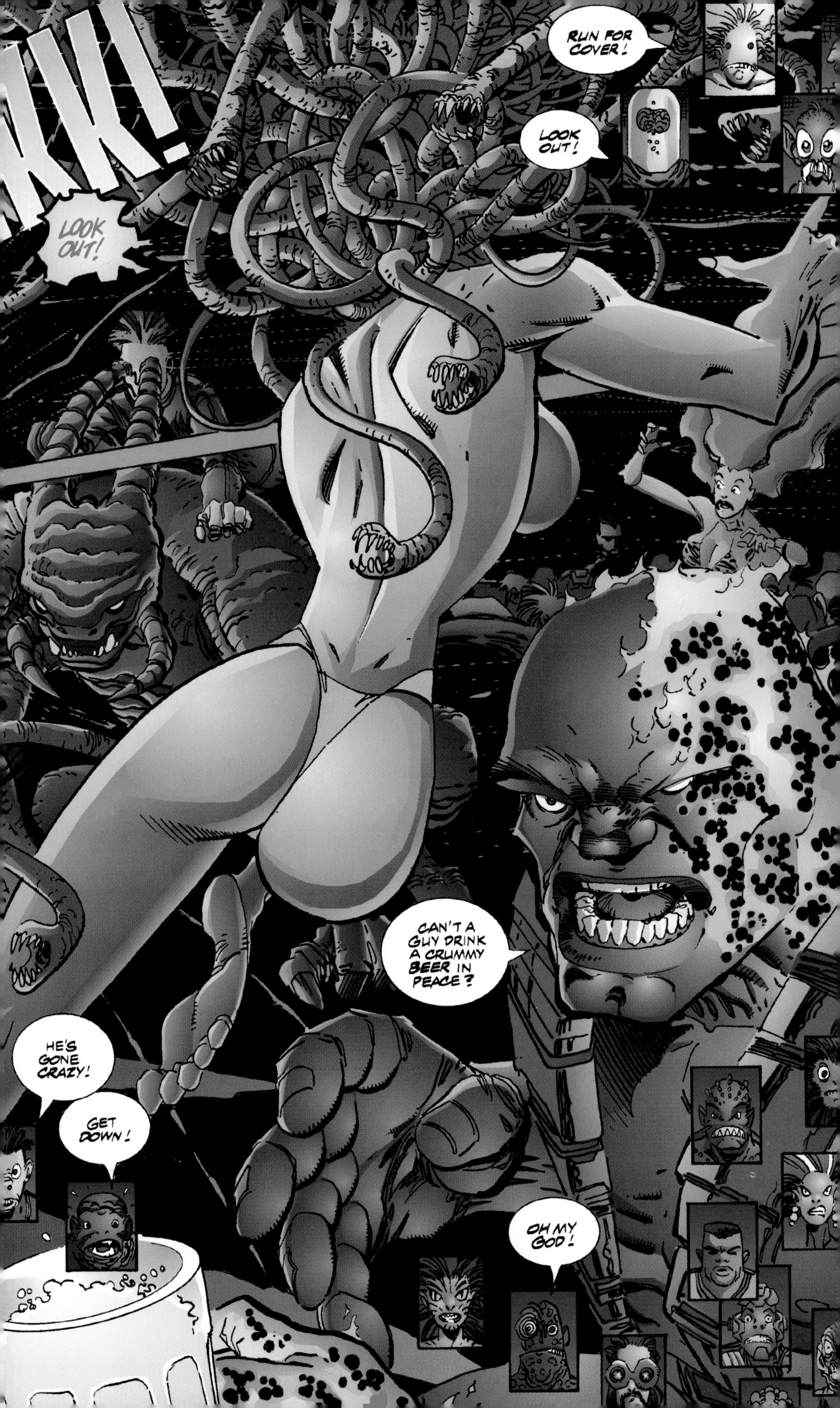

LOOK OUT!
RUN FOR COVER!
LOOK OUT!
CAN'T A GUY DRINK A CRUMMY BEER IN PEACE?
HE'S GONE CRAZY!
GET DOWN!
OH MY GOD!

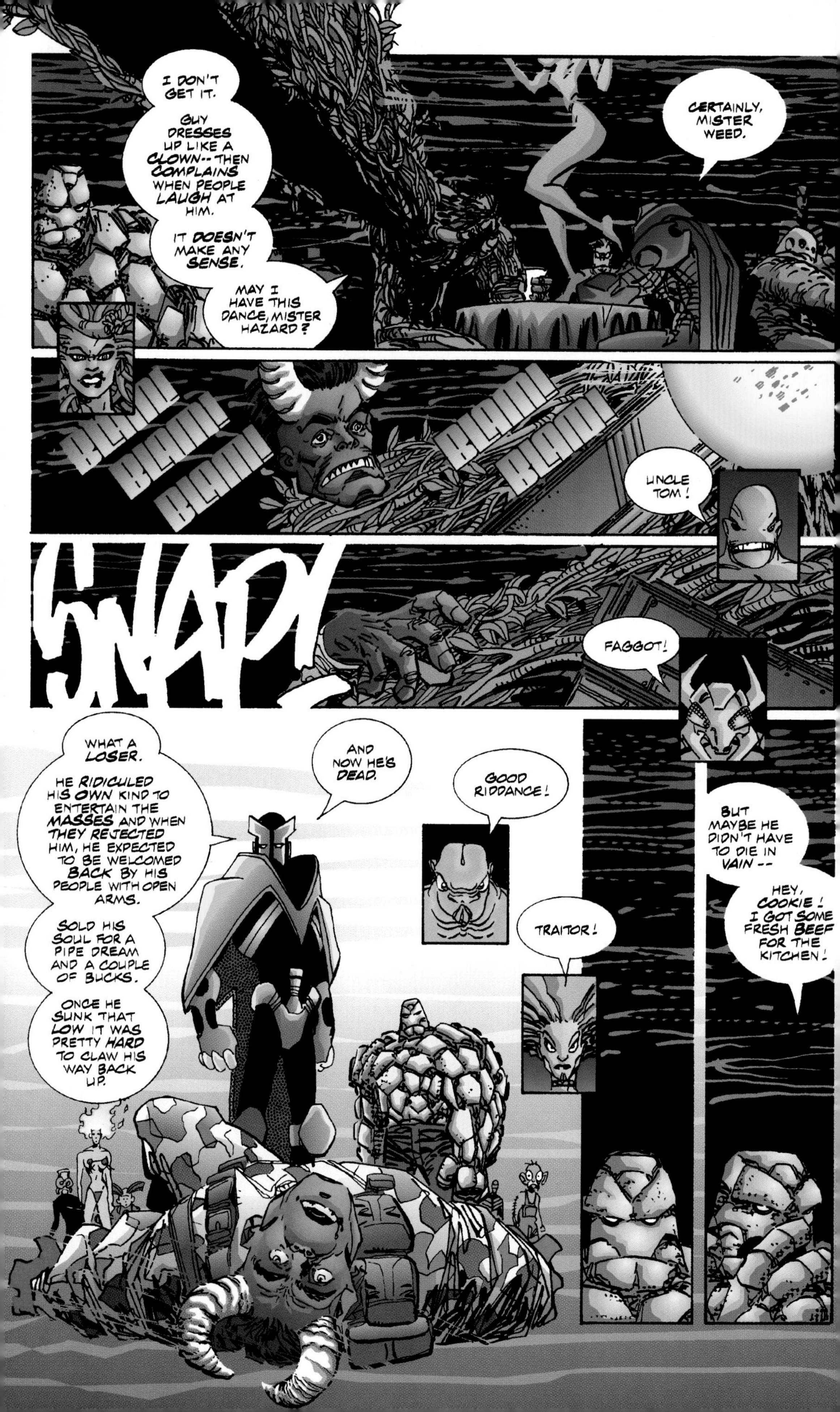

I DON'T GET IT.
GUY DRESSES UP LIKE A CLOWN-- THEN COMPLAINS WHEN PEOPLE LAUGH AT HIM.
IT DOESN'T MAKE ANY SENSE.
CERTAINLY, MISTER WEED.
MAY I HAVE THIS DANCE, MISTER HAZARD?
UNCLE TOM!
SNAP!
FAGGOT!
WHAT A LOSER.
HE RIDICULED HIS OWN KIND TO ENTERTAIN THE MASSES AND WHEN THEY REJECTED HIM, HE EXPECTED TO BE WELCOMED BACK BY HIS PEOPLE WITH OPEN ARMS.
SOLD HIS SOUL FOR A PIPE DREAM AND A COUPLE OF BUCKS.
ONCE HE SUNK THAT LOW IT WAS PRETTY HARD TO CLAW HIS WAY BACK UP.
AND NOW HE'S DEAD.
GOOD RIDDANCE!
TRAITOR!
BUT MAYBE HE DIDN'T HAVE TO DIE IN VAIN --
HEY, COOKIE! I GOT SOME FRESH BEEF FOR THE KITCHEN!

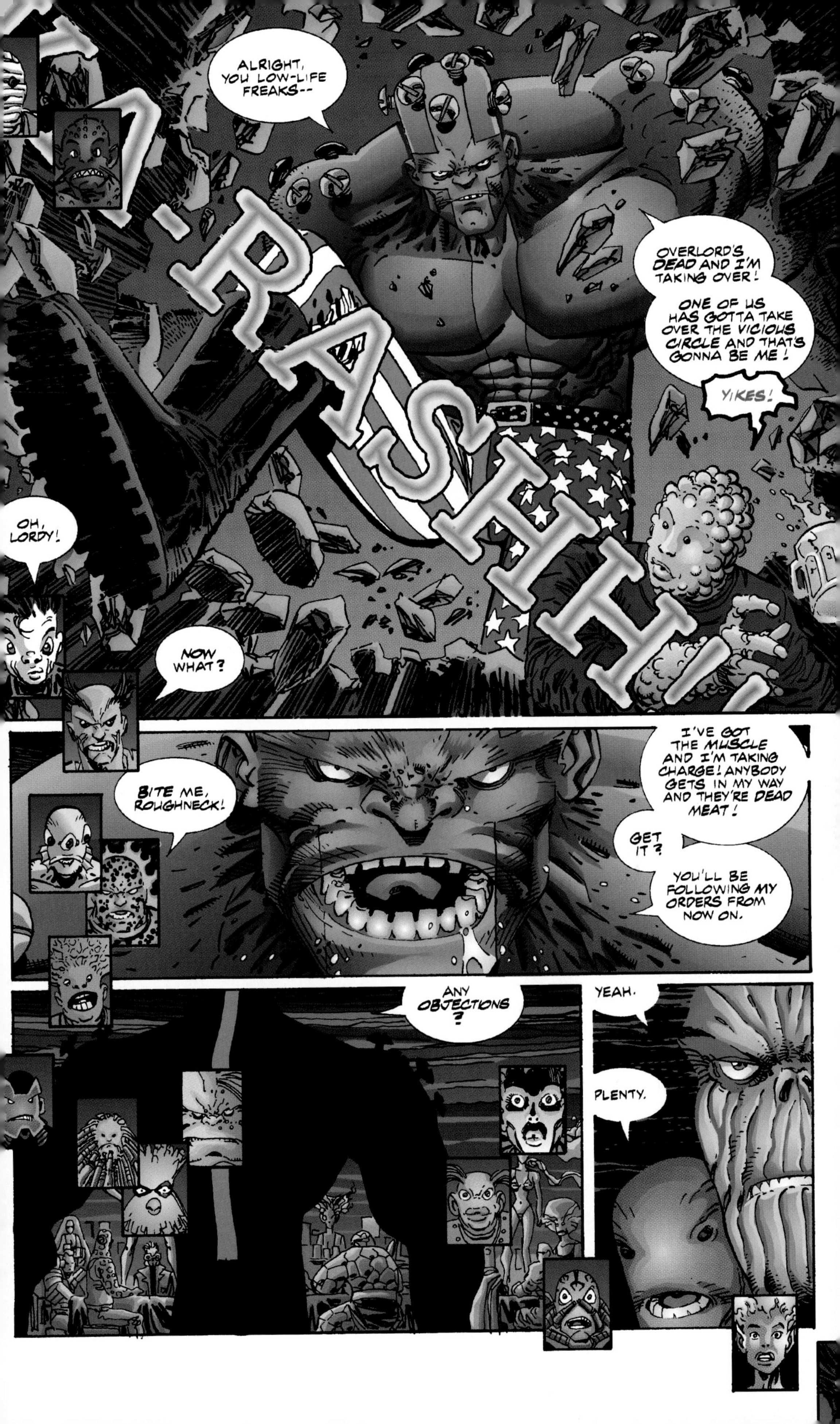
ALRIGHT, YOU LOW-LIFE FREAKS--
'RASHH!
OVERLORD'S DEAD AND I'M TAKING OVER!
ONE OF US HAS GOTTA TAKE OVER THE VICIOUS CIRCLE AND THAT'S GONNA BE ME!
YIKES!
OH, LORDY!
NOW WHAT?
I'VE GOT THE MUSCLE AND I'M TAKING CHARGE! ANYBODY GETS IN MY WAY AND THEY'RE DEAD MEAT!
BITE ME, ROUGHNECK!
GET IT?
YOU'LL BE FOLLOWING MY ORDERS FROM NOW ON.
ANY OBJECTIONS?
YEAH.
PLENTY.

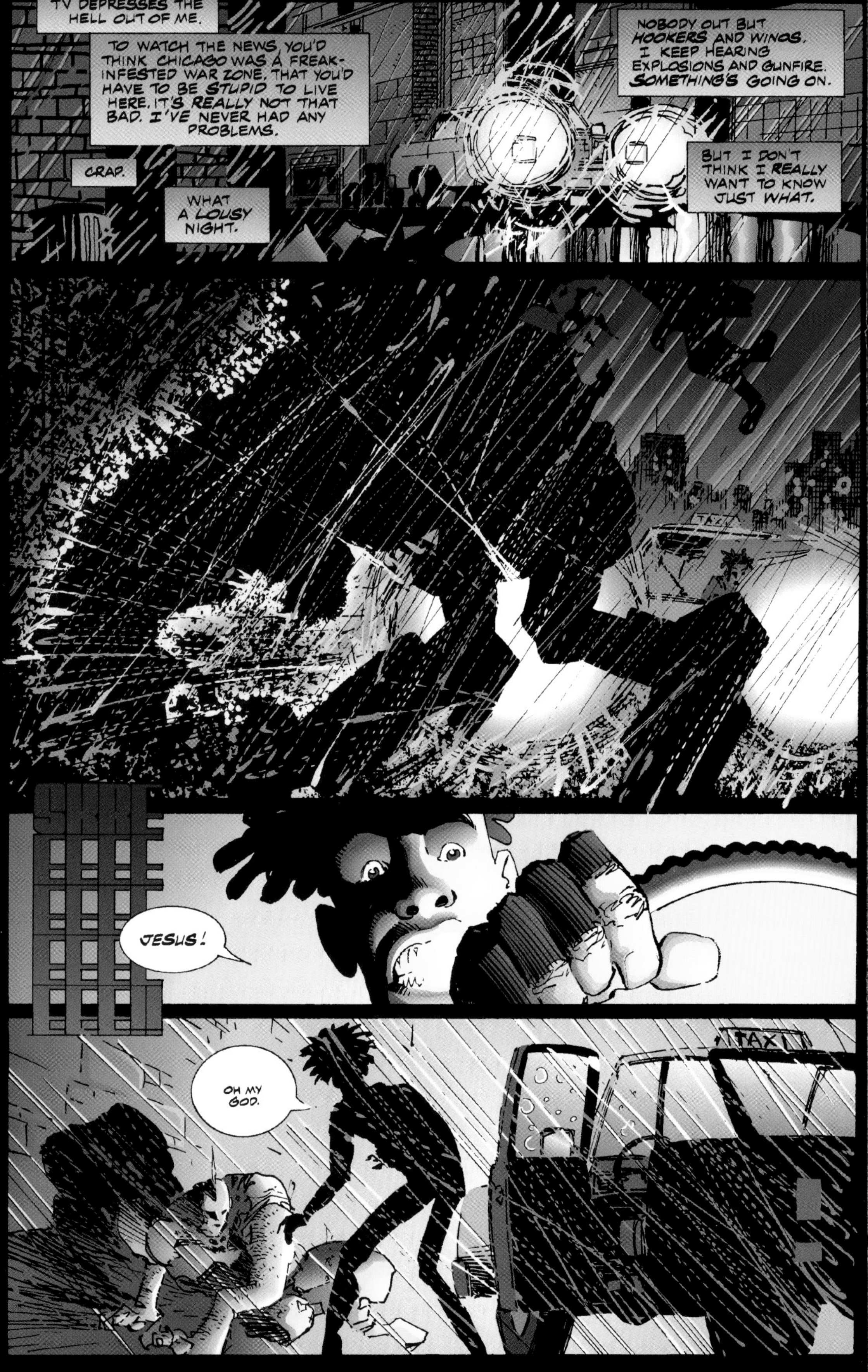
TV DEPRESSES THE HELL OUT OF ME.
TO WATCH THE NEWS, YOU'D THINK CHICAGO WAS A FREAK-INFESTED WAR ZONE. THAT YOU'D HAVE TO BE STUPID TO LIVE HERE. IT'S REALLY NOT THAT BAD. I'VE NEVER HAD ANY PROBLEMS.
CRAP.
WHAT A LOUSY NIGHT.
NOBODY OUT BUT HOOKERS AND WINOS. I KEEP HEARING EXPLOSIONS AND GUNFIRE. SOMETHING'S GOING ON.
BUT I DON'T THINK I REALLY WANT TO KNOW JUST WHAT.
TAXI
JESUS!
TAXI
OH MY GOD.

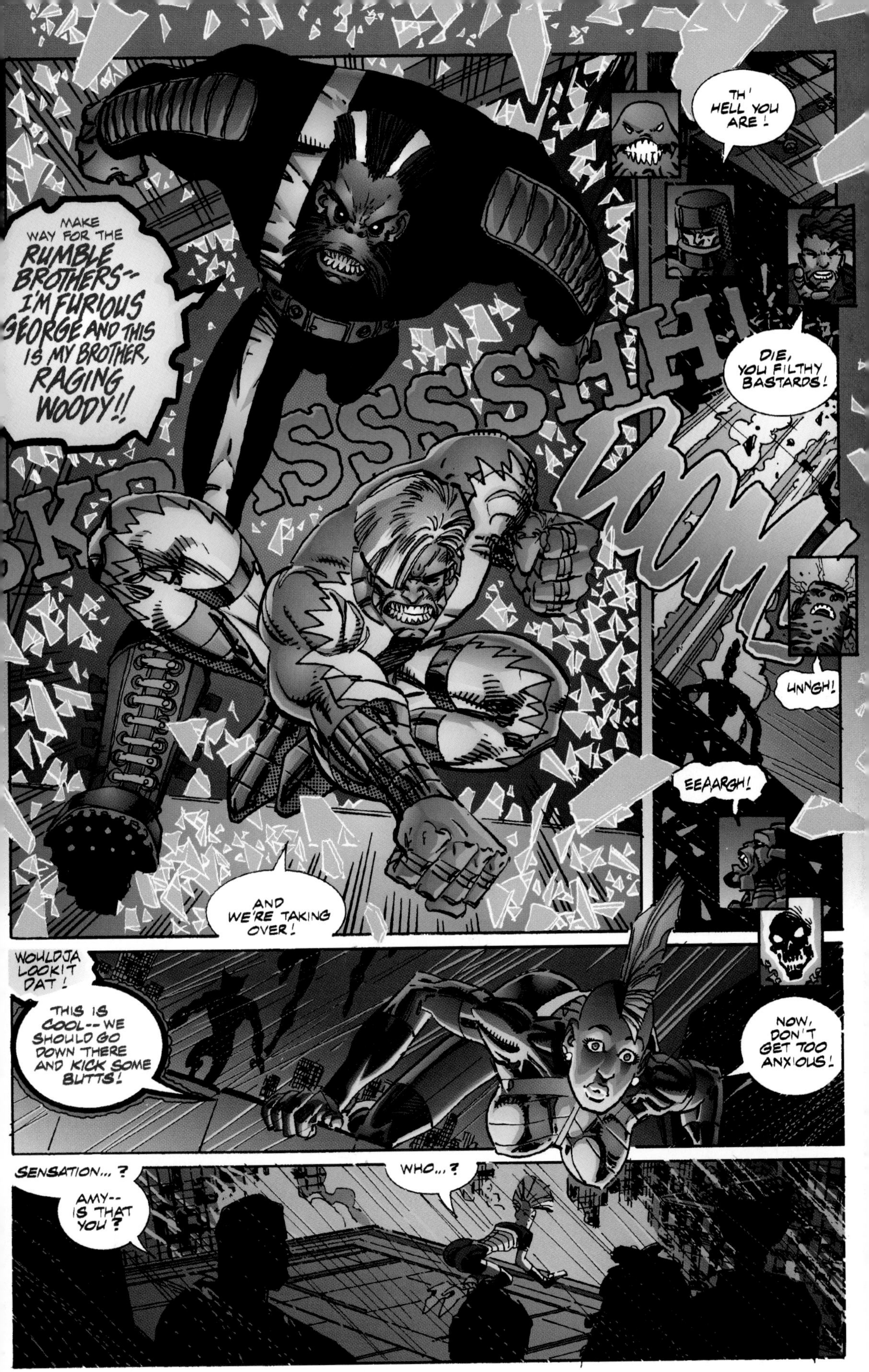
TH' HELL YOU ARE!
MAKE WAY FOR THE RUMBLE BROTHERS-- I'M FURIOUS GEORGE AND THIS IS MY BROTHER, RAGING WOODY!!
DIE, YOU FILTHY BASTARDS!
UNNGH!
EEAARGH!
AND WE'RE TAKING OVER!
WOULDJA LOOKIT DAT!
THIS IS COOL-- WE SHOULD GO DOWN THERE AND KICK SOME BUTTS!
NOW, DON'T GET TOO ANXIOUS!
SENSATION...?
AMY-- IS THAT YOU?
WHO...?

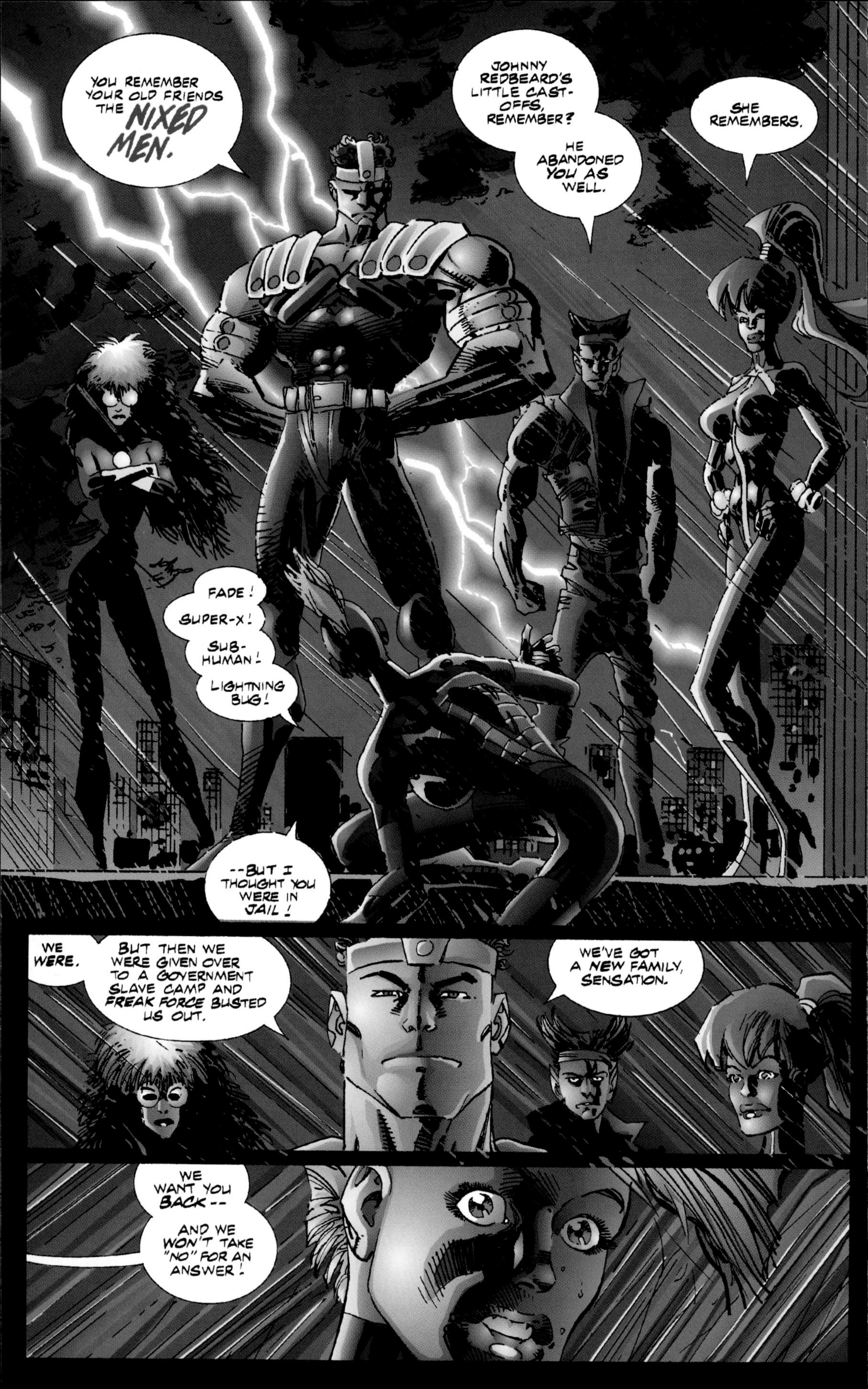
YOU REMEMBER YOUR OLD FRIENDS THE NIXED MEN.
JOHNNY REDBEARD'S LITTLE CAST-OFFS, REMEMBER?
HE ABANDONED YOU AS WELL.
SHE REMEMBERS.
FADE!
SUPER-X!
SUB-HUMAN!
LIGHTNING BUG!
--BUT I THOUGHT YOU WERE IN JAIL!
WE WERE.
BUT THEN WE WERE GIVEN OVER TO A GOVERNMENT SLAVE CAMP AND FREAK FORCE BUSTED US OUT.
WE'VE GOT A NEW FAMILY, SENSATION.
WE WANT YOU BACK--
AND WE WON'T TAKE "NO" FOR AN ANSWER!

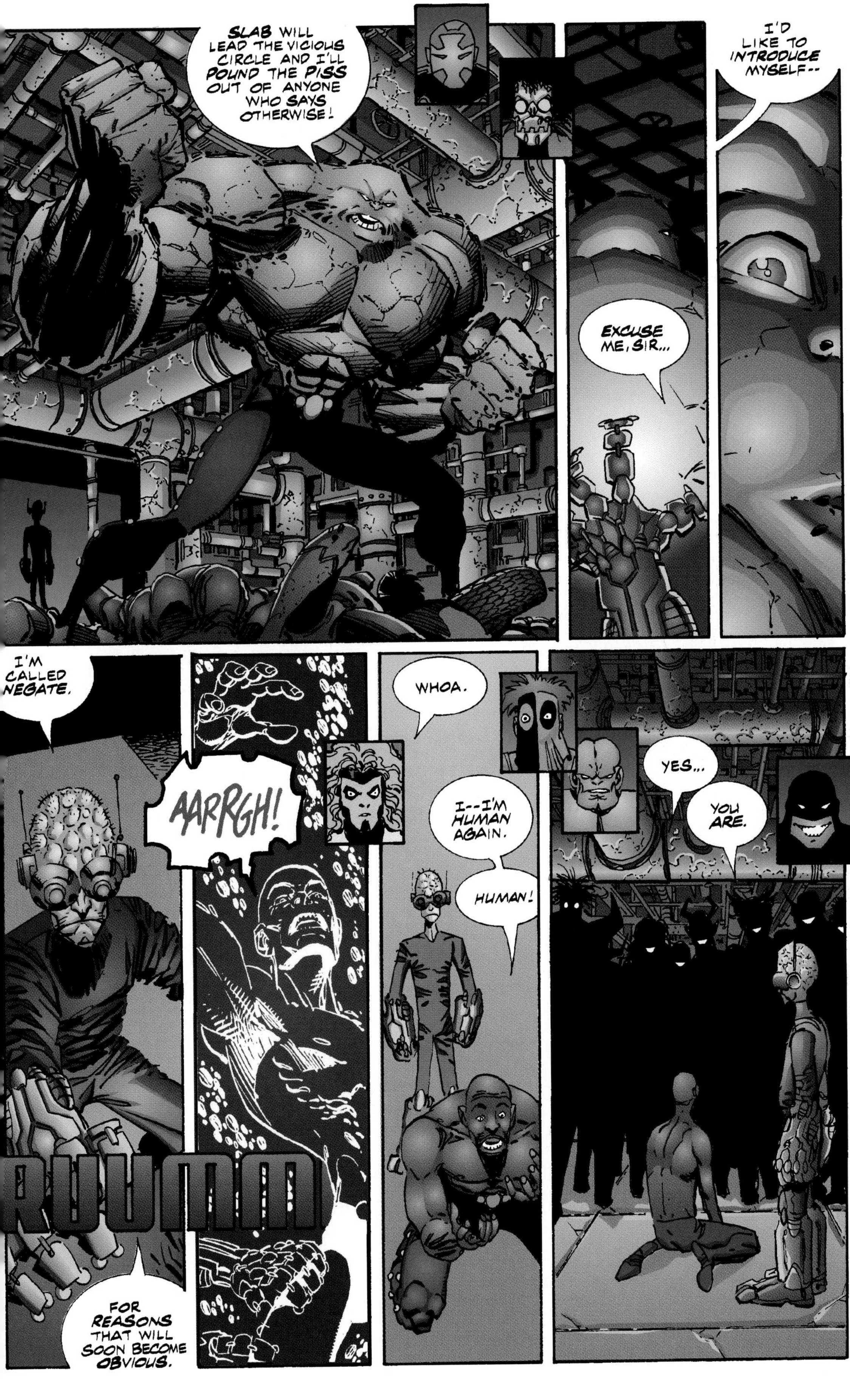
SLAB WILL LEAD THE VICIOUS CIRCLE AND I'LL POUND THE PISS OUT OF ANYONE WHO SAYS OTHERWISE!
EXCUSE ME, SIR...
I'D LIKE TO INTRODUCE MYSELF--
I'M CALLED NEGATE.
RUUMM
FOR REASONS THAT WILL SOON BECOME OBVIOUS.
AARRGH!
WHOA.
I--I'M HUMAN AGAIN.
HUMAN!
YES...
YOU ARE.

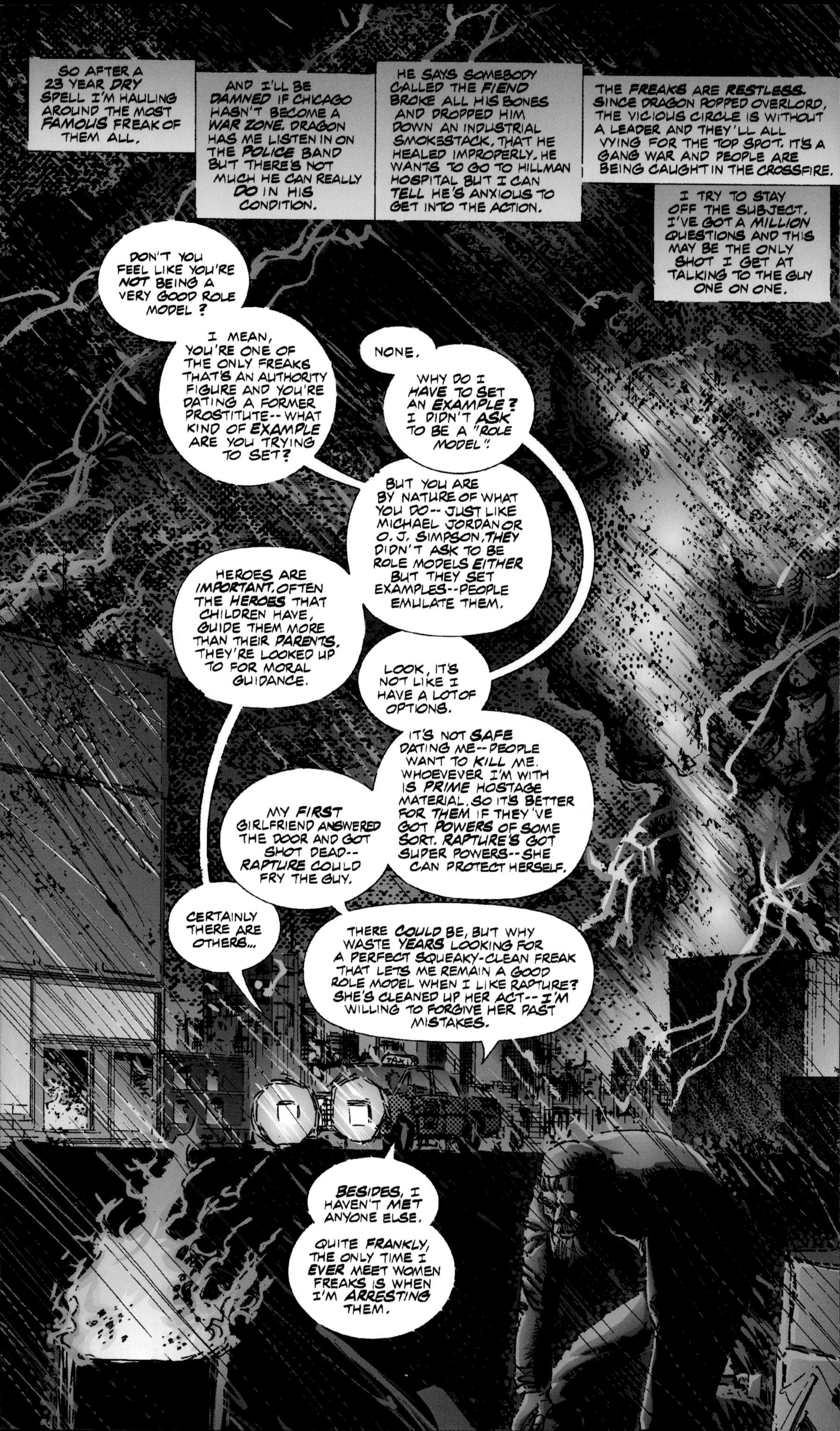
SO AFTER A 23 YEAR DRY SPELL I'M HAULING AROUND THE MOST FAMOUS FREAK OF THEM ALL.
AND I'LL BE DAMNED IF CHICAGO HASN'T BECOME A WAR ZONE. DRAGON HAS ME LISTEN IN ON THE POLICE BAND BUT THERE'S NOT MUCH HE CAN REALLY DO IN HIS CONDITION.
HE SAYS SOMEBODY CALLED THE FIEND BROKE ALL HIS BONES AND DROPPED HIM DOWN AN INDUSTRIAL SMOKESTACK, THAT HE HEALED IMPROPERLY. HE WANTS TO GO TO HILLMAN HOSPITAL BUT I CAN TELL HE'S ANXIOUS TO GET INTO THE ACTION.
THE FREAKS ARE RESTLESS. SINCE DRAGON POPPED OVERLORD, THE VICIOUS CIRCLE IS WITHOUT A LEADER AND THEY'LL ALL VYING FOR THE TOP SPOT. IT'S A GANG WAR AND PEOPLE ARE BEING CAUGHT IN THE CROSSFIRE.
I TRY TO STAY OFF THE SUBJECT. I'VE GOT A MILLION QUESTIONS AND THIS MAY BE THE ONLY SHOT I GET AT TALKING TO THE GUY ONE ON ONE.
DON'T YOU FEEL LIKE YOU'RE NOT BEING A VERY GOOD ROLE MODEL ?
I MEAN, YOU'RE ONE OF THE ONLY FREAKS THAT'S AN AUTHORITY FIGURE AND YOU'RE DATING A FORMER PROSTITUTE-- WHAT KIND OF EXAMPLE ARE YOU TRYING TO SET?
NONE.
WHY DO I HAVE TO SET AN EXAMPLE ? I DIDN'T ASK TO BE A "ROLE MODEL".
BUT YOU ARE BY NATURE OF WHAT YOU DO-- JUST LIKE MICHAEL JORDAN OR O. J. SIMPSON, THEY DIDN'T ASK TO BE ROLE MODELS EITHER BUT THEY SET EXAMPLES--PEOPLE EMULATE THEM.
HEROES ARE IMPORTANT. OFTEN THE HEROES THAT CHILDREN HAVE, GUIDE THEM MORE THAN THEIR PARENTS. THEY'RE LOOKED UP TO FOR MORAL GUIDANCE.
LOOK, IT'S NOT LIKE I HAVE A LOT OF OPTIONS.
IT'S NOT SAFE DATING ME--PEOPLE WANT TO KILL ME. WHOEVEVER I'M WITH IS PRIME HOSTAGE MATERIAL, SO IT'S BETTER FOR THEM IF THEY'VE GOT POWERS OF SOME SORT. RAPTURE'S GOT SUPER POWERS--SHE CAN PROTECT HERSELF.
MY FIRST GIRLFRIEND ANSWERED THE DOOR AND GOT SHOT DEAD-- RAPTURE COULD FRY THE GUY.
CERTAINLY THERE ARE OTHERS...
THERE COULD BE, BUT WHY WASTE YEARS LOOKING FOR A PERFECT SQUEAKY-CLEAN FREAK THAT LETS ME REMAIN A GOOD ROLE MODEL WHEN I LIKE RAPTURE? SHE'S CLEANED UP HER ACT-- I'M WILLING TO FORGIVE HER PAST MISTAKES.
BESIDES, I HAVEN'T MET ANYONE ELSE.
QUITE FRANKLY, THE ONLY TIME I EVER MEET WOMEN FREAKS IS WHEN I'M ARRESTING THEM.
TAXI

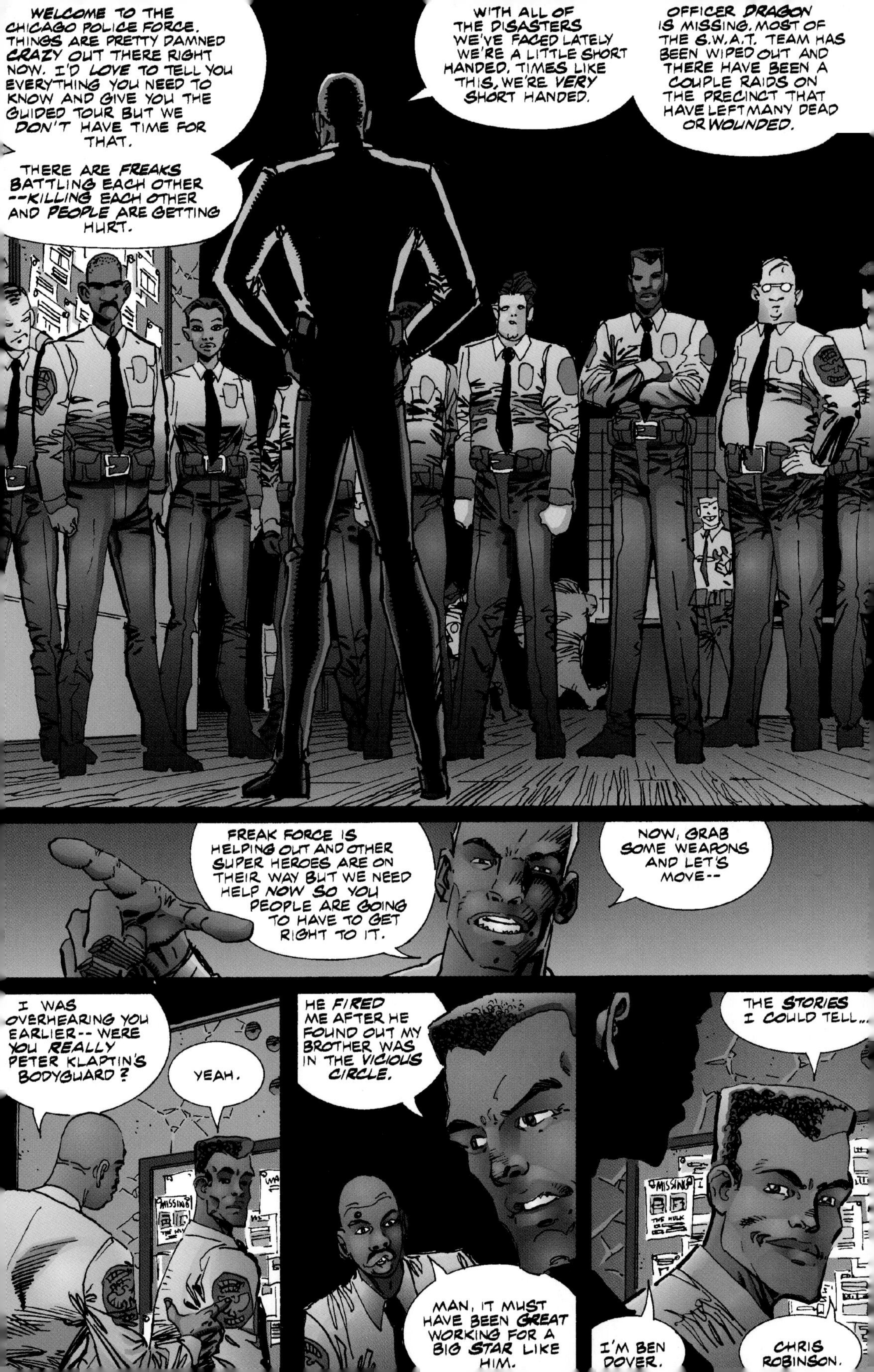
WELCOME TO THE CHICAGO POLICE FORCE. THINGS ARE PRETTY DAMNED CRAZY OUT THERE RIGHT NOW. I'D LOVE TO TELL YOU EVERYTHING YOU NEED TO KNOW AND GIVE YOU THE GUIDED TOUR BUT WE DON'T HAVE TIME FOR THAT.
THERE ARE FREAKS BATTLING EACH OTHER --KILLING EACH OTHER AND PEOPLE ARE GETTING HURT.
WITH ALL OF THE DISASTERS WE'VE FACED LATELY WE'RE A LITTLE SHORT HANDED. TIMES LIKE THIS, WE'RE VERY SHORT HANDED.
OFFICER DRAGON IS MISSING. MOST OF THE S.W.A.T. TEAM HAS BEEN WIPED OUT AND THERE HAVE BEEN A COUPLE RAIDS ON THE PRECINCT THAT HAVE LEFT MANY DEAD OR WOUNDED.
FREAK FORCE IS HELPING OUT AND OTHER SUPER HEROES ARE ON THEIR WAY BUT WE NEED HELP NOW SO YOU PEOPLE ARE GOING TO HAVE TO GET RIGHT TO IT.
NOW, GRAB SOME WEAPONS AND LET'S MOVE--
I WAS OVERHEARING YOU EARLIER-- WERE YOU REALLY PETER KLAPTIN'S BODYGUARD?
YEAH.
HE FIRED ME AFTER HE FOUND OUT MY BROTHER WAS IN THE VICIOUS CIRCLE.
MAN, IT MUST HAVE BEEN GREAT WORKING FOR A BIG STAR LIKE HIM.
THE STORIES I COULD TELL...
I'M BEN DOVER.
CHRIS ROBINSON.

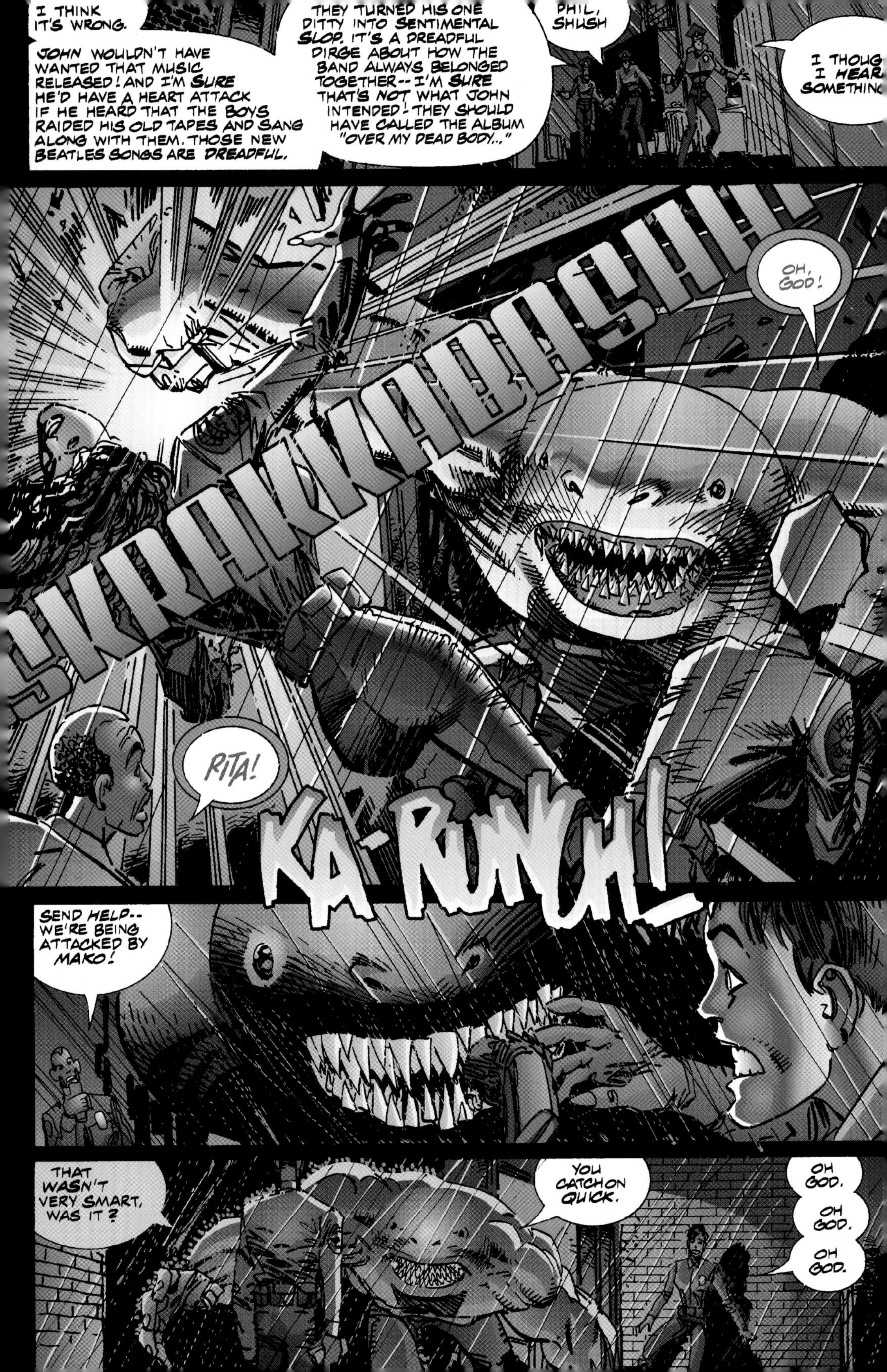

I THINK IT'S WRONG.
JOHN WOULDN'T HAVE WANTED THAT MUSIC RELEASED! AND I'M SURE HE'D HAVE A HEART ATTACK IF HE HEARD THAT THE BOYS RAIDED HIS OLD TAPES AND SANG ALONG WITH THEM. THOSE NEW BEATLES SONGS ARE DREADFUL.
THEY TURNED HIS ONE DITTY INTO SENTIMENTAL SLOP. IT'S A DREADFUL DIRGE ABOUT HOW THE BAND ALWAYS BELONGED TOGETHER-- I'M SURE THAT'S NOT WHAT JOHN INTENDED! THEY SHOULD HAVE CALLED THE ALBUM "OVER MY DEAD BODY..."
PHIL, SHUSH
OH, GOD!
RITA!
KA-RUNCH!
SEND HELP-- WE'RE BEING ATTACKED BY MAKO!
THAT WASN'T VERY SMART, WAS IT?
YOU CATCH ON QUICK.
OH GOD.
OH GOD.
OH GOD.

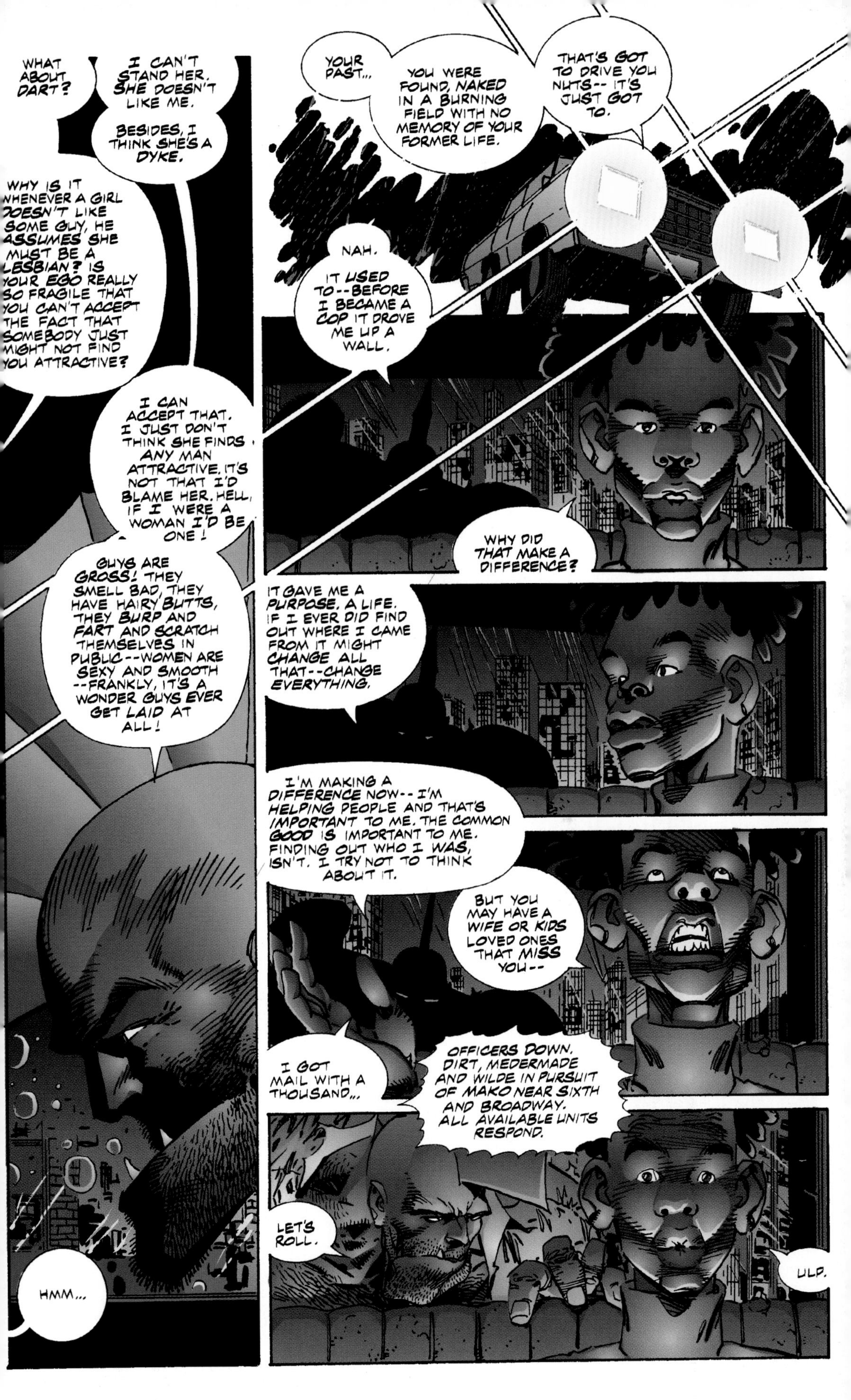

WHAT ABOUT DART?
I CAN'T STAND HER. SHE DOESN'T LIKE ME.
BESIDES, I THINK SHE'S A DYKE.
WHY IS IT WHENEVER A GIRL DOESN'T LIKE SOME GUY, HE ASSUMES SHE MUST BE A LESBIAN? IS YOUR EGO REALLY SO FRAGILE THAT YOU CAN'T ACCEPT THE FACT THAT SOMEBODY JUST MIGHT NOT FIND YOU ATTRACTIVE?
I CAN ACCEPT THAT. I JUST DON'T THINK SHE FINDS ANY MAN ATTRACTIVE. IT'S NOT THAT I'D BLAME HER. HELL, IF I WERE A WOMAN I'D BE ONE!
GUYS ARE GROSS! THEY SMELL BAD, THEY HAVE HAIRY BUTTS, THEY BURP AND FART AND SCRATCH THEMSELVES IN PUBLIC--WOMEN ARE SEXY AND SMOOTH --FRANKLY, IT'S A WONDER GUYS EVER GET LAID AT ALL!
HMM...
YOUR PAST...
YOU WERE FOUND, NAKED IN A BURNING FIELD WITH NO MEMORY OF YOUR FORMER LIFE.
THAT'S GOT TO DRIVE YOU NUTS-- IT'S JUST GOT TO.
NAH.
IT USED TO--BEFORE I BECAME A COP IT DROVE ME UP A WALL.
WHY DID THAT MAKE A DIFFERENCE?
IT GAVE ME A PURPOSE. A LIFE. IF I EVER DID FIND OUT WHERE I CAME FROM IT MIGHT CHANGE ALL THAT--CHANGE EVERYTHING.
I'M MAKING A DIFFERENCE NOW-- I'M HELPING PEOPLE AND THAT'S IMPORTANT TO ME. THE COMMON GOOD IS IMPORTANT TO ME. FINDING OUT WHO I WAS, ISN'T. I TRY NOT TO THINK ABOUT IT.
BUT YOU MAY HAVE A WIFE OR KIDS LOVED ONES THAT MISS YOU--
I GOT MAIL WITH A THOUSAND...
OFFICERS DOWN. DIRT, MEDERMADE AND WILDE IN PURSUIT OF MAKO NEAR SIXTH AND BROADWAY. ALL AVAILABLE UNITS RESPOND.
LET'S ROLL.
ULP.

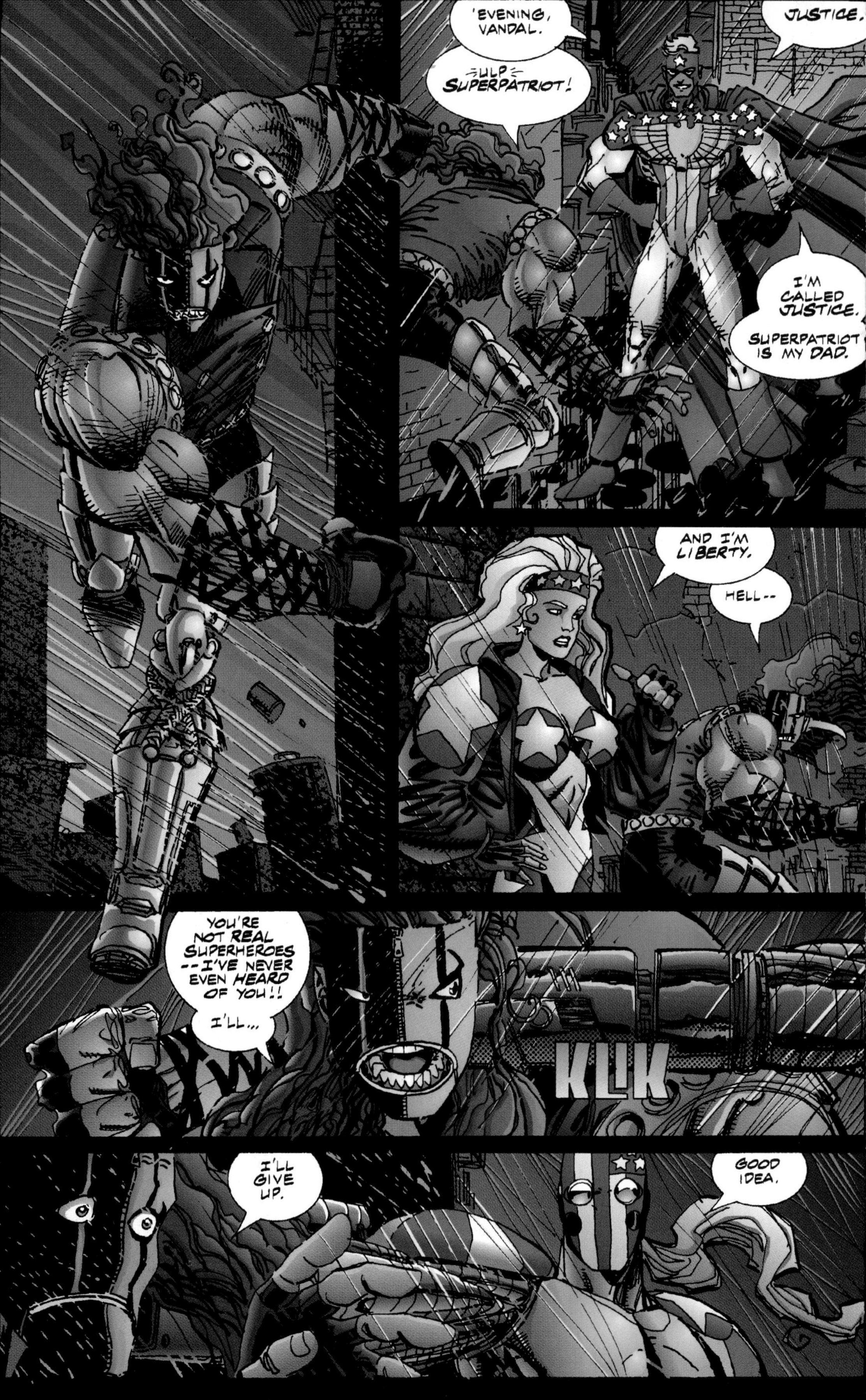

'EVENING, VANDAL.
ULP SUPERPATRIOT!
JUSTICE.
I'M CALLED JUSTICE.
SUPERPATRIOT IS MY DAD.
AND I'M LIBERTY.
HELL--
YOU'RE NOT REAL SUPERHEROES --I'VE NEVER EVEN HEARD OF YOU!!
I'LL...
KLIK
I'LL GIVE UP.
GOOD IDEA.

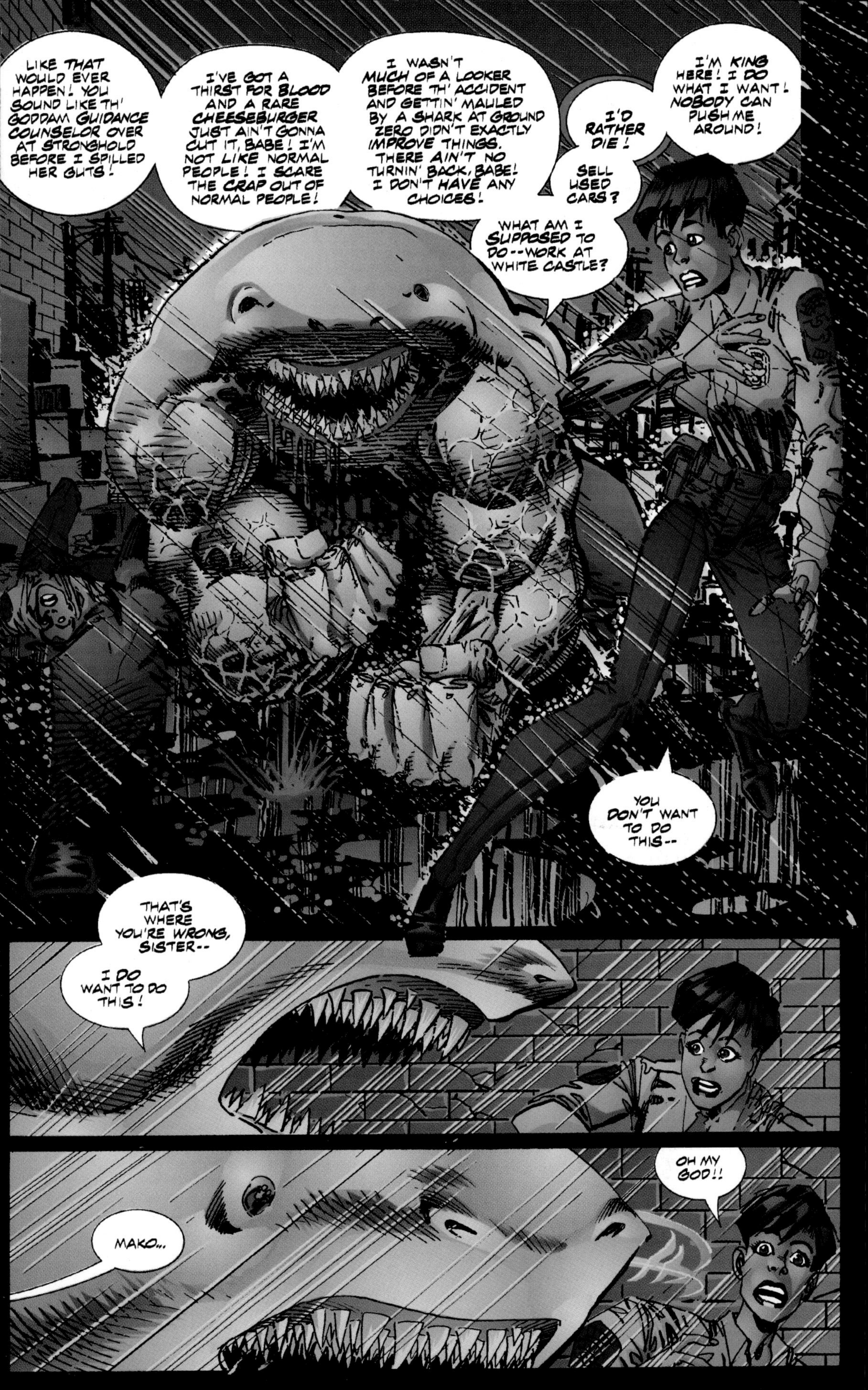
LIKE THAT WOULD EVER HAPPEN! YOU SOUND LIKE TH' GODDAM GUIDANCE COUNSELOR OVER AT STRONGHOLD BEFORE I SPILLED HER GUTS!
I'VE GOT A THIRST FOR BLOOD AND A RARE CHEESEBURGER JUST AIN'T GONNA CUT IT, BABE! I'M NOT LIKE NORMAL PEOPLE! I SCARE THE CRAP OUT OF NORMAL PEOPLE!
I WASN'T MUCH OF A LOOKER BEFORE TH' ACCIDENT AND GETTIN' MAULED BY A SHARK AT GROUND ZERO DIDN'T EXACTLY IMPROVE THINGS. THERE AIN'T NO TURNIN' BACK, BABE! I DON'T HAVE ANY CHOICES!
I'M KING HERE! I DO WHAT I WANT! NOBODY CAN PUSH ME AROUND!
I'D RATHER DIE!
SELL USED CARS?
WHAT AM I SUPPOSED TO DO--WORK AT WHITE CASTLE?
YOU DON'T WANT TO DO THIS--
THAT'S WHERE YOU'RE WRONG, SISTER--
I DO WANT TO DO THIS!
OH MY GOD!!
MAKO...

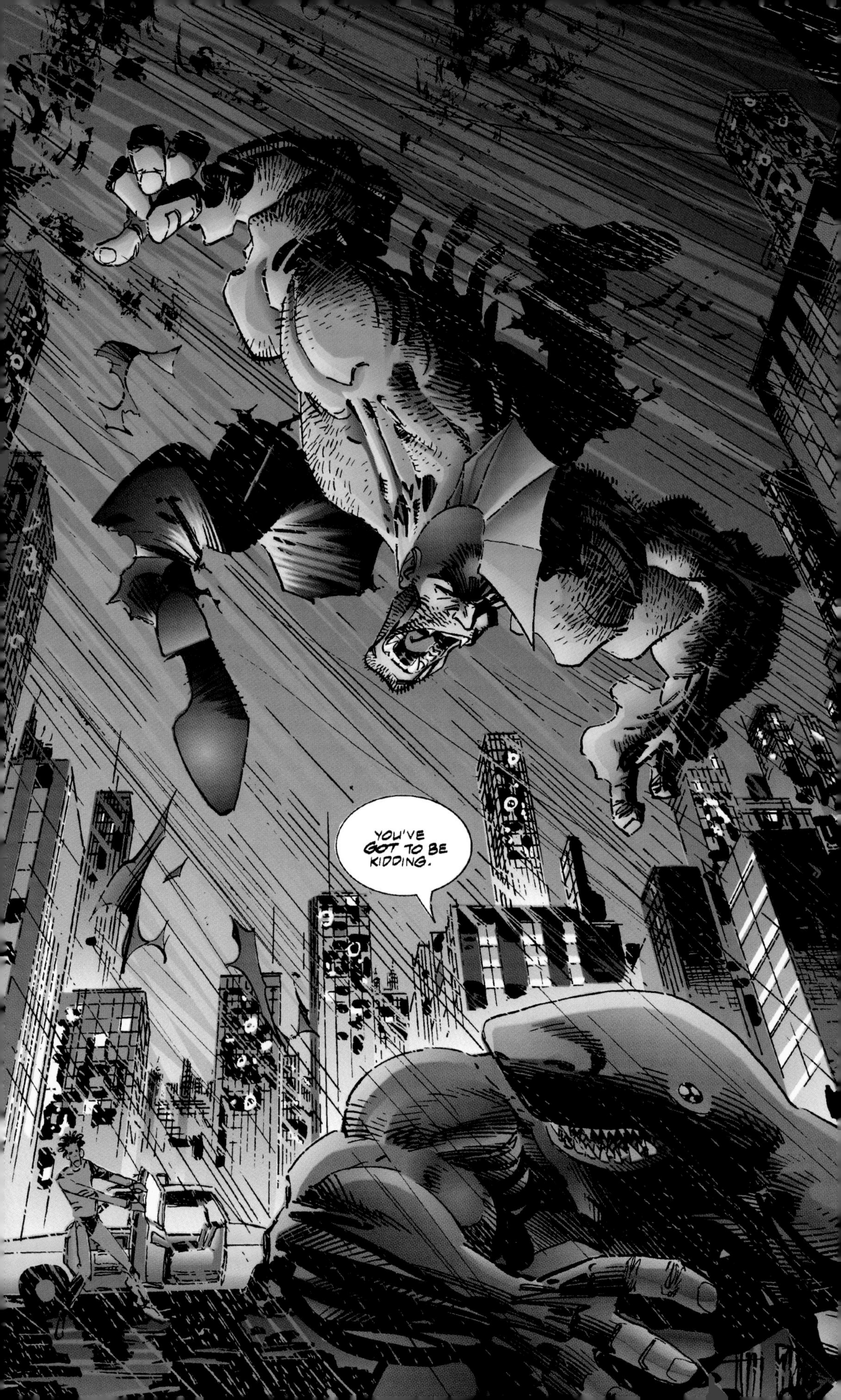
YOU'VE GOT TO BE KIDDING.

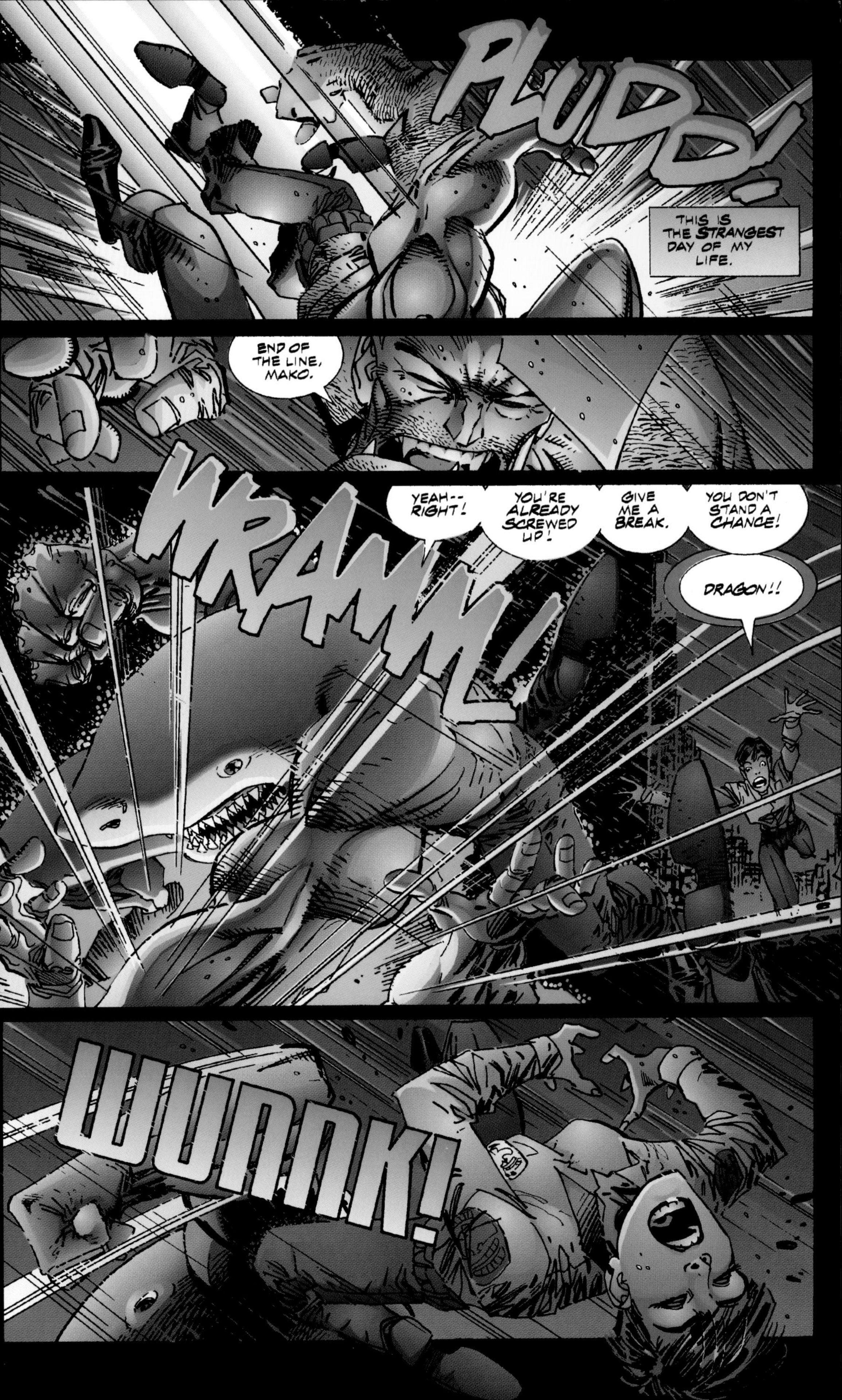
PLUDD!
THIS IS THE STRANGEST DAY OF MY LIFE.
END OF THE LINE, MAKO.
WRAMM!
YEAH-- RIGHT!
YOU'RE ALREADY SCREWED UP!
GIVE ME A BREAK.
YOU DON'T STAND A CHANCE!
DRAGON!!
WUNNK!

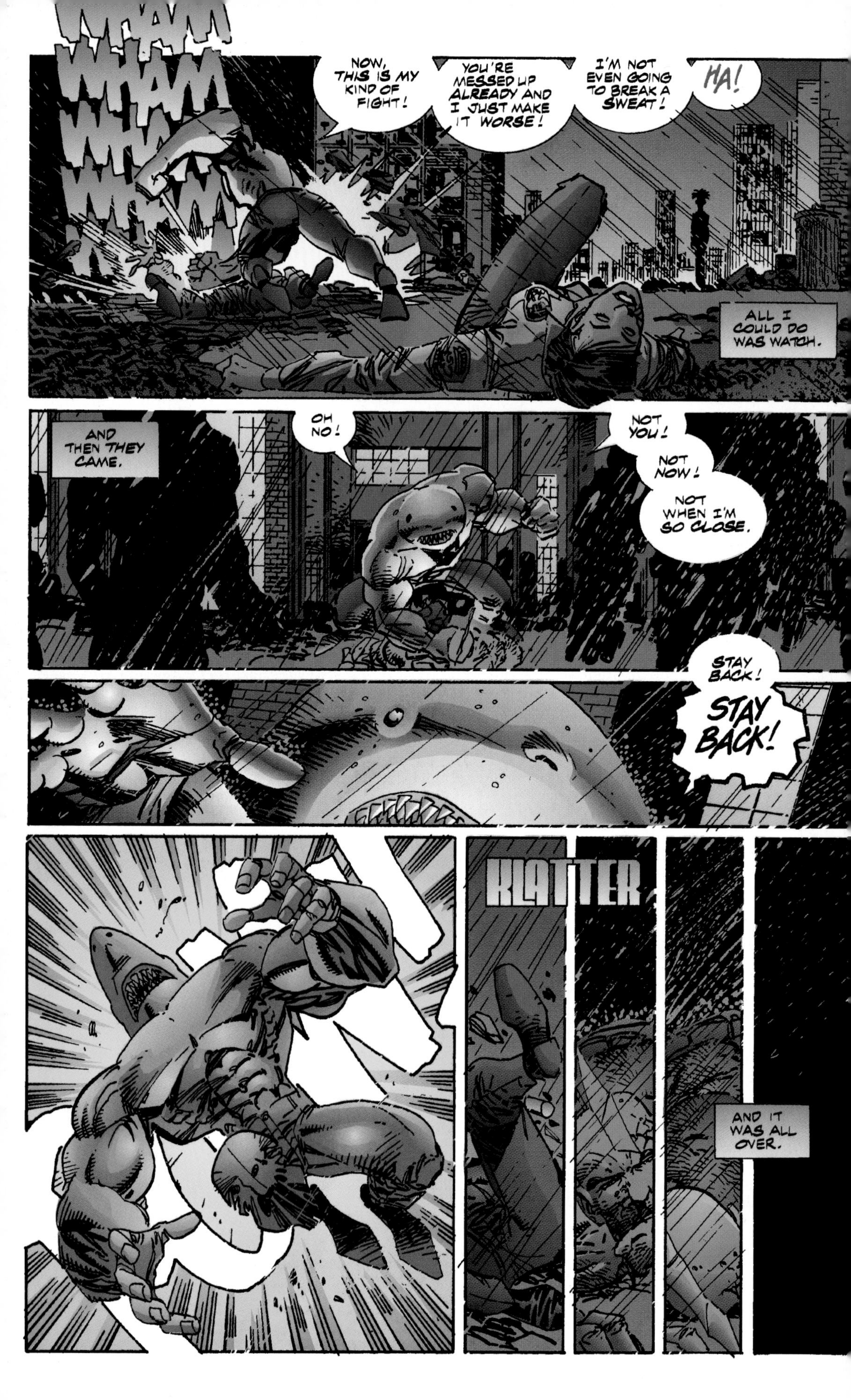
WHAM WHAM WHAM WHAM WHAM
NOW, THIS IS MY KIND OF FIGHT!
YOU'RE MESSED UP ALREADY AND I JUST MAKE IT WORSE!
I'M NOT EVEN GOING TO BREAK A SWEAT!
HA!
ALL I COULD DO WAS WATCH.
AND THEN THEY CAME.
OH NO!
NOT YOU!
NOT NOW!
NOT WHEN I'M SO CLOSE.
STAY BACK!
STAY BACK!
KLATTER
AND IT WAS ALL OVER.

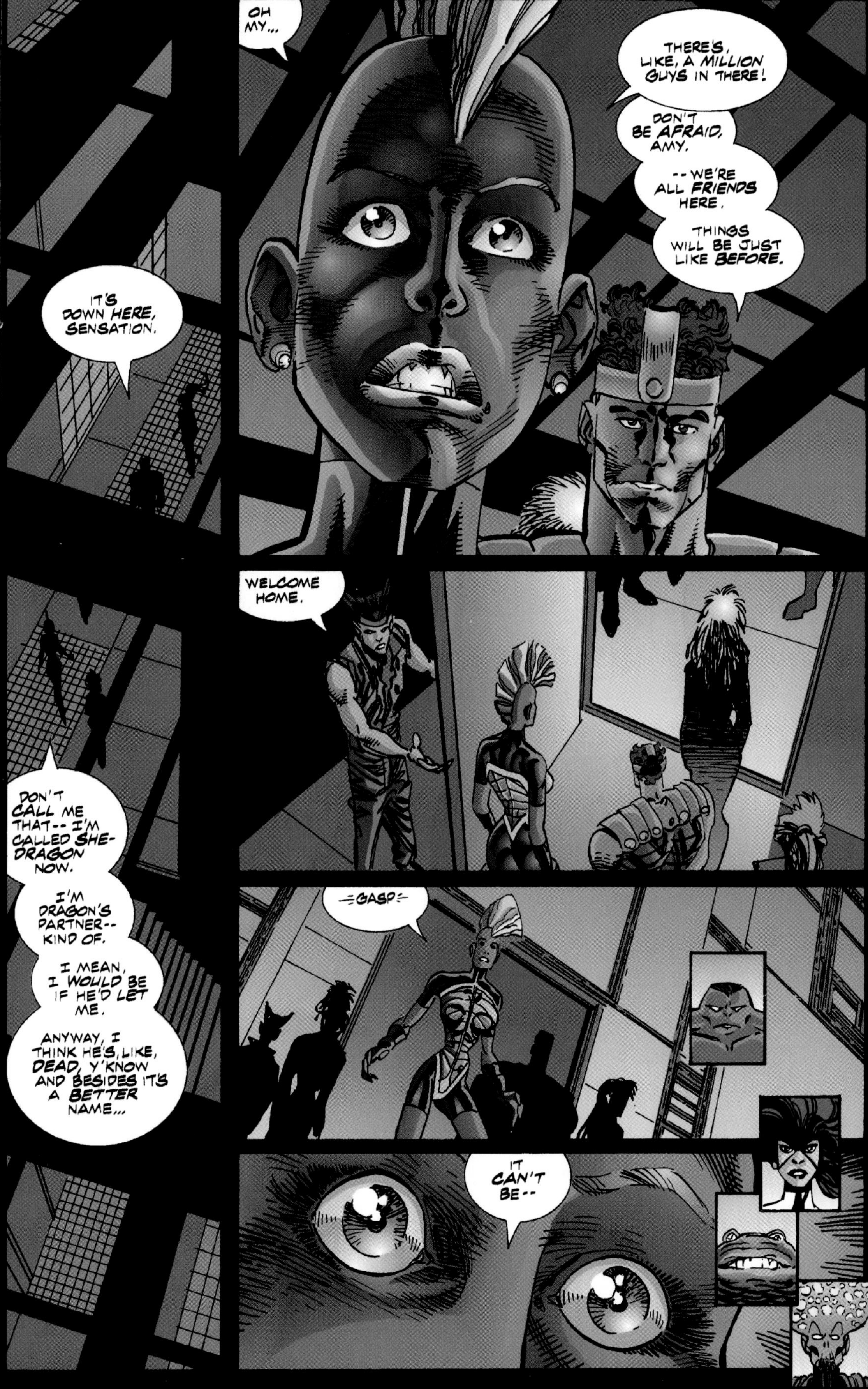

OH MY...
THERE'S, LIKE, A MILLION GUYS IN THERE!
DON'T BE AFRAID, AMY.
-- WE'RE ALL FRIENDS HERE.
THINGS WILL BE JUST LIKE BEFORE.
IT'S DOWN HERE, SENSATION.
WELCOME HOME.
DON'T CALL ME THAT-- I'M CALLED SHE-DRAGON NOW.
I'M DRAGON'S PARTNER-- KIND OF.
I MEAN, I WOULD BE IF HE'D LET ME.
ANYWAY, I THINK HE'S, LIKE, DEAD, Y'KNOW AND BESIDES IT'S A BETTER NAME...
-GASP-
IT CAN'T BE--

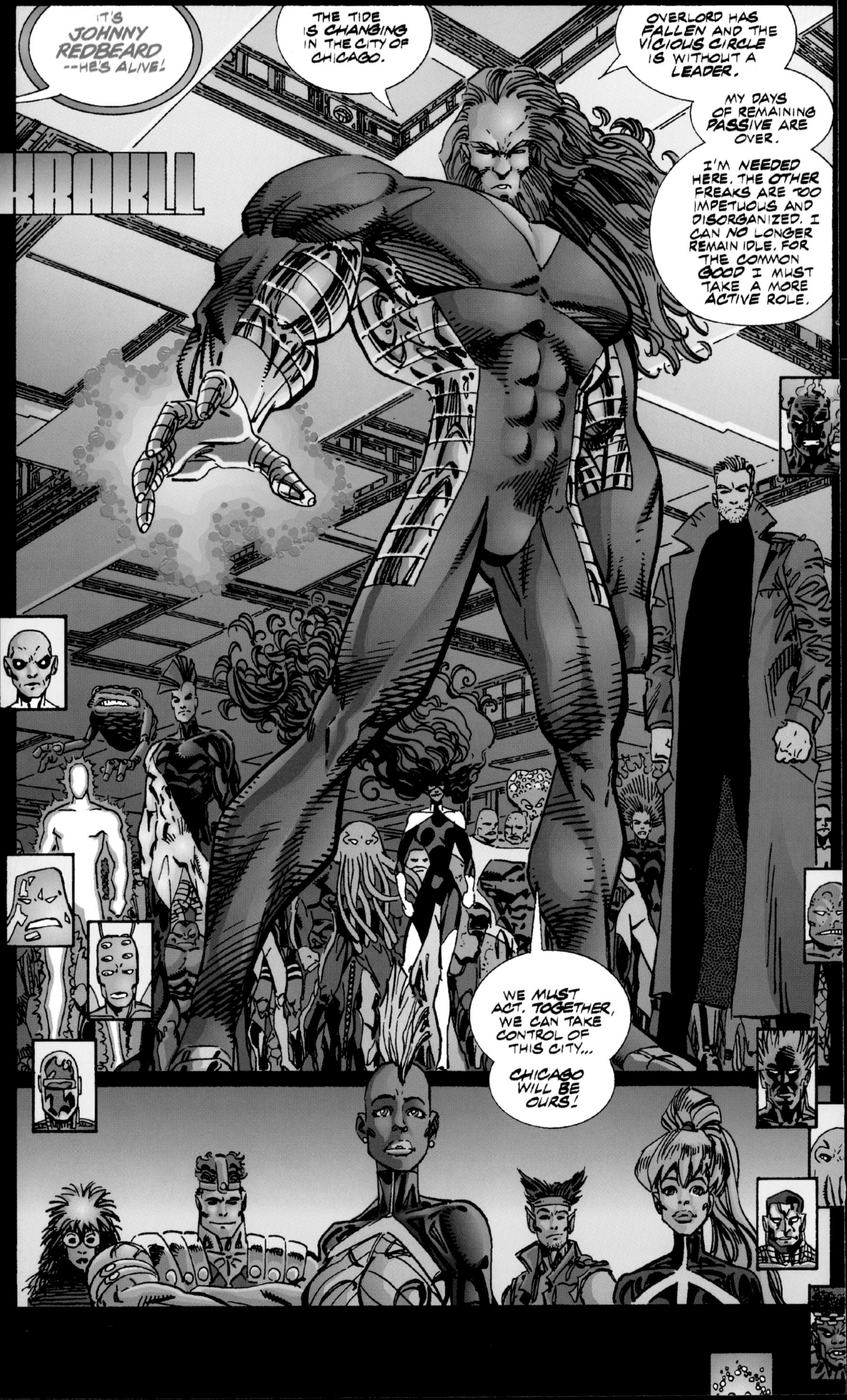
IT'S JOHNNY REDBEARD --HE'S ALIVE!
THE TIDE IS CHANGING IN THE CITY OF CHICAGO.
OVERLORD HAS FALLEN AND THE VICIOUS CIRCLE IS WITHOUT A LEADER.
MY DAYS OF REMAINING PASSIVE ARE OVER.
I'M NEEDED HERE. THE OTHER FREAKS ARE TOO IMPETUOUS AND DISORGANIZED. I CAN NO LONGER REMAIN IDLE. FOR THE COMMON GOOD I MUST TAKE A MORE ACTIVE ROLE.
KRAKLL
WE MUST ACT. TOGETHER, WE CAN TAKE CONTROL OF THIS CITY...
CHICAGO WILL BE OURS!

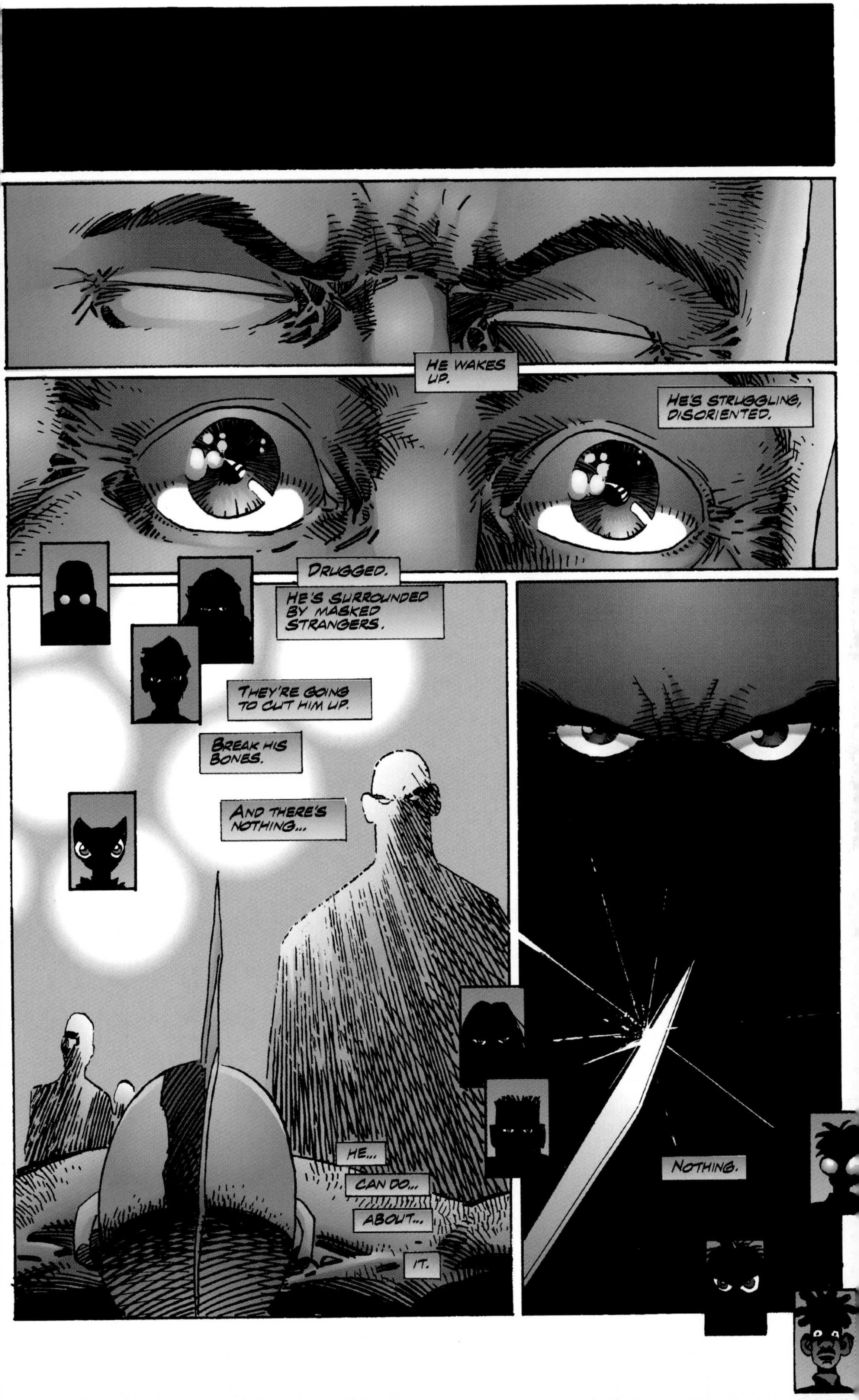
HE WAKES UP.
HE'S STRUGGLING, DISORIENTED.
DRUGGED.
HE'S SURROUNDED BY MASKED STRANGERS.
THEY'RE GOING TO CUT HIM UP.
BREAK HIS BONES.
AND THERE'S NOTHING...
HE...
CAN DO...
ABOUT...
IT.
NOTHING.

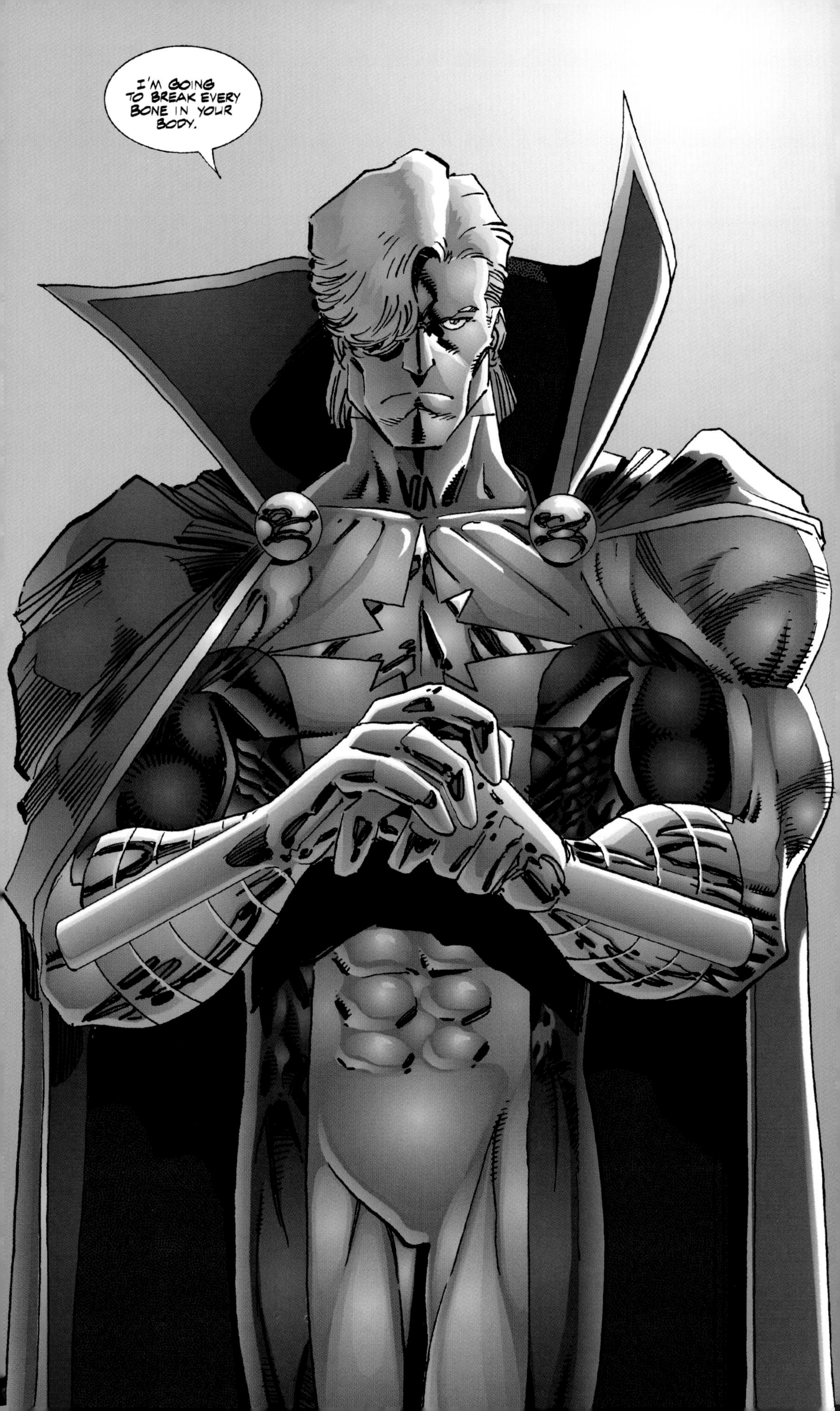
I'M GOING TO BREAK EVERY BONE IN YOUR BODY.

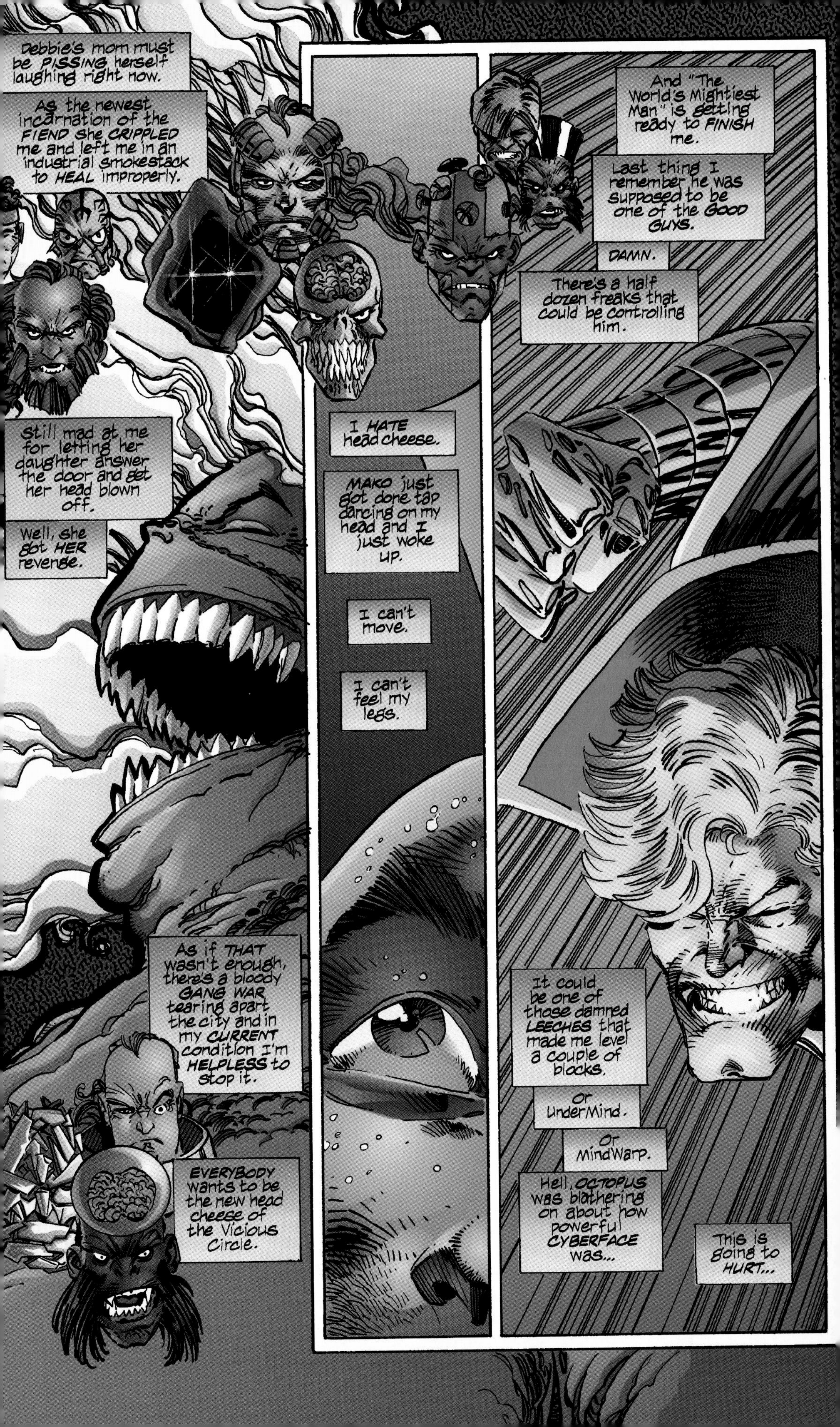

Debbie's mom must be PISSING herself laughing right now.
As the newest incarnation of the FIEND she CRIPPLED me and left me in an industrial smokestack to HEAL improperly.
Still mad at me for letting her daughter answer the door and get her head blown off.
Well, she got HER revenge.
As if THAT wasn't enough, there's a bloody GANG WAR tearing apart the city and in my CURRENT condition I'm HELPLESS to stop it.
EVERYBODY wants to be the new head cheese of the Vicious Circle.
I HATE head cheese.
MAKO just got done tap dancing on my head and I just woke up.
I can't move.
I can't feel my legs.
And "The World's Mightiest Man" is getting ready to FINISH me.
Last thing I remember he was supposed to be one of the GOOD GUYS.
DAMN.
There's a half dozen freaks that could be controlling him.
It could be one of those damned LEECHES that made me level a couple of blocks.
Or UnderMind.
Or MindWarp.
Hell, OCTOPUS was blathering on about how powerful CYBERFACE was...
This is going to HURT...

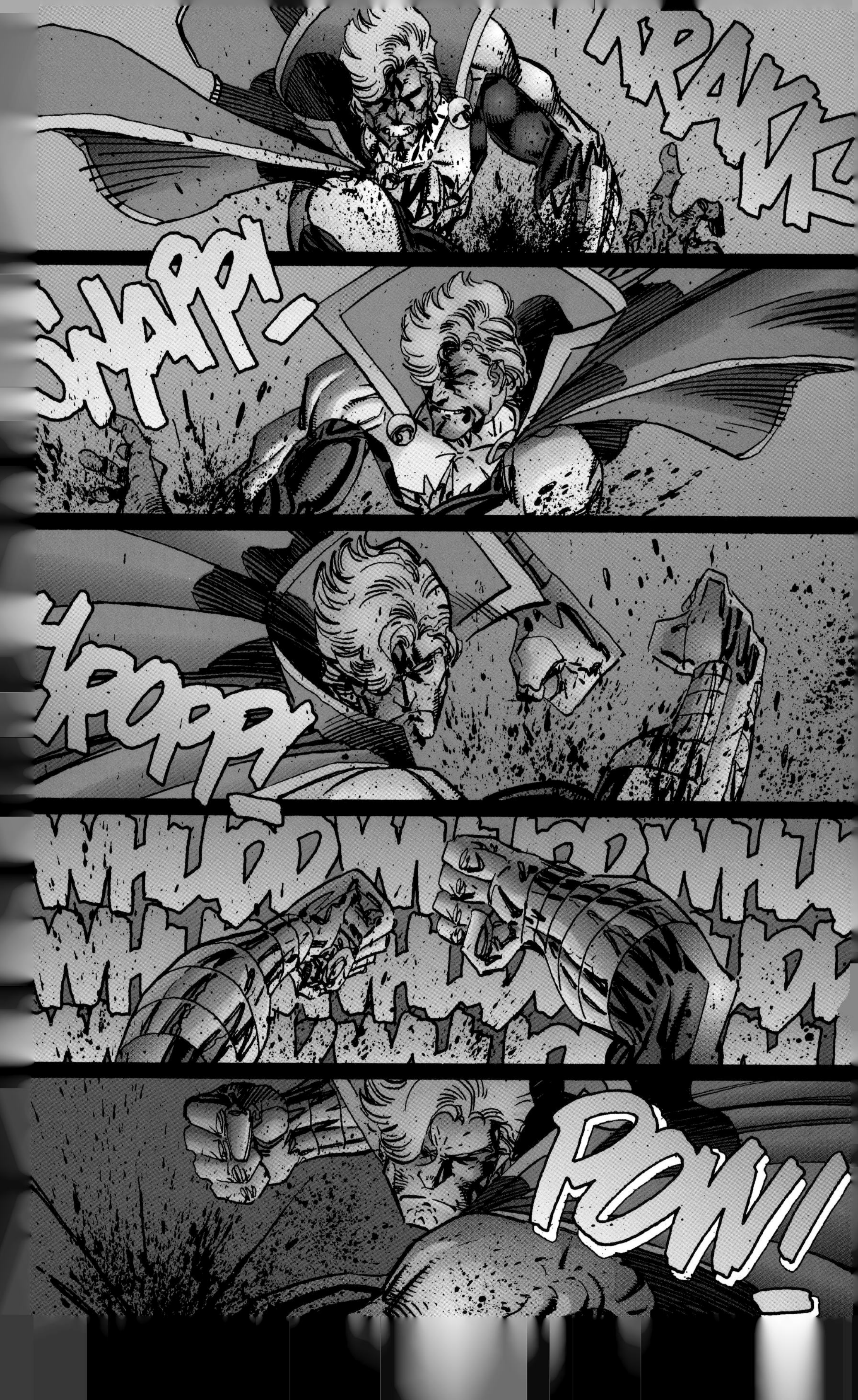
SHAPP!
KROPP
POW!

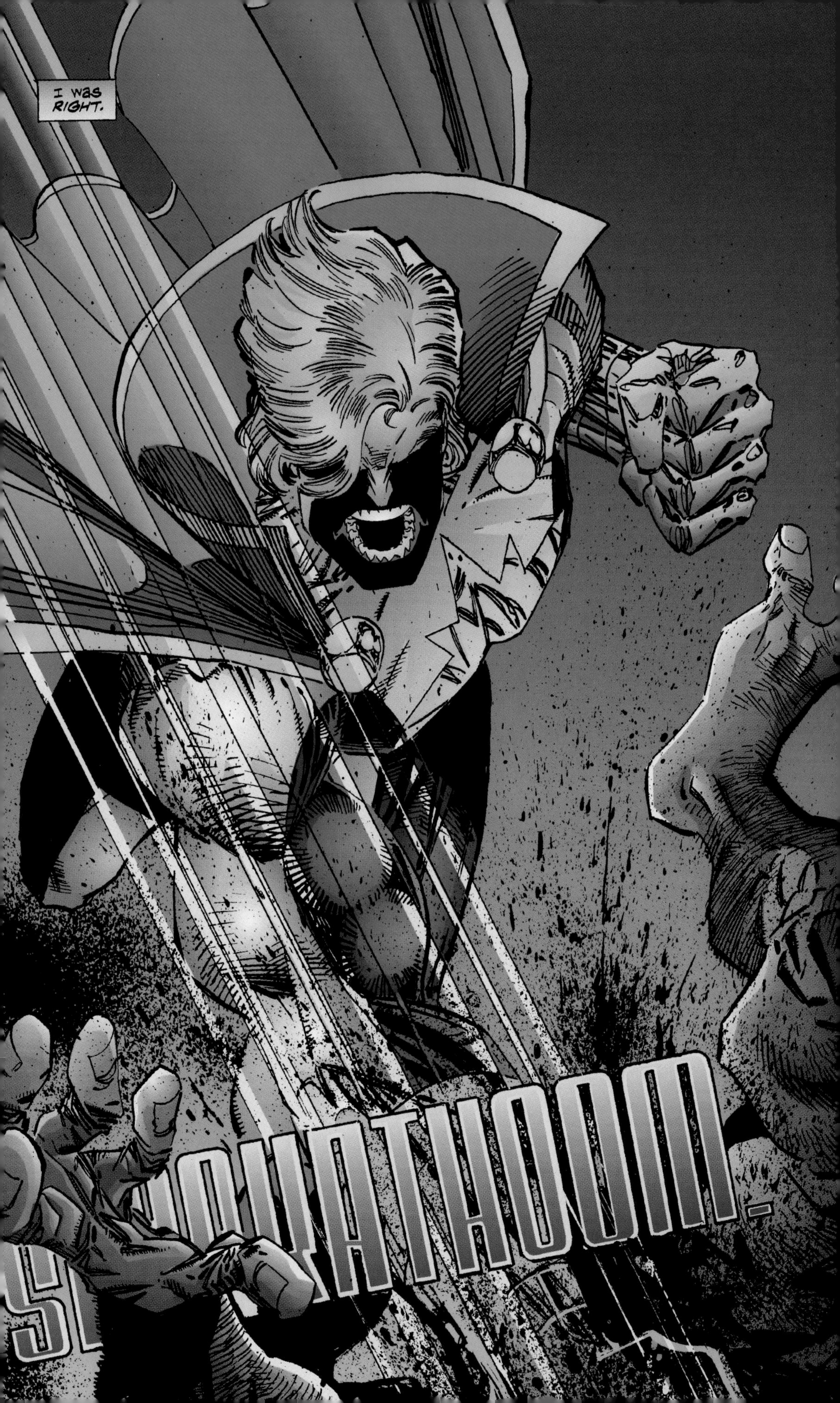
I WAS RIGHT.

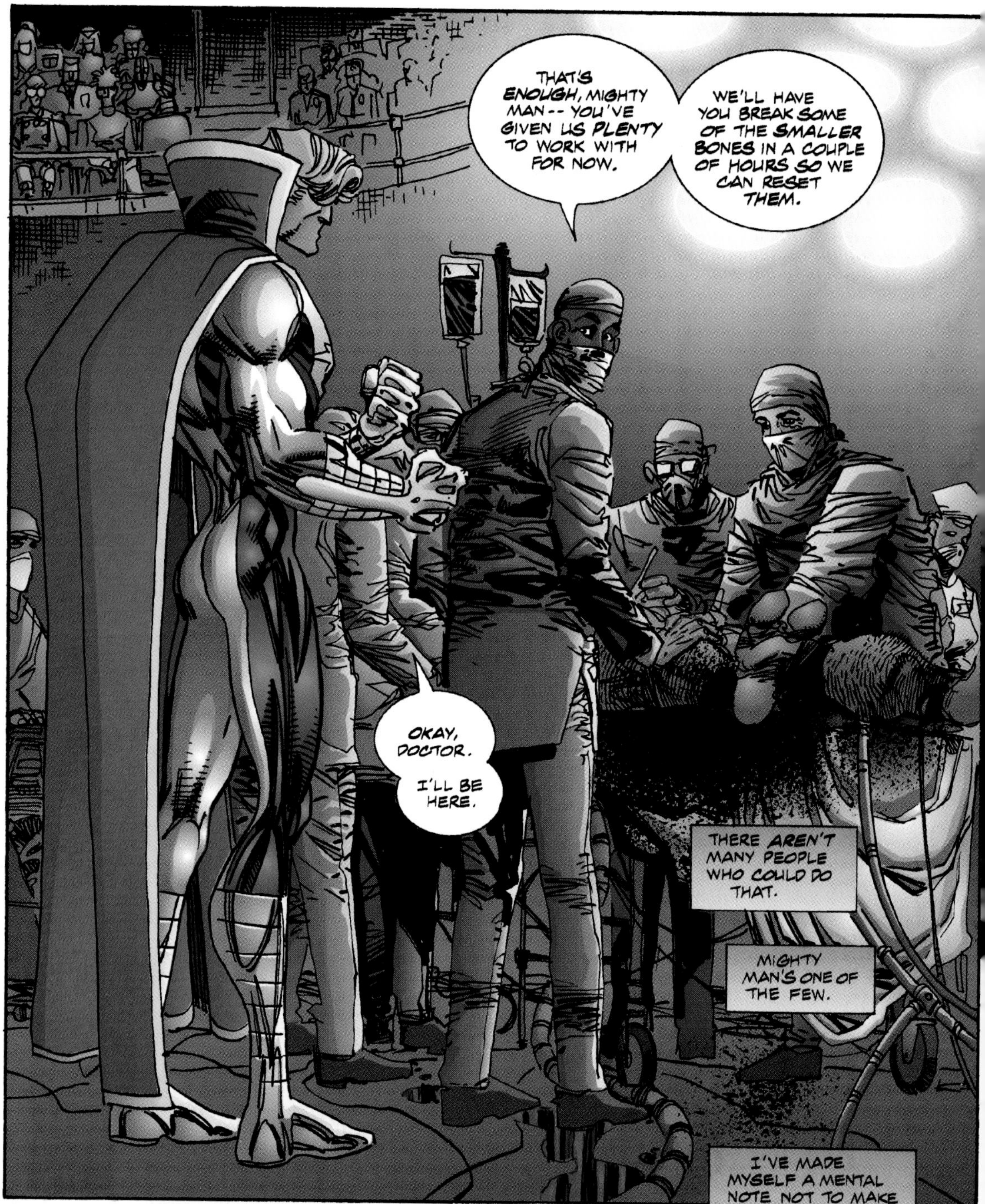
THAT'S ENOUGH, MIGHTY MAN -- YOU'VE GIVEN US PLENTY TO WORK WITH FOR NOW.
WE'LL HAVE YOU BREAK SOME OF THE SMALLER BONES IN A COUPLE OF HOURS SO WE CAN RESET THEM.
OKAY, DOCTOR.
I'LL BE HERE.
THERE AREN'T MANY PEOPLE WHO COULD DO THAT.
MIGHTY MAN'S ONE OF THE FEW.
I'VE MADE MYSELF A MENTAL NOTE NOT TO MAKE FUN OF HIM FOR WEARING HIS UNDERWEAR IN PUBLIC.
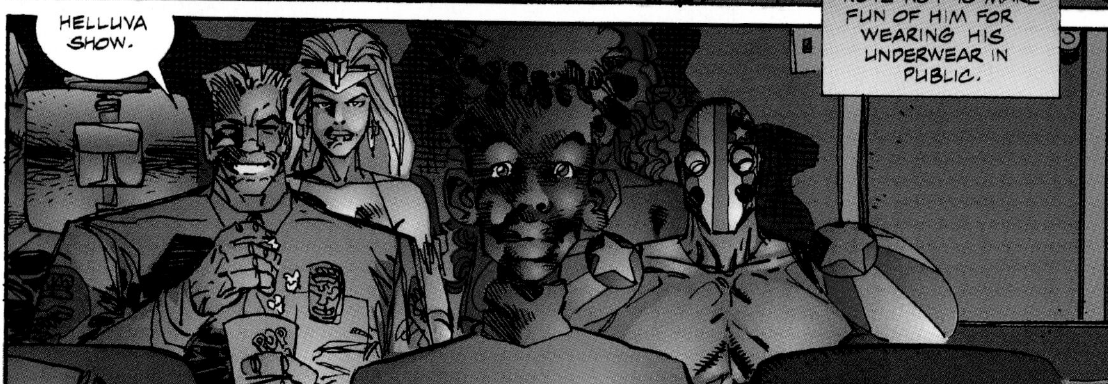
HELLUVA SHOW.
POP

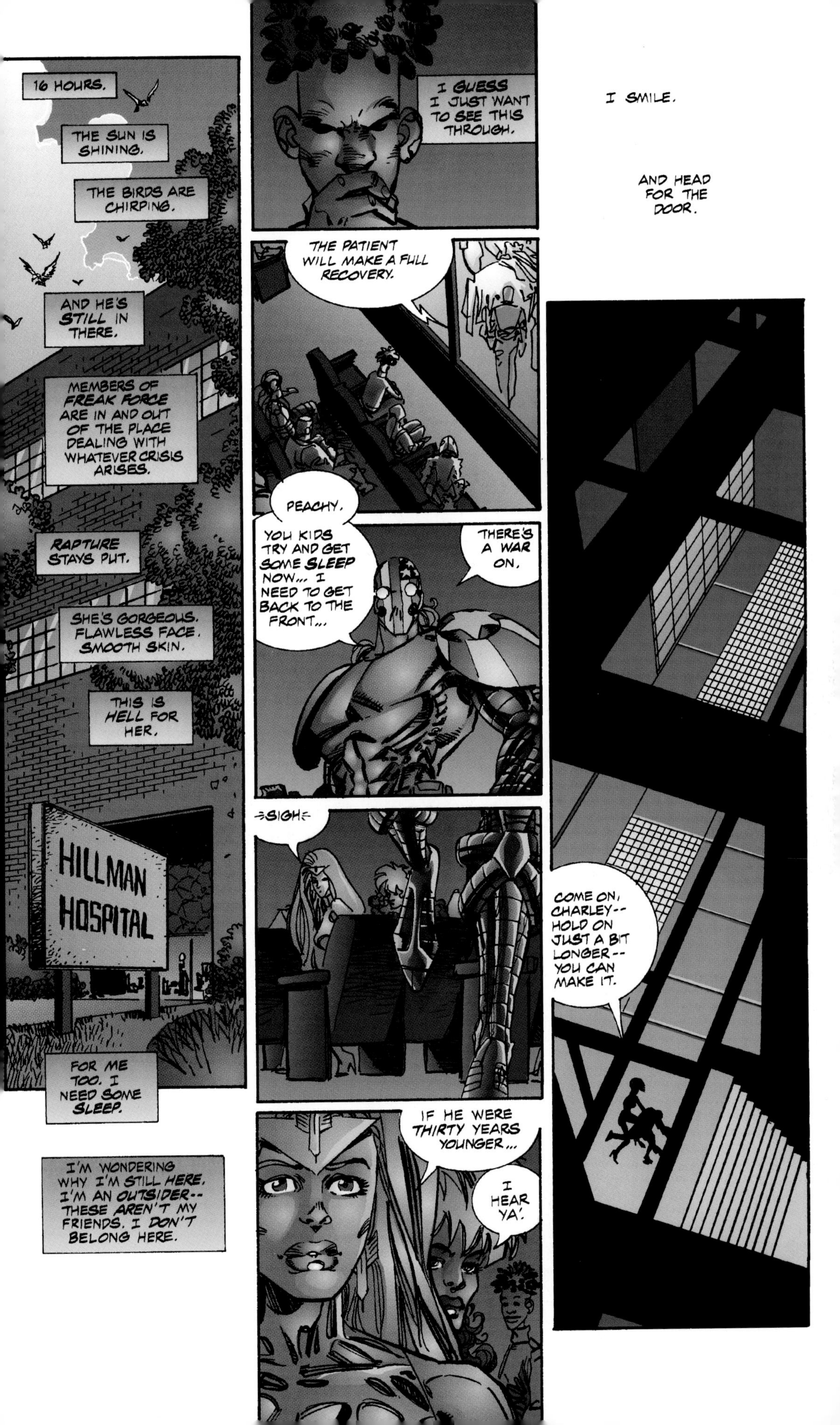

16 HOURS.
THE SUN IS SHINING.
THE BIRDS ARE CHIRPING.
AND HE'S STILL IN THERE.
MEMBERS OF FREAK FORCE ARE IN AND OUT OF THE PLACE DEALING WITH WHATEVER CRISIS ARISES.
RAPTURE STAYS PUT.
SHE'S GORGEOUS. FLAWLESS FACE. SMOOTH SKIN.
THIS IS HELL FOR HER.
HILLMAN HOSPITAL
FOR ME TOO. I NEED SOME SLEEP.
I'M WONDERING WHY I'M STILL HERE. I'M AN OUTSIDER-- THESE AREN'T MY FRIENDS. I DON'T BELONG HERE.
I GUESS I JUST WANT TO SEE THIS THROUGH.
THE PATIENT WILL MAKE A FULL RECOVERY.
PEACHY.
YOU KIDS TRY AND GET SOME SLEEP NOW... I NEED TO GET BACK TO THE FRONT...
THERE'S A WAR ON.
=SIGH=
IF HE WERE THIRTY YEARS YOUNGER...
I HEAR YA'.
I SMILE.
AND HEAD FOR THE DOOR.
COME ON, CHARLEY-- HOLD ON JUST A BIT LONGER-- YOU CAN MAKE IT.

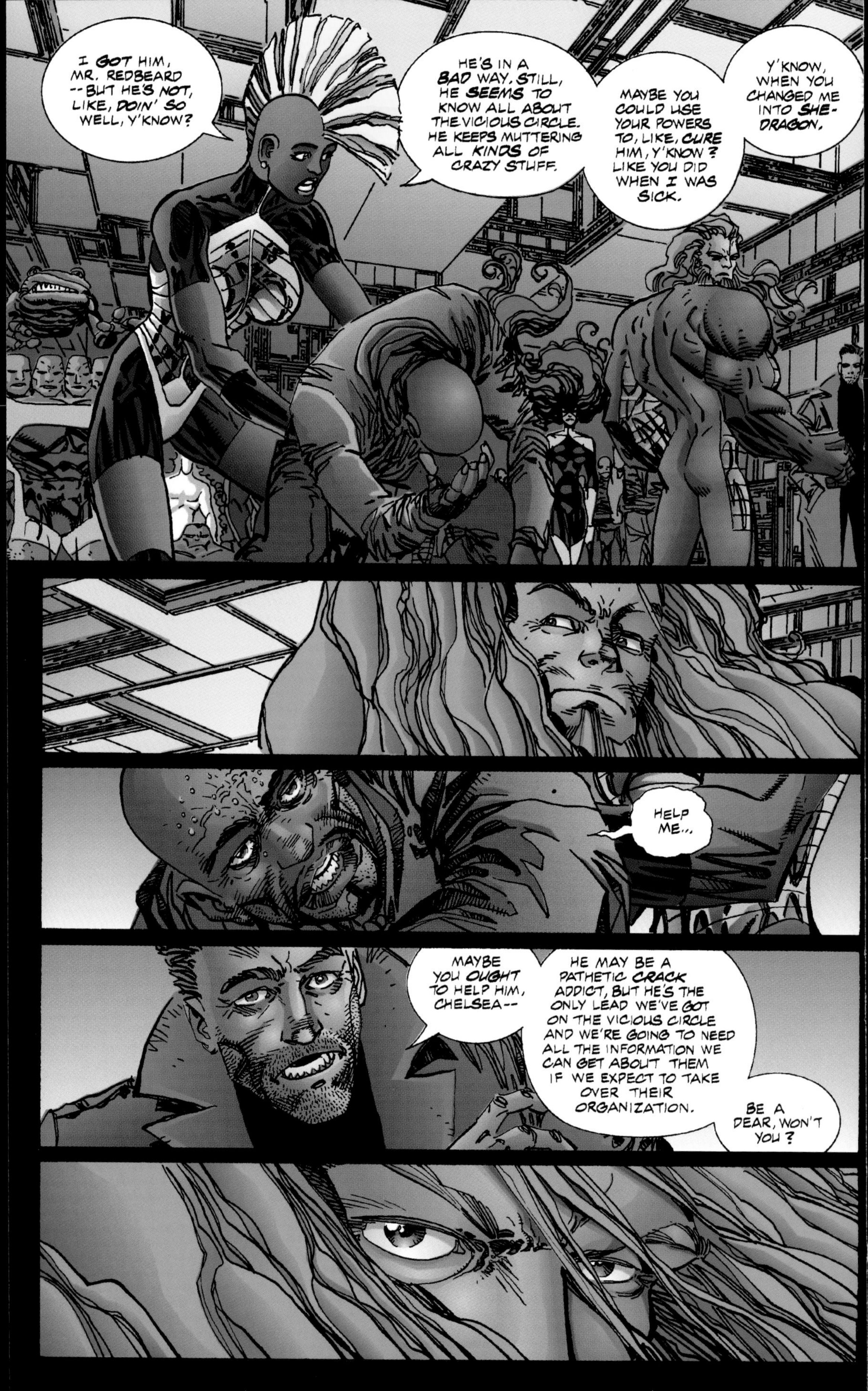
I GOT HIM, MR. REDBEARD --BUT HE'S NOT, LIKE, DOIN' SO WELL, Y'KNOW?
HE'S IN A BAD WAY. STILL, HE SEEMS TO KNOW ALL ABOUT THE VICIOUS CIRCLE. HE KEEPS MUTTERING ALL KINDS OF CRAZY STUFF.
MAYBE YOU COULD USE YOUR POWERS TO, LIKE, CURE HIM, Y'KNOW? LIKE YOU DID WHEN I WAS SICK.
Y'KNOW, WHEN YOU CHANGED ME INTO SHE-DRAGON.
HELP ME...
MAYBE YOU OUGHT TO HELP HIM, CHELSEA--
HE MAY BE A PATHETIC CRACK ADDICT, BUT HE'S THE ONLY LEAD WE'VE GOT ON THE VICIOUS CIRCLE AND WE'RE GOING TO NEED ALL THE INFORMATION WE CAN GET ABOUT THEM IF WE EXPECT TO TAKE OVER THEIR ORGANIZATION.
BE A DEAR, WON'T YOU?

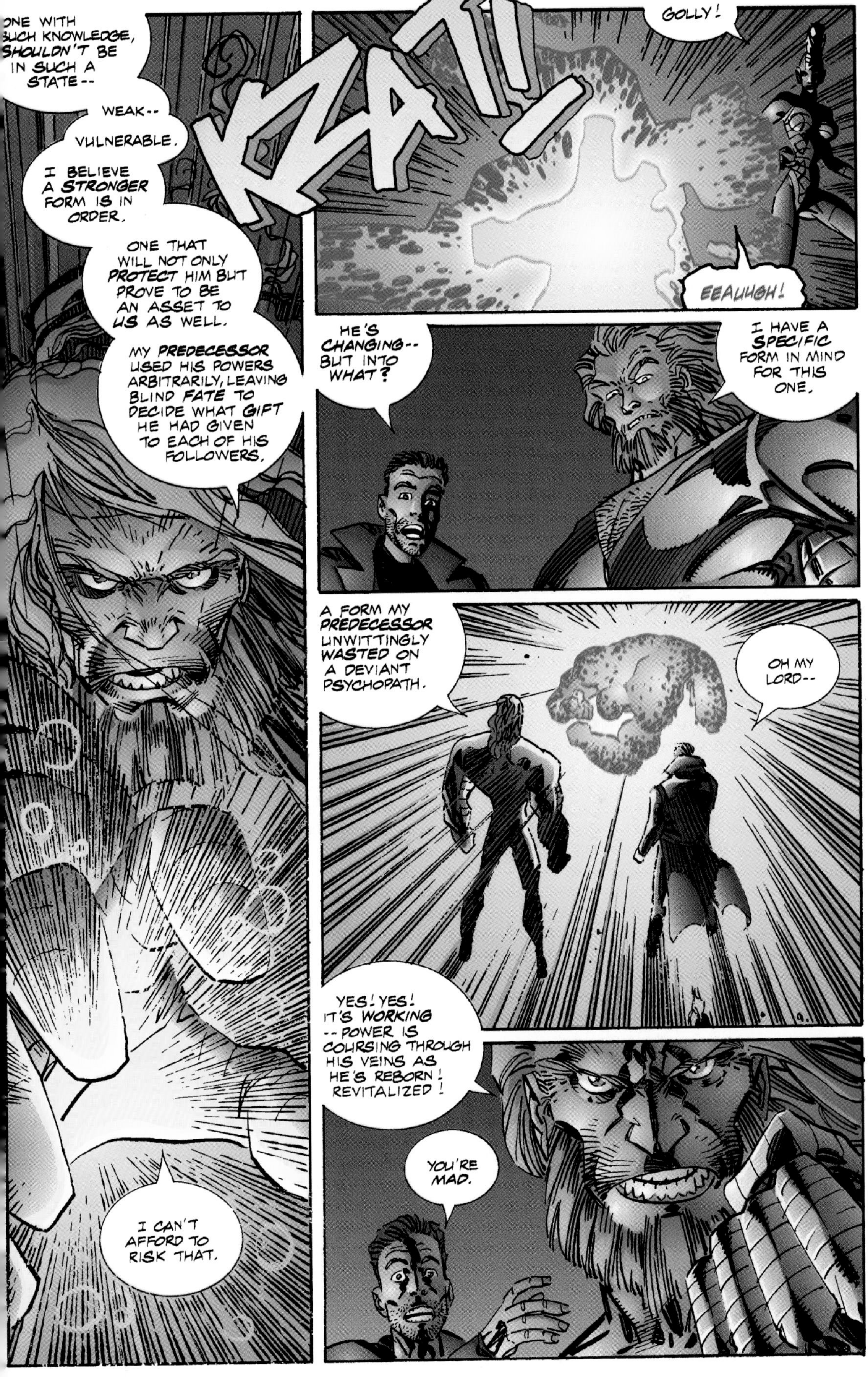

ONE WITH SUCH KNOWLEDGE, SHOULDN'T BE IN SUCH A STATE --
WEAK --
VULNERABLE.
I BELIEVE A STRONGER FORM IS IN ORDER.
ONE THAT WILL NOT ONLY PROTECT HIM BUT PROVE TO BE AN ASSET TO US AS WELL.
MY PREDECESSOR USED HIS POWERS ARBITRARILY, LEAVING BLIND FATE TO DECIDE WHAT GIFT HE HAD GIVEN TO EACH OF HIS FOLLOWERS.
I CAN'T AFFORD TO RISK THAT.
KZAT!!
GOLLY!
EEAUUGH!
HE'S CHANGING -- BUT INTO WHAT?
I HAVE A SPECIFIC FORM IN MIND FOR THIS ONE.
A FORM MY PREDECESSOR UNWITTINGLY WASTED ON A DEVIANT PSYCHOPATH.
OH MY LORD --
YES! YES! IT'S WORKING -- POWER IS COURSING THROUGH HIS VEINS AS HE'S REBORN! REVITALIZED!
YOU'RE MAD.

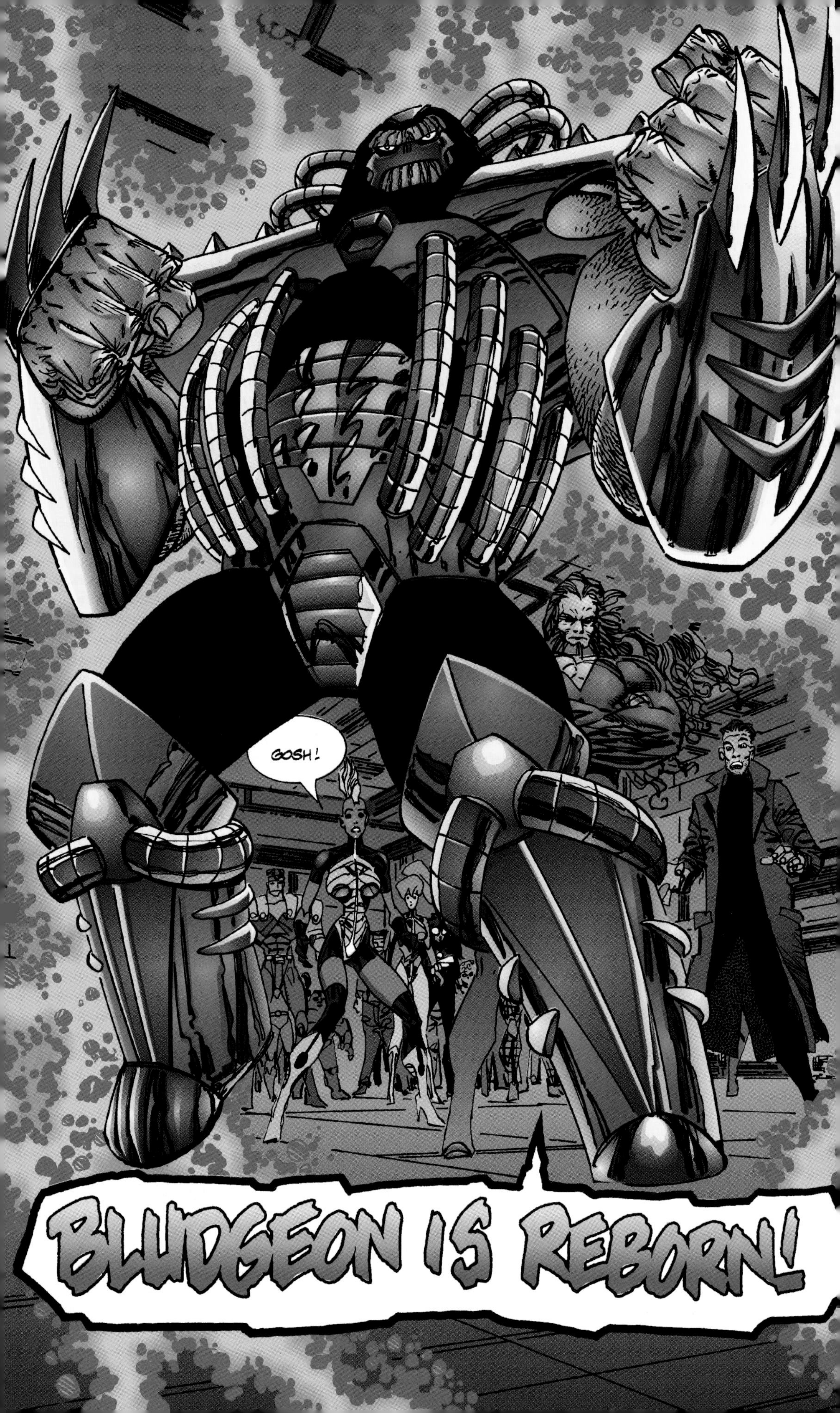
GOSH!
BLUDGEON IS REBORN!

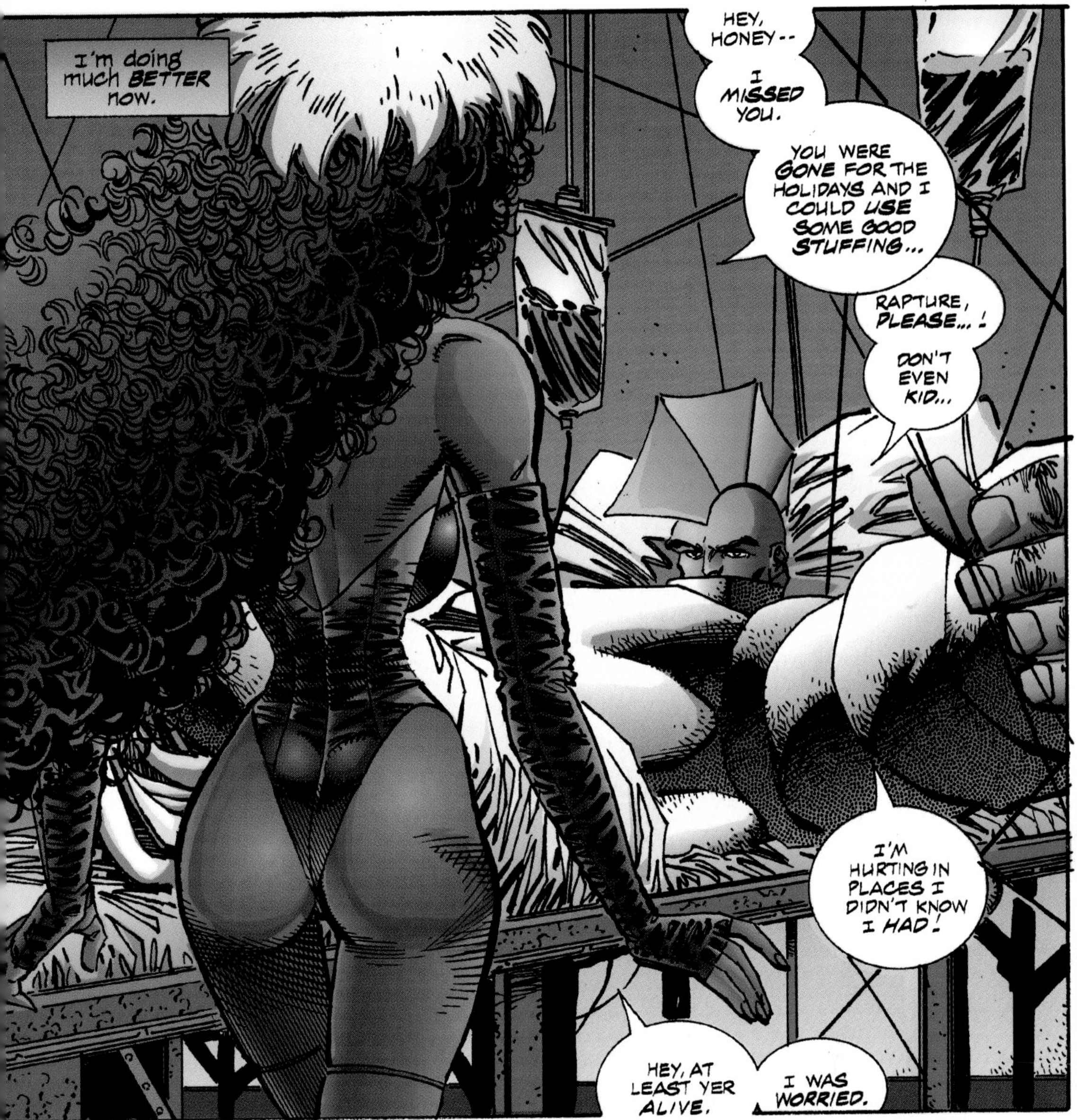
I'm doing much BETTER now.
HEY, HONEY--
I MISSED YOU.
YOU WERE GONE FOR THE HOLIDAYS AND I COULD USE SOME GOOD STUFFING...
RAPTURE, PLEASE...!
DON'T EVEN KID...
I'M HURTING IN PLACES I DIDN'T KNOW I HAD!
HEY, AT LEAST YER ALIVE.
I WAS WORRIED.

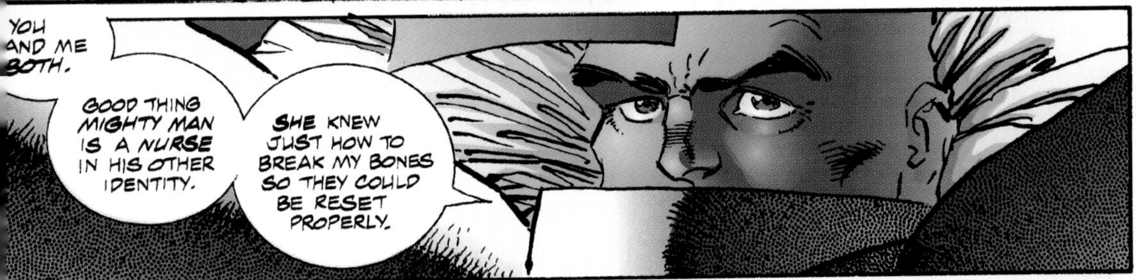
YOU AND ME BOTH.
GOOD THING MIGHTY MAN IS A NURSE IN HIS OTHER IDENTITY.
SHE KNEW JUST HOW TO BREAK MY BONES SO THEY COULD BE RESET PROPERLY.

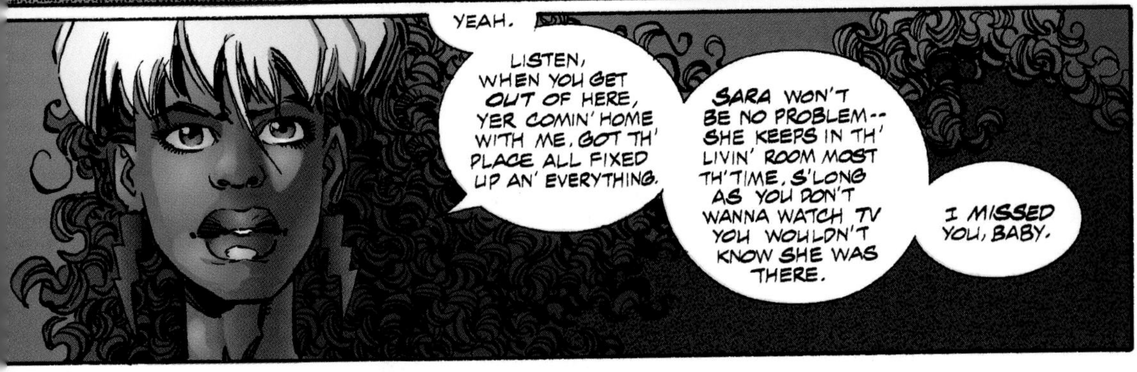
YEAH.
LISTEN, WHEN YOU GET OUT OF HERE, YER COMIN' HOME WITH ME. GOT TH' PLACE ALL FIXED UP AN' EVERYTHING.
SARA WON'T BE NO PROBLEM-- SHE KEEPS IN TH' LIVIN' ROOM MOST TH' TIME. S'LONG AS YOU DON'T WANNA WATCH TV YOU WOULDN'T KNOW SHE WAS THERE.
I MISSED YOU, BABY.

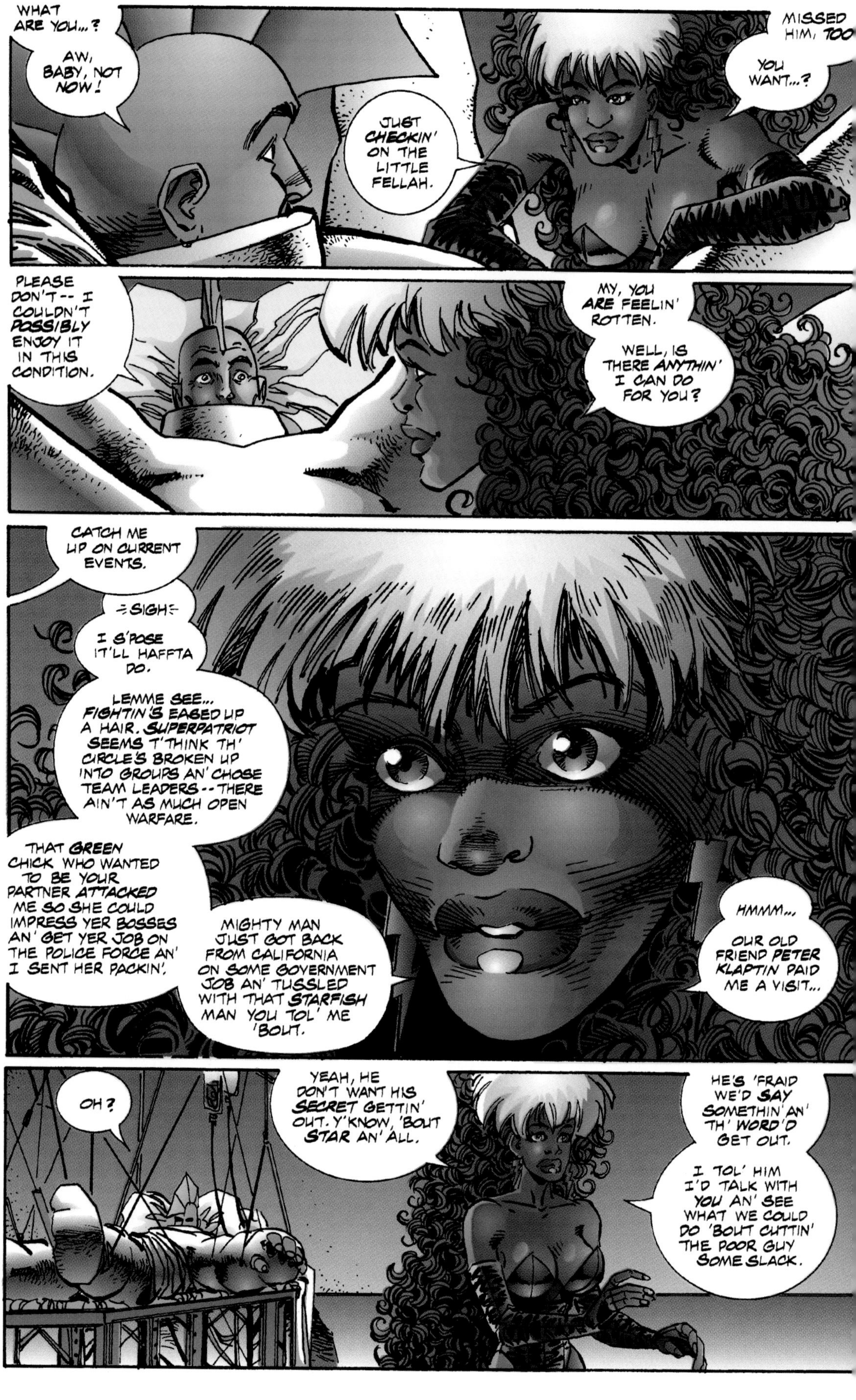
WHAT ARE YOU...?
AW, BABY, NOT NOW!
JUST CHECKIN' ON THE LITTLE FELLAH.
MISSED HIM, TOO
YOU WANT...?
PLEASE DON'T -- I COULDN'T POSSIBLY ENJOY IT IN THIS CONDITION.
MY, YOU ARE FEELIN' ROTTEN.
WELL, IS THERE ANYTHIN' I CAN DO FOR YOU?
CATCH ME UP ON CURRENT EVENTS.
=SIGH=
I S'POSE IT'LL HAFFTA DO.
LEMME SEE... FIGHTIN'S EASED UP A HAIR. SUPERPATRIOT SEEMS T'THINK TH' CIRCLE'S BROKEN UP INTO GROUPS AN' CHOSE TEAM LEADERS -- THERE AIN'T AS MUCH OPEN WARFARE.
THAT GREEN CHICK WHO WANTED TO BE YOUR PARTNER ATTACKED ME SO SHE COULD IMPRESS YER BOSSES AN' GET YER JOB ON THE POLICE FORCE AN' I SENT HER PACKIN'.
MIGHTY MAN JUST GOT BACK FROM CALIFORNIA ON SOME GOVERNMENT JOB AN' TUSSLED WITH THAT STARFISH MAN YOU TOL' ME 'BOUT.
HMMM...
OUR OLD FRIEND PETER KLAPTIN PAID ME A VISIT...
OH?
YEAH, HE DON'T WANT HIS SECRET GETTIN' OUT. Y'KNOW, 'BOUT STAR AN' ALL.
HE'S 'FRAID WE'D SAY SOMETHIN' AN' TH' WORD'D GET OUT.
I TOL' HIM I'D TALK WITH YOU AN' SEE WHAT WE COULD DO 'BOUT CUTTIN' THE POOR GUY SOME SLACK.

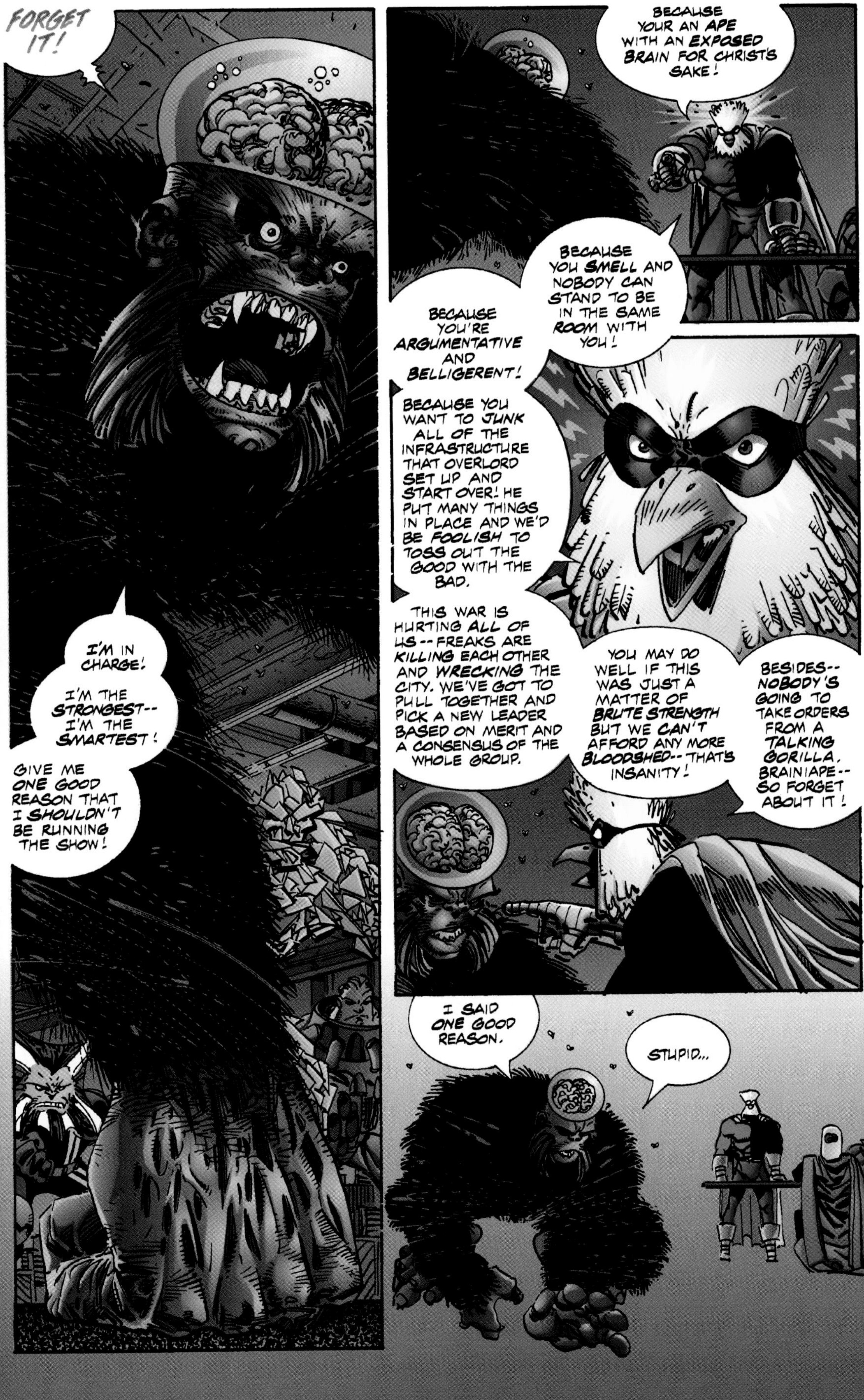
FORGET IT!
I'M IN CHARGE!
I'M THE STRONGEST-- I'M THE SMARTEST!
GIVE ME ONE GOOD REASON THAT I SHOULDN'T BE RUNNING THE SHOW!
BECAUSE YOUR AN APE WITH AN EXPOSED BRAIN FOR CHRIST'S SAKE!
BECAUSE YOU SMELL AND NOBODY CAN STAND TO BE IN THE SAME ROOM WITH YOU!
BECAUSE YOU'RE ARGUMENTATIVE AND BELLIGERENT!
BECAUSE YOU WANT TO JUNK ALL OF THE INFRASTRUCTURE THAT OVERLORD SET UP AND START OVER! HE PUT MANY THINGS IN PLACE AND WE'D BE FOOLISH TO TOSS OUT THE GOOD WITH THE BAD.
THIS WAR IS HURTING ALL OF US -- FREAKS ARE KILLING EACH OTHER AND WRECKING THE CITY. WE'VE GOT TO PULL TOGETHER AND PICK A NEW LEADER BASED ON MERIT AND A CONSENSUS OF THE WHOLE GROUP.
YOU MAY DO WELL IF THIS WAS JUST A MATTER OF BRUTE STRENGTH BUT WE CAN'T AFFORD ANY MORE BLOODSHED-- THAT'S INSANITY!
BESIDES-- NOBODY'S GOING TO TAKE ORDERS FROM A TALKING GORILLA, BRAINIAPE-- SO FORGET ABOUT IT!
I SAID ONE GOOD REASON.
STUPID...

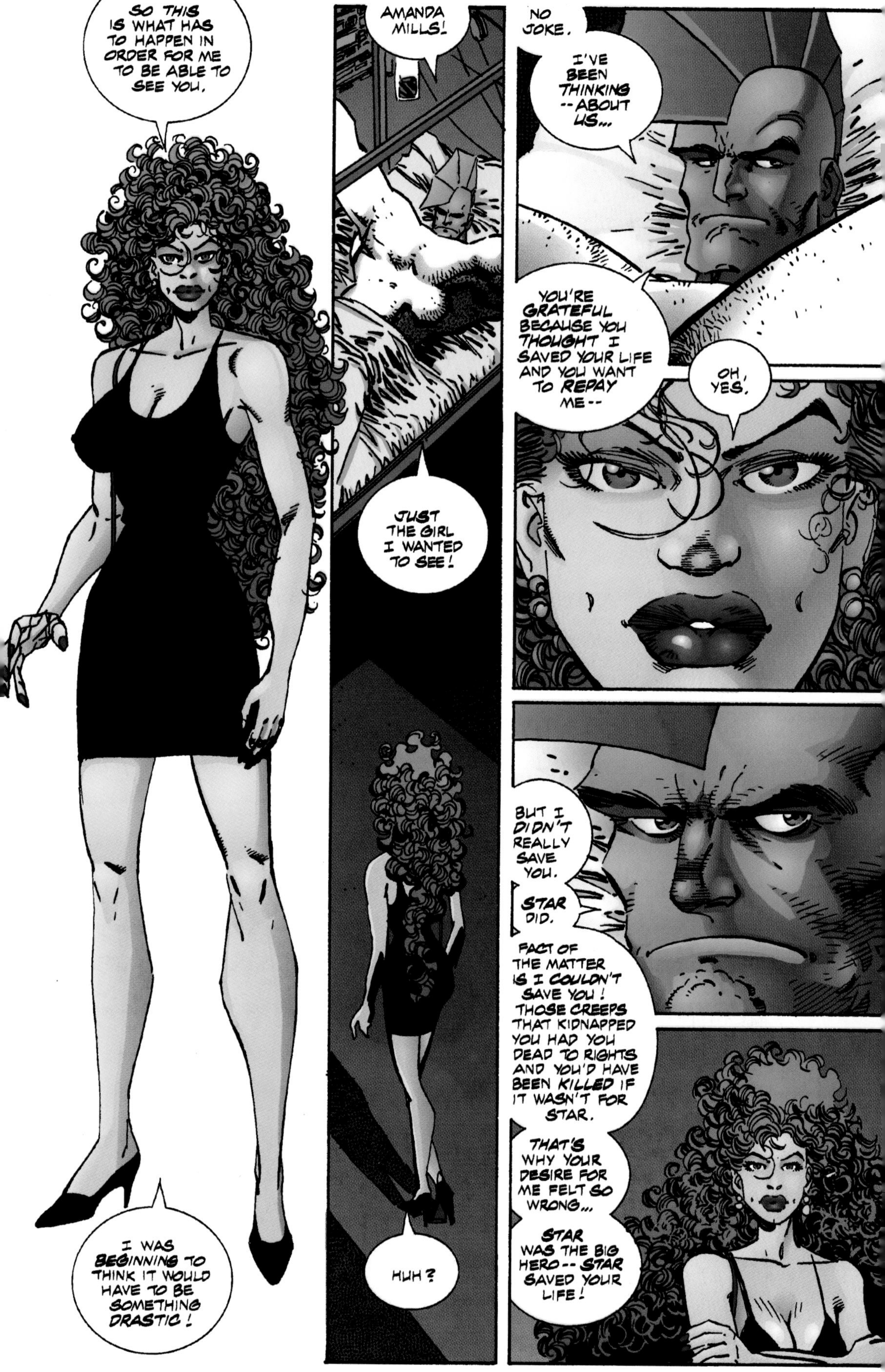

SO THIS IS WHAT HAS TO HAPPEN IN ORDER FOR ME TO BE ABLE TO SEE YOU.
I WAS BEGINNING TO THINK IT WOULD HAVE TO BE SOMETHING DRASTIC!
AMANDA MILLS!
JUST THE GIRL I WANTED TO SEE!
HUH?
NO JOKE.
I'VE BEEN THINKING --ABOUT US...
YOU'RE GRATEFUL BECAUSE YOU THOUGHT I SAVED YOUR LIFE AND YOU WANT TO REPAY ME--
OH, YES.
BUT I DIDN'T REALLY SAVE YOU.
STAR DID.
FACT OF THE MATTER IS I COULDN'T SAVE YOU! THOSE CREEPS THAT KIDNAPPED YOU HAD YOU DEAD TO RIGHTS AND YOU'D HAVE BEEN KILLED IF IT WASN'T FOR STAR.
THAT'S WHY YOUR DESIRE FOR ME FELT SO WRONG...
STAR WAS THE BIG HERO-- STAR SAVED YOUR LIFE!

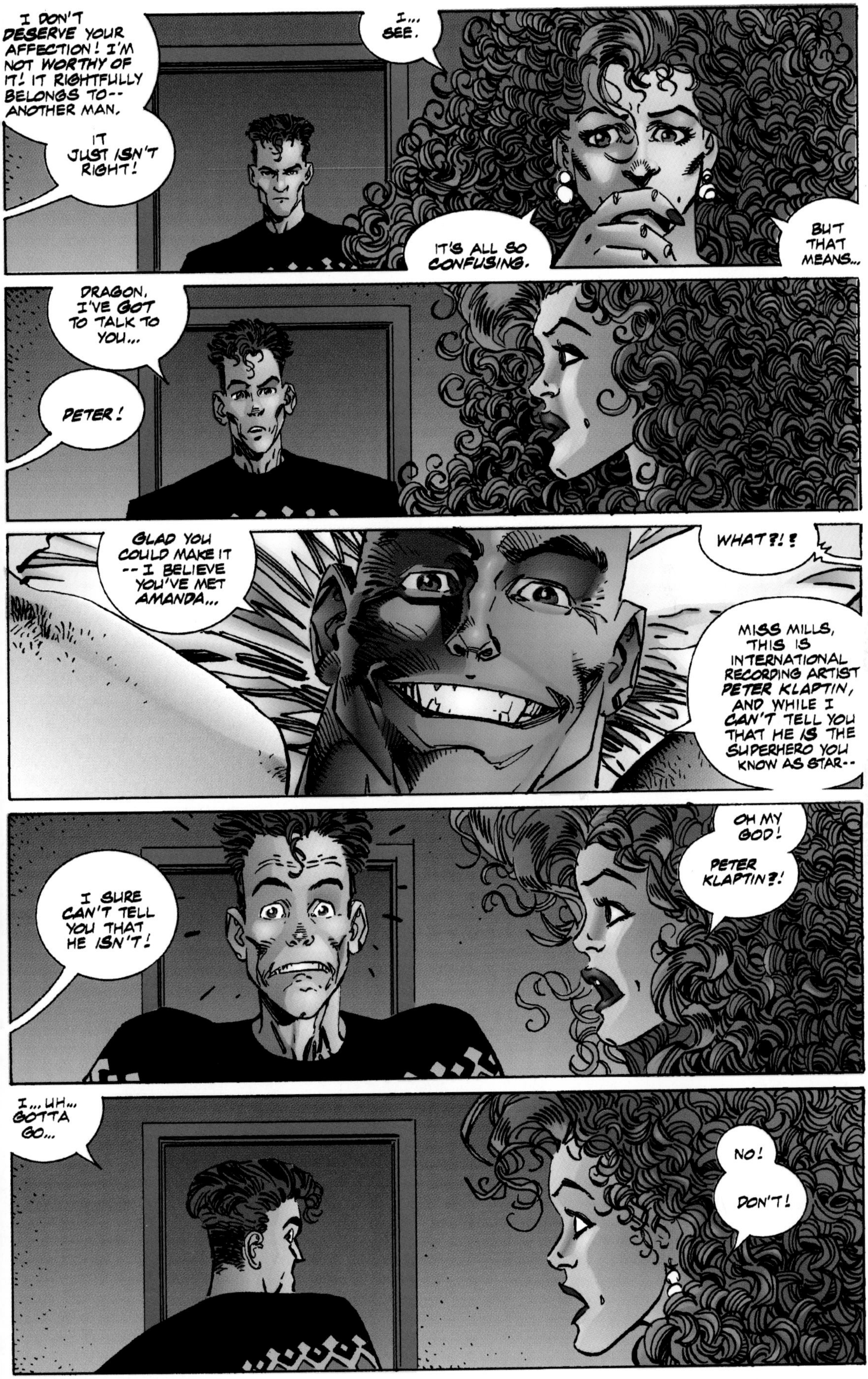
I DON'T DESERVE YOUR AFFECTION! I'M NOT WORTHY OF IT! IT RIGHTFULLY BELONGS TO--ANOTHER MAN.
IT JUST ISN'T RIGHT!
I... SEE.
IT'S ALL SO CONFUSING.
BUT THAT MEANS...
DRAGON, I'VE GOT TO TALK TO YOU...
PETER!
GLAD YOU COULD MAKE IT --I BELIEVE YOU'VE MET AMANDA...
WHAT?!!
MISS MILLS, THIS IS INTERNATIONAL RECORDING ARTIST PETER KLAPTIN, AND WHILE I CAN'T TELL YOU THAT HE IS THE SUPERHERO YOU KNOW AS STAR--
I SURE CAN'T TELL YOU THAT HE ISN'T!
OH MY GOD!
PETER KLAPTIN?!
I... UH... GOTTA GO...
NO!
DON'T!

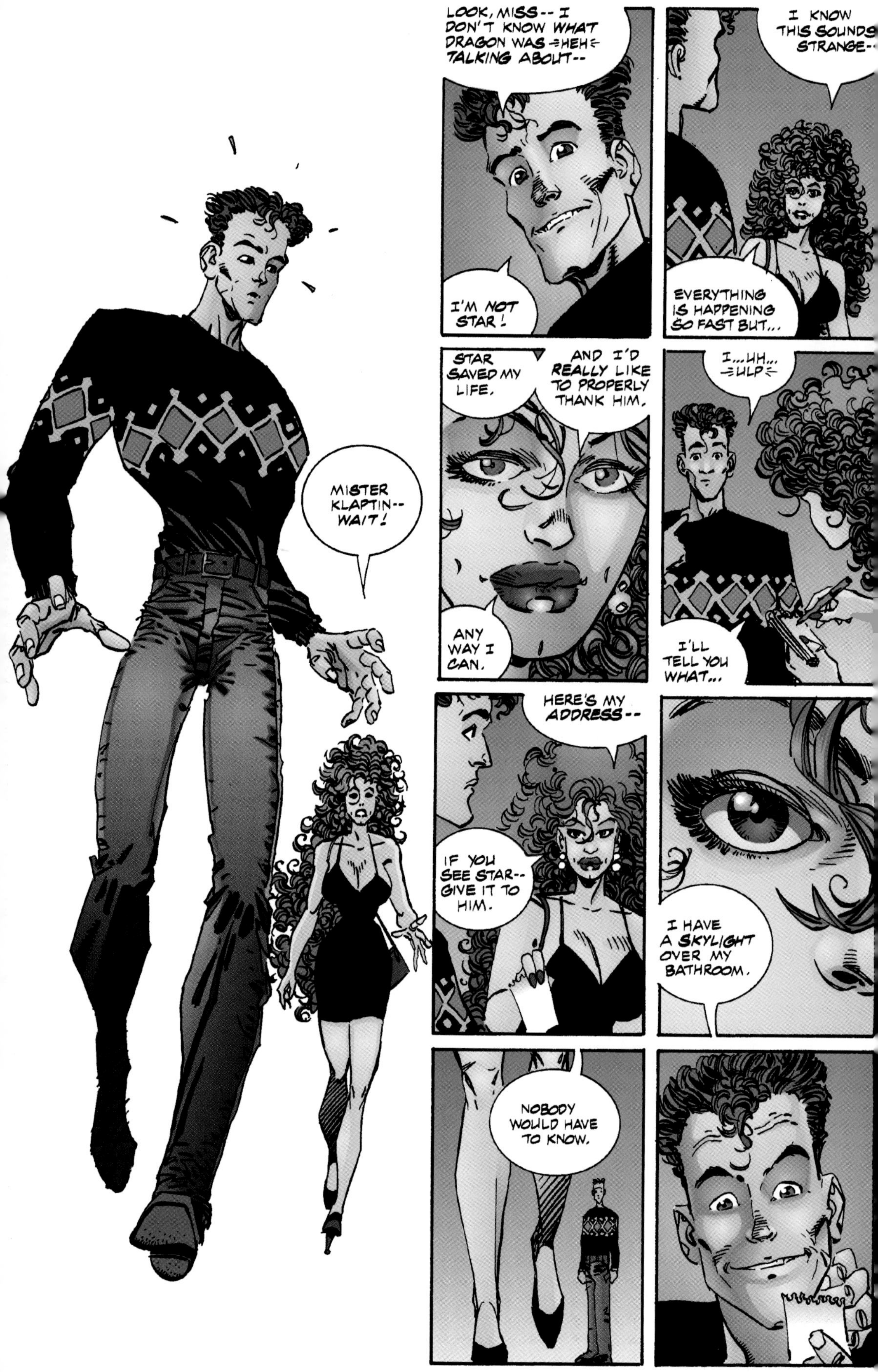
MISTER KLAPTIN-- WAIT!
LOOK, MISS-- I DON'T KNOW WHAT DRAGON WAS =HEH= TALKING ABOUT--
I'M NOT STAR!
I KNOW THIS SOUNDS STRANGE--
EVERYTHING IS HAPPENING SO FAST BUT...
STAR SAVED MY LIFE.
AND I'D REALLY LIKE TO PROPERLY THANK HIM.
ANY WAY I CAN.
I...UH... =ULP=
I'LL TELL YOU WHAT...
HERE'S MY ADDRESS--
IF YOU SEE STAR-- GIVE IT TO HIM.
I HAVE A SKYLIGHT OVER MY BATHROOM.
NOBODY WOULD HAVE TO KNOW.

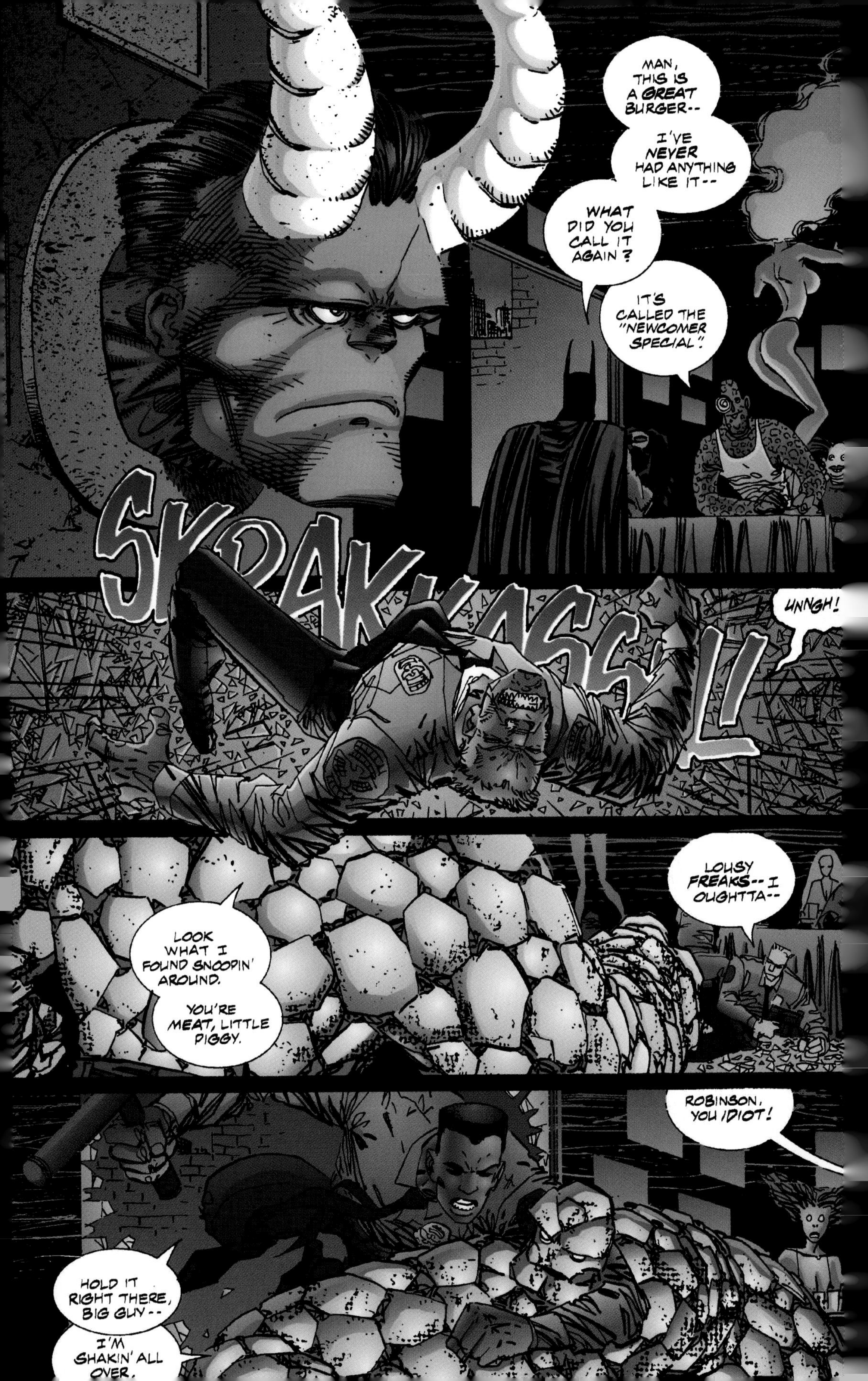

MAN, THIS IS A GREAT BURGER--
I'VE NEVER HAD ANYTHING LIKE IT--
WHAT DID YOU CALL IT AGAIN?
IT'S CALLED THE "NEWCOMER SPECIAL".
UNNGH!
LOUSY FREAKS-- I OUGHTTA--
LOOK WHAT I FOUND SNOOPIN' AROUND.
YOU'RE MEAT, LITTLE PIGGY.
ROBINSON, YOU IDIOT!
HOLD IT RIGHT THERE, BIG GUY--
I'M SHAKIN' ALL OVER.

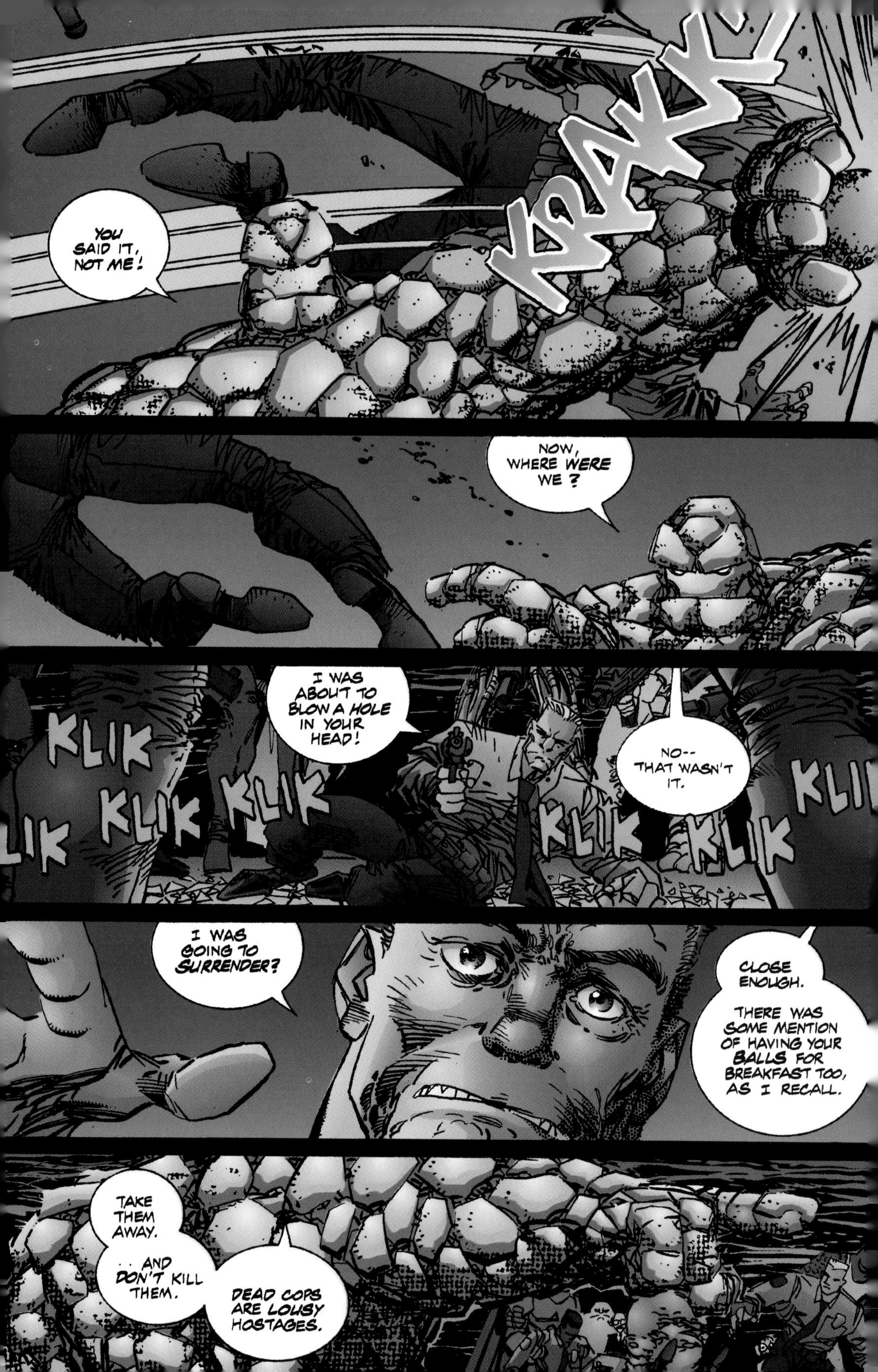
YOU SAID IT, NOT ME!
KRAKK
NOW, WHERE WERE WE?
KLIK KLIK KLIK KLIK
I WAS ABOUT TO BLOW A HOLE IN YOUR HEAD!
NO-- THAT WASN'T IT.
KLIK KLIK KLIK
I WAS GOING TO SURRENDER?
CLOSE ENOUGH.
THERE WAS SOME MENTION OF HAVING YOUR BALLS FOR BREAKFAST TOO, AS I RECALL.
TAKE THEM AWAY.
.. AND DON'T KILL THEM.
DEAD COPS ARE LOUSY HOSTAGES.

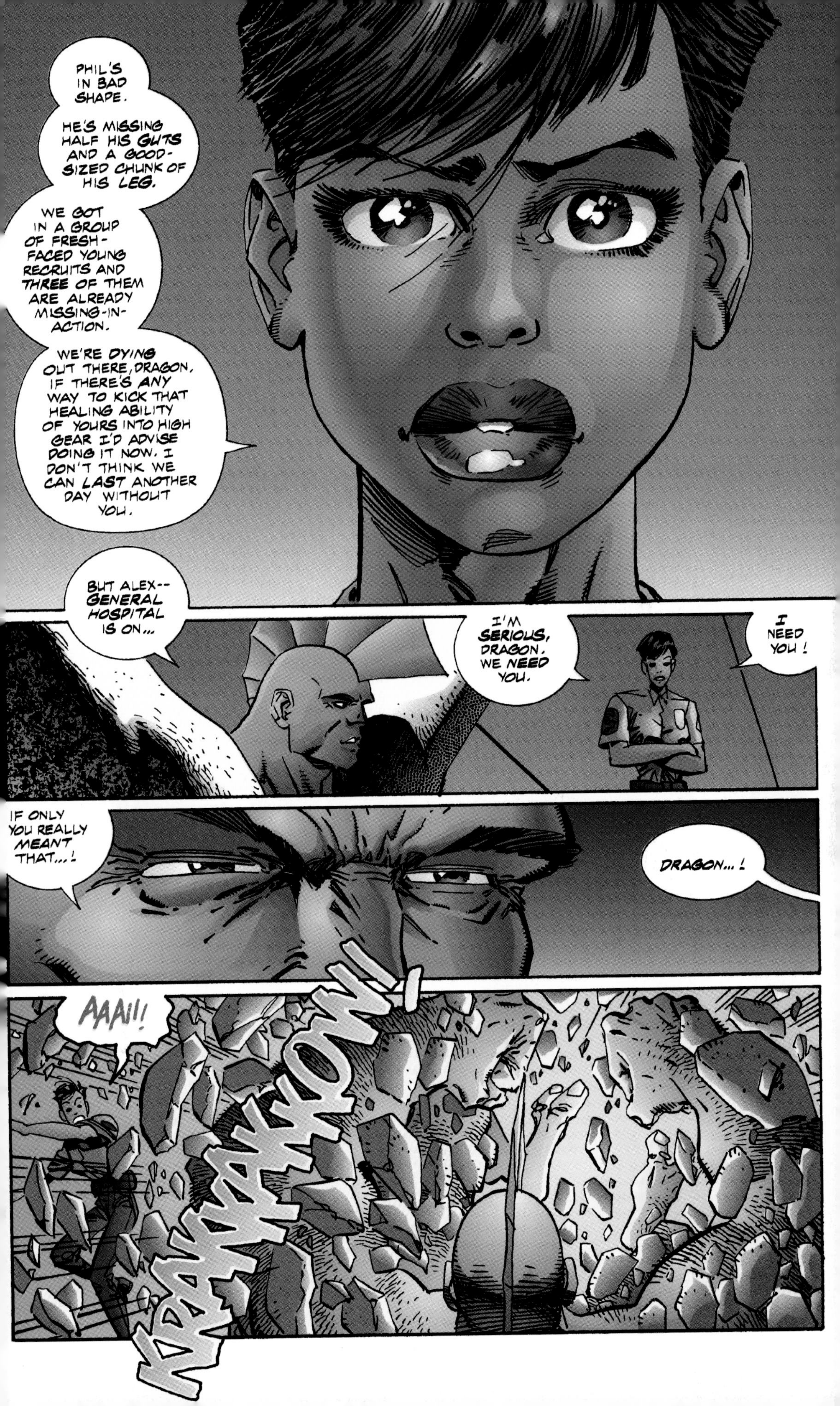
PHIL'S IN BAD SHAPE.
HE'S MISSING HALF HIS GUTS AND A GOOD-SIZED CHUNK OF HIS LEG.
WE GOT IN A GROUP OF FRESH-FACED YOUNG RECRUITS AND THREE OF THEM ARE ALREADY MISSING-IN-ACTION.
WE'RE DYING OUT THERE, DRAGON, IF THERE'S ANY WAY TO KICK THAT HEALING ABILITY OF YOURS INTO HIGH GEAR I'D ADVISE DOING IT NOW. I DON'T THINK WE CAN LAST ANOTHER DAY WITHOUT YOU.
BUT ALEX-- GENERAL HOSPITAL IS ON...
I'M SERIOUS, DRAGON. WE NEED YOU.
I NEED YOU!
IF ONLY YOU REALLY MEANT THAT...!
DRAGON...!
AAAII!
KRAKAKAKOOM!

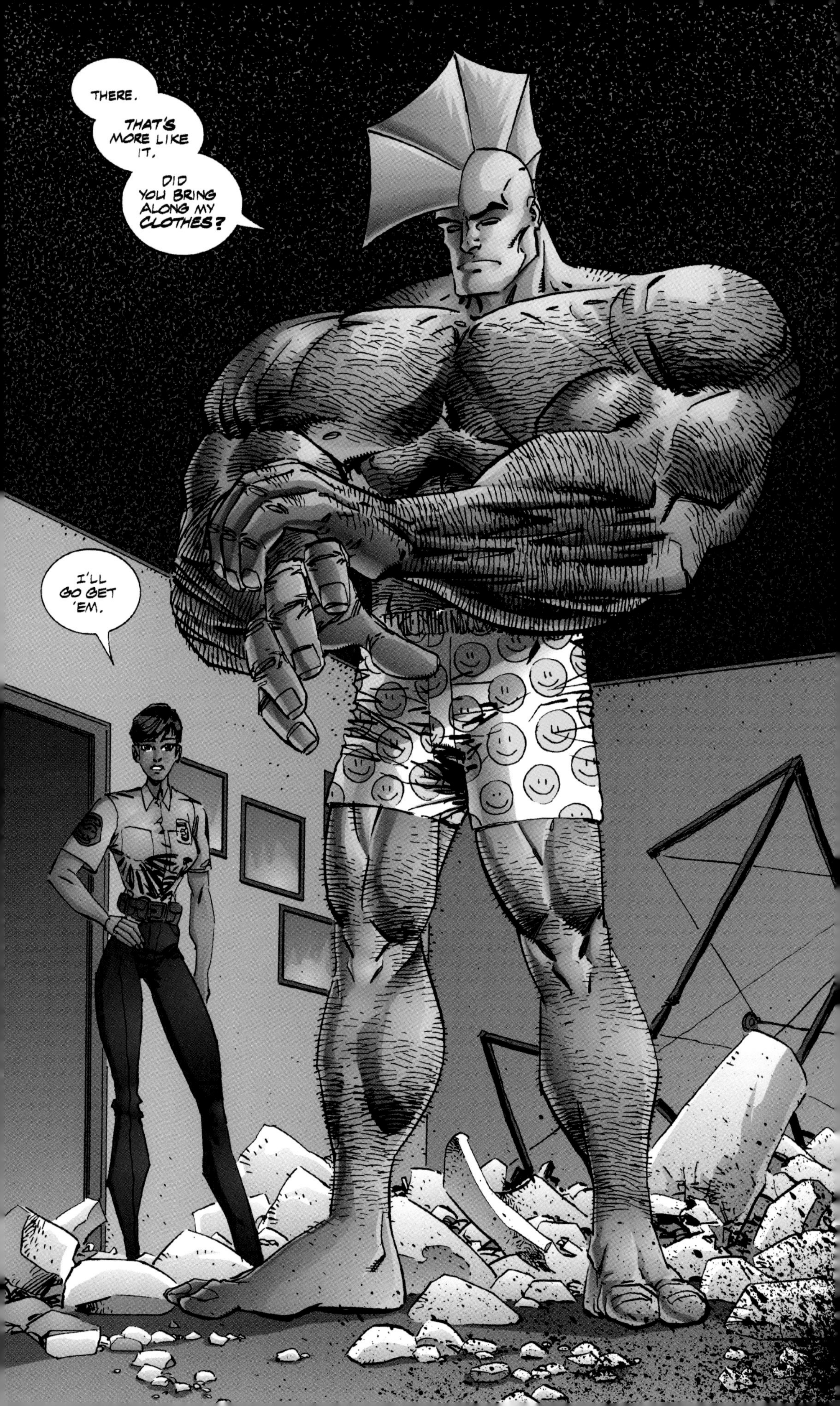

THERE.
THAT'S MORE LIKE IT.
DID YOU BRING ALONG MY CLOTHES?
I'LL GO GET 'EM.

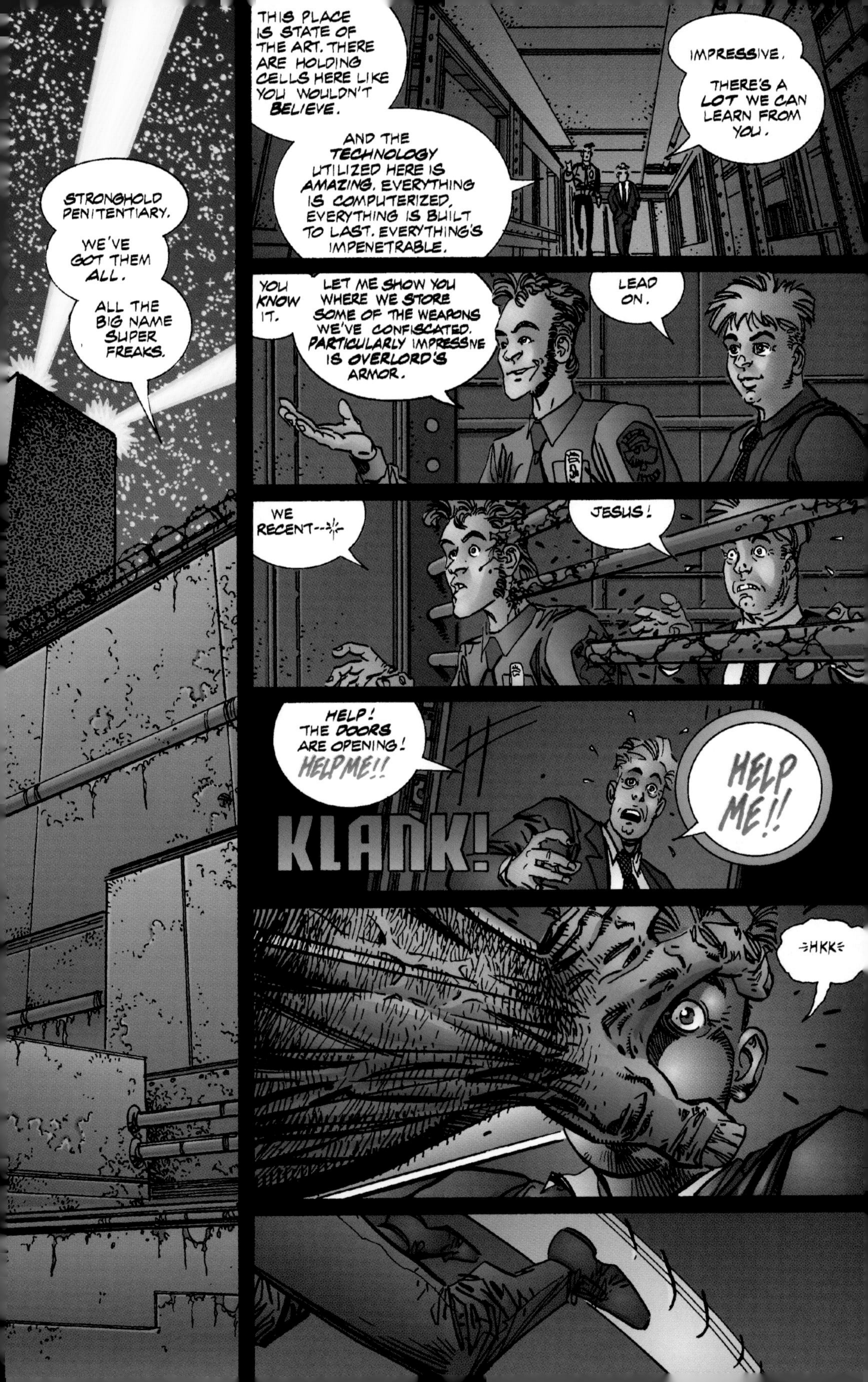
STRONGHOLD PENITENTIARY.
WE'VE GOT THEM ALL.
ALL THE BIG NAME SUPER FREAKS.
THIS PLACE IS STATE OF THE ART. THERE ARE HOLDING CELLS HERE LIKE YOU WOULDN'T BELIEVE.
AND THE TECHNOLOGY UTILIZED HERE IS AMAZING. EVERYTHING IS COMPUTERIZED. EVERYTHING IS BUILT TO LAST. EVERYTHING'S IMPENETRABLE.
IMPRESSIVE.
THERE'S A LOT WE CAN LEARN FROM YOU.
YOU KNOW IT.
LET ME SHOW YOU WHERE WE STORE SOME OF THE WEAPONS WE'VE CONFISCATED. PARTICULARLY IMPRESSIVE IS OVERLORD'S ARMOR.
LEAD ON.
WE RECENT--
JESUS!
HELP! THE DOORS ARE OPENING! HELP ME!!
KLANK!
HELP ME!!
HKK

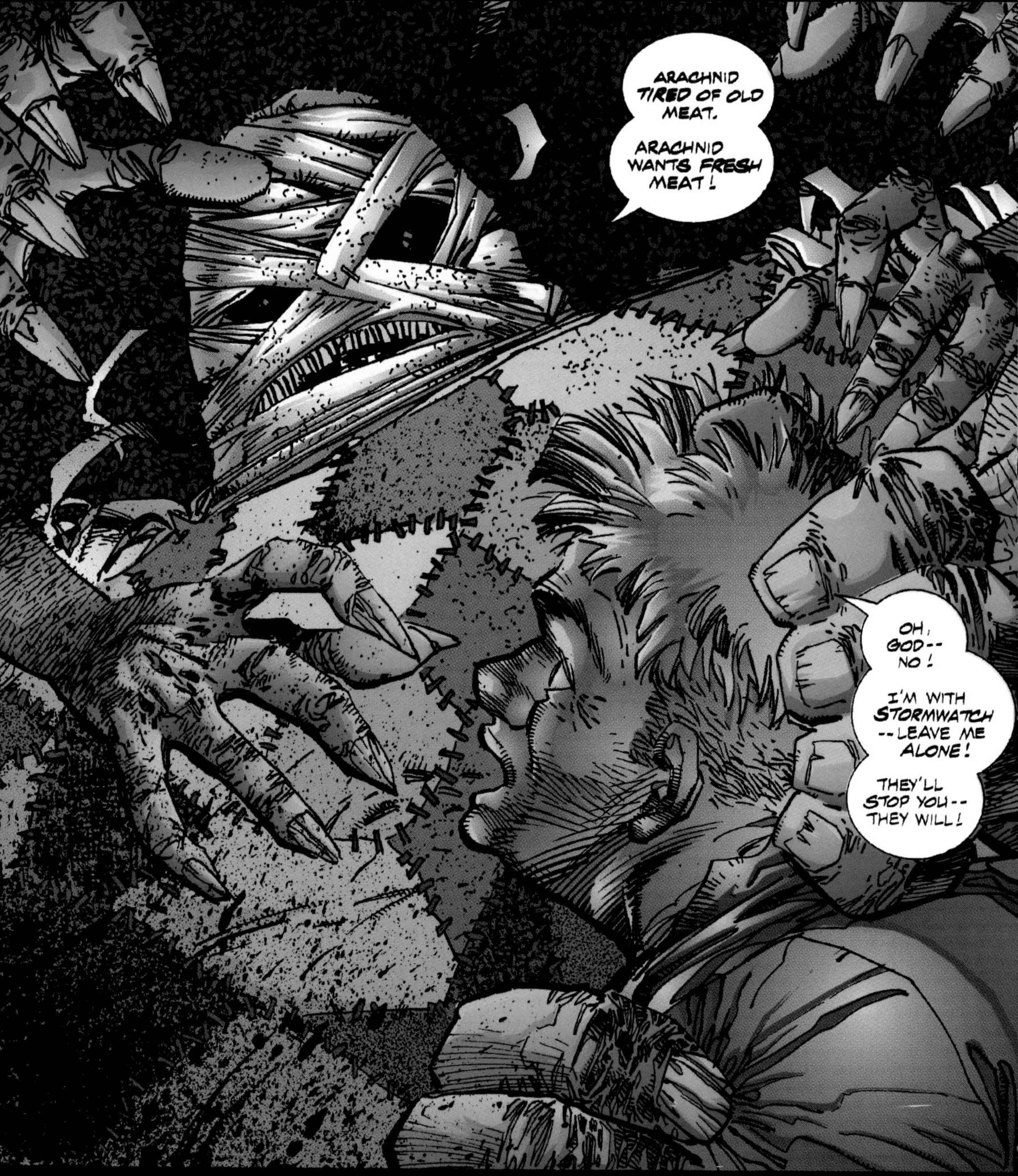
ARACHNID TIRED OF OLD MEAT.
ARACHNID WANTS FRESH MEAT!
OH, GOD--NO!
I'M WITH STORMWATCH--LEAVE ME ALONE!
THEY'LL STOP YOU--THEY WILL!
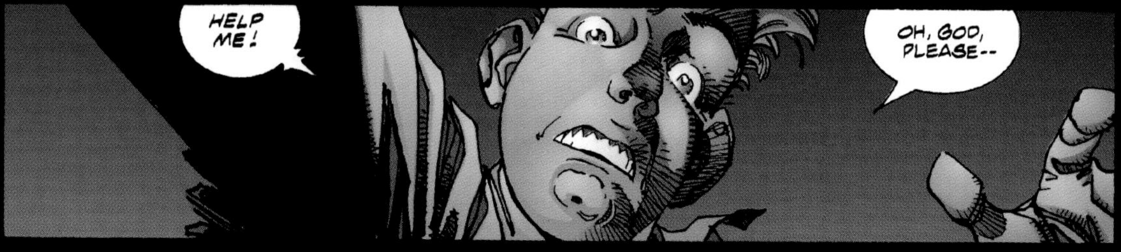
HELP ME!
OH, GOD, PLEASE--
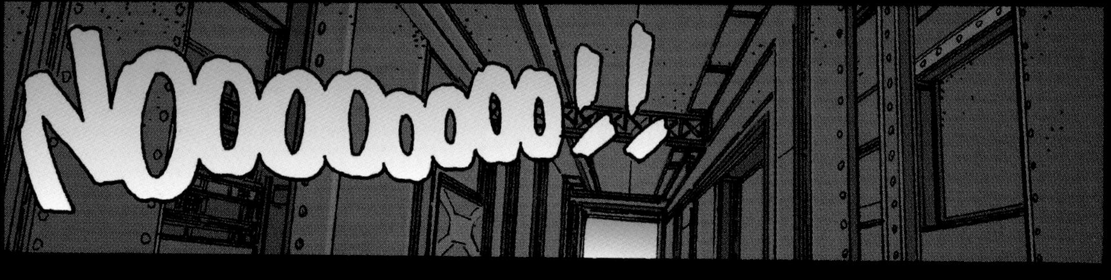
NOOOOOOOO!!

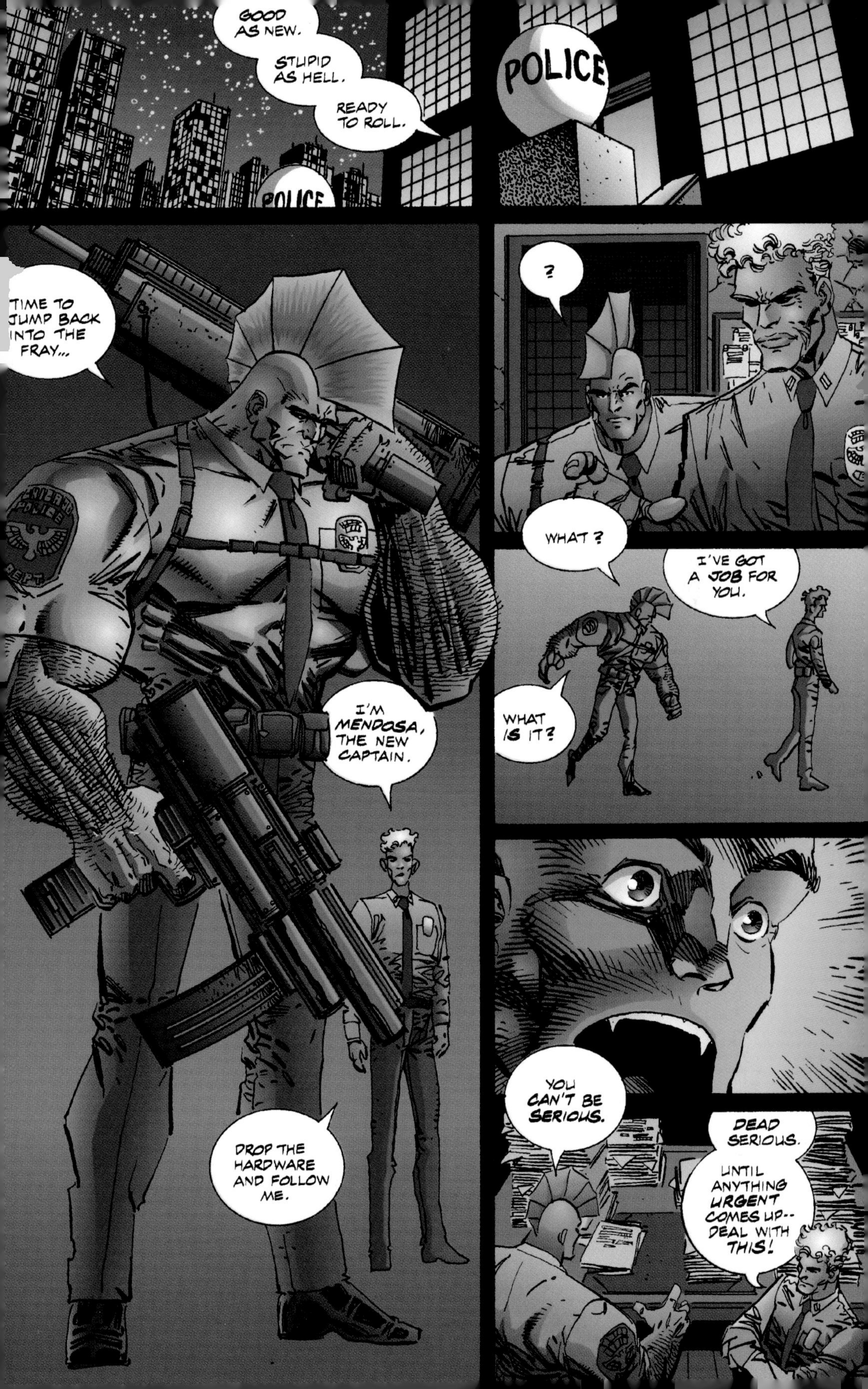
GOOD AS NEW.
STUPID AS HELL.
READY TO ROLL.
POLICE
POLICE
TIME TO JUMP BACK INTO THE FRAY...
I'M MENDOSA, THE NEW CAPTAIN.
DROP THE HARDWARE AND FOLLOW ME.
?
WHAT ?
I'VE GOT A JOB FOR YOU.
WHAT IS IT?
YOU CAN'T BE SERIOUS.
DEAD SERIOUS.
UNTIL ANYTHING URGENT COMES UP-- DEAL WITH THIS!

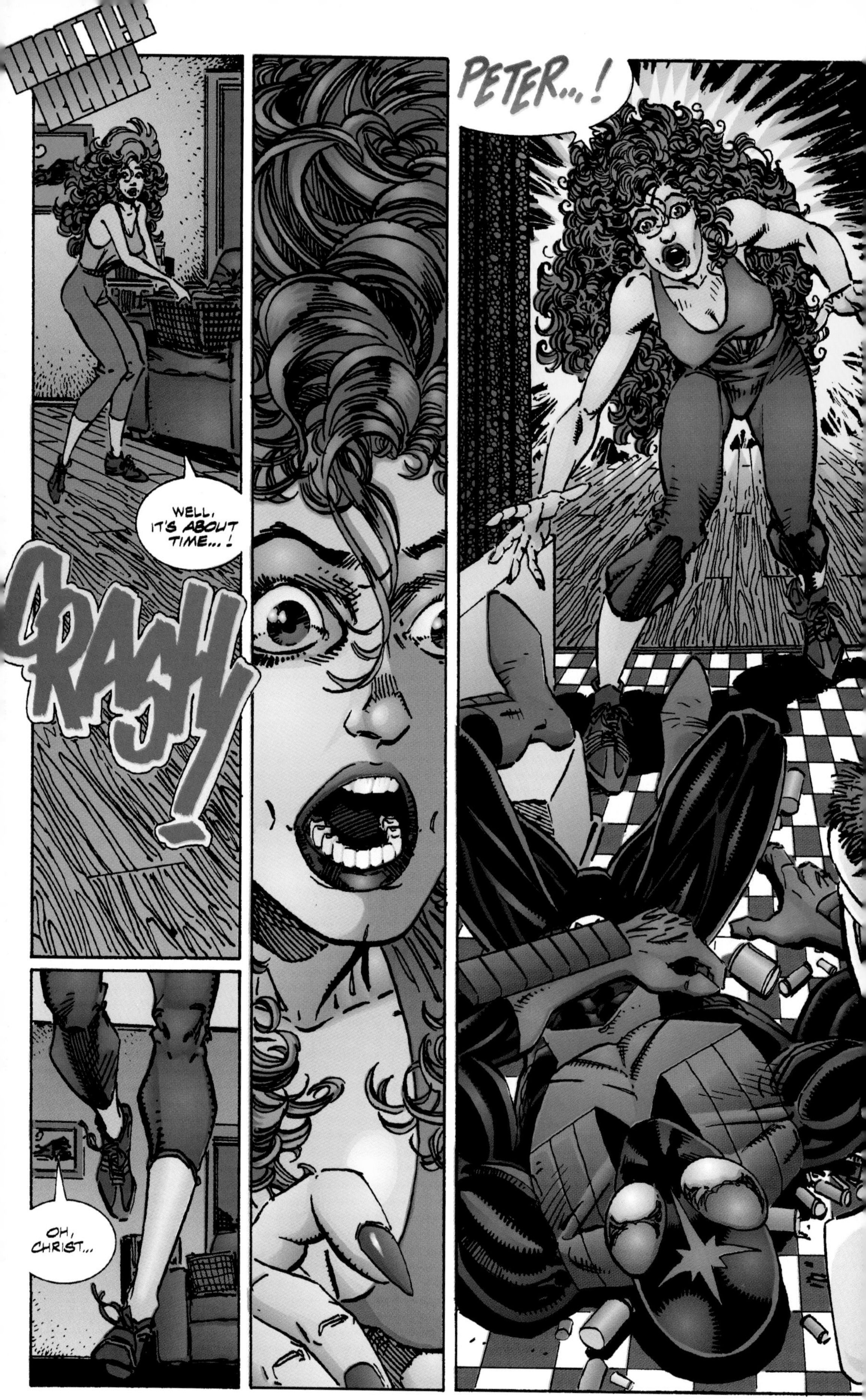
WELL, IT'S ABOUT TIME...!
CRASH
OH, CHRIST...
PETER...!

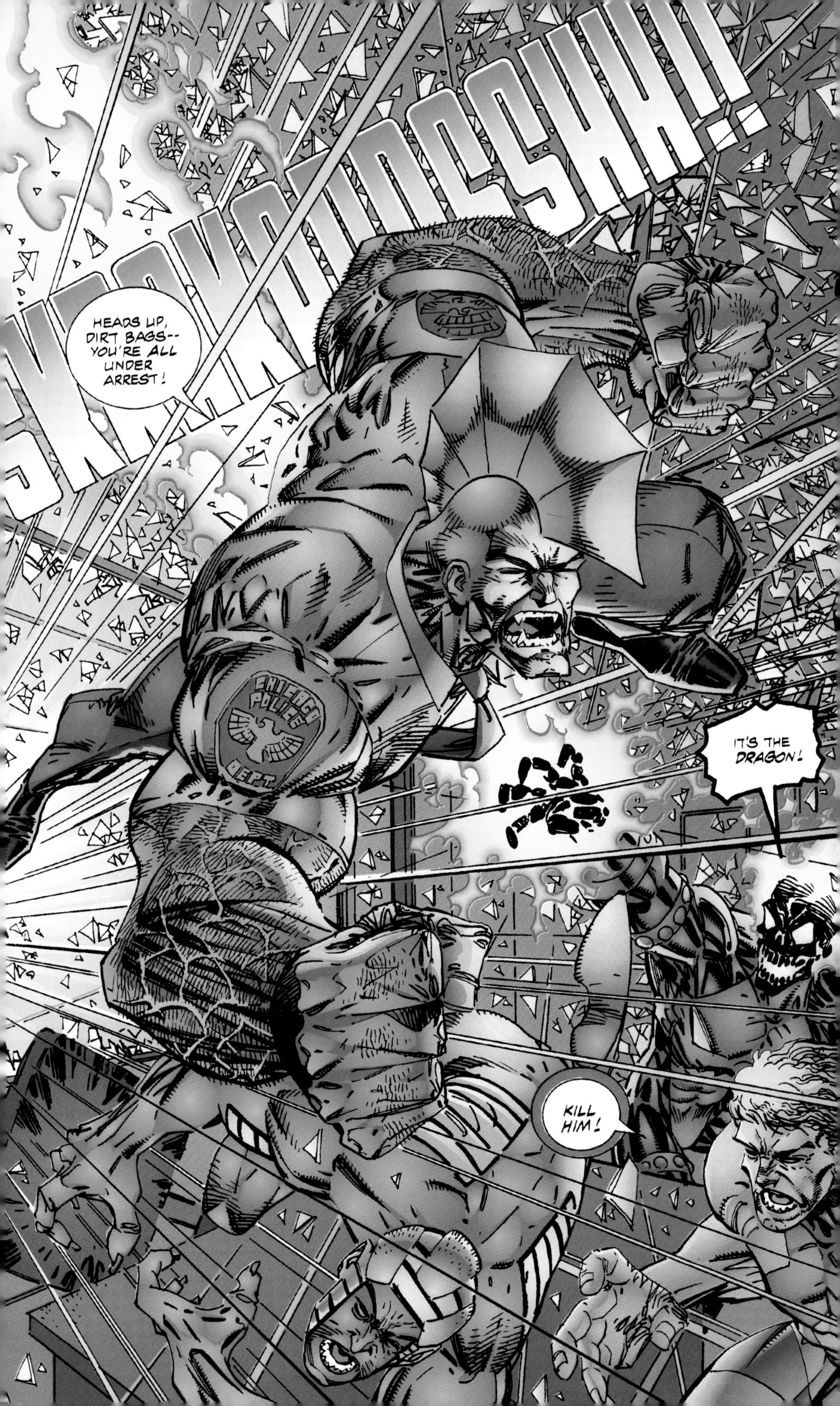
SKRAKATHOOOSHH!!
HEADS UP, DIRT BAGS-- YOU'RE ALL UNDER ARREST!
IT'S THE DRAGON!
KILL HIM!

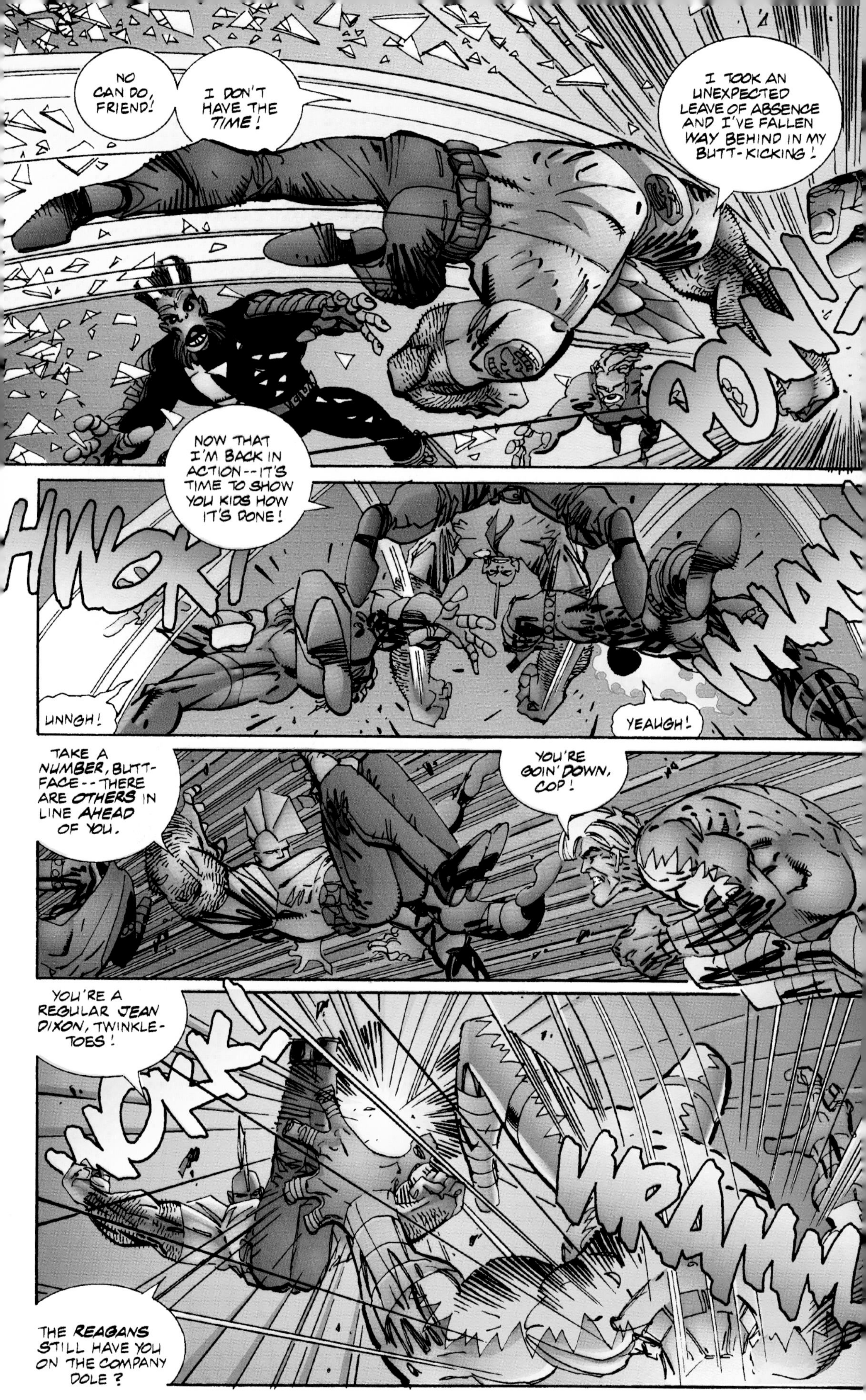
NO CAN DO, FRIEND!
I DON'T HAVE THE TIME!
I TOOK AN UNEXPECTED LEAVE OF ABSENCE AND I'VE FALLEN WAY BEHIND IN MY BUTT-KICKING!
NOW THAT I'M BACK IN ACTION--IT'S TIME TO SHOW YOU KIDS HOW IT'S DONE!
UNNGH!
YEAUGH!
TAKE A NUMBER, BUTT-FACE--THERE ARE OTHERS IN LINE AHEAD OF YOU.
YOU'RE GOIN' DOWN, COP!
YOU'RE A REGULAR JEAN DIXON, TWINKLE-TOES!
THE REAGANS STILL HAVE YOU ON THE COMPANY DOLE?

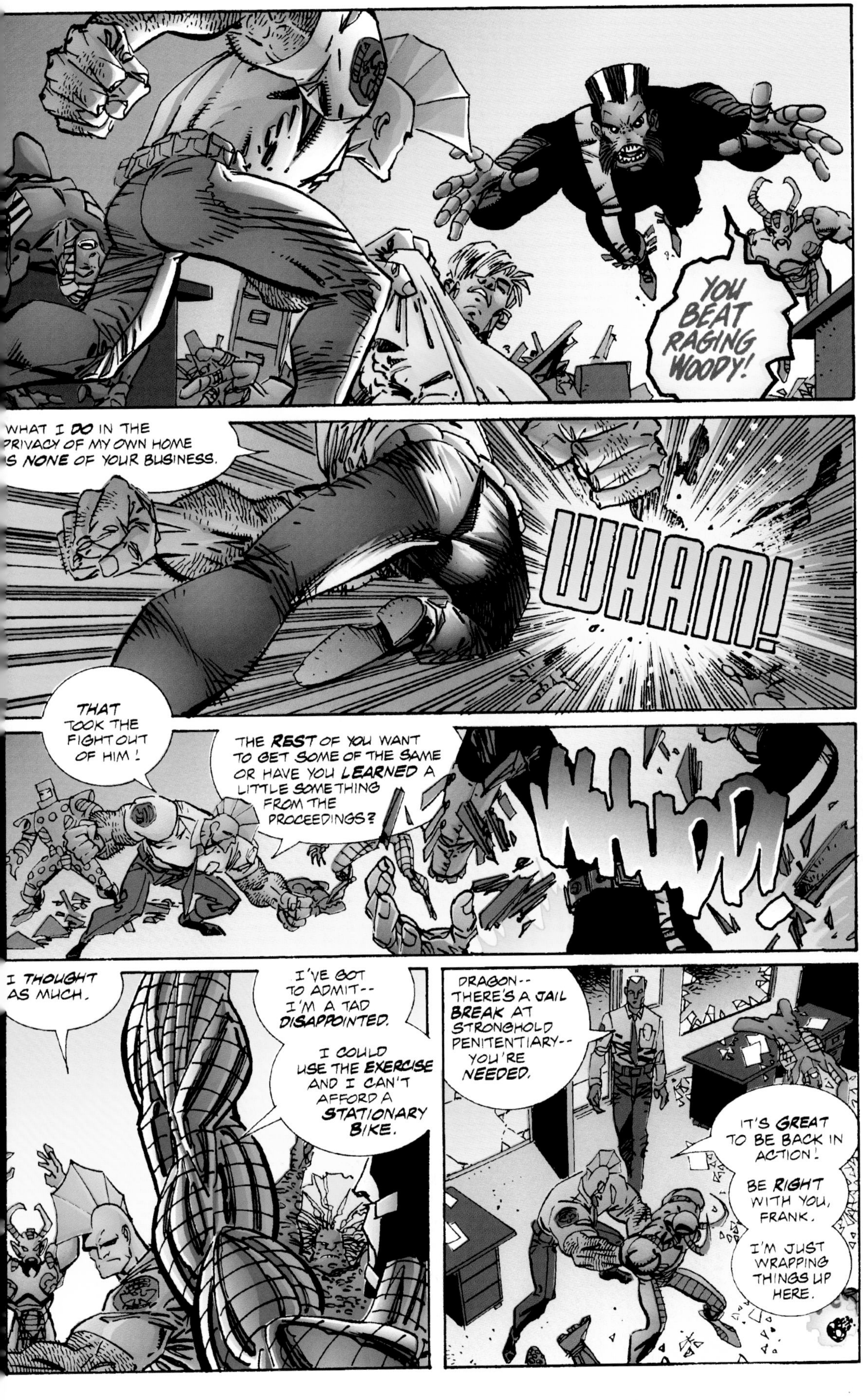

YOU BEAT RAGING WOODY!
WHAT I DO IN THE PRIVACY OF MY OWN HOME IS NONE OF YOUR BUSINESS.
WHAM!
THAT TOOK THE FIGHT OUT OF HIM!
THE REST OF YOU WANT TO GET SOME OF THE SAME OR HAVE YOU LEARNED A LITTLE SOMETHING FROM THE PROCEEDINGS?
WHOOM
I THOUGHT AS MUCH.
I'VE GOT TO ADMIT-- I'M A TAD DISAPPOINTED.
I COULD USE THE EXERCISE AND I CAN'T AFFORD A STATIONARY BIKE.
DRAGON-- THERE'S A JAIL BREAK AT STRONGHOLD PENITENTIARY-- YOU'RE NEEDED.
IT'S GREAT TO BE BACK IN ACTION!
BE RIGHT WITH YOU, FRANK.
I'M JUST WRAPPING THINGS UP HERE.

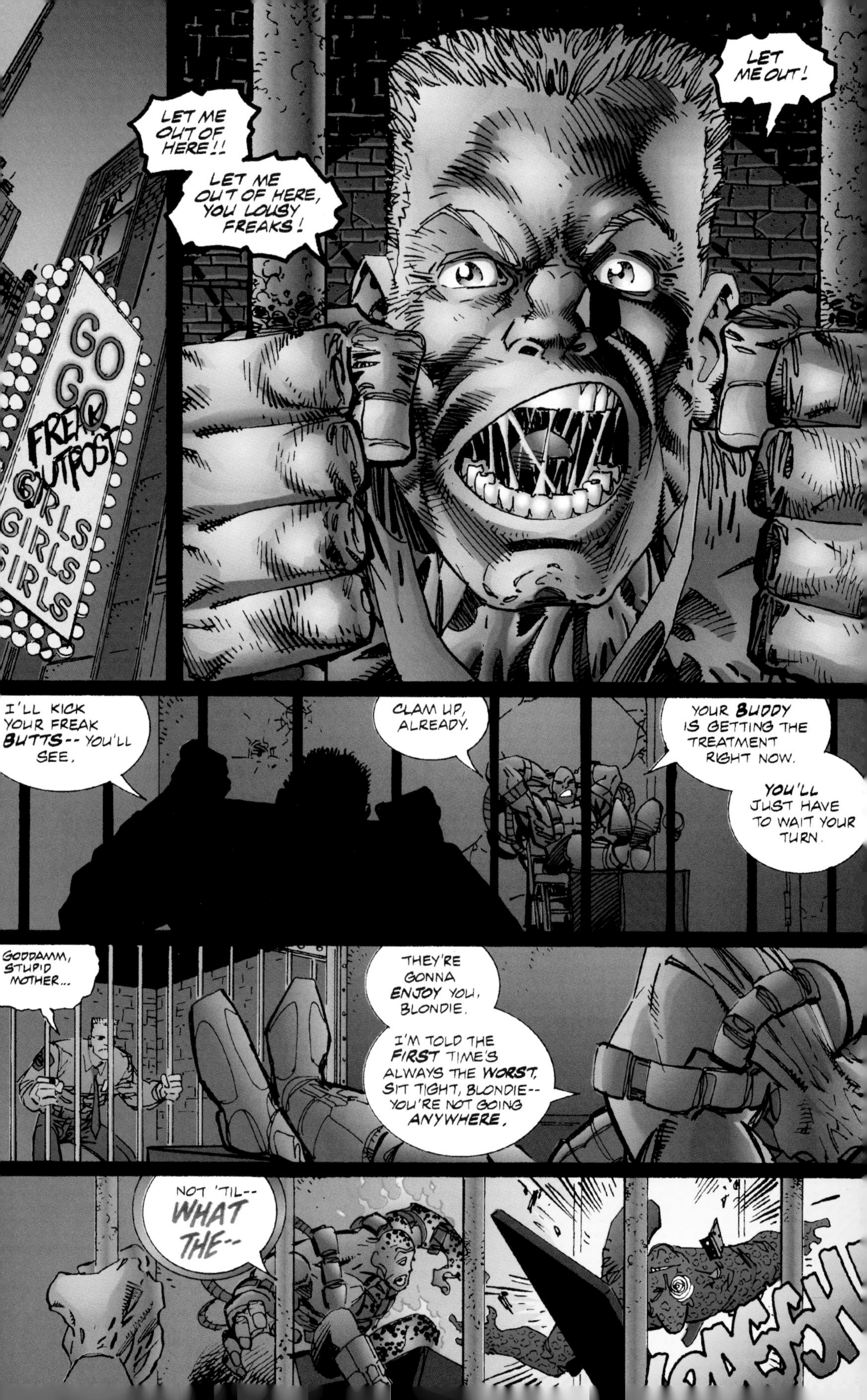
LET ME OUT OF HERE!!
LET ME OUT OF HERE, YOU LOUSY FREAKS!
LET ME OUT!
GO GO
FREAK OUTPOST
GIRLS
GIRLS
I'LL KICK YOUR FREAK BUTTS-- YOU'LL SEE.
CLAM UP, ALREADY.
YOUR BUDDY IS GETTING THE TREATMENT RIGHT NOW.
YOU'LL JUST HAVE TO WAIT YOUR TURN.
GODDAMM, STUPID MOTHER...
THEY'RE GONNA ENJOY YOU, BLONDIE.
I'M TOLD THE FIRST TIME'S ALWAYS THE WORST. SIT TIGHT, BLONDIE-- YOU'RE NOT GOING ANYWHERE.
NOT 'TIL-- WHAT THE--

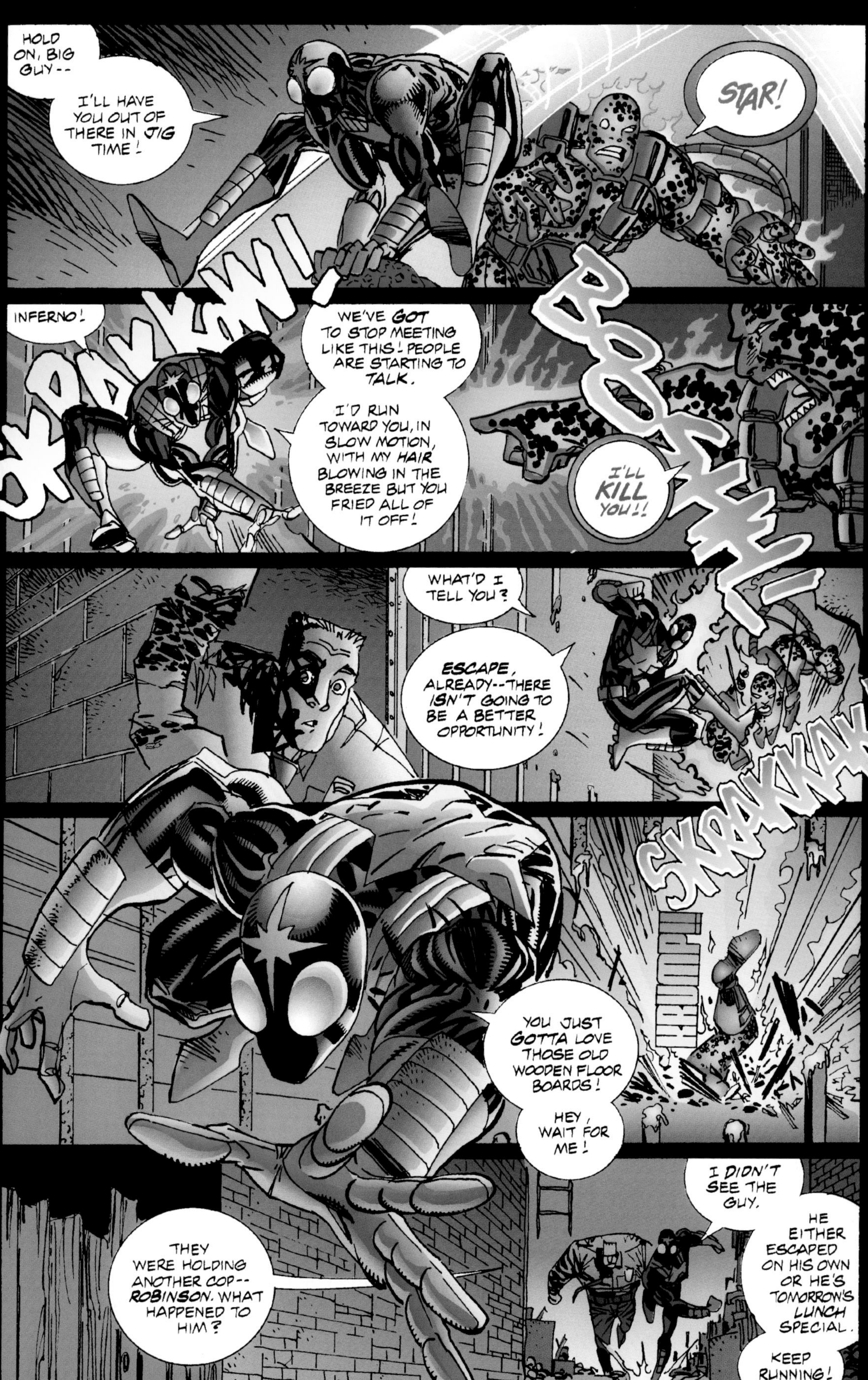
HOLD ON, BIG GUY--
I'LL HAVE YOU OUT OF THERE IN JIG TIME!
STAR!
SKRAKKW!
INFERNO!
WE'VE GOT TO STOP MEETING LIKE THIS! PEOPLE ARE STARTING TO TALK.
I'D RUN TOWARD YOU, IN SLOW MOTION, WITH MY HAIR BLOWING IN THE BREEZE BUT YOU FRIED ALL OF IT OFF!
BOOSHH!
I'LL KILL YOU!!
WHAT'D I TELL YOU?
ESCAPE, ALREADY--THERE ISN'T GOING TO BE A BETTER OPPORTUNITY!
SKRAKKAK
KRUMP!!
YOU JUST GOTTA LOVE THOSE OLD WOODEN FLOOR BOARDS!
HEY, WAIT FOR ME!
THEY WERE HOLDING ANOTHER COP--ROBINSON. WHAT HAPPENED TO HIM?
I DIDN'T SEE THE GUY.
HE EITHER ESCAPED ON HIS OWN OR HE'S TOMORROW'S LUNCH SPECIAL.
KEEP RUNNING!

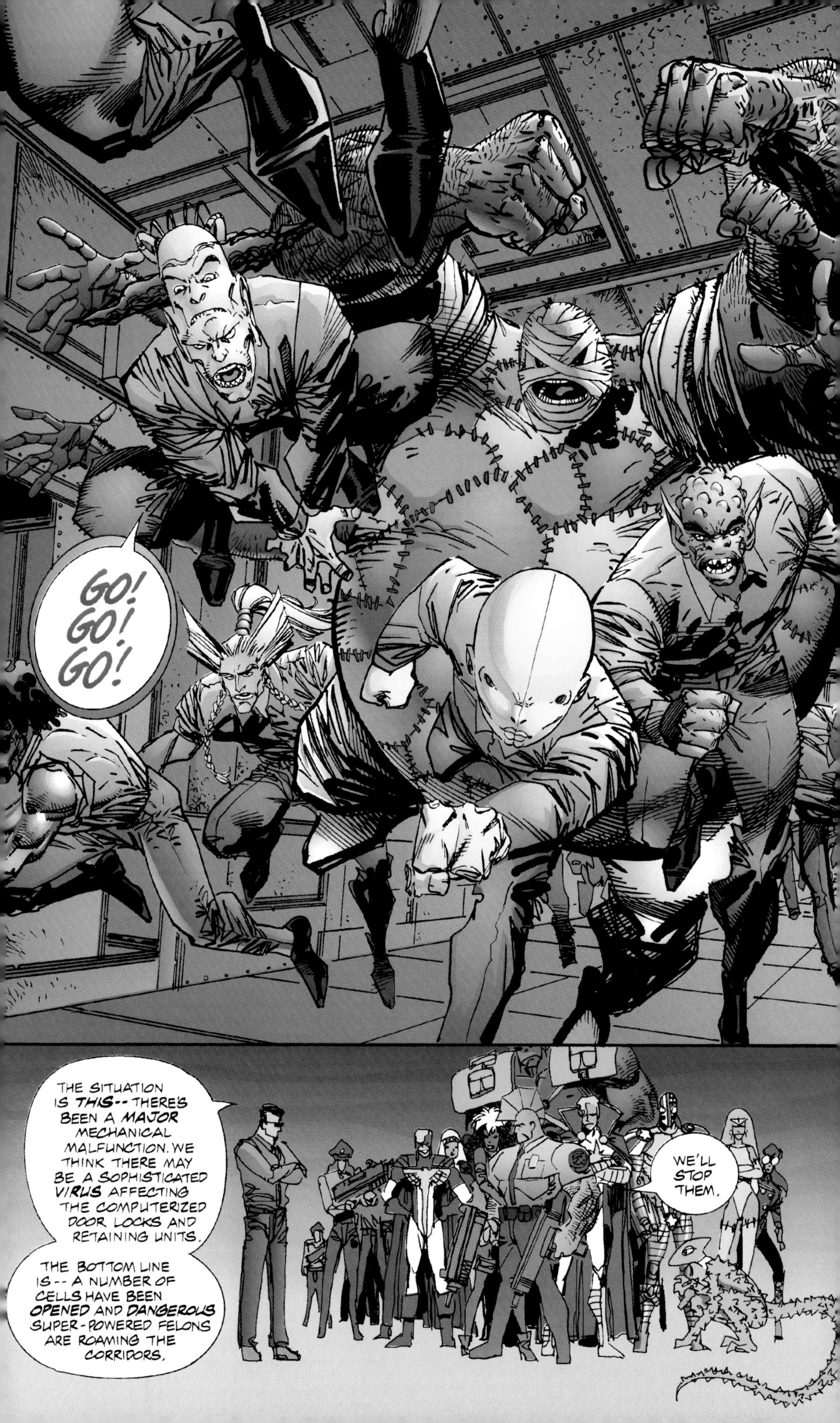
GO! GO! GO!
THE SITUATION IS THIS-- THERE'S BEEN A MAJOR MECHANICAL MALFUNCTION. WE THINK THERE MAY BE A SOPHISTICATED VIRUS AFFECTING THE COMPUTERIZED DOOR LOCKS AND RETAINING UNITS.
THE BOTTOM LINE IS-- A NUMBER OF CELLS HAVE BEEN OPENED AND DANGEROUS SUPER-POWERED FELONS ARE ROAMING THE CORRIDORS.
WE'LL STOP THEM.

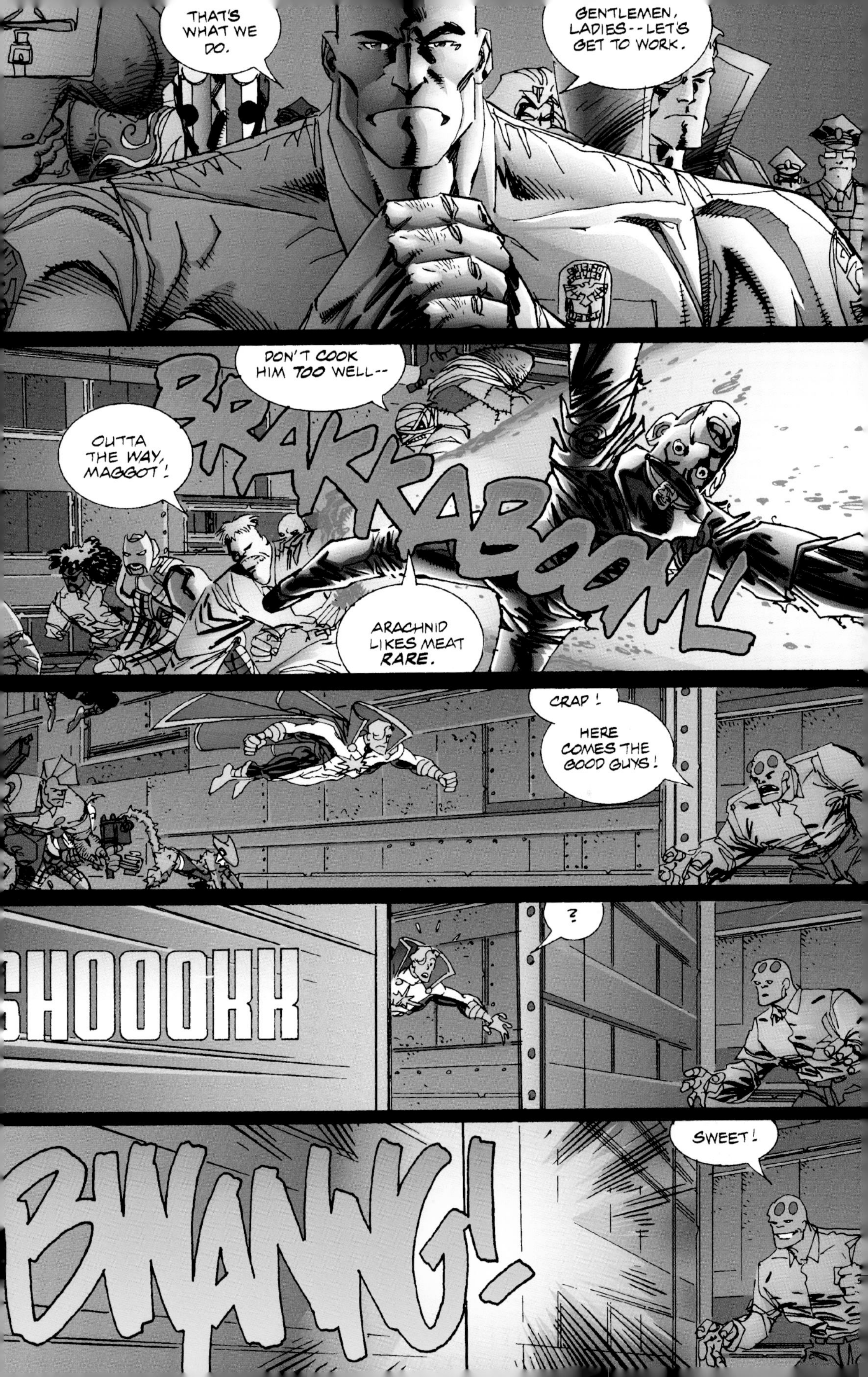
THAT'S WHAT WE DO.
GENTLEMEN, LADIES--LET'S GET TO WORK.
DON'T COOK HIM TOO WELL--
BRAKKABOOM!
OUTTA THE WAY, MAGGOT!
ARACHNID LIKES MEAT RARE.
CRAP!
HERE COMES THE GOOD GUYS!
?
SHOOOKK
SWEET!
BWANG!

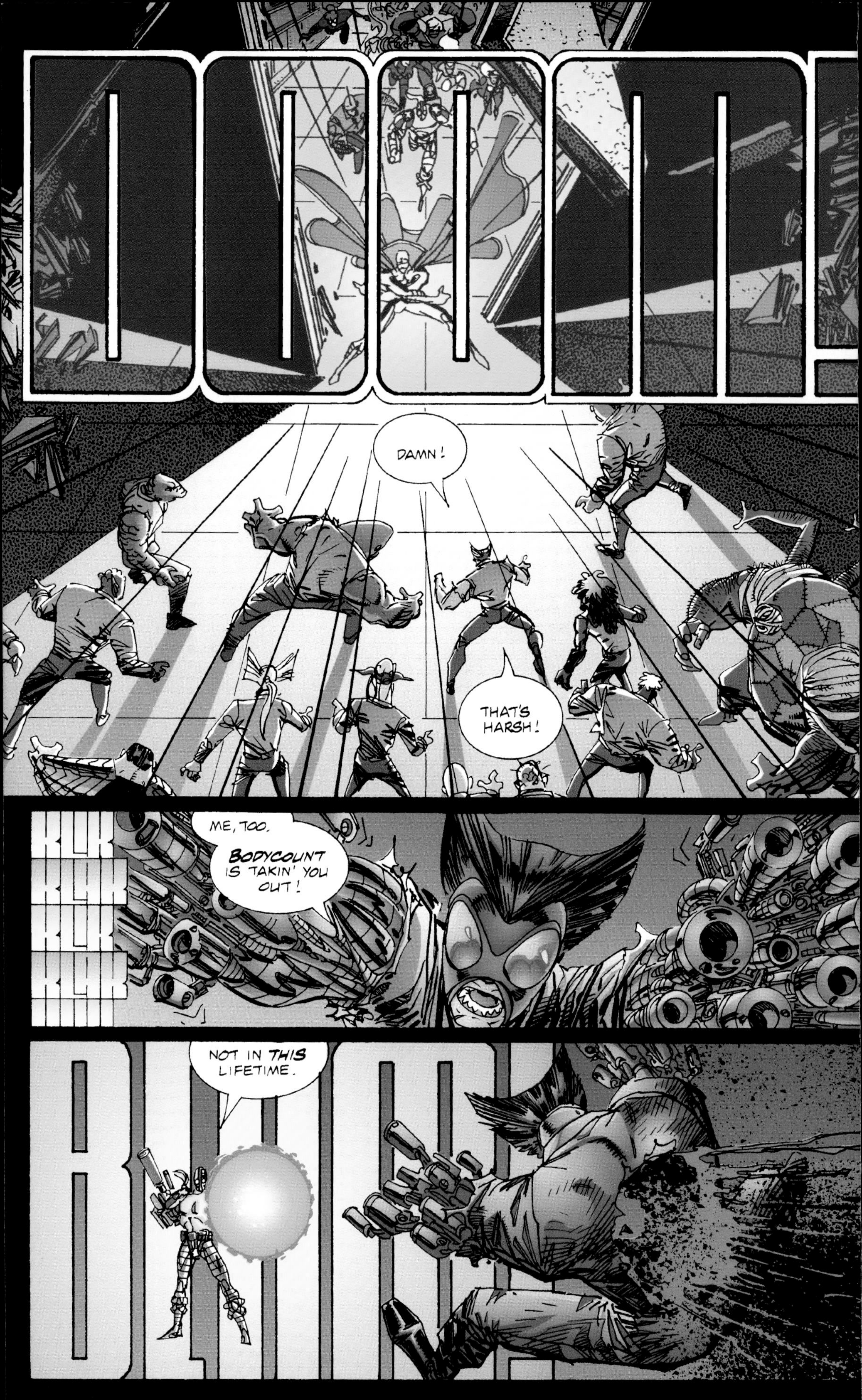

BOOOM!
DAMN!
THAT'S HARSH!
ME, TOO. BODYCOUNT IS TAKIN' YOU OUT!
KLIK KLAK KLIK KLAK
NOT IN THIS LIFETIME.

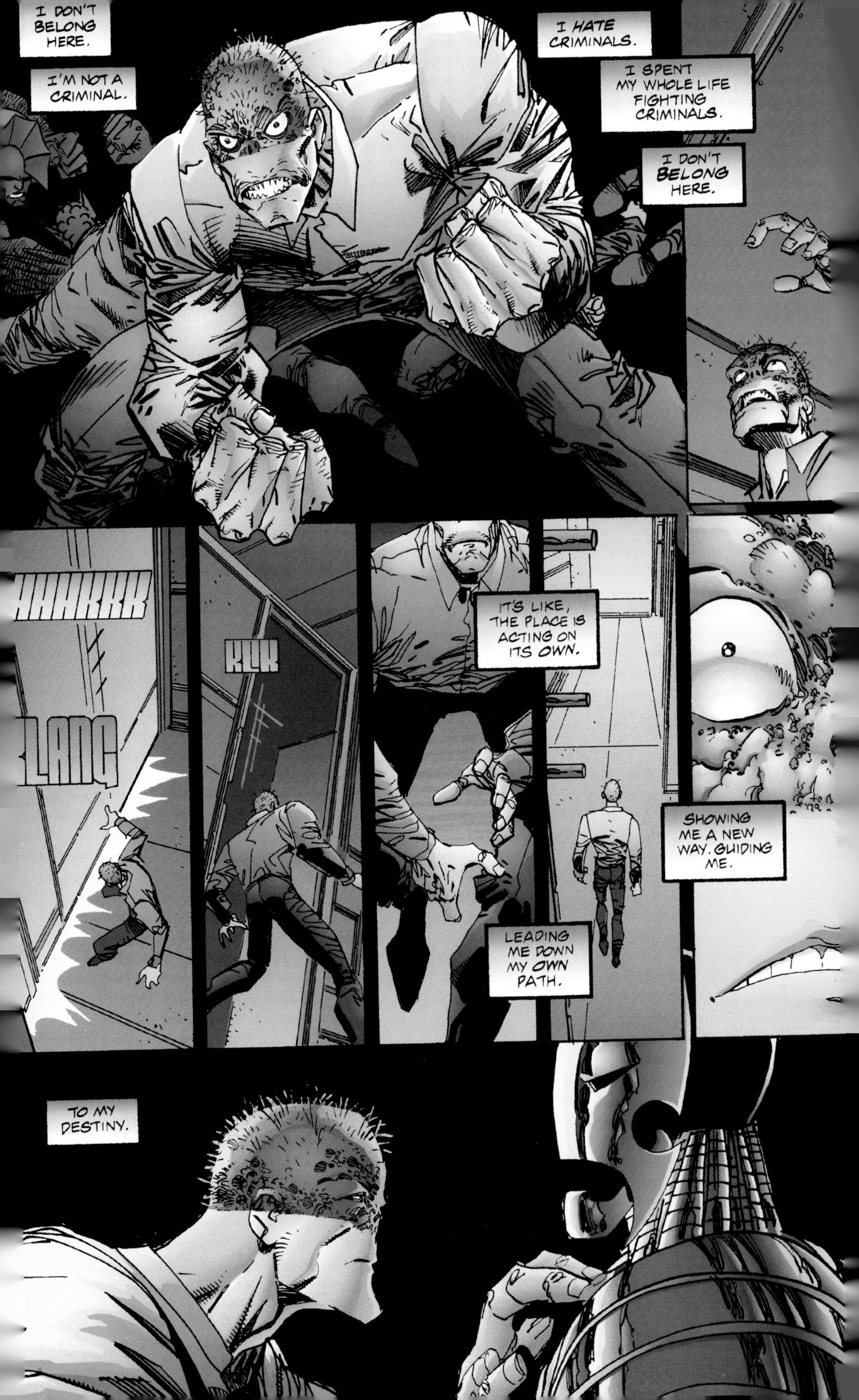

I DON'T BELONG HERE.
I'M NOT A CRIMINAL.
I HATE CRIMINALS.
I SPENT MY WHOLE LIFE FIGHTING CRIMINALS.
I DON'T BELONG HERE.
HHHAKKK
CLANG
KLK
IT'S LIKE, THE PLACE IS ACTING ON ITS OWN.
LEADING ME DOWN MY OWN PATH.
SHOWING ME A NEW WAY. GUIDING ME.
TO MY DESTINY.

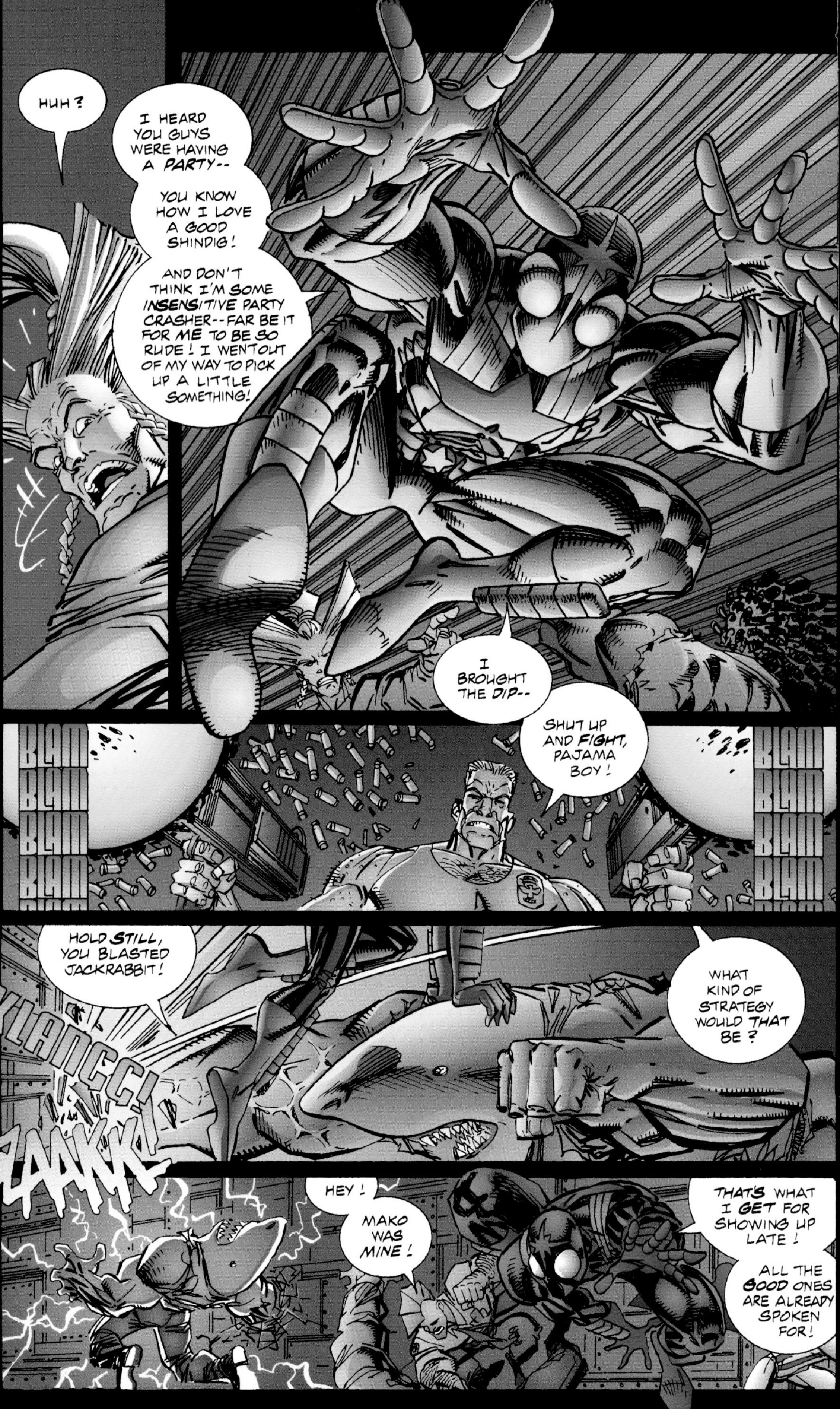
HUH ?
I HEARD YOU GUYS WERE HAVING A PARTY--
YOU KNOW HOW I LOVE A GOOD SHINDIG!
AND DON'T THINK I'M SOME INSENSITIVE PARTY CRASHER--FAR BE IT FOR ME TO BE SO RUDE! I WENT OUT OF MY WAY TO PICK UP A LITTLE SOMETHING!
I BROUGHT THE DIP--
BLAM BLAM BLAM BLAM BLAM
SHUT UP AND FIGHT, PAJAMA BOY!
BLAM BLAM BLAM BLAM BLAM
HOLD STILL, YOU BLASTED JACKRABBIT!
WHAT KIND OF STRATEGY WOULD THAT BE ?
KLANCC!
SZAAKK!
HEY!
MAKO WAS MINE!
THAT'S WHAT I GET FOR SHOWING UP LATE!
ALL THE GOOD ONES ARE ALREADY SPOKEN FOR!

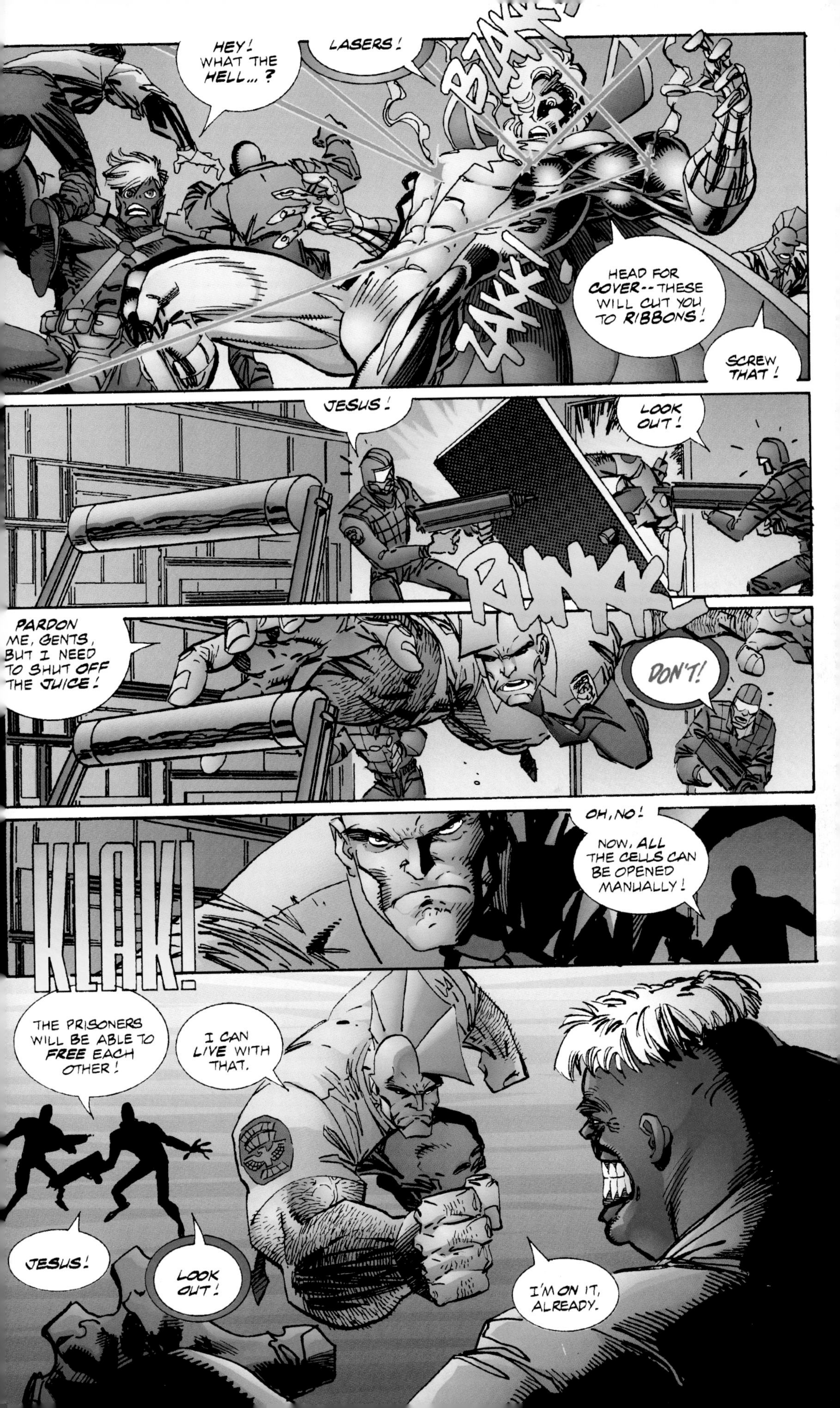
HEY! WHAT THE HELL...?
LASERS!
BZAK!
ZAKK!
HEAD FOR COVER--THESE WILL CUT YOU TO RIBBONS!
SCREW THAT!
JESUS!
LOOK OUT!
RUNK!
PARDON ME, GENTS, BUT I NEED TO SHUT OFF THE JUICE!
DON'T!
KLAK!
OH, NO!
NOW, ALL THE CELLS CAN BE OPENED MANUALLY!
THE PRISONERS WILL BE ABLE TO FREE EACH OTHER!
I CAN LIVE WITH THAT.
JESUS!
LOOK OUT!
I'M ON IT, ALREADY.

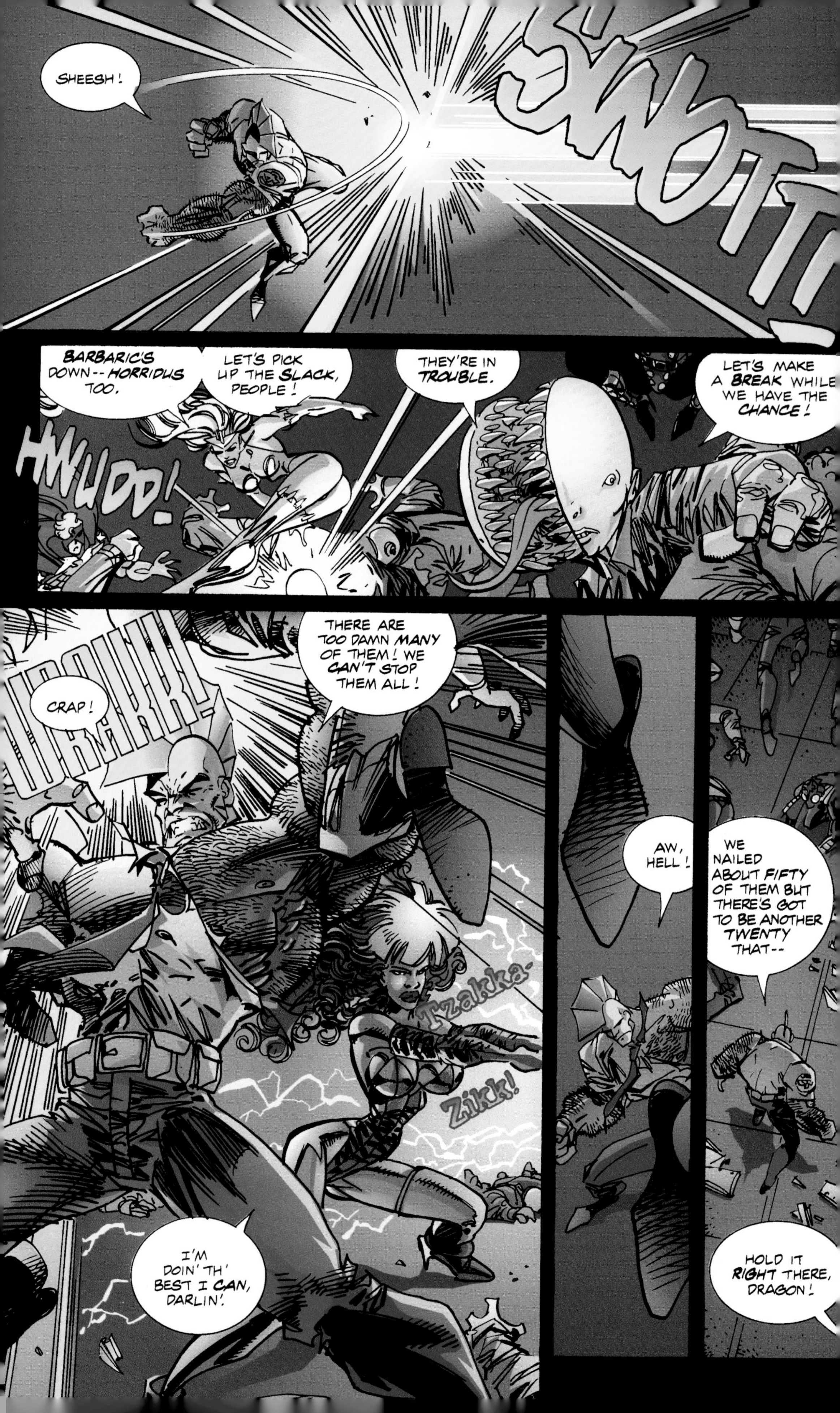
SHEESH!
SNOTT!
BARBARIC'S DOWN--HORRIDUS TOO.
LET'S PICK UP THE SLACK, PEOPLE!
THEY'RE IN TROUBLE.
LET'S MAKE A BREAK WHILE WE HAVE THE CHANCE!
HWUDD!
CRAP!
THERE ARE TOO DAMN MANY OF THEM! WE CAN'T STOP THEM ALL!
Tzakka
Zikk!
I'M DOIN' TH' BEST I CAN, DARLIN'.
AW, HELL!
WE NAILED ABOUT FIFTY OF THEM BUT THERE'S GOT TO BE ANOTHER TWENTY THAT--
HOLD IT RIGHT THERE, DRAGON!

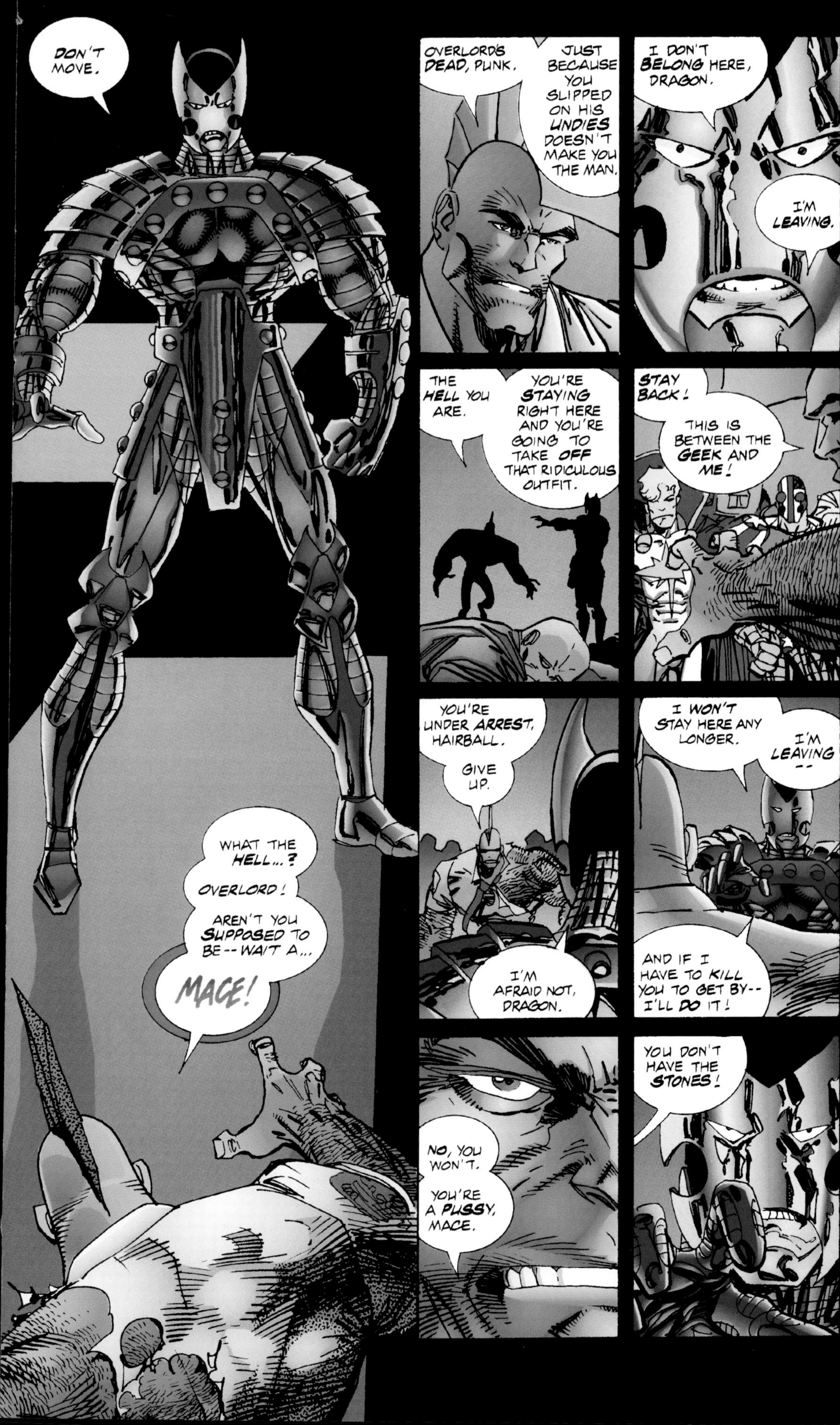
DON'T MOVE.
WHAT THE HELL...?
OVERLORD!
AREN'T YOU SUPPOSED TO BE--WAIT A...
MACE!
OVERLORD'S DEAD, PUNK.
JUST BECAUSE YOU SLIPPED ON HIS UNDIES DOESN'T MAKE YOU THE MAN.
I DON'T BELONG HERE, DRAGON.
I'M LEAVING.
THE HELL YOU ARE.
YOU'RE STAYING RIGHT HERE AND YOU'RE GOING TO TAKE OFF THAT RIDICULOUS OUTFIT.
STAY BACK!
THIS IS BETWEEN THE GEEK AND ME!
YOU'RE UNDER ARREST, HAIRBALL.
GIVE UP.
I'M AFRAID NOT, DRAGON.
I WON'T STAY HERE ANY LONGER.
I'M LEAVING--
AND IF I HAVE TO KILL YOU TO GET BY--I'LL DO IT!
NO, YOU WON'T.
YOU'RE A PUSSY, MACE.
YOU DON'T HAVE THE STONES!

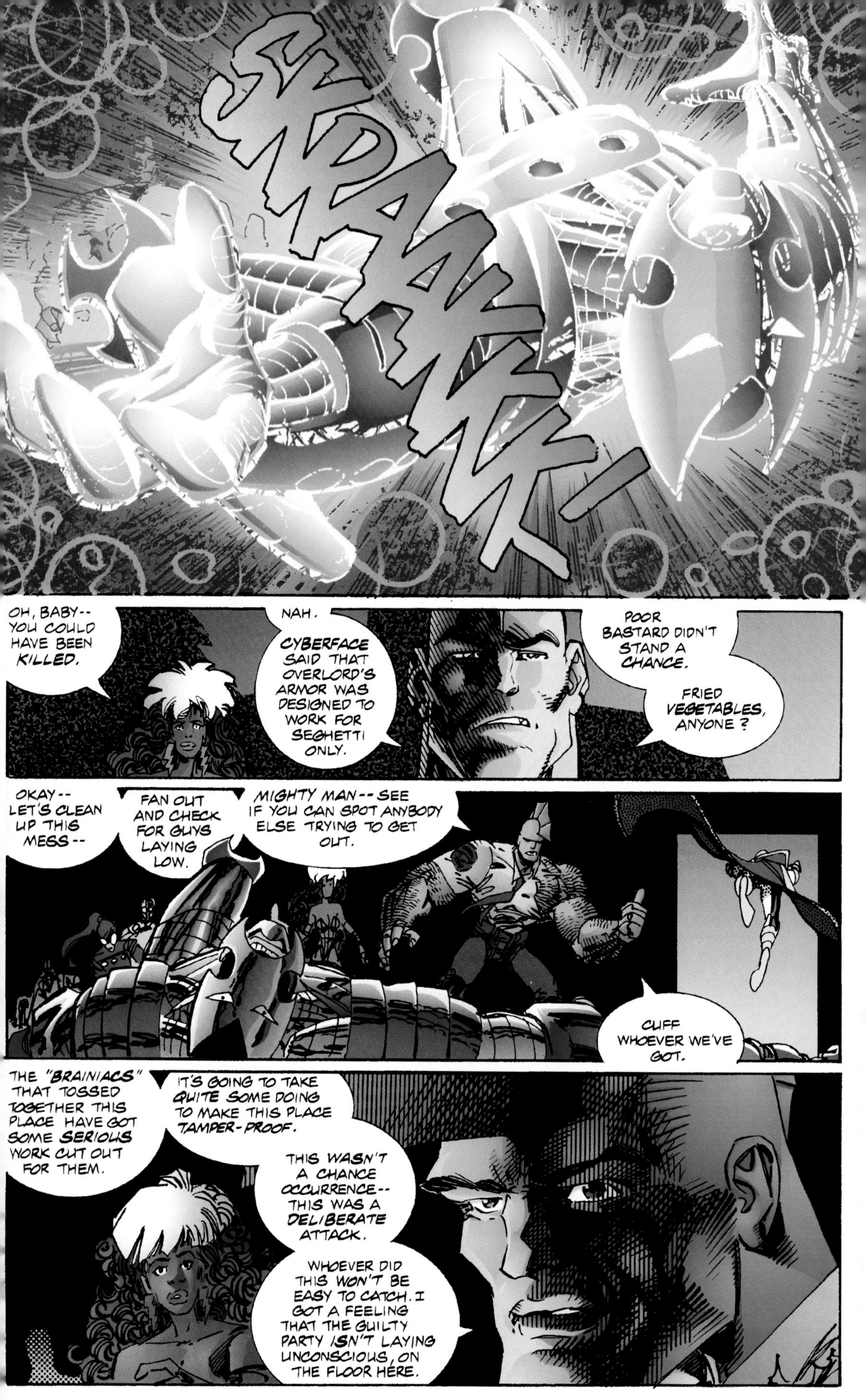
SKRAAKKK!
OH, BABY-- YOU COULD HAVE BEEN KILLED.
NAH.
CYBERFACE SAID THAT OVERLORD'S ARMOR WAS DESIGNED TO WORK FOR SEGHETTI ONLY.
POOR BASTARD DIDN'T STAND A CHANCE.
FRIED VEGETABLES, ANYONE ?
OKAY-- LET'S CLEAN UP THIS MESS--
FAN OUT AND CHECK FOR GUYS LAYING LOW.
MIGHTY MAN-- SEE IF YOU CAN SPOT ANYBODY ELSE TRYING TO GET OUT.
CUFF WHOEVER WE'VE GOT.
THE "BRAINIACS" THAT TOSSED TOGETHER THIS PLACE HAVE GOT SOME SERIOUS WORK CUT OUT FOR THEM.
IT'S GOING TO TAKE QUITE SOME DOING TO MAKE THIS PLACE TAMPER-PROOF.
THIS WASN'T A CHANCE OCCURRENCE-- THIS WAS A DELIBERATE ATTACK.
WHOEVER DID THIS WON'T BE EASY TO CATCH. I GOT A FEELING THAT THE GUILTY PARTY ISN'T LAYING UNCONSCIOUS, ON THE FLOOR HERE.

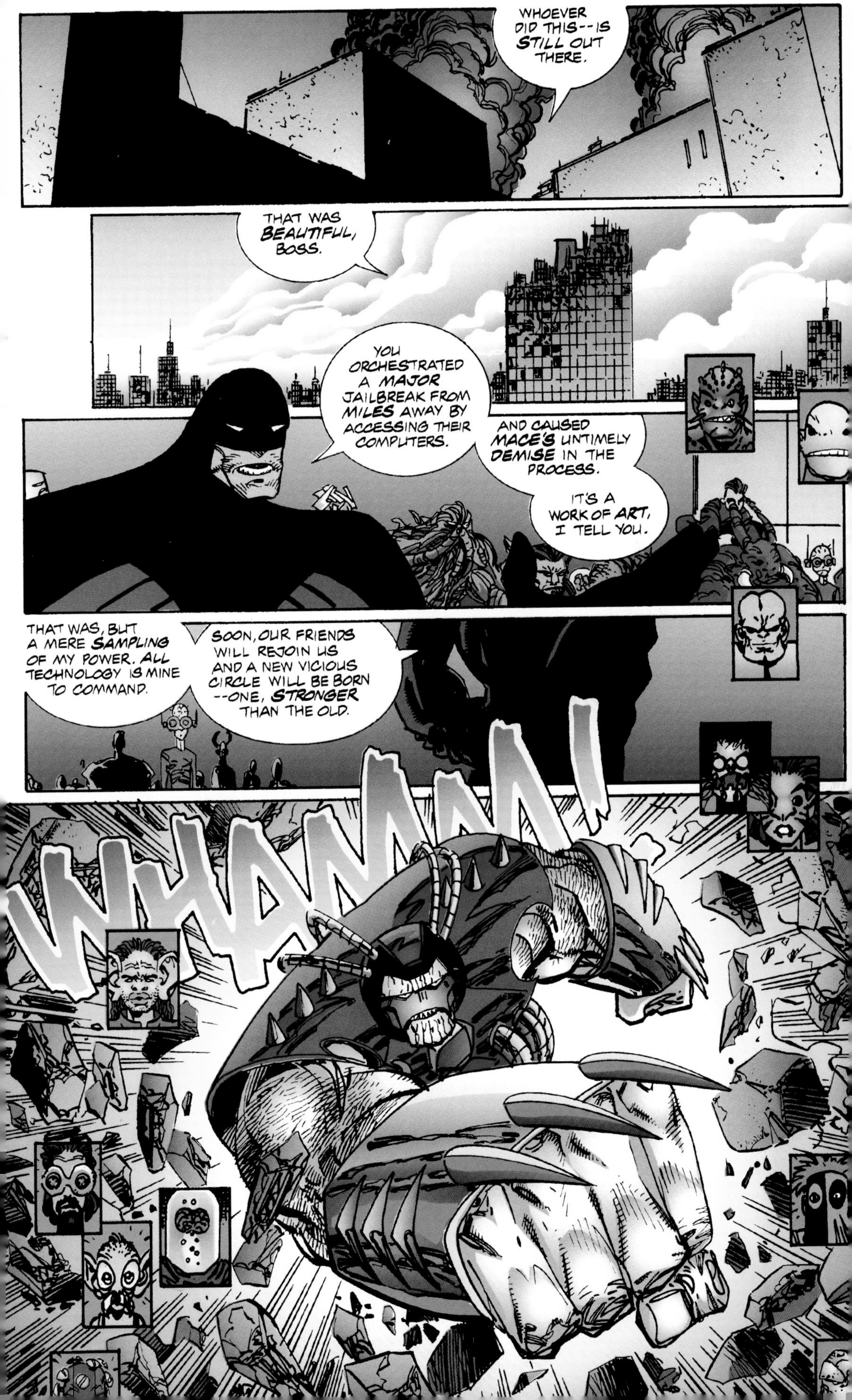
WHOEVER DID THIS--IS STILL OUT THERE.
THAT WAS BEAUTIFUL, BOSS.
YOU ORCHESTRATED A MAJOR JAILBREAK FROM MILES AWAY BY ACCESSING THEIR COMPUTERS.
AND CAUSED MACE'S UNTIMELY DEMISE IN THE PROCESS.
IT'S A WORK OF ART, I TELL YOU.
THAT WAS, BUT A MERE SAMPLING OF MY POWER. ALL TECHNOLOGY IS MINE TO COMMAND.
SOON, OUR FRIENDS WILL REJOIN US AND A NEW VICIOUS CIRCLE WILL BE BORN --ONE, STRONGER THAN THE OLD.
WHAMM!

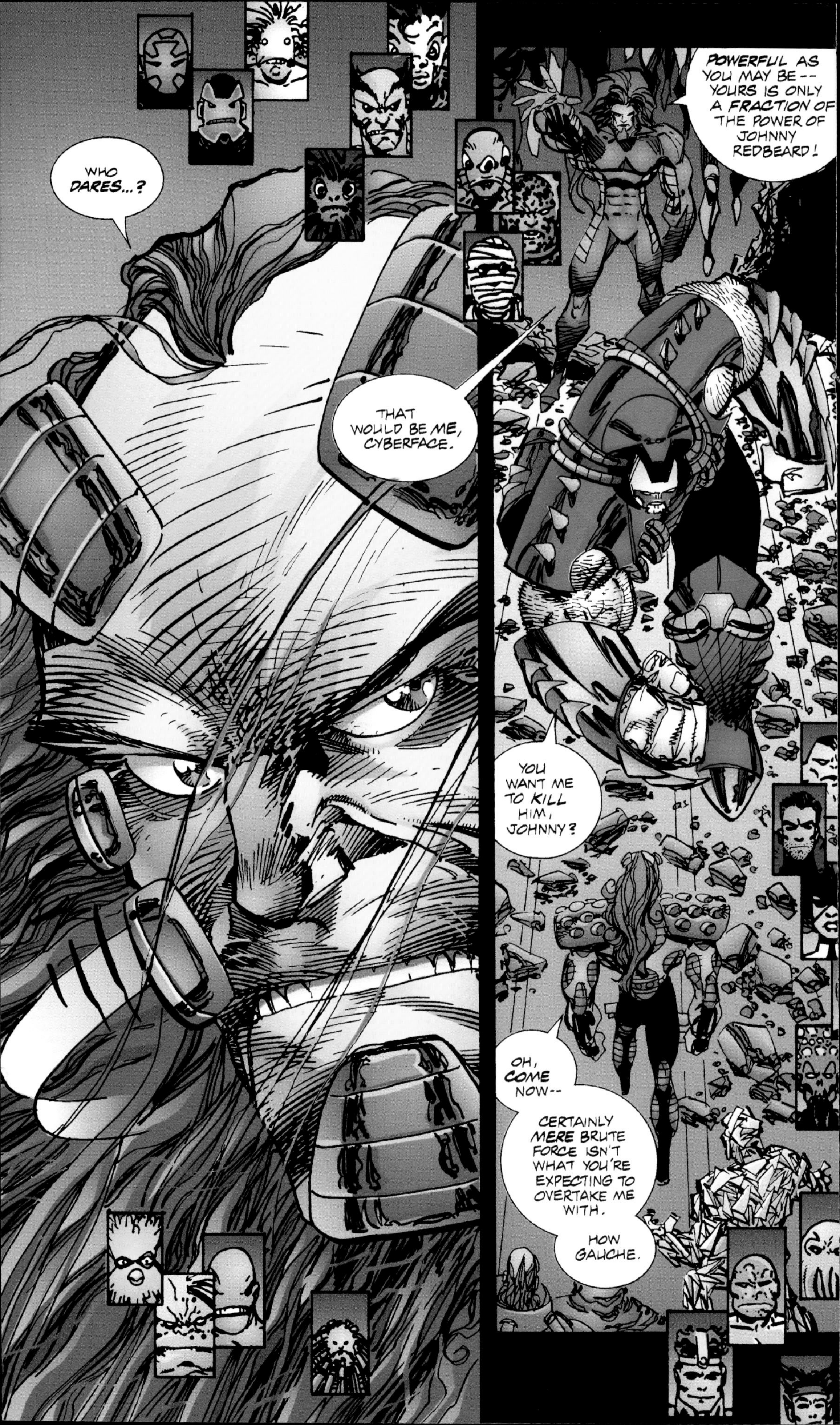
WHO DARES...?
THAT WOULD BE ME, CYBERFACE.
POWERFUL AS YOU MAY BE -- YOURS IS ONLY A FRACTION OF THE POWER OF JOHNNY REDBEARD!
YOU WANT ME TO KILL HIM, JOHNNY?
OH, COME NOW--
CERTAINLY MERE BRUTE FORCE ISN'T WHAT YOU'RE EXPECTING TO OVERTAKE ME WITH.
HOW GAUCHE.

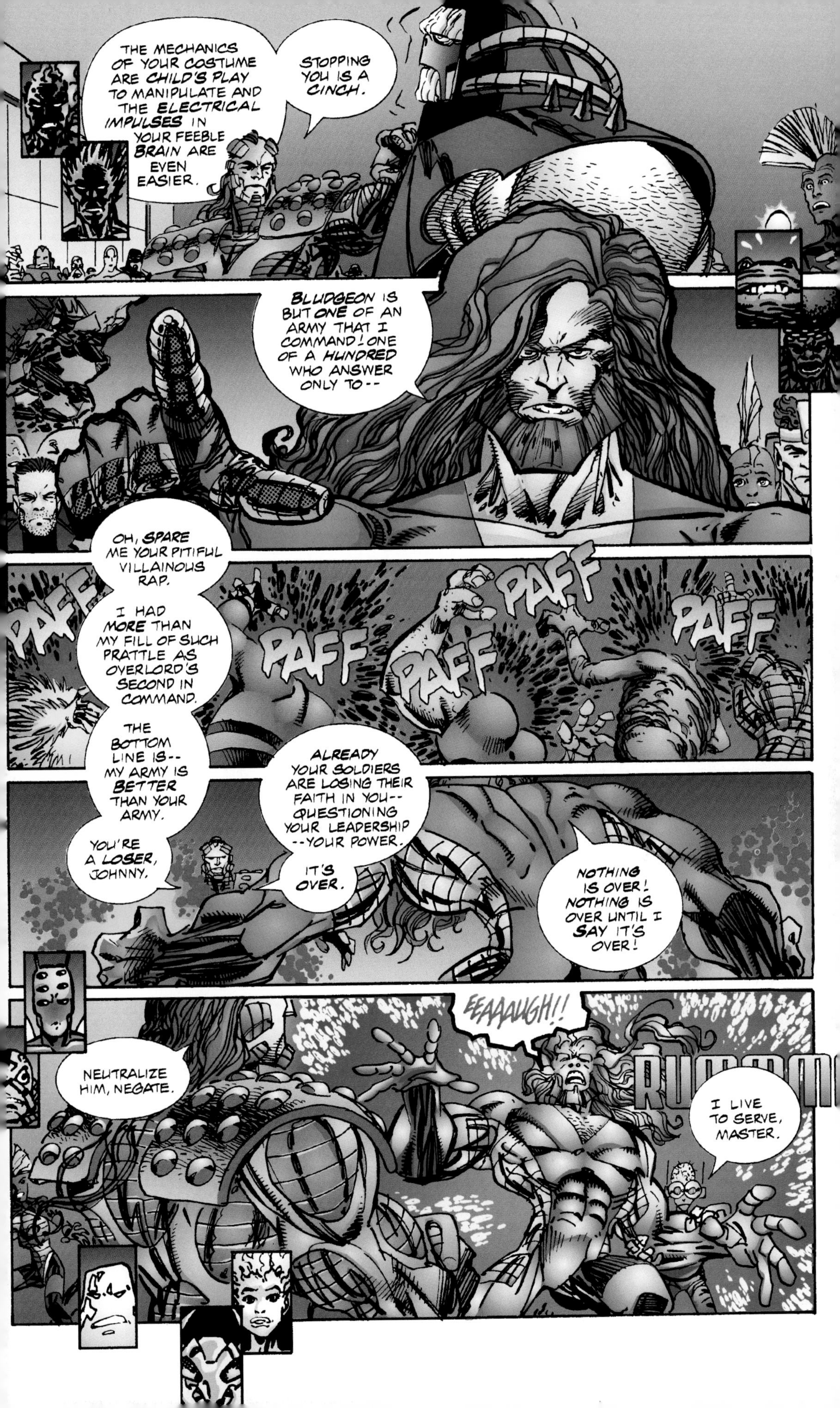

THE MECHANICS OF YOUR COSTUME ARE CHILD'S PLAY TO MANIPULATE AND THE ELECTRICAL IMPULSES IN YOUR FEEBLE BRAIN ARE EVEN EASIER.
STOPPING YOU IS A CINCH.
BLUDGEON IS BUT ONE OF AN ARMY THAT I COMMAND! ONE OF A HUNDRED WHO ANSWER ONLY TO--
OH, SPARE ME YOUR PITIFUL VILLAINOUS RAP.
I HAD MORE THAN MY FILL OF SUCH PRATTLE AS OVERLORD'S SECOND IN COMMAND.
PAFF
PAFF
PAFF
PAFF
PAFF
THE BOTTOM LINE IS-- MY ARMY IS BETTER THAN YOUR ARMY.
YOU'RE A LOSER, JOHNNY.
ALREADY YOUR SOLDIERS ARE LOSING THEIR FAITH IN YOU-- QUESTIONING YOUR LEADERSHIP --YOUR POWER.
IT'S OVER.
NOTHING IS OVER! NOTHING IS OVER UNTIL I SAY IT'S OVER!
NEUTRALIZE HIM, NEGATE.
EEAAAUGH!!
I LIVE TO SERVE, MASTER.

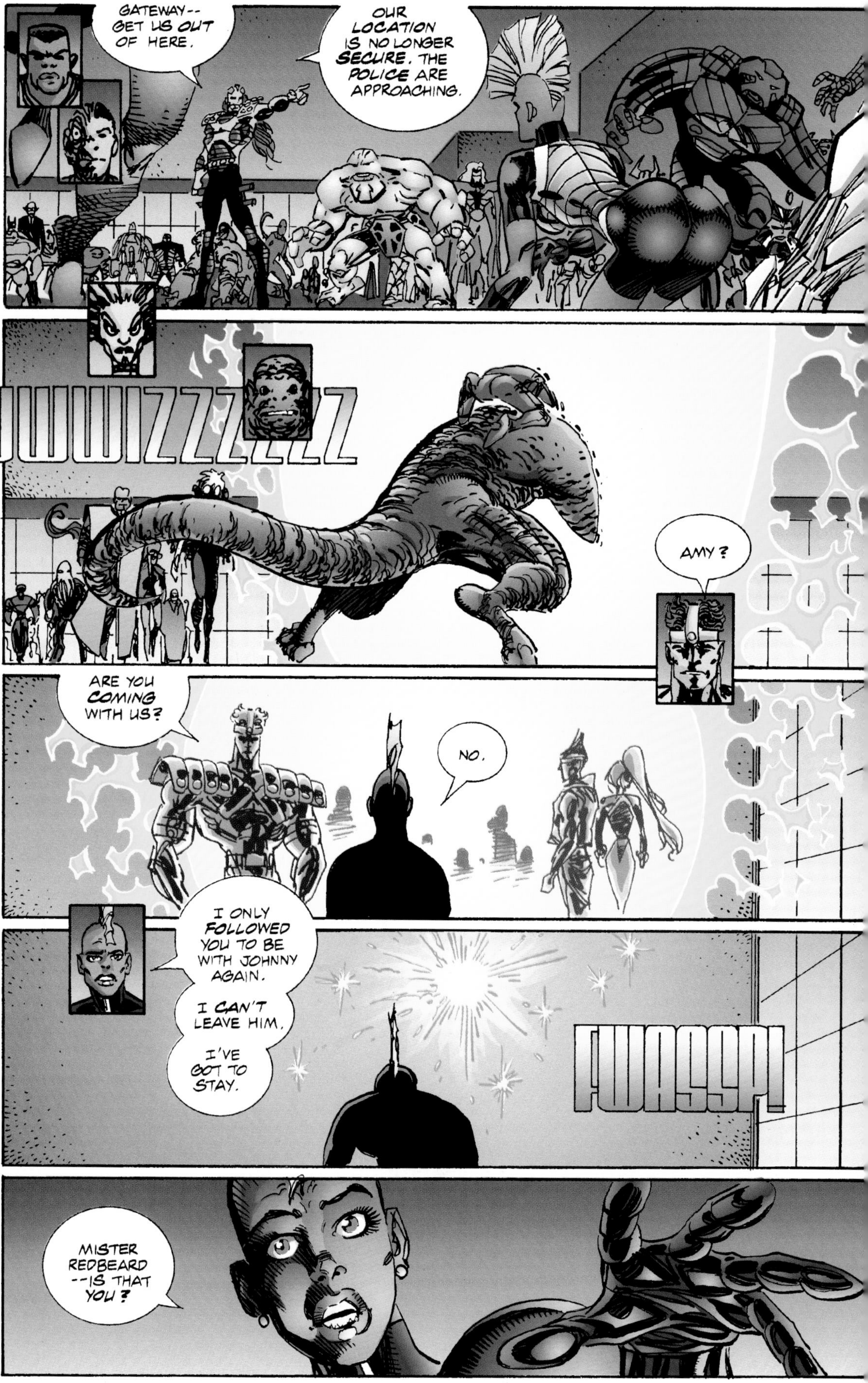

GATEWAY-- GET US OUT OF HERE.
OUR LOCATION IS NO LONGER SECURE. THE POLICE ARE APPROACHING.
VWWIZZZZZZZ
AMY?
ARE YOU COMING WITH US?
NO.
I ONLY FOLLOWED YOU TO BE WITH JOHNNY AGAIN.
I CAN'T LEAVE HIM.
I'VE GOT TO STAY.
FWASSP!
MISTER REDBEARD --IS THAT YOU?

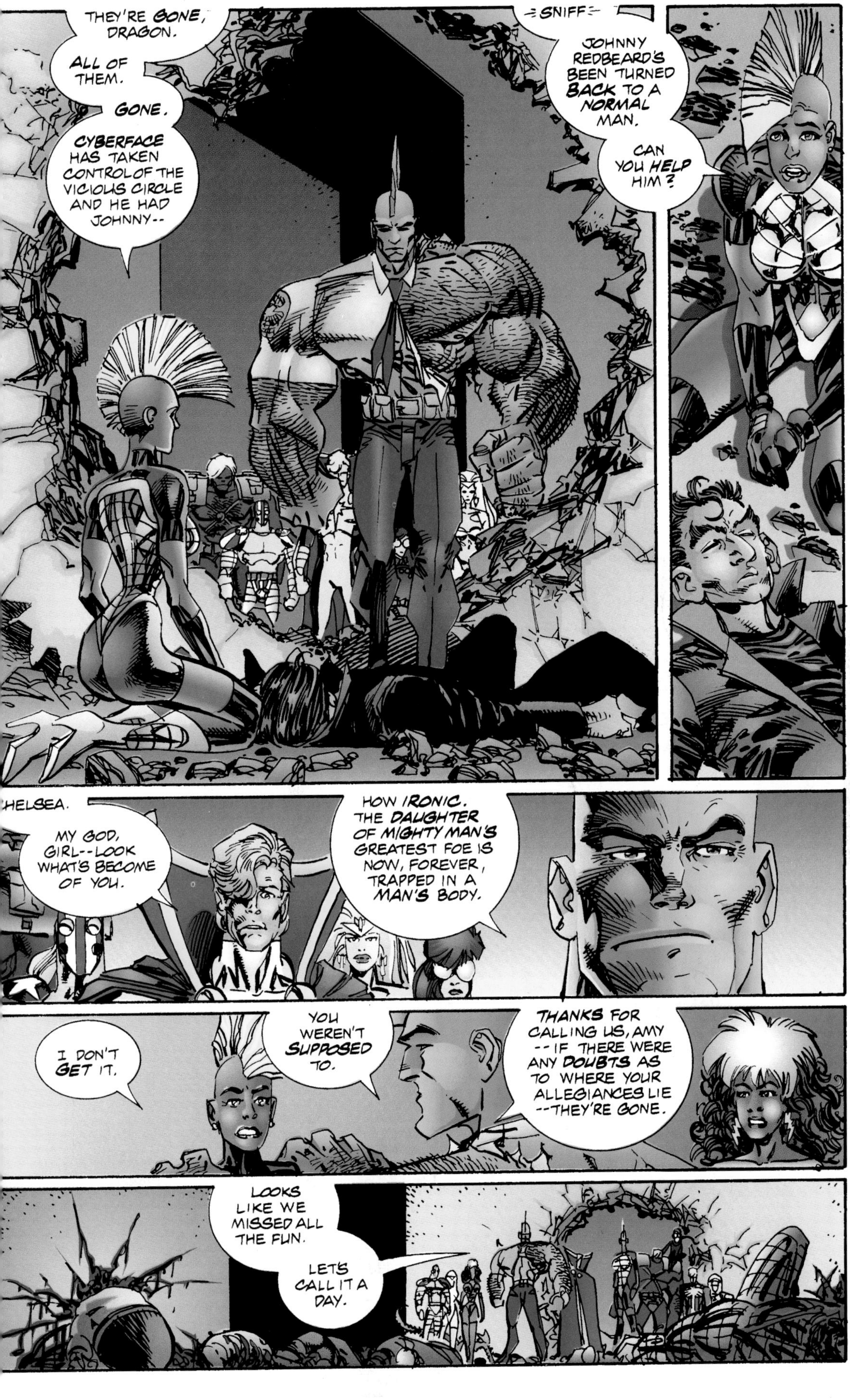
THEY'RE GONE, DRAGON.
ALL OF THEM.
GONE.
CYBERFACE HAS TAKEN CONTROL OF THE VICIOUS CIRCLE AND HE HAD JOHNNY--
=SNIFF=
JOHNNY REDBEARD'S BEEN TURNED BACK TO A NORMAL MAN.
CAN YOU HELP HIM?
HELSEA.
MY GOD, GIRL--LOOK WHAT'S BECOME OF YOU.
HOW IRONIC. THE DAUGHTER OF MIGHTY MAN'S GREATEST FOE IS NOW, FOREVER, TRAPPED IN A MAN'S BODY.
I DON'T GET IT.
YOU WEREN'T SUPPOSED TO.
THANKS FOR CALLING US, AMY --IF THERE WERE ANY DOUBTS AS TO WHERE YOUR ALLEGIANCES LIE --THEY'RE GONE.
LOOKS LIKE WE MISSED ALL THE FUN.
LET'S CALL IT A DAY.

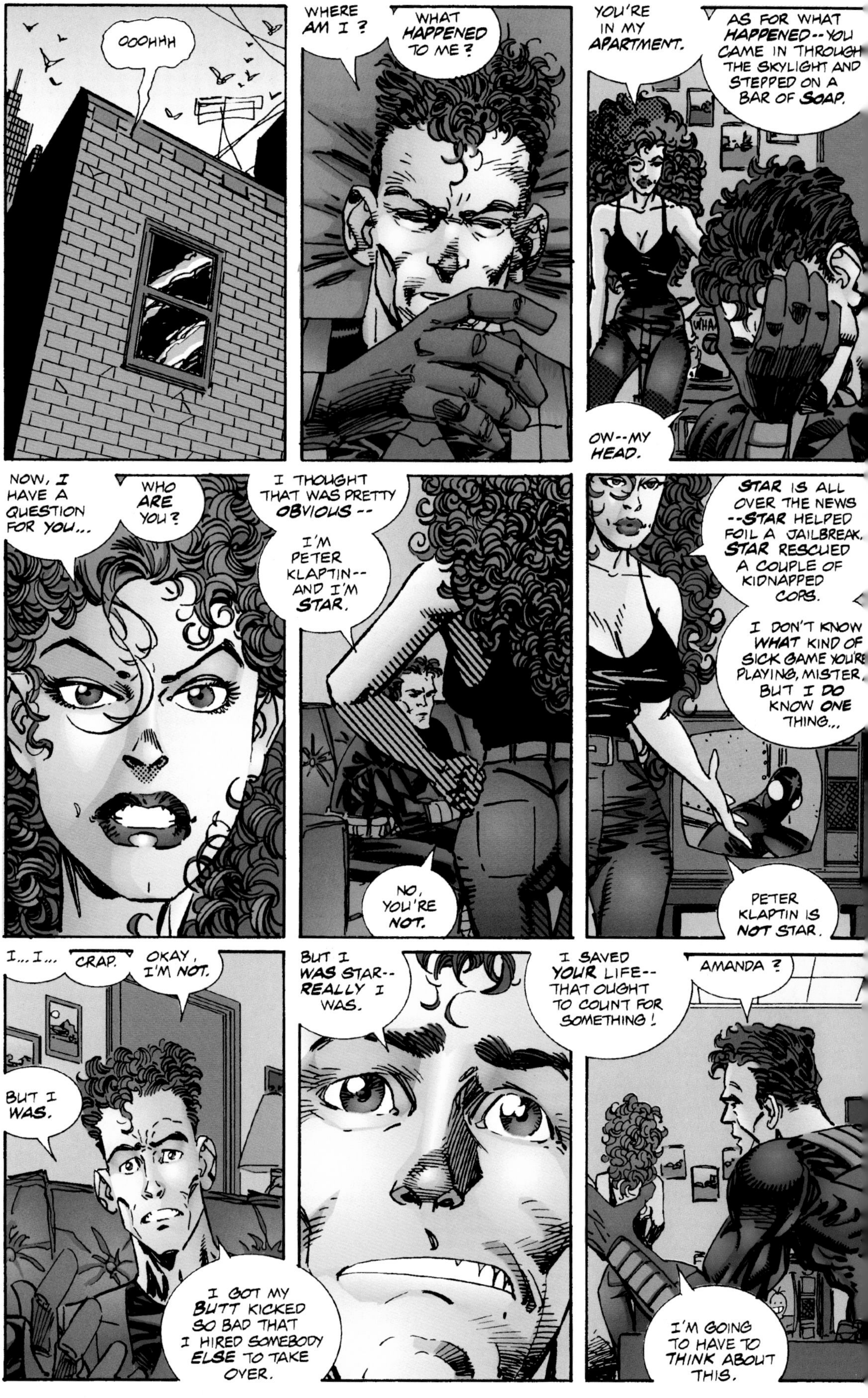
OOOHHH
WHERE AM I?
WHAT HAPPENED TO ME?
YOU'RE IN MY APARTMENT.
AS FOR WHAT HAPPENED--YOU CAME IN THROUGH THE SKYLIGHT AND STEPPED ON A BAR OF SOAP.
OW--MY HEAD.
NOW, I HAVE A QUESTION FOR YOU...
WHO ARE YOU?
I THOUGHT THAT WAS PRETTY OBVIOUS--
I'M PETER KLAPTIN--AND I'M STAR.
NO, YOU'RE NOT.
STAR IS ALL OVER THE NEWS --STAR HELPED FOIL A JAILBREAK. STAR RESCUED A COUPLE OF KIDNAPPED COPS.
I DON'T KNOW WHAT KIND OF SICK GAME YOU'RE PLAYING, MISTER, BUT I DO KNOW ONE THING...
PETER KLAPTIN IS NOT STAR.
I... I...
CRAP.
OKAY, I'M NOT.
BUT I WAS.
I GOT MY BUTT KICKED SO BAD THAT I HIRED SOMEBODY ELSE TO TAKE OVER.
BUT I WAS STAR--REALLY I WAS.
I SAVED YOUR LIFE--THAT OUGHT TO COUNT FOR SOMETHING!
AMANDA?
I'M GOING TO HAVE TO THINK ABOUT THIS.

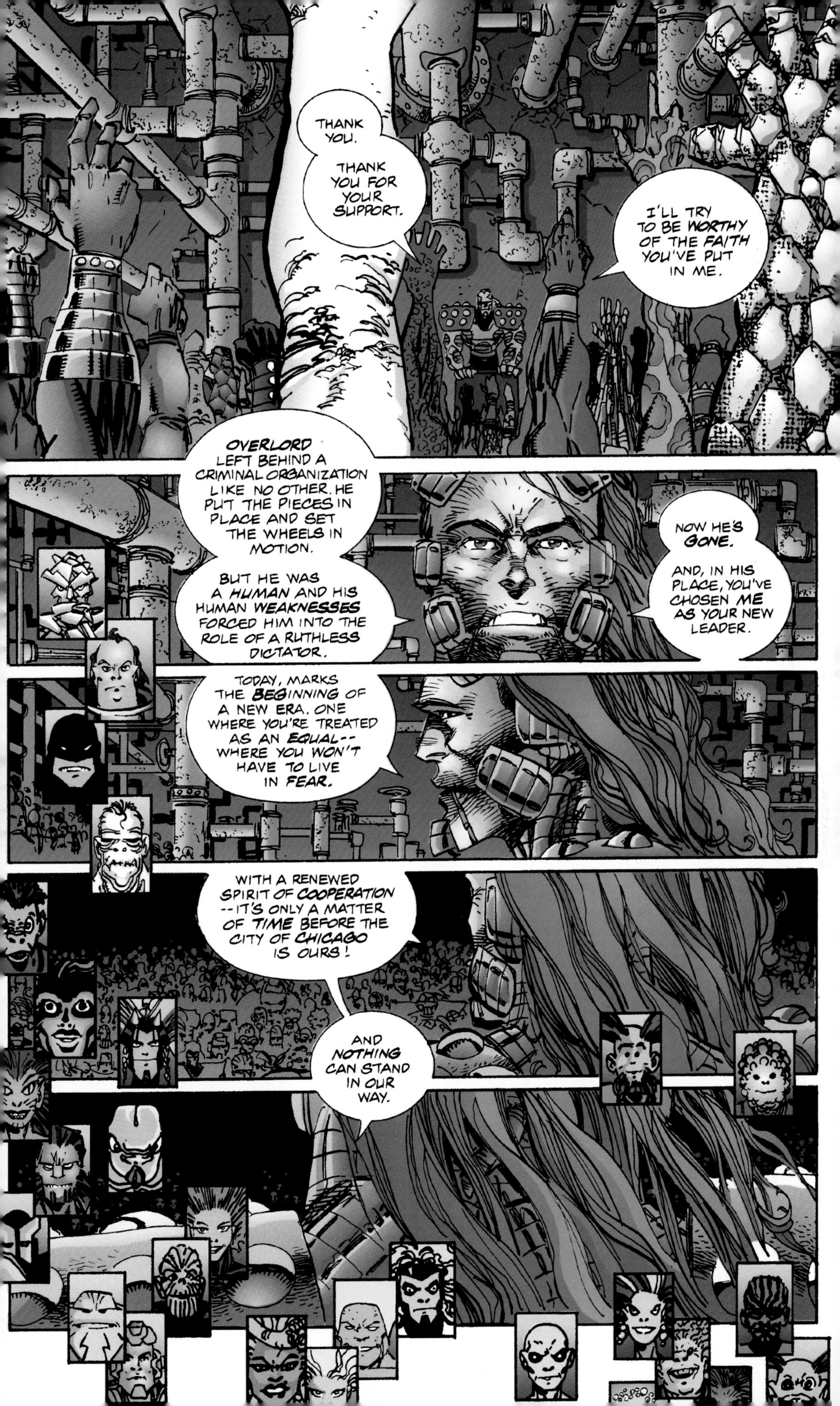

THANK YOU.
THANK YOU FOR YOUR SUPPORT.
I'LL TRY TO BE WORTHY OF THE FAITH YOU'VE PUT IN ME.
OVERLORD LEFT BEHIND A CRIMINAL ORGANIZATION LIKE NO OTHER. HE PUT THE PIECES IN PLACE AND SET THE WHEELS IN MOTION.
BUT HE WAS A HUMAN AND HIS HUMAN WEAKNESSES FORCED HIM INTO THE ROLE OF A RUTHLESS DICTATOR.
NOW HE'S GONE.
AND, IN HIS PLACE, YOU'VE CHOSEN ME AS YOUR NEW LEADER.
TODAY, MARKS THE BEGINNING OF A NEW ERA. ONE WHERE YOU'RE TREATED AS AN EQUAL-- WHERE YOU WON'T HAVE TO LIVE IN FEAR.
WITH A RENEWED SPIRIT OF COOPERATION --IT'S ONLY A MATTER OF TIME BEFORE THE CITY OF CHICAGO IS OURS!
AND NOTHING CAN STAND IN OUR WAY.

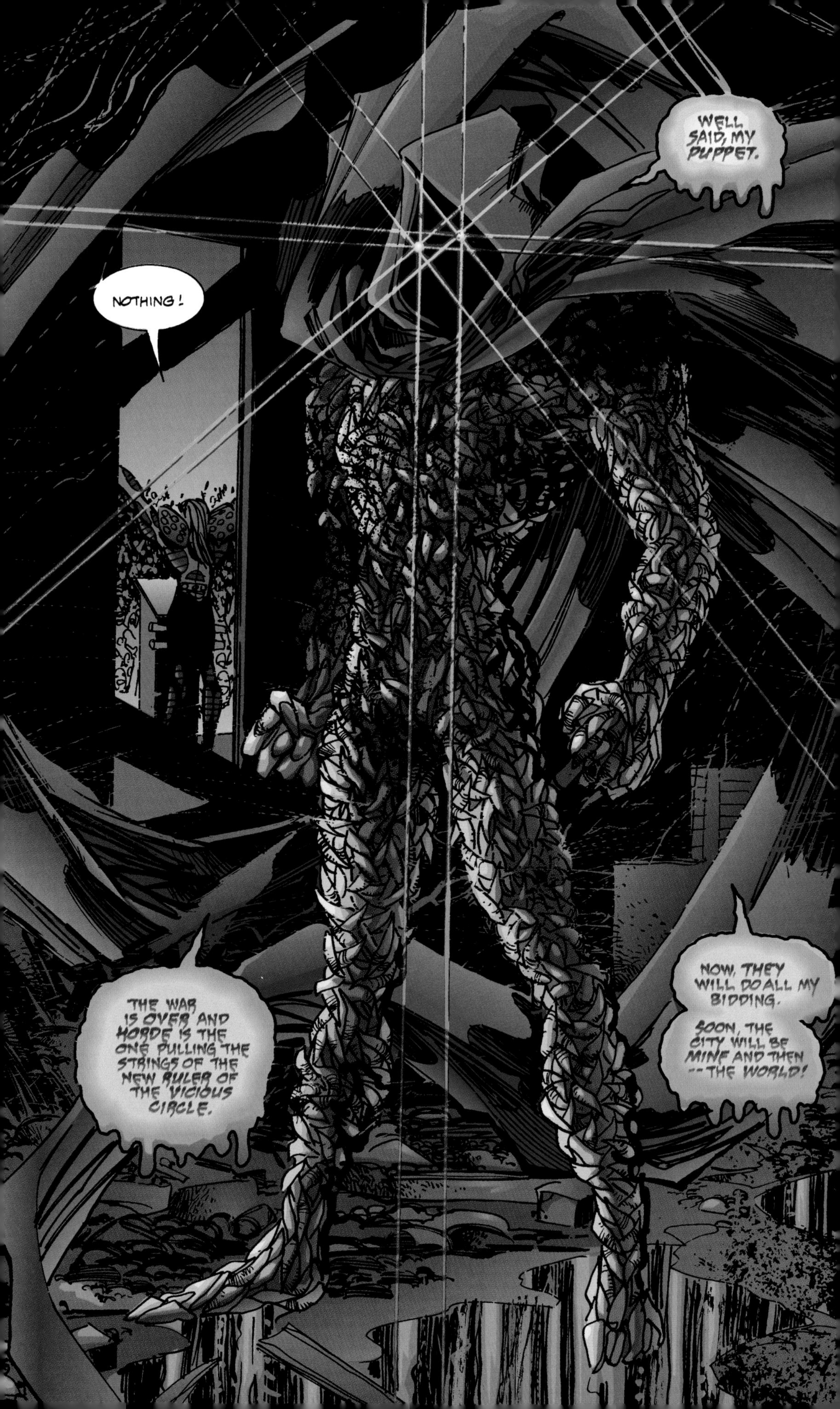
WELL SAID, MY PUPPET.
NOTHING!
THE WAR IS OVER AND HORDE IS THE ONE PULLING THE STRINGS OF THE NEW RULER OF THE VICIOUS CIRCLE.
NOW, THEY WILL DO ALL MY BIDDING.
SOON, THE CITY WILL BE MINE AND THEN -- THE WORLD!

COVERS

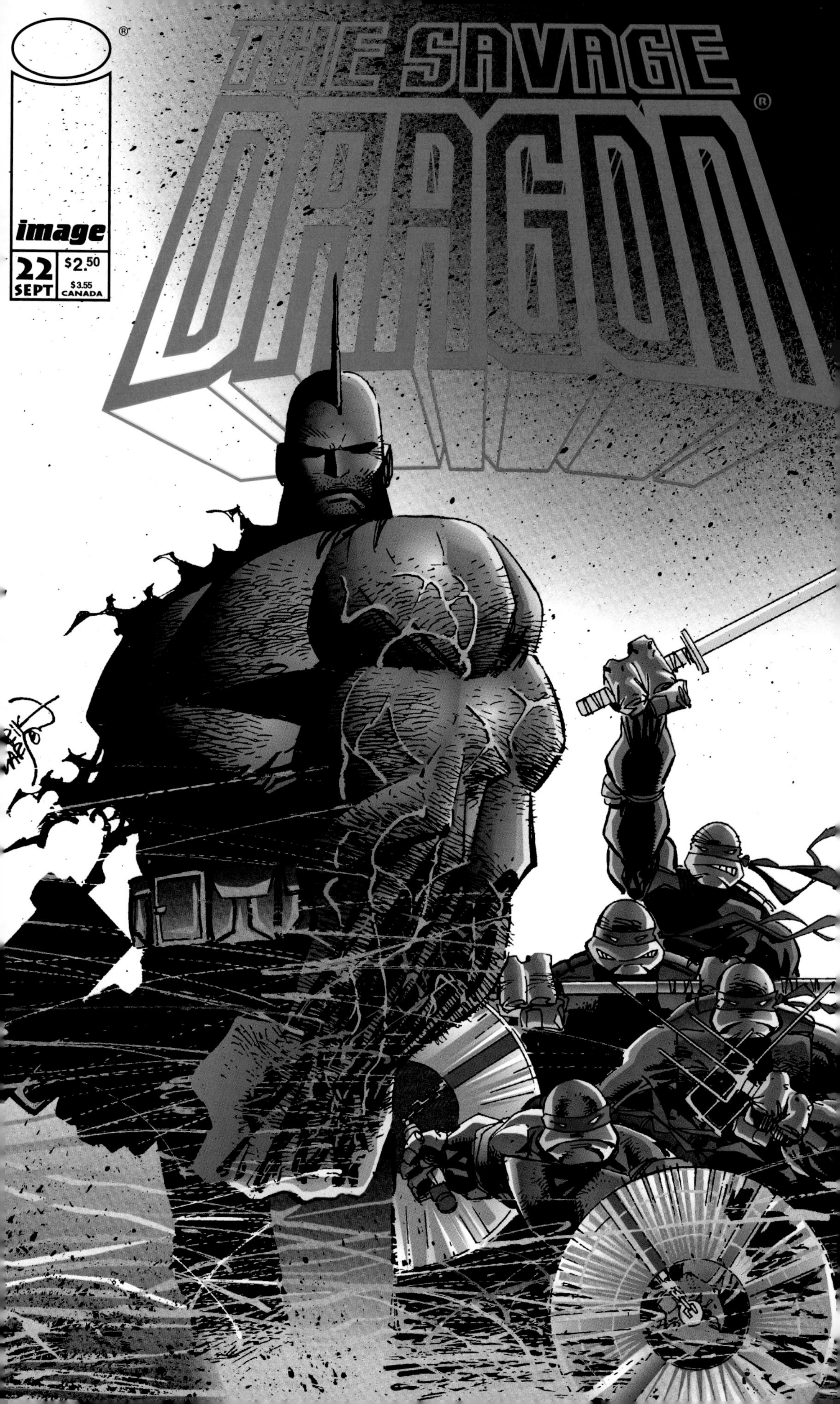

THE SAVAGE DRAGON
image
22
SEPT
$2.50
$3.55 CANADA

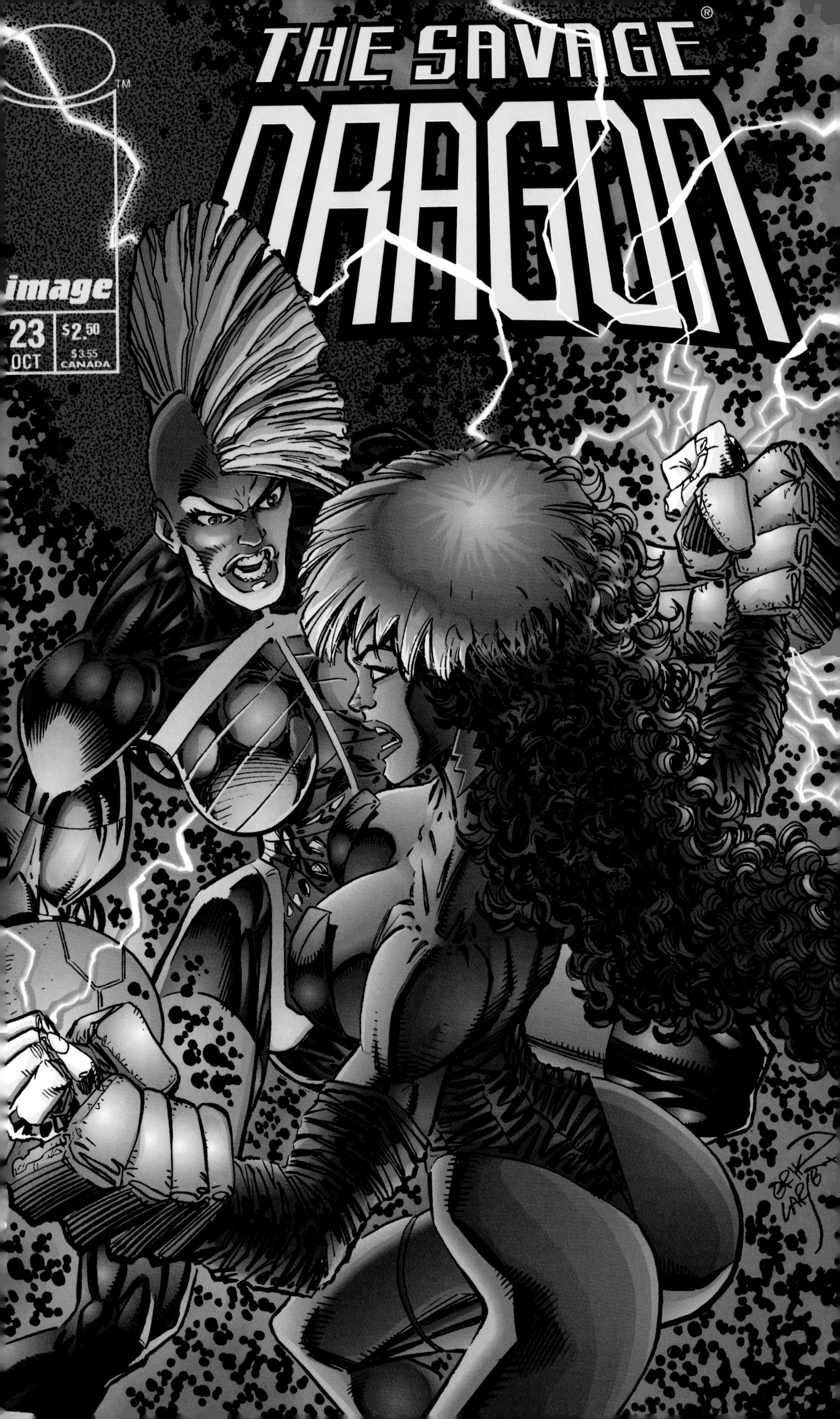
THE SAVAGE DRAGON®
image™
image
23
OCT
$2.50
$3.55 CANADA
ERIK LARSEN

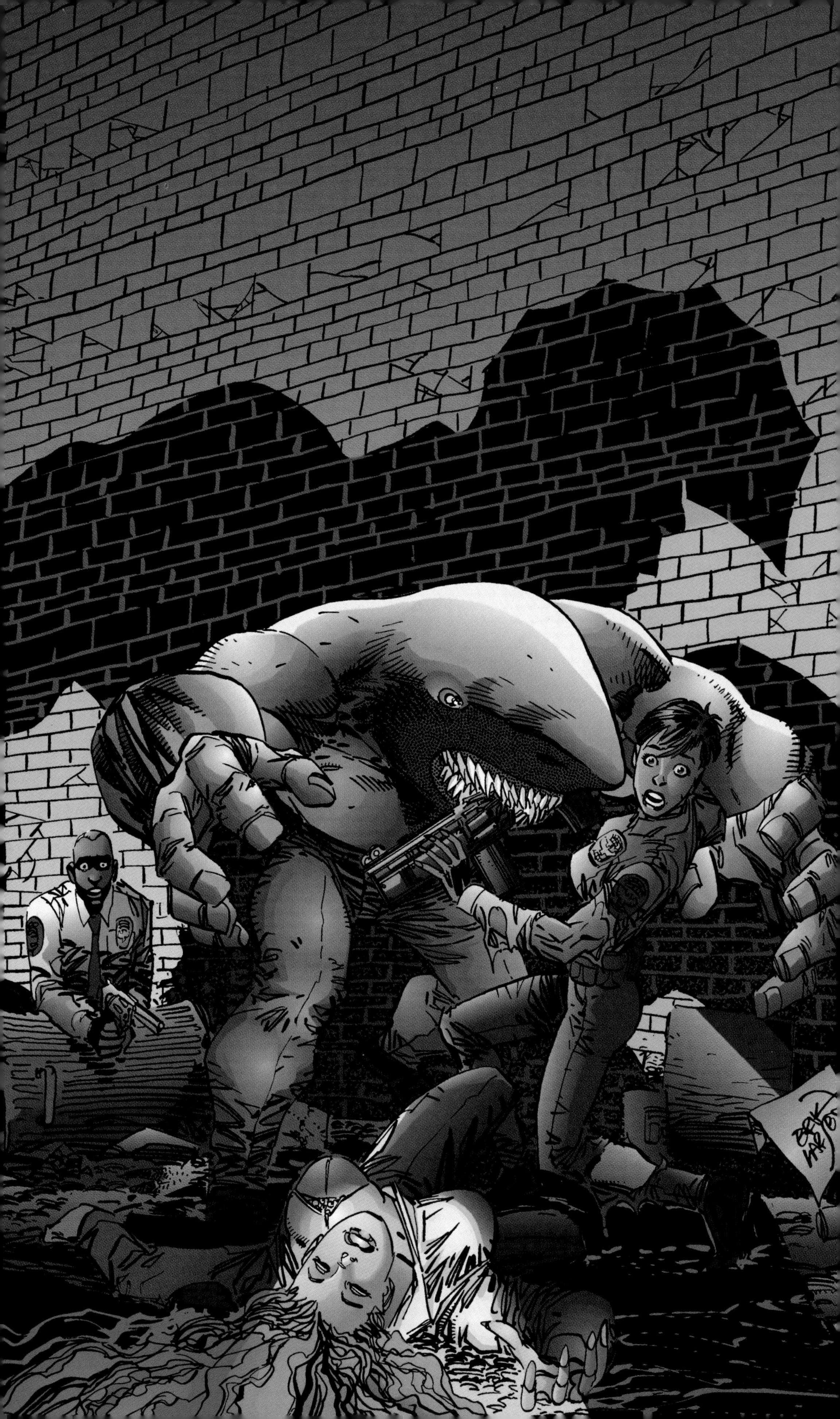

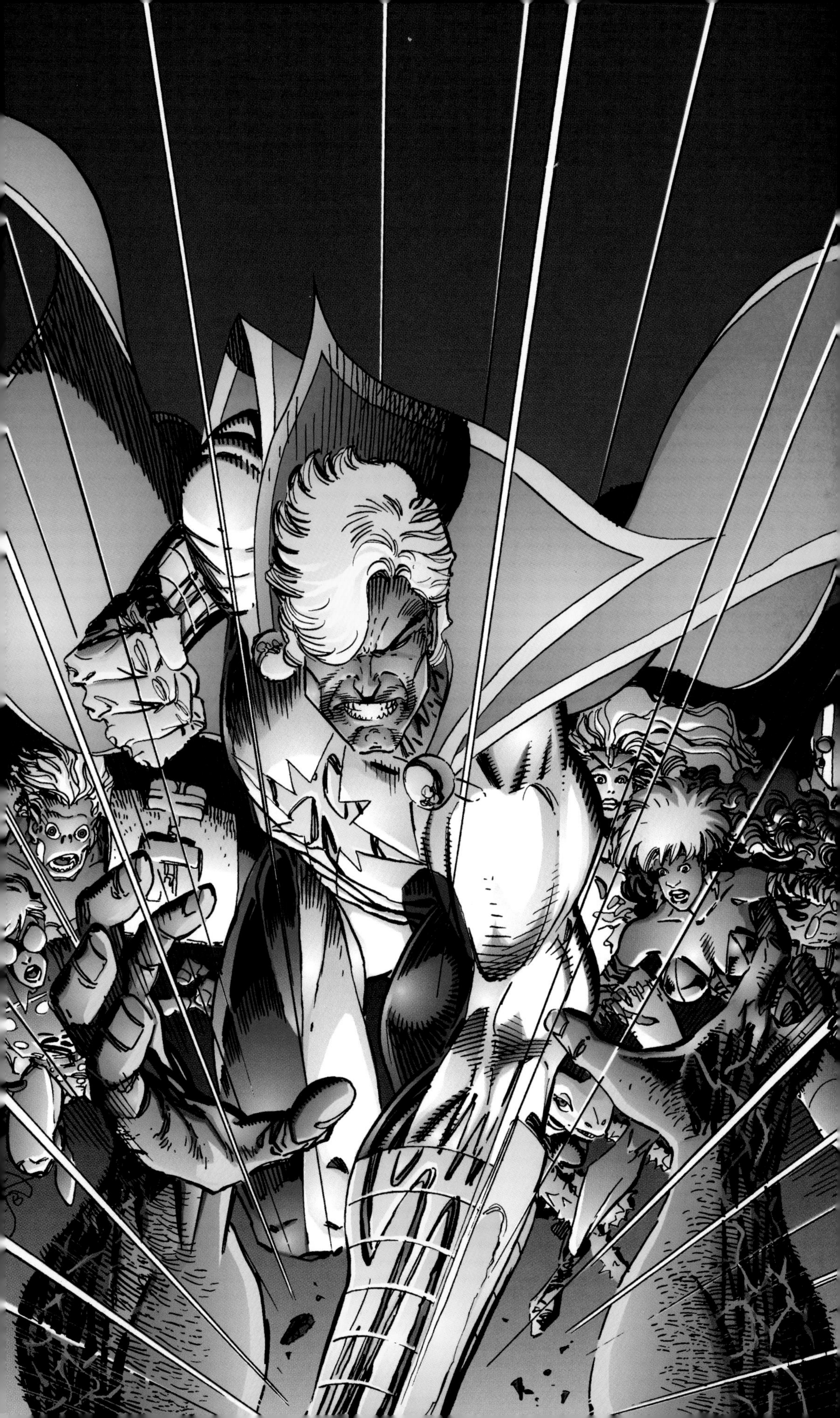

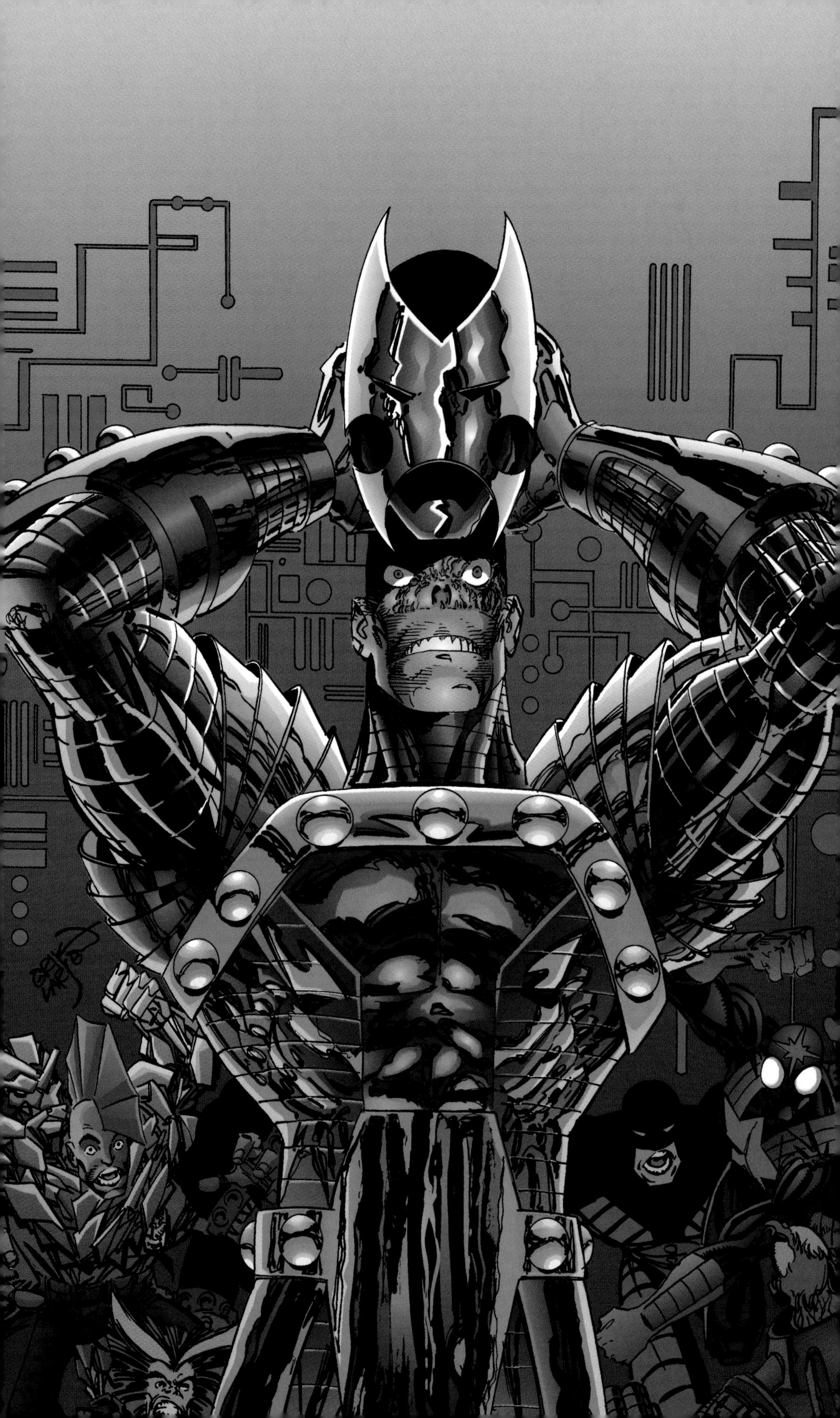

SAVAGE DRAGON: GANG WAR SKETCHBOOK

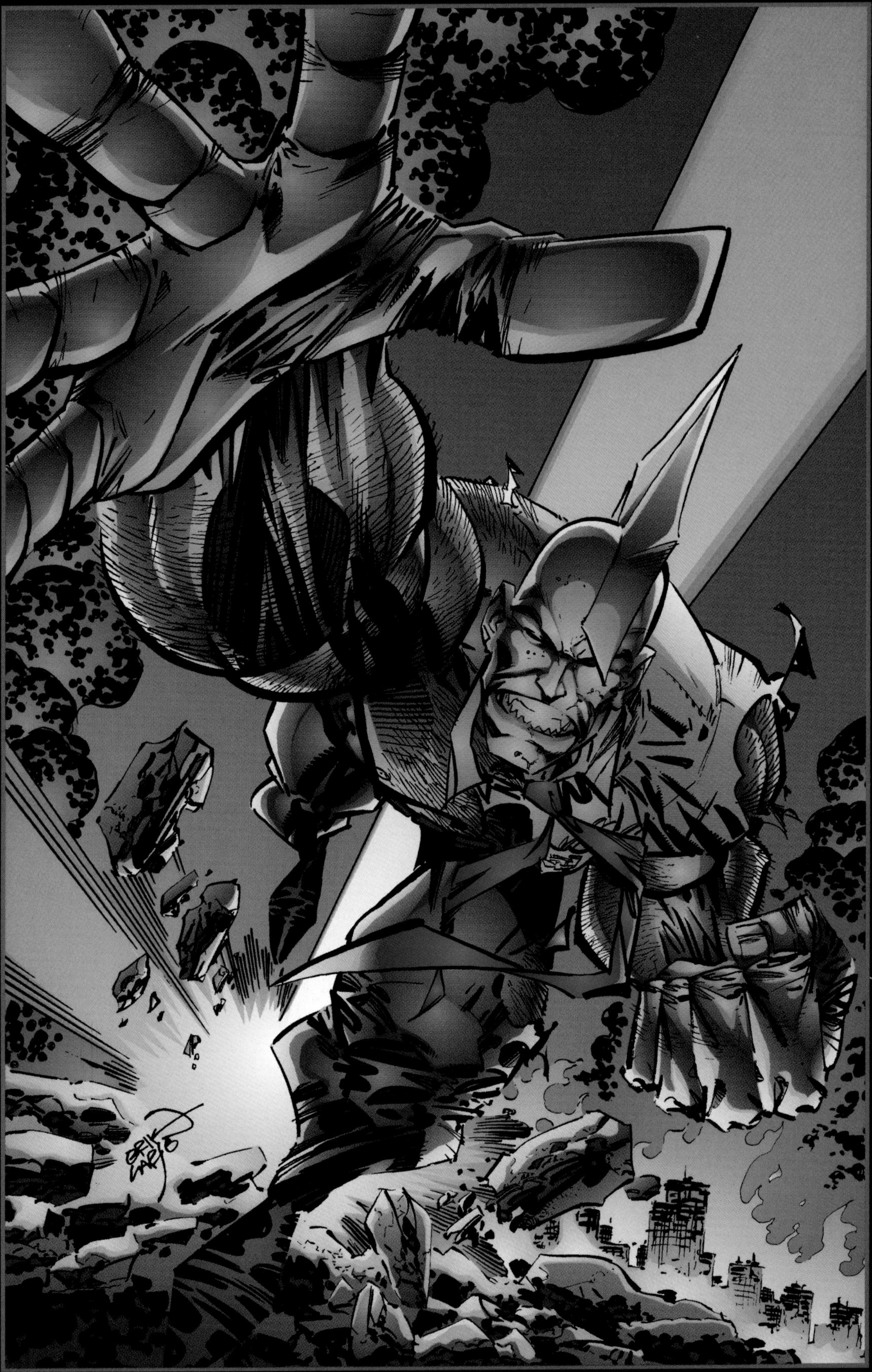

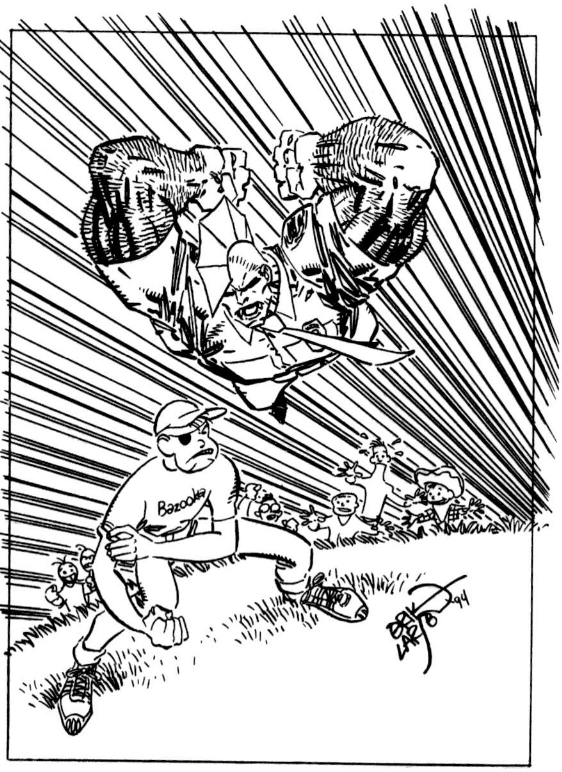
Bazooka

Here are a few drawings from various card sets. This one was from the Topps "Image Universe" series, it featured the Dragon facing off against the Topps mainstay, Bazooka Joe.

More cards from the Topps set, the Deadly Duo & Star,

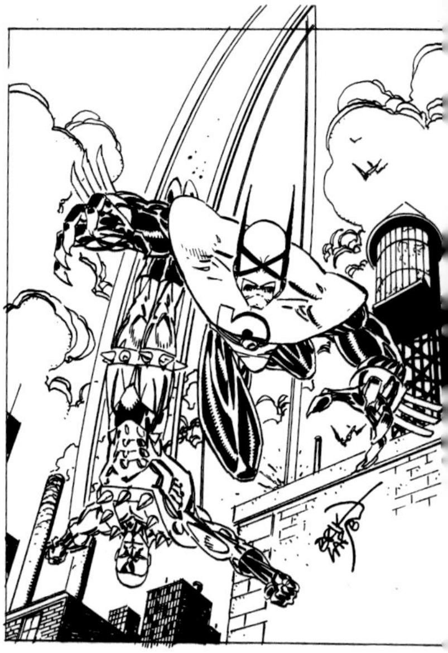

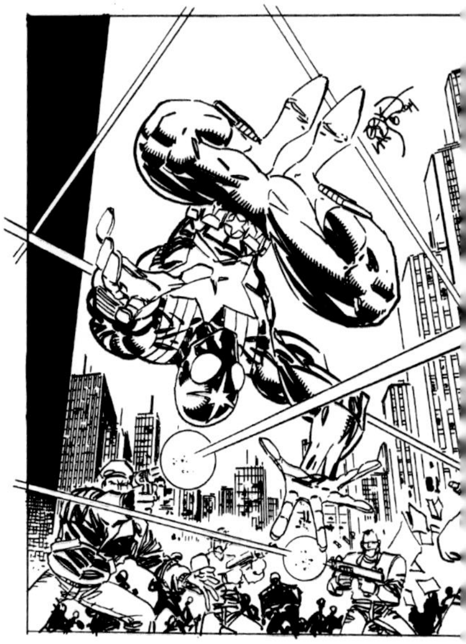

Below was a card for the Overpower card set—some nutty card game that I never did play, actually.

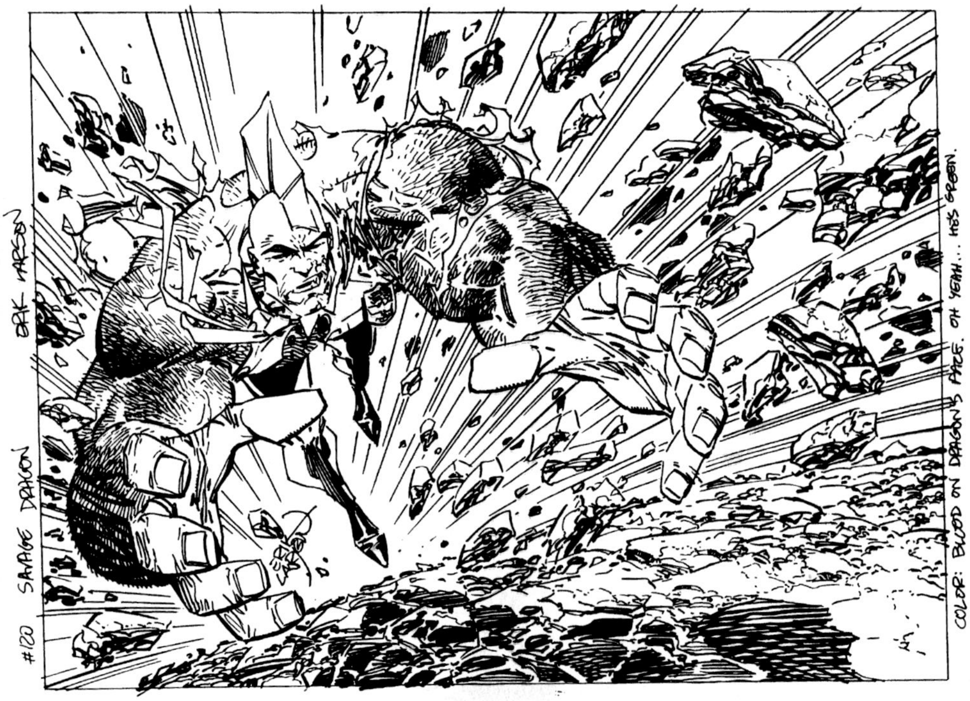
ERIK LARSEN
#120 SAVAGE DRAGON
COLOR: BLOOD ON DRAGON'S FACE. OH YEAH... HE'S GREEN.

Two more cards from the Topps set. A photo of me was placed in the drawing (below). Dragon and Rature (right). These folks did a fine job on this set. I was pretty taken by the whole thing.

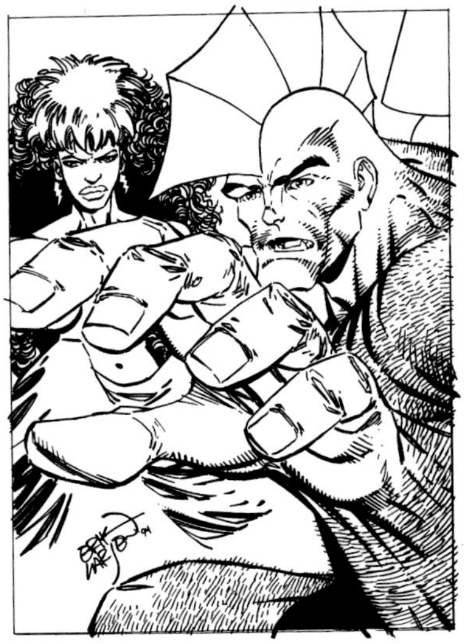

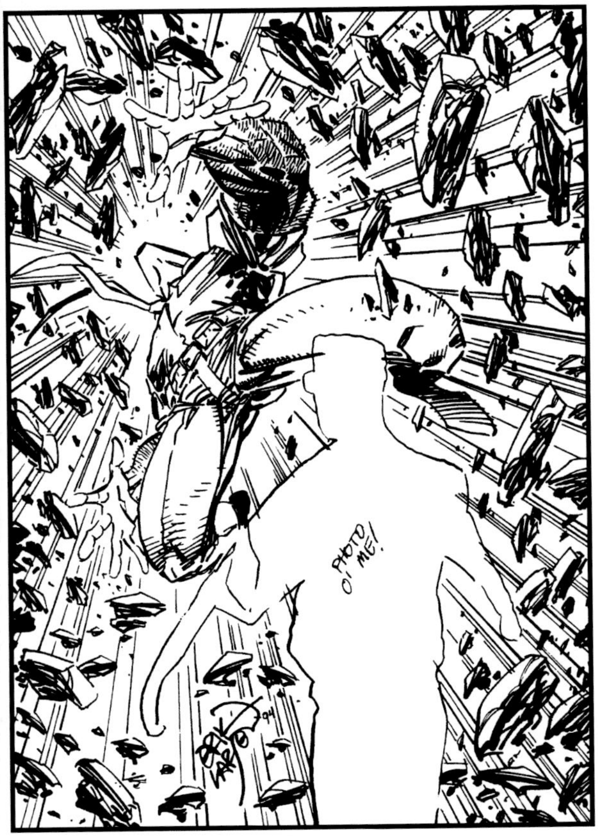
PHOTO O' ME!

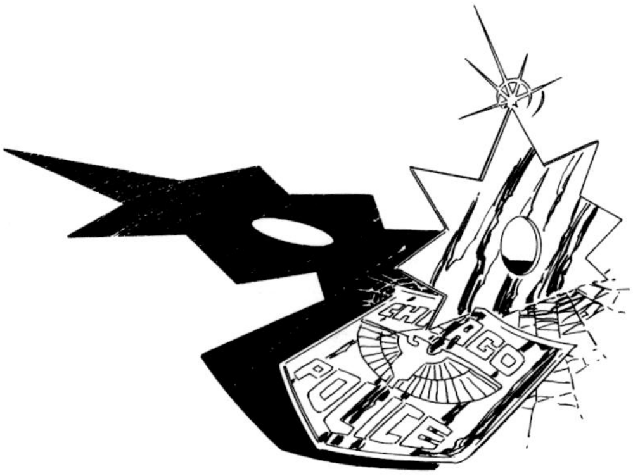
POLICE

These were title cards for the Savage Dragon cartoon. They were my heavy-handed inks over Craig Wilson's layouts (and some of those were based on drawings of mine from the comic book - go figure).

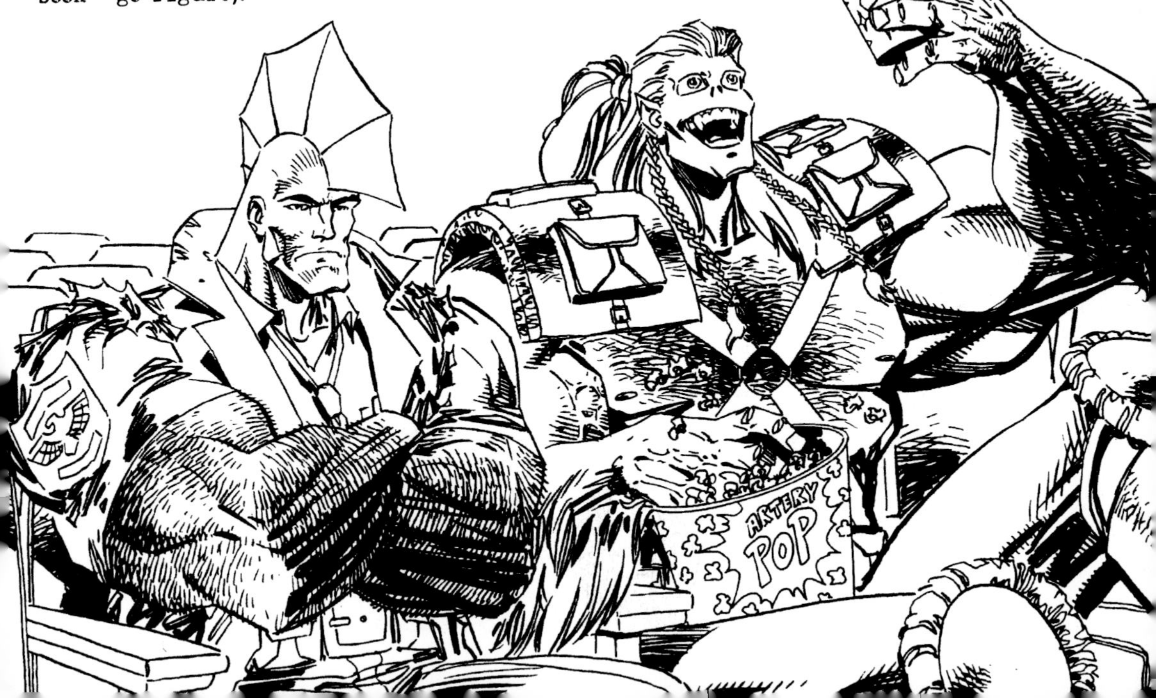
ARTERY
POP

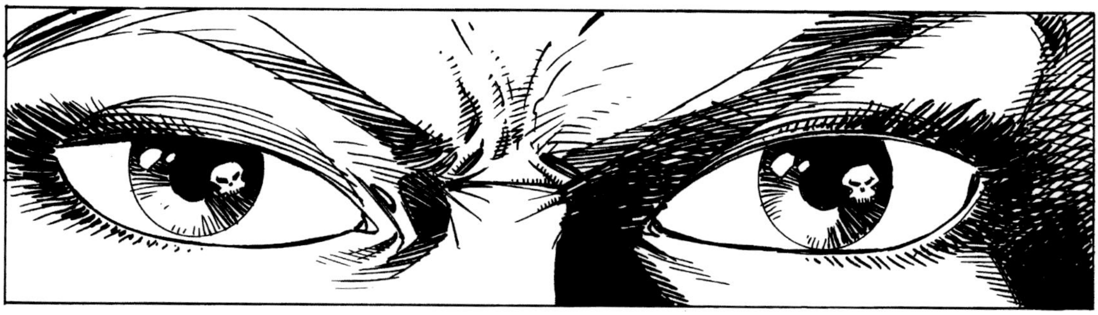

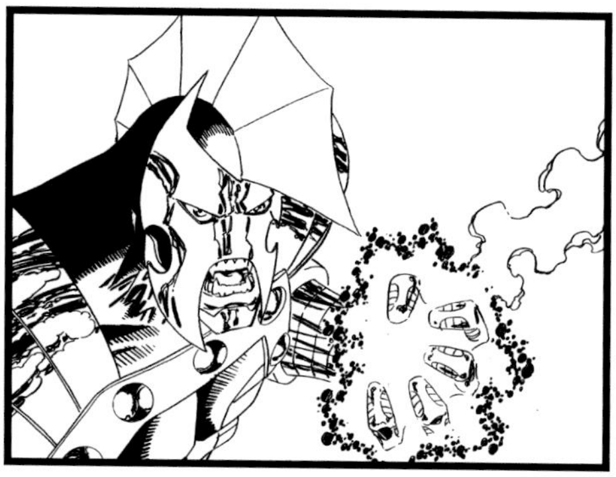

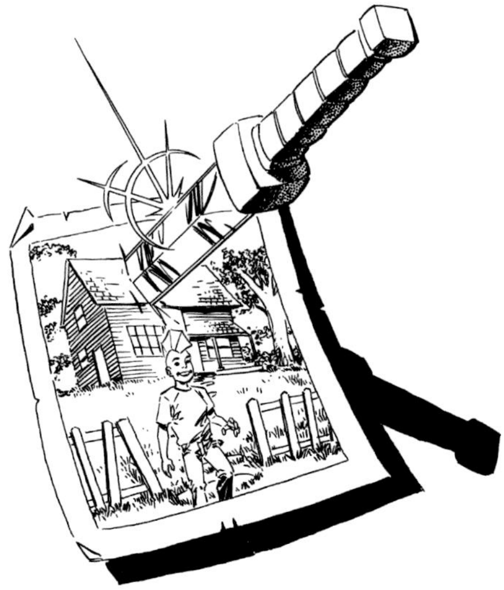

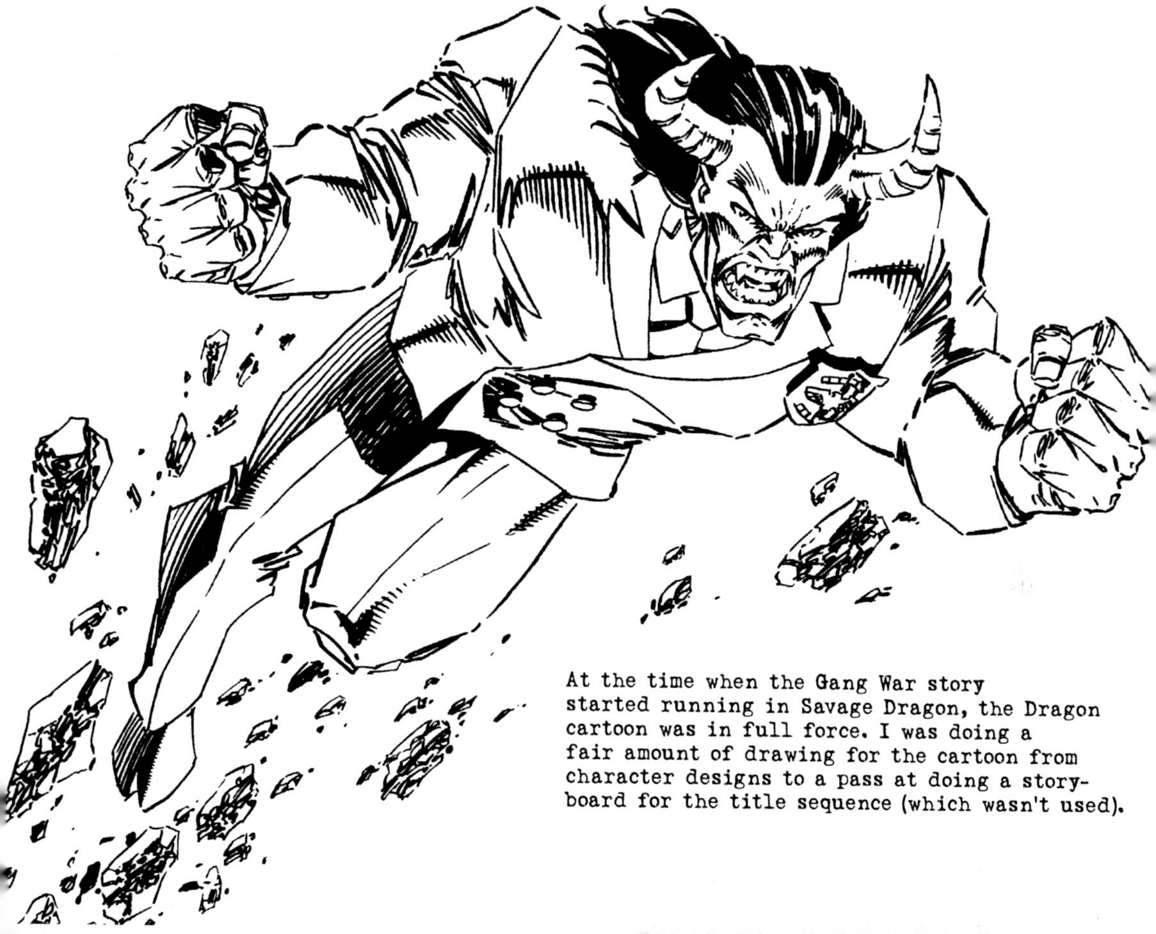

At the time when the Gang War story started running in Savage Dragon, the Dragon cartoon was in full force. I was doing a fair amount of drawing for the cartoon from character designs to a pass at doing a storyboard for the title sequence (which wasn't used).

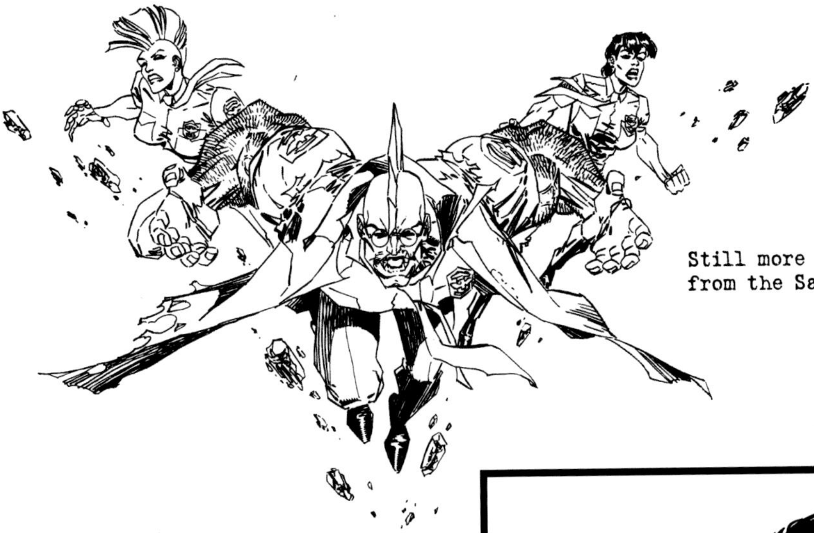

Still more title cards
from the Savage Dragon cartoon.

This spider-woman was designed by somebody at Universal Studios. She was a "bride" for the character Arachnid. She doesn't look much like a character I'd design— although they got a couple of things right.

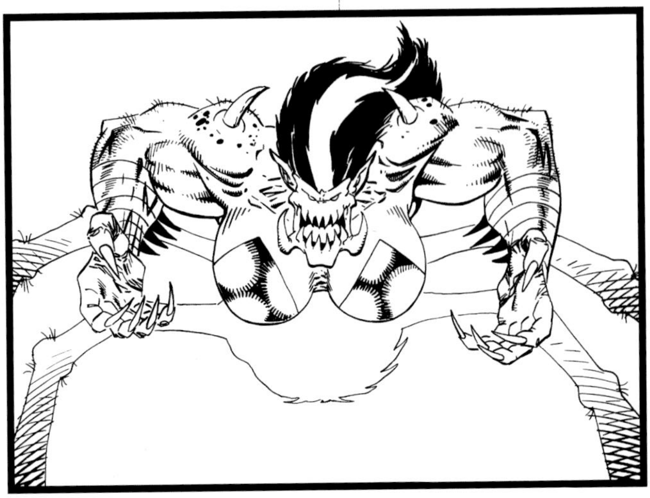

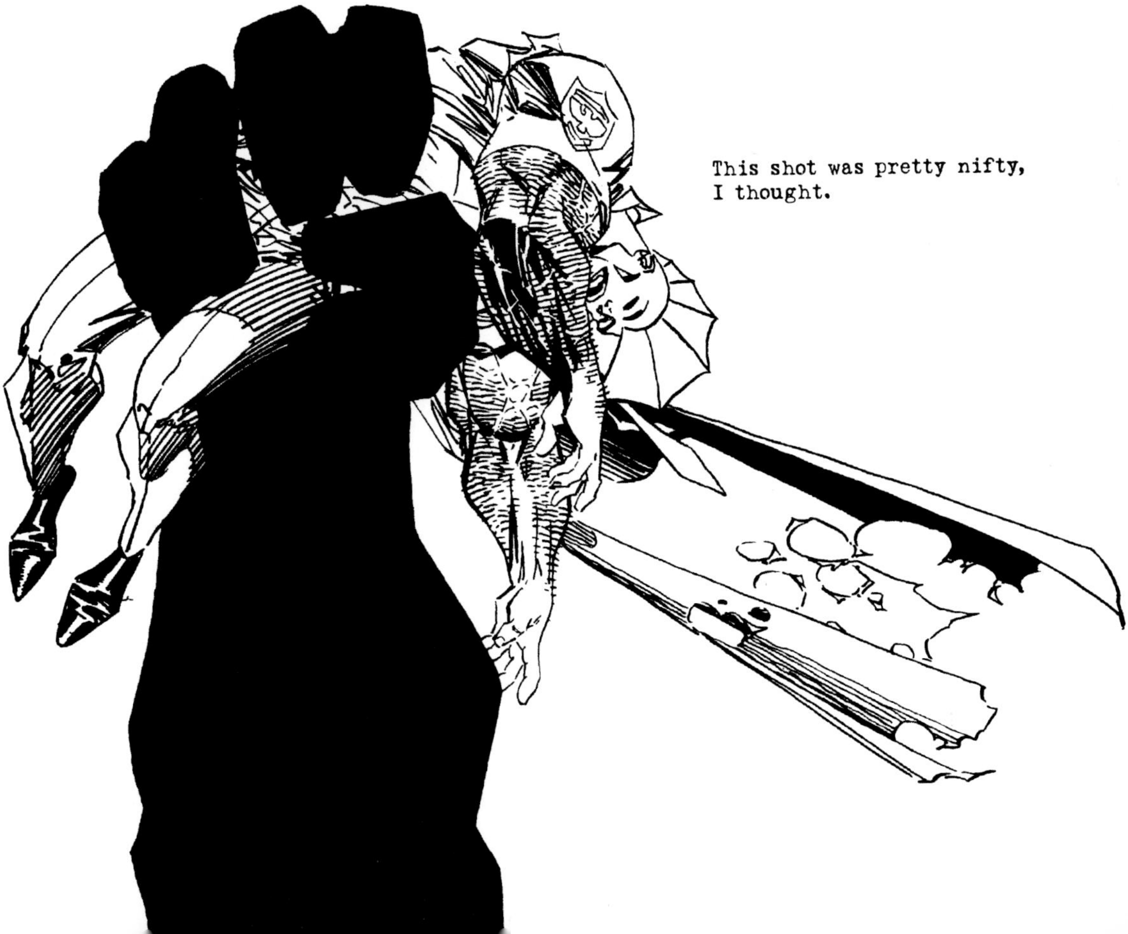

This shot was pretty nifty, I thought.

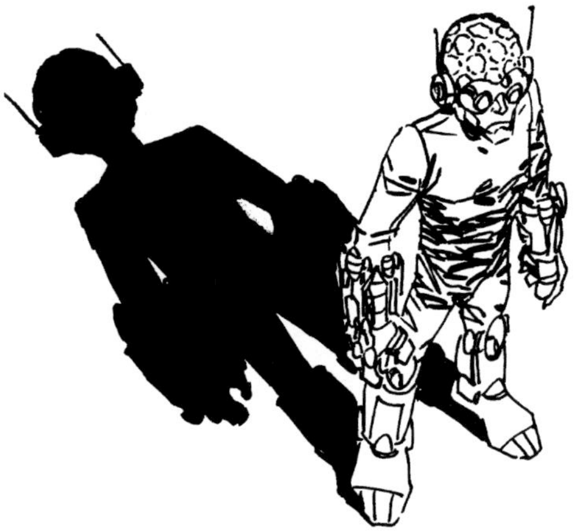

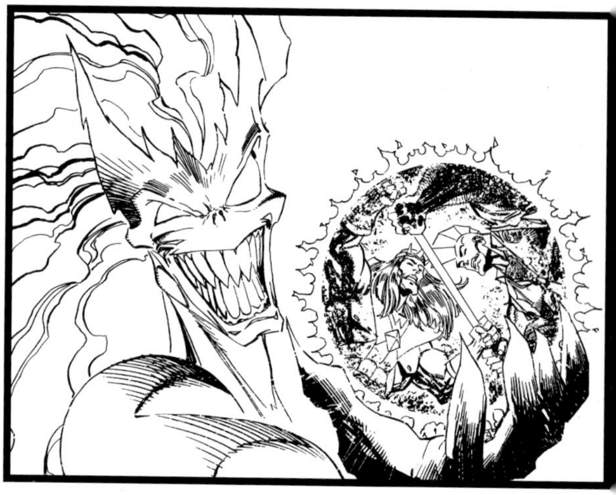

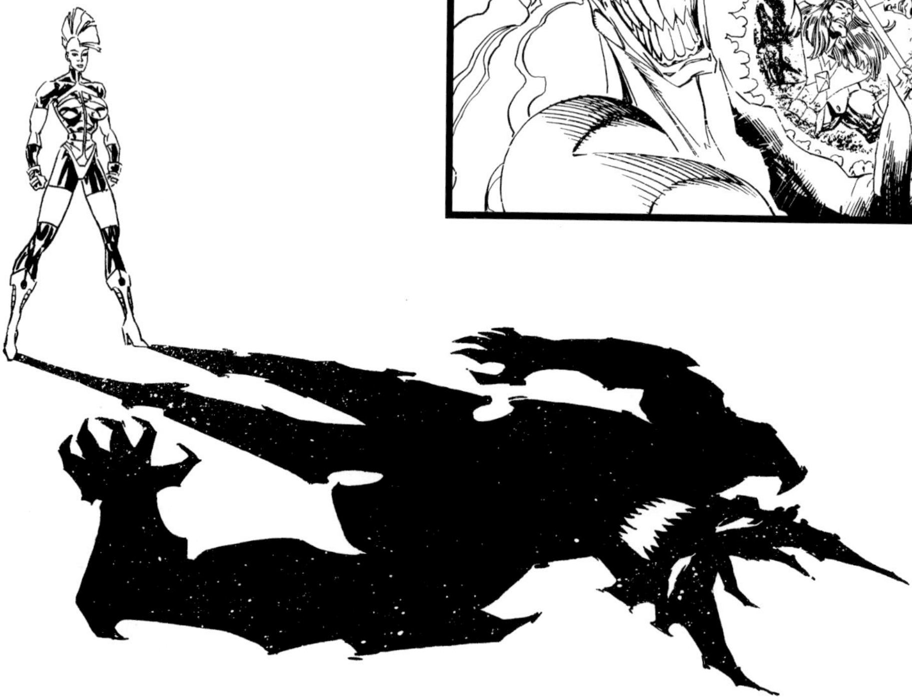

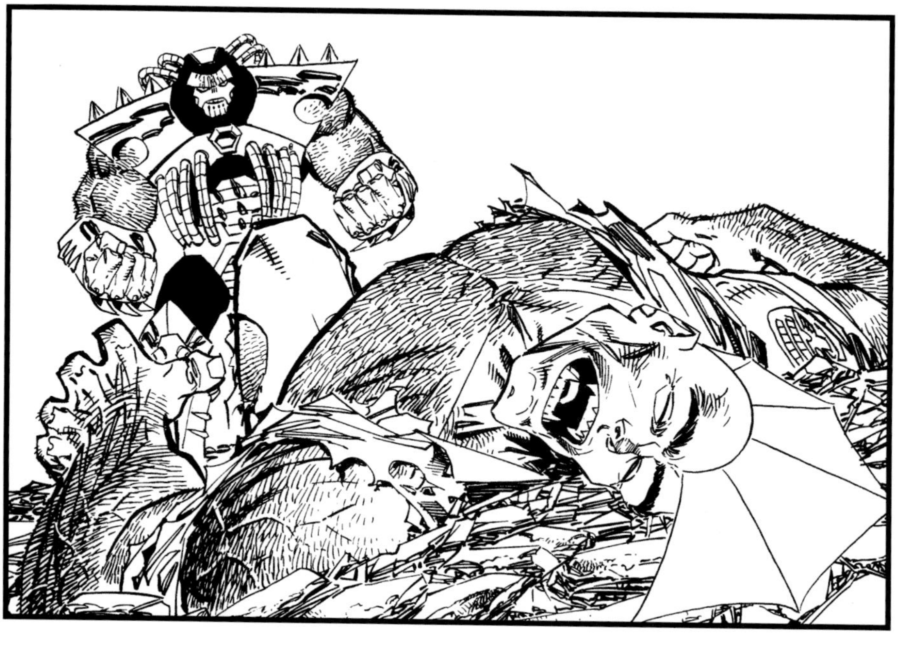

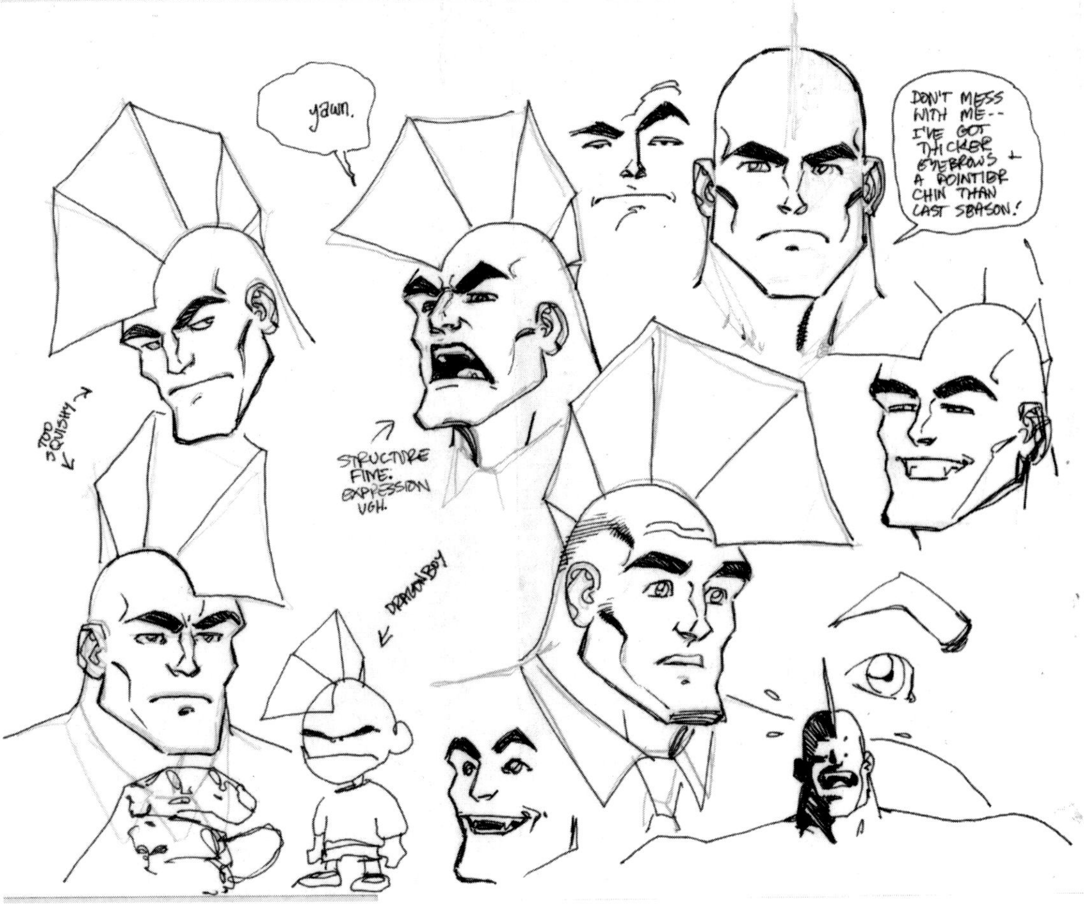

yawn.
DON'T MESS WITH ME-- I'VE GOT THICKER EYEBROWS + A POINTIER CHIN THAN LAST SEASON!
TOO SQUISHY
STRUCTURE FINE. EXPRESSION UGH.
DRAGON BOY

Drawings for the cartoon— trying desperately to give Dragon that distinctive Dragon look from the comic book. Ultimately, however, it looked like hell. If I were to do it over again, I'd go for a much more exaggerated style like Dexter's Lab or Ren & Stimpy. Despite some damned talented folks putting in a great deal of effort, the Savage Dragon show looked just plain awful. It's painful to watch.

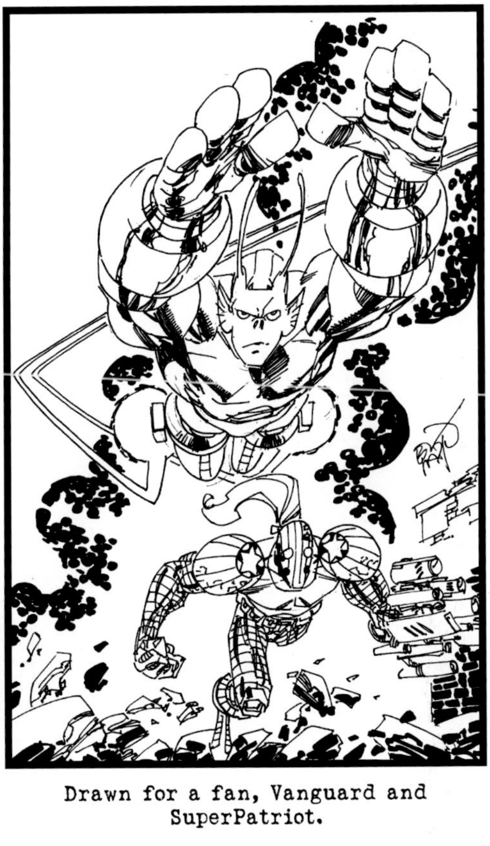

Drawn for a fan, Vanguard and SuperPatriot.

BulkHead. A character created for the Dragon cartoon. I later used him in a Freak Force mini-series. For whatever reason, despite having a gazillion characters at their sdisposal, the folks in charge of the cartoon wanted more. I was happy to oblige.

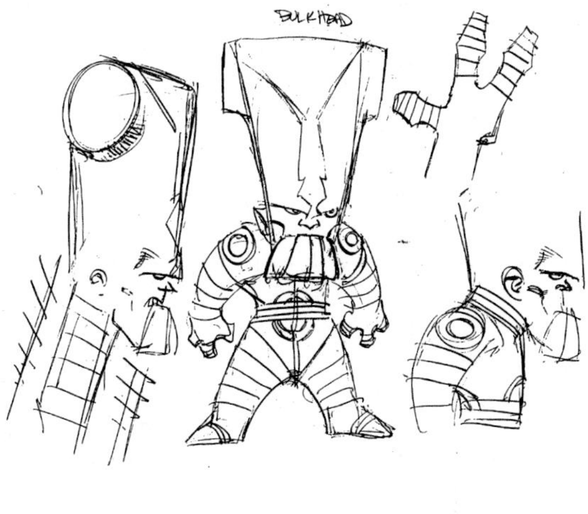

BULKHEAD

I started this as a cover for the Revenge trade paperback. Dragon's arms were simply way out of control. I ended up tossing out the whole mess after I came up with a design that I liked better.

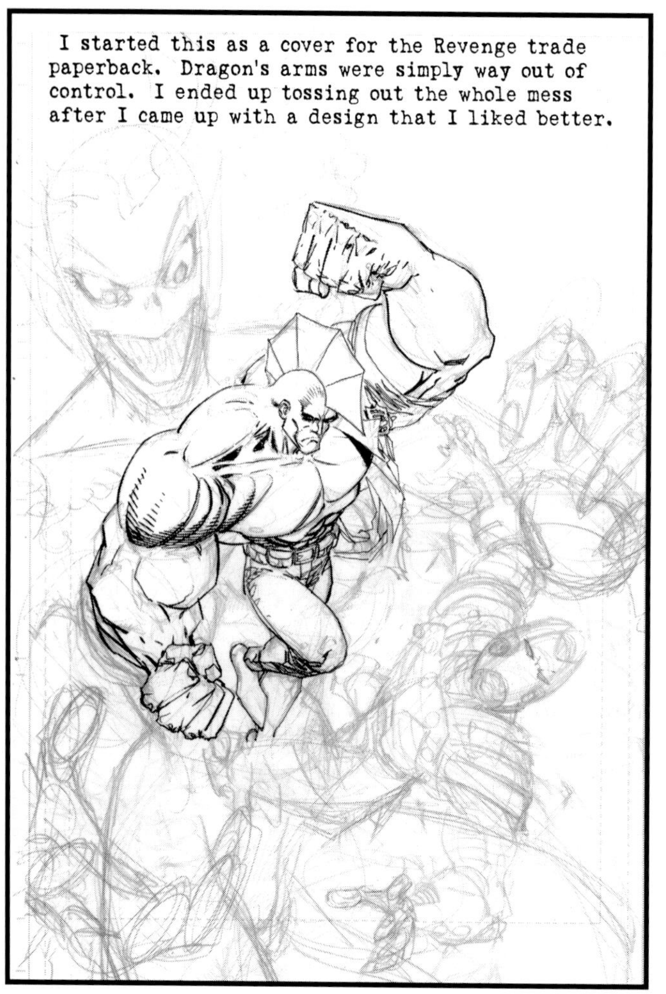

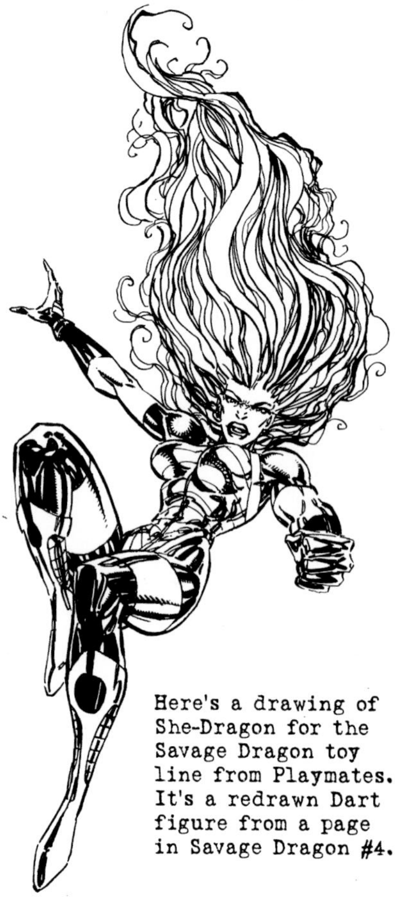

Here's a drawing of She-Dragon for the Savage Dragon toy line from Playmates. It's a redrawn Dart figure from a page in Savage Dragon #4.

I do a lot of scribbles on paper to keep fresh—if I hit on something particularly striking, I'll often work it into the actual book. No such luck with either of these.

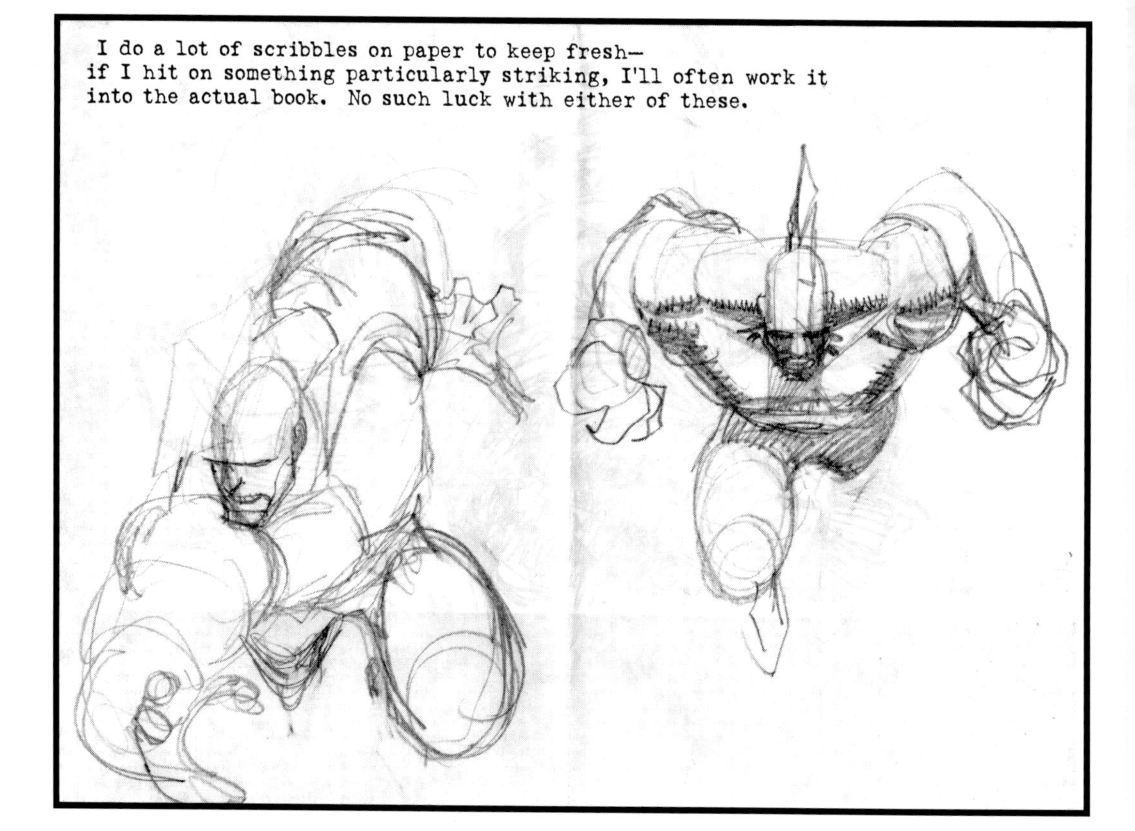

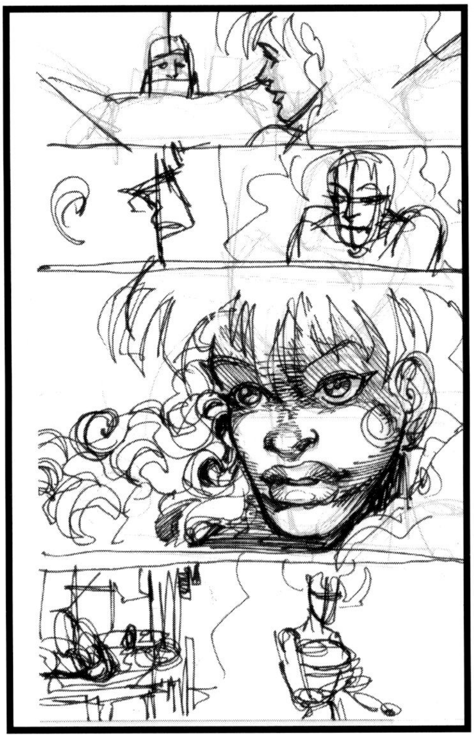

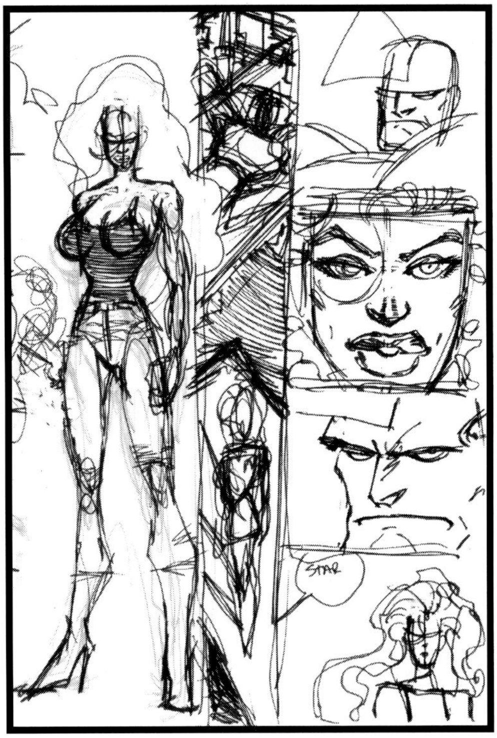
STAR

These two translated pretty literally into pages of Savage Dragon #25.

I did a bunch of drawings of Rapture and She-Dragon mixing it up. The idea here was to get in as much gratuitous T&A shots as possible. I thought I did a pretty good job on that front.

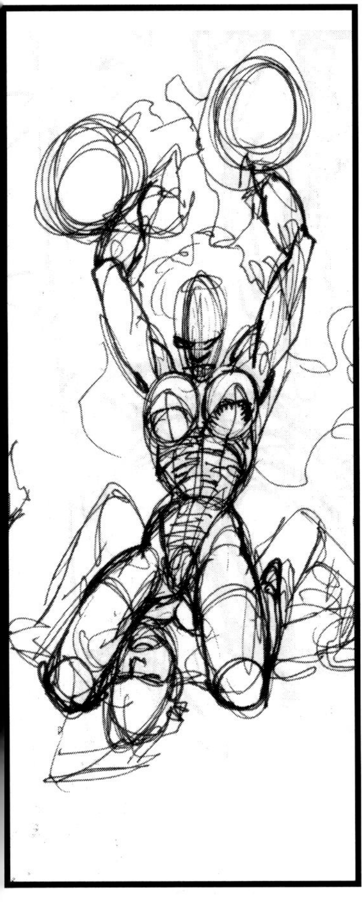

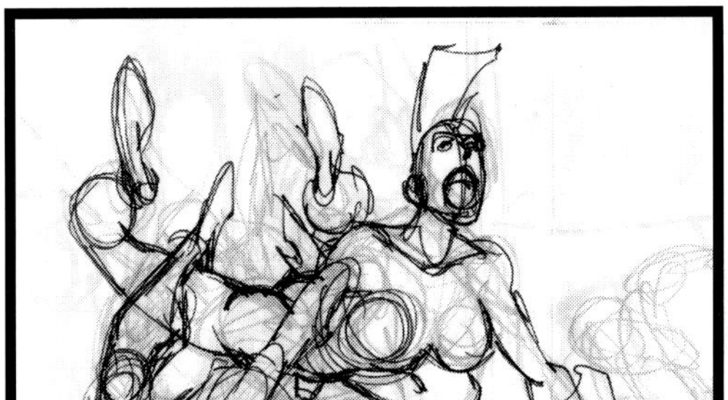

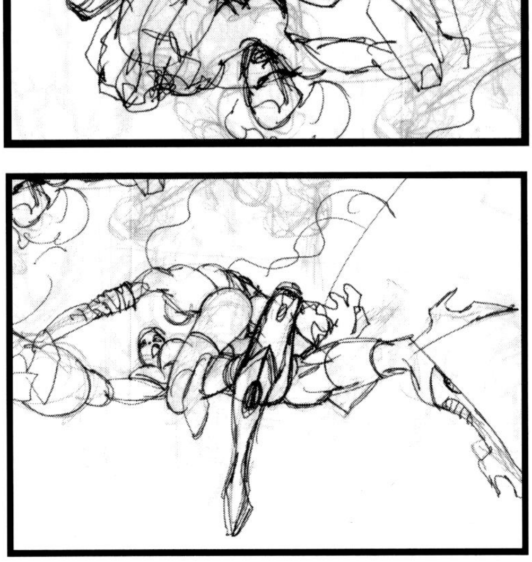

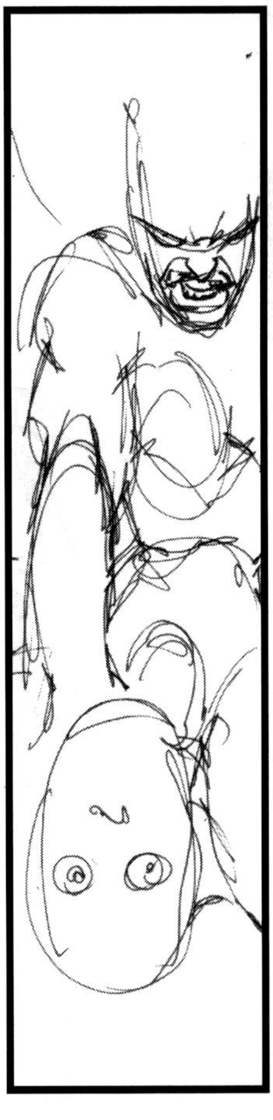

An aborted design for the female version of the Fiend— a cover half-finished and abandoned. I do a lot of this sort of thing.

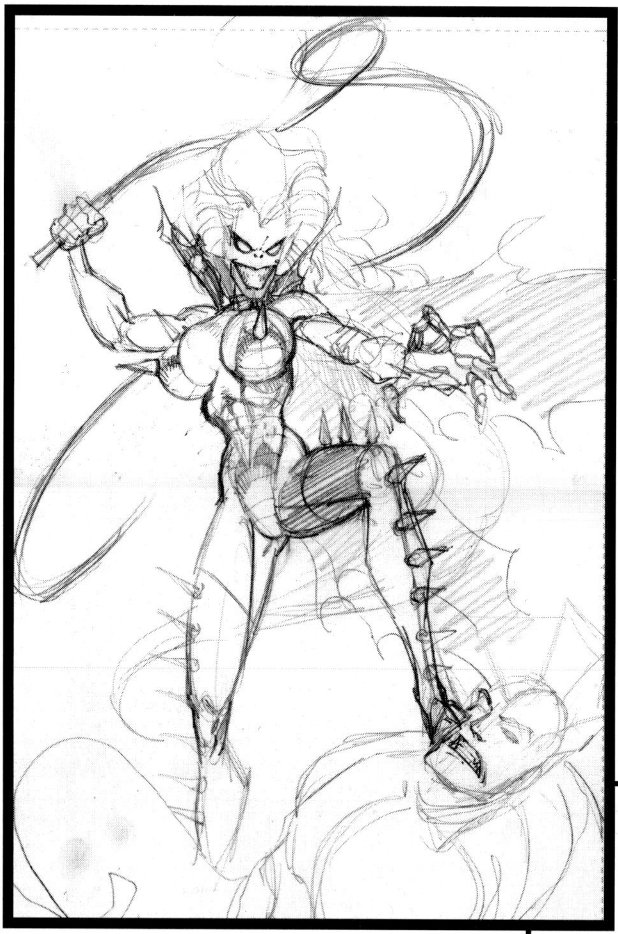

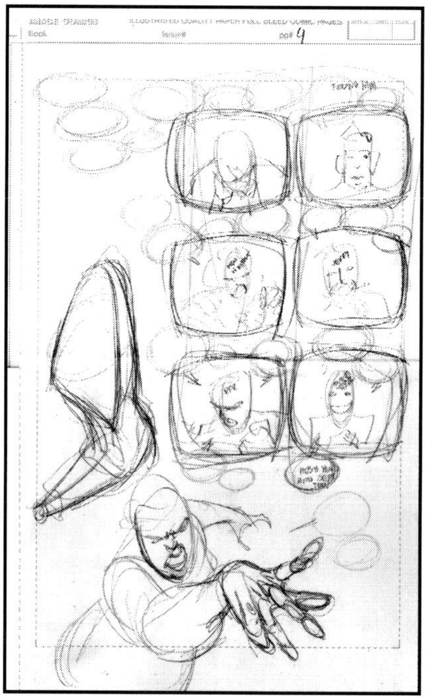

A started page that didn't make the cut. Still, I liked the design of this. It was intended for Savage Dragon #11.

(right)
There's a good reason some drawings stay on the cutting room floor. This beauty was drawn back when I started the initial Savage Dragon mini-series. Not only is the fin on Dragon's head way out of whack but the overall look just bites hard. Not my proudest moment.

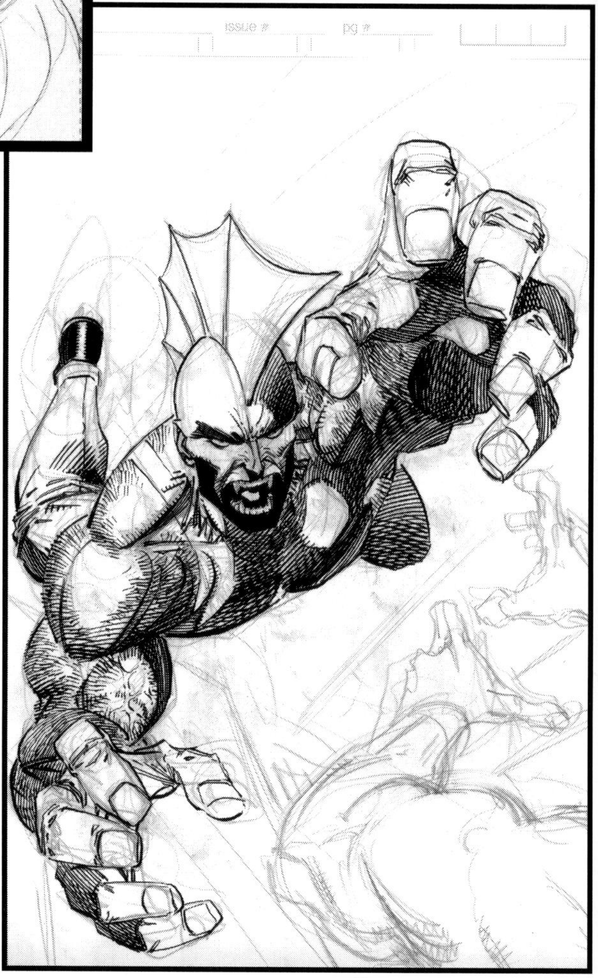

A stab at a TPB cover— still not sure that I like it.

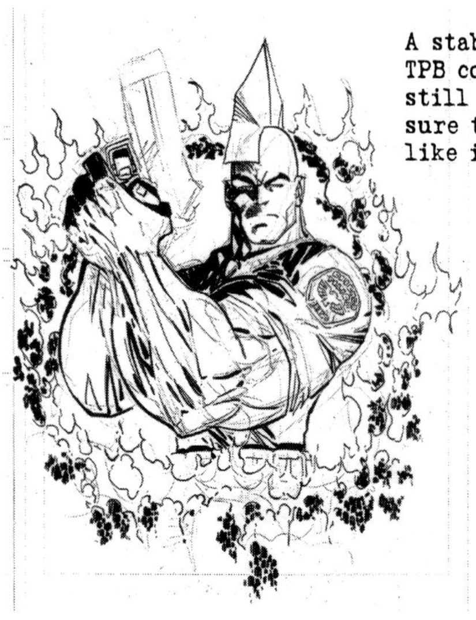

This was an attempt to combine two pages of layouts into a single page. The story was (as usual) running long and I thought I could buy a page by combining two— no such luck. It ended up looking too cramped and the long panel on the right hand side made it so reading the panels out of order was a strong probability.

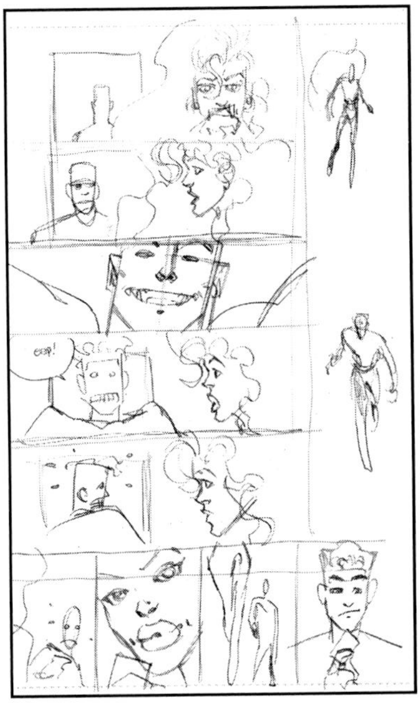

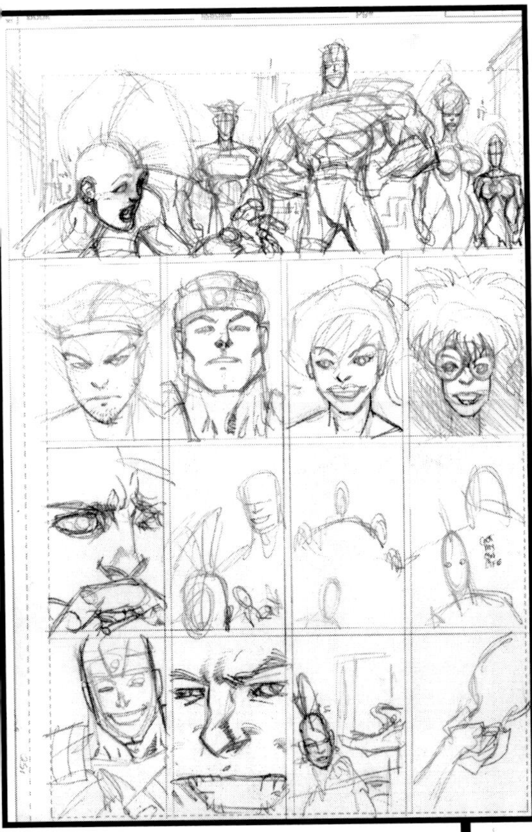

(above)
Initially, I thought of doing the Gang War story on a rigid 4-panel by 4-panel grid. I ditched that notion pretty quick. This saga was ambitious enough with so many characters appearing— complicating matter with a grid like this would have done me in. I eventually did do an issue based on a 4 x 4 grid— Savage Dragon #47.

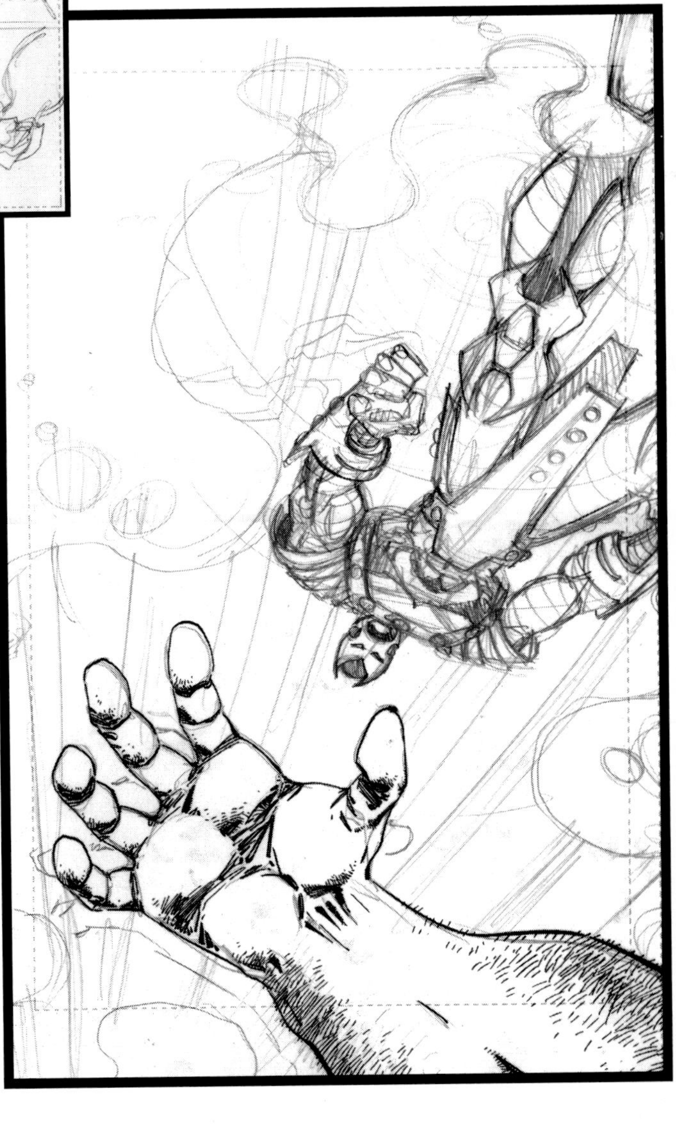

An aborted cover for Savage Dragon #20. The logo would have rendered it unreadable.

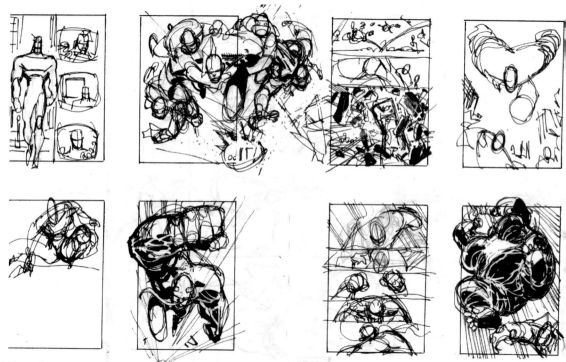

The tiny layouts above are from issue #22.

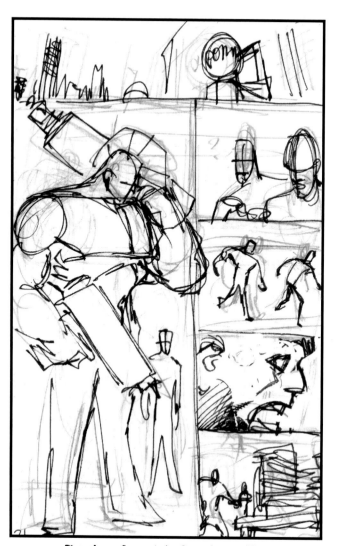

This was an aborted page intended for issue #24. Dragon versus Mako.

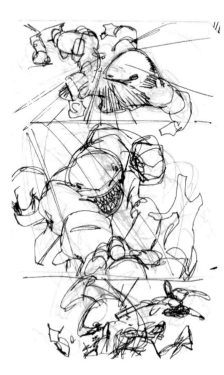

The above layout is from issue #25.

(below)
An initial layout for a cover for the magazine "Combo." I ended up doing something else entirely.

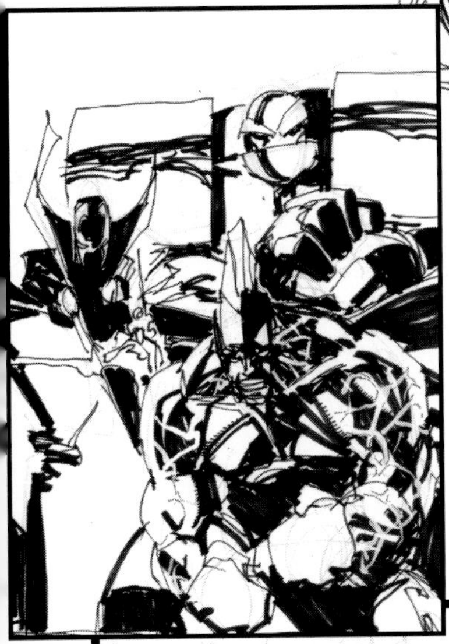

Dragon gettin' punched!

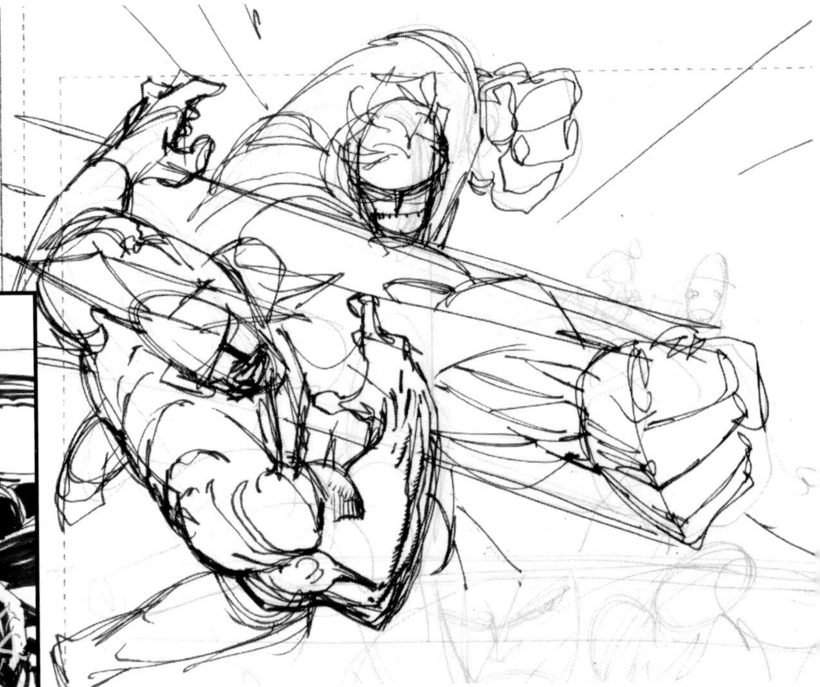

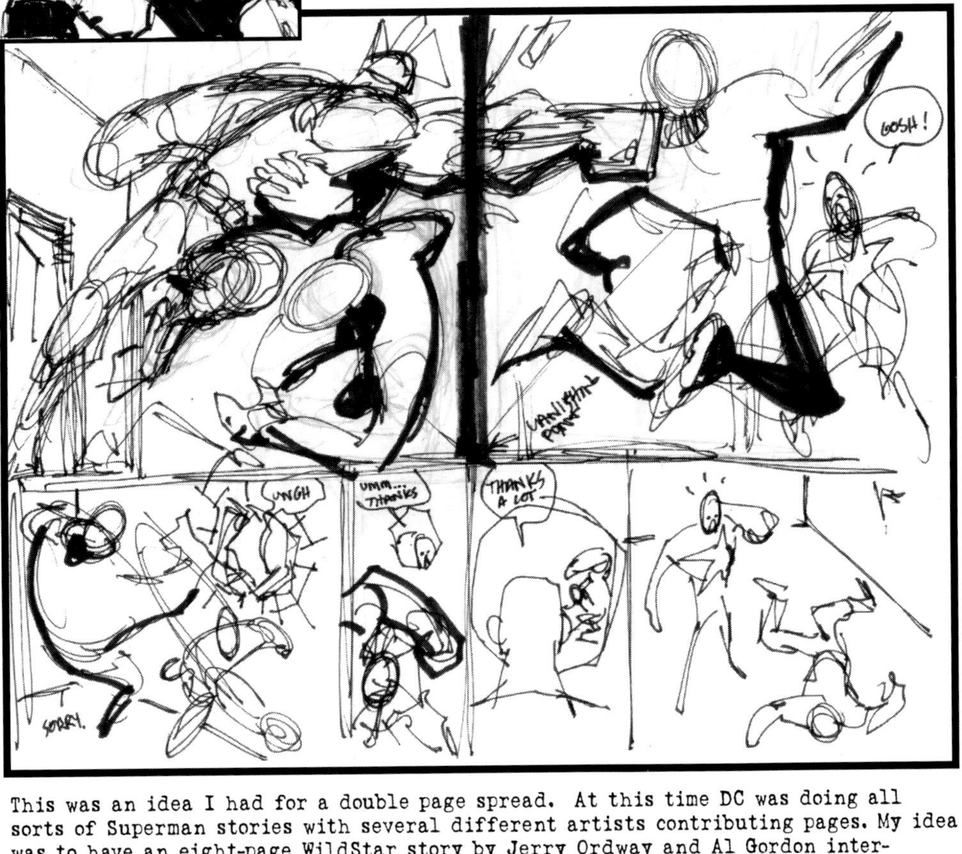
GOSH!
UNGH
UMM... THANKS
THANKS A LOT
SORRY.

This was an idea I had for a double page spread. At this time DC was doing all sorts of Superman stories with several different artists contributing pages. My idea was to have an eight-page WildStar story by Jerry Ordway and Al Gordon interspersed among a Dragon story by me. Both stories could be read independently of each other on in the order in which they were printed. The end of the WildStar story would crossover with the Dragon story. This layout was intended as the crossover spread— as Dragon tried to nail a villain on my half, the bad guy ducked and Dragon's hand went through the wall. On Jerry & Al's half, Dragon's fist would come through the wall, knocking unconscious the villain who menaced WildStar. It was a fun idea, which was never executed. Maybe another time.

Scribbles aplenty. Just trying to work out a few kinks. I wanted Dragon to explode onto the scene as Savage Dragon #26 started. He'd been out of action or messed up for a few months and I wanted his comeback to be as dramatic as possible!

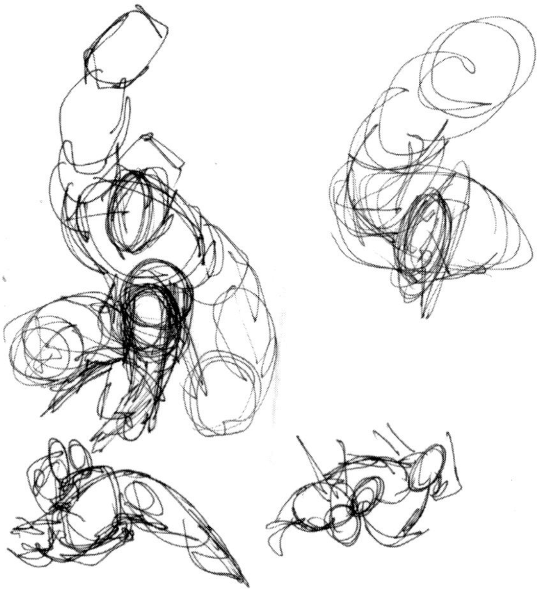

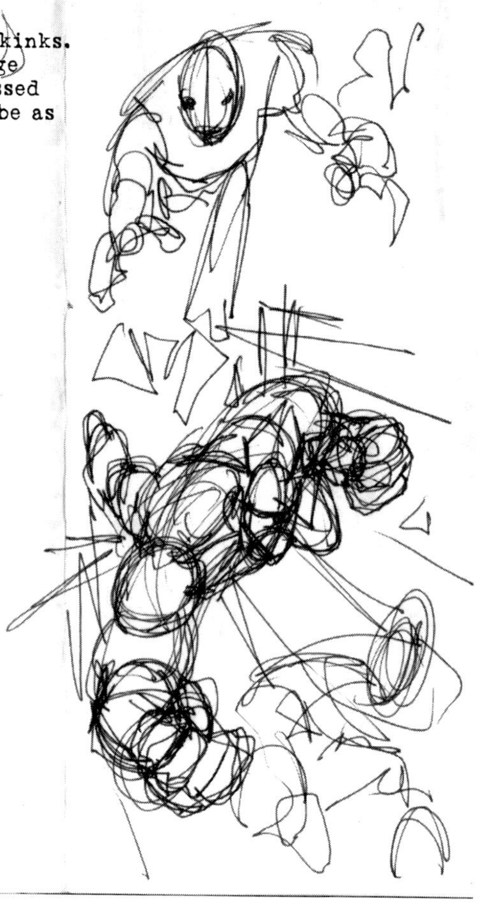

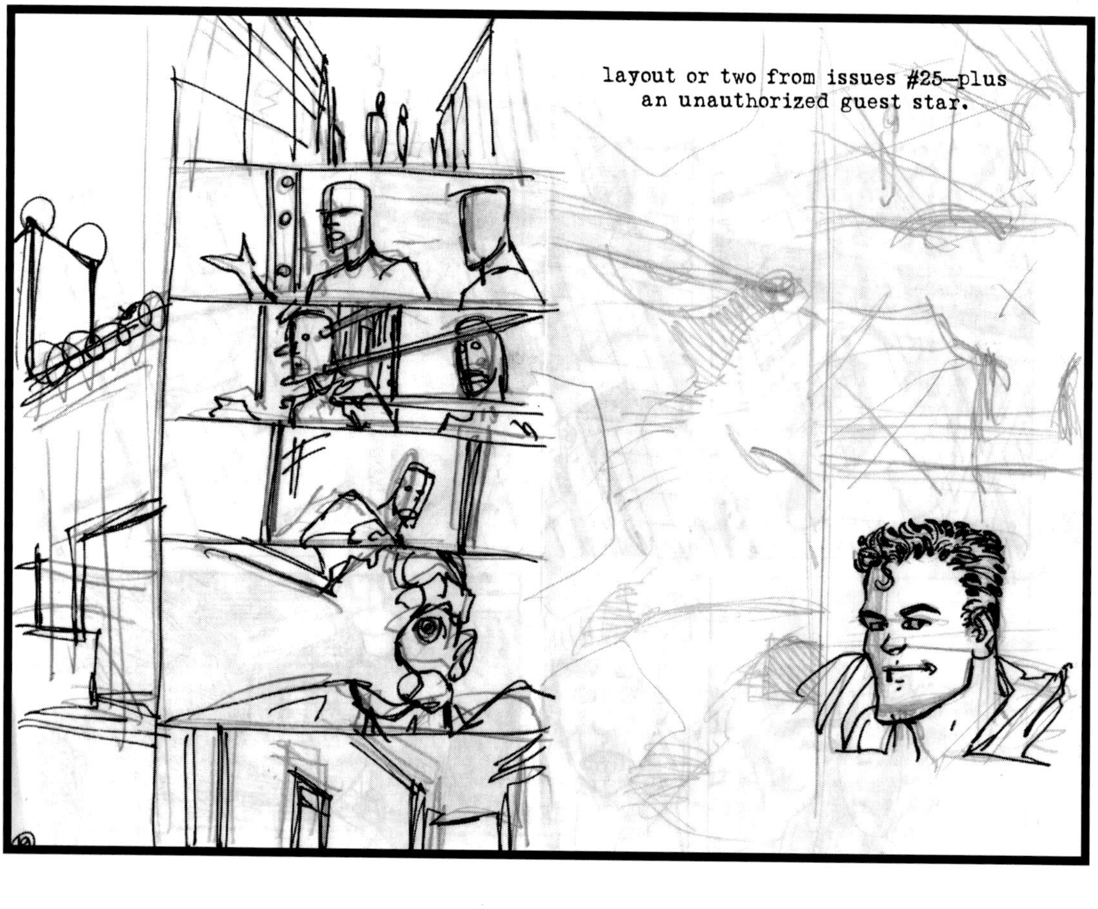

layout or two from issues #25—plus an unauthorized guest star.

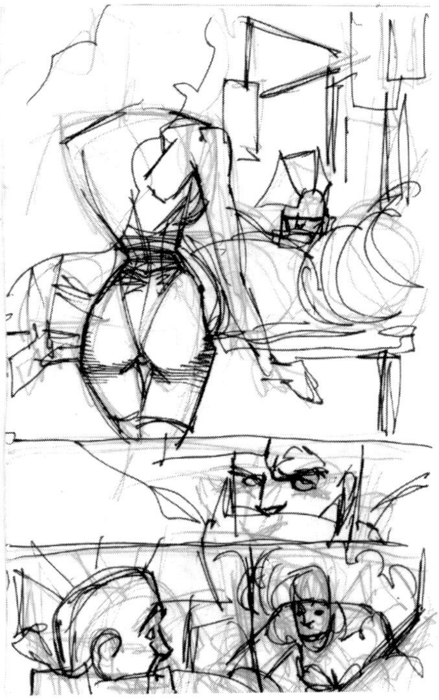

(above)
A layout from Savage Dragon #25. Rapture's butt ended up turning out far more oddly shaped than I'd intended in the printed version of #25— it bothered me enough that I actually went to the trouble of re-drawing it for this collection. Talk about an anal cartoonist.

Rejected cover idea for issue #23.

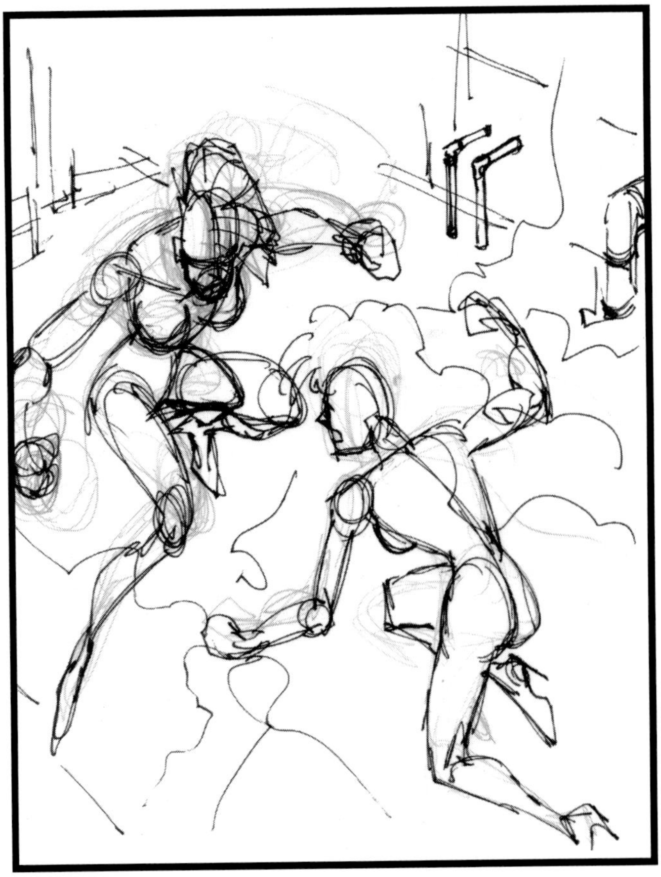

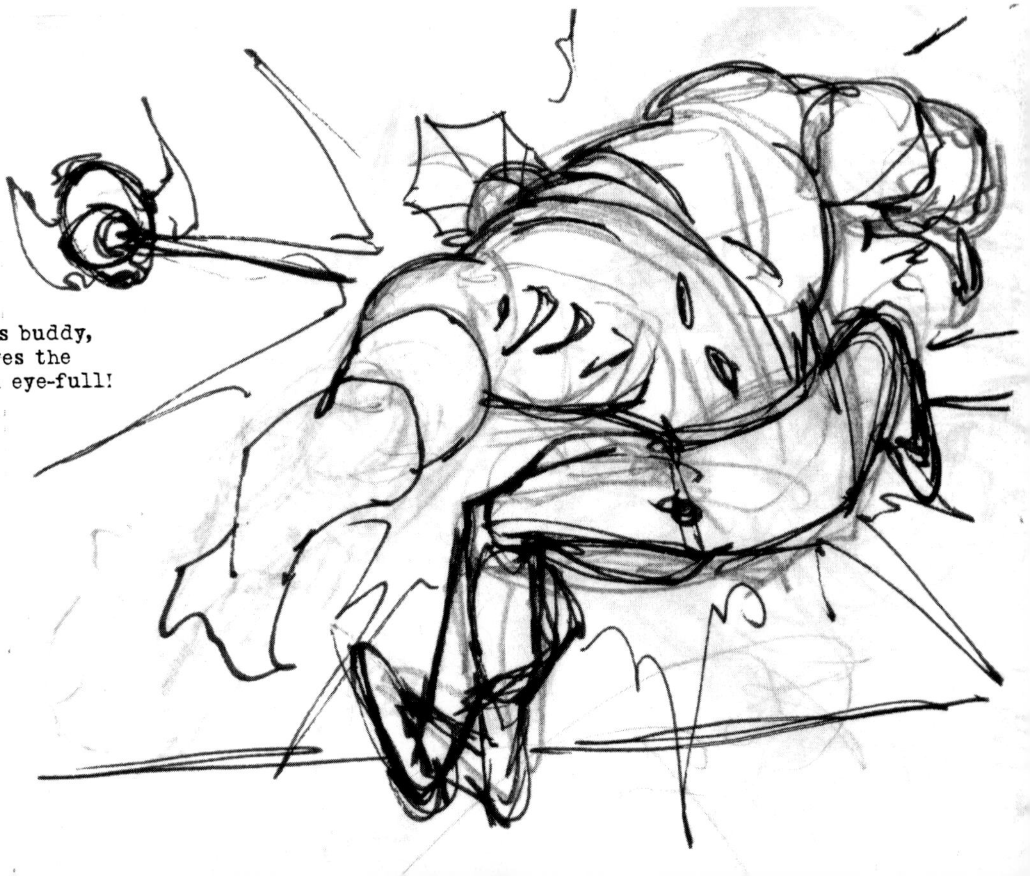

Vanguard's buddy, Wally, gives the Dragon an eye-full!

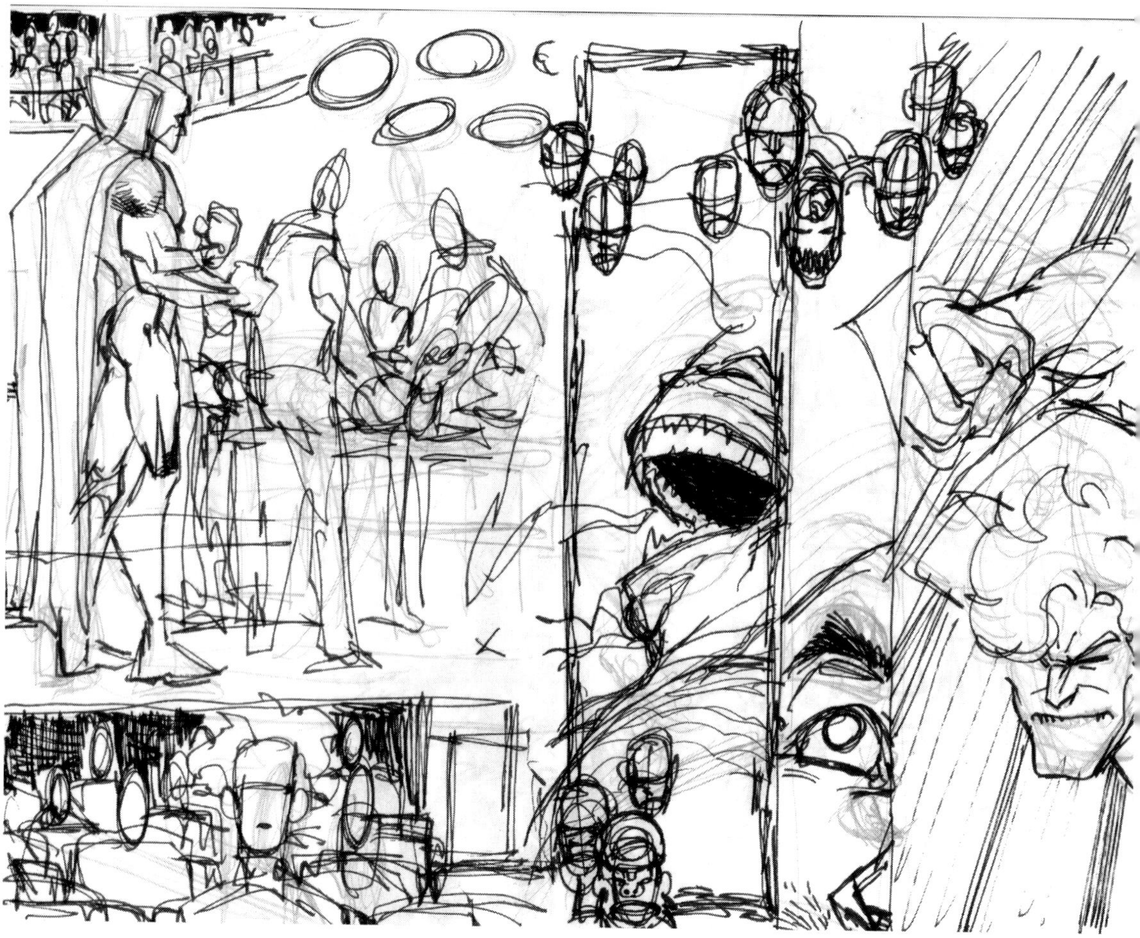

More layouts!...the above 2 are from issue #25, below from #24.

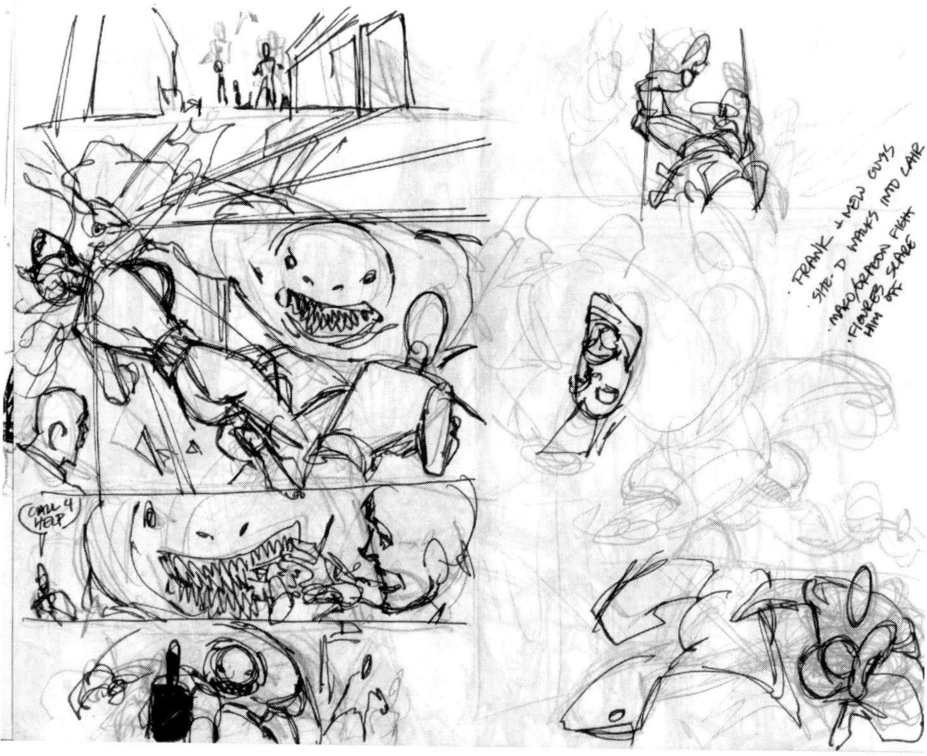
CALL 4 HELP
· FRANK + NEW GUYS
· SHE-D WALKS INTO LAIR
· MAKO/DRAGON FIGHT
· FLAVEGS HIM OFF
SLAPE

The layout for the drawing on the next couple of pages. The sketch looked pretty decent, I thought.

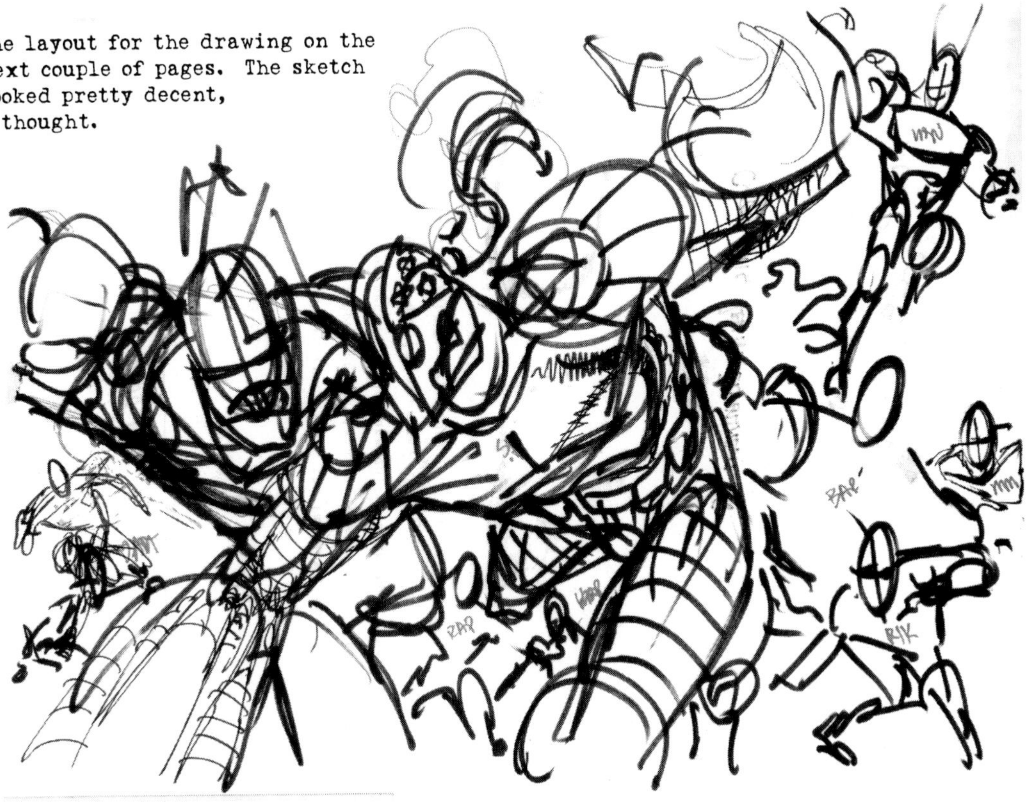

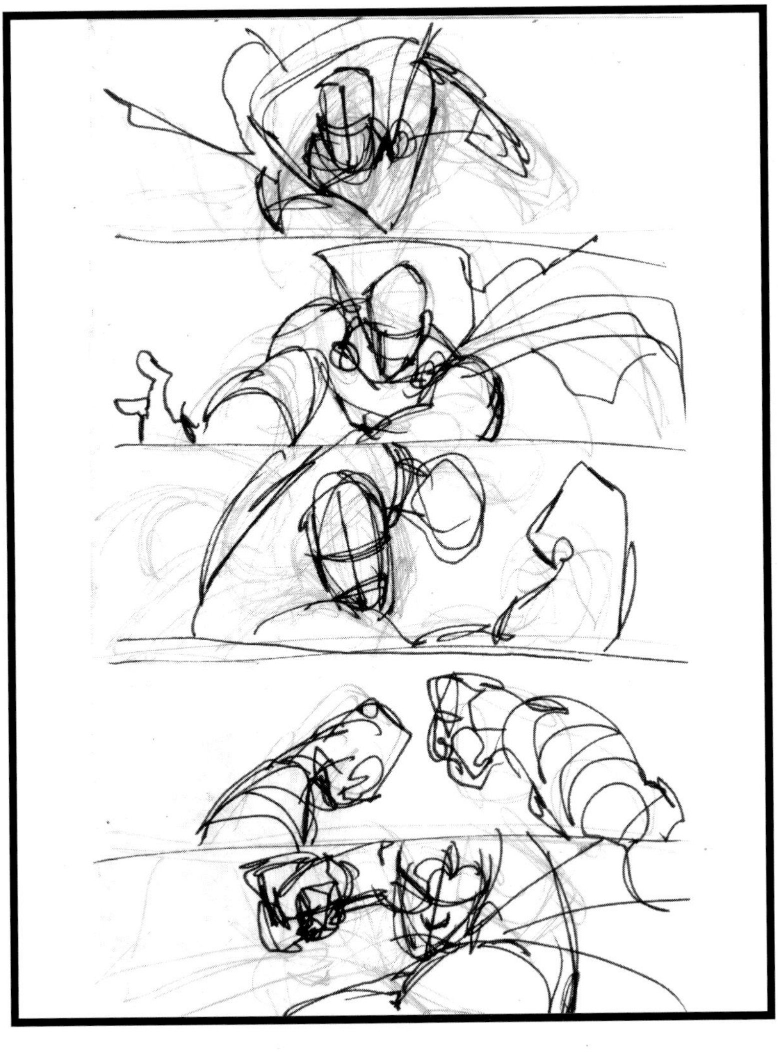

Another layout from Savage Dragon #25. This scene pretty much followed one that was similar from Savage Dragon #22 where the Fiend attacked the Dragon. I often use scenes that parallel ones from other issues—it gives the reader a sense of familiarity, which sets them up for a similar payoff. By doing this, I can pull off surprises that would be more difficult otherwise.

An attempt at a wrap around cover for Wizard. The longer I drew on it, the worse it got.

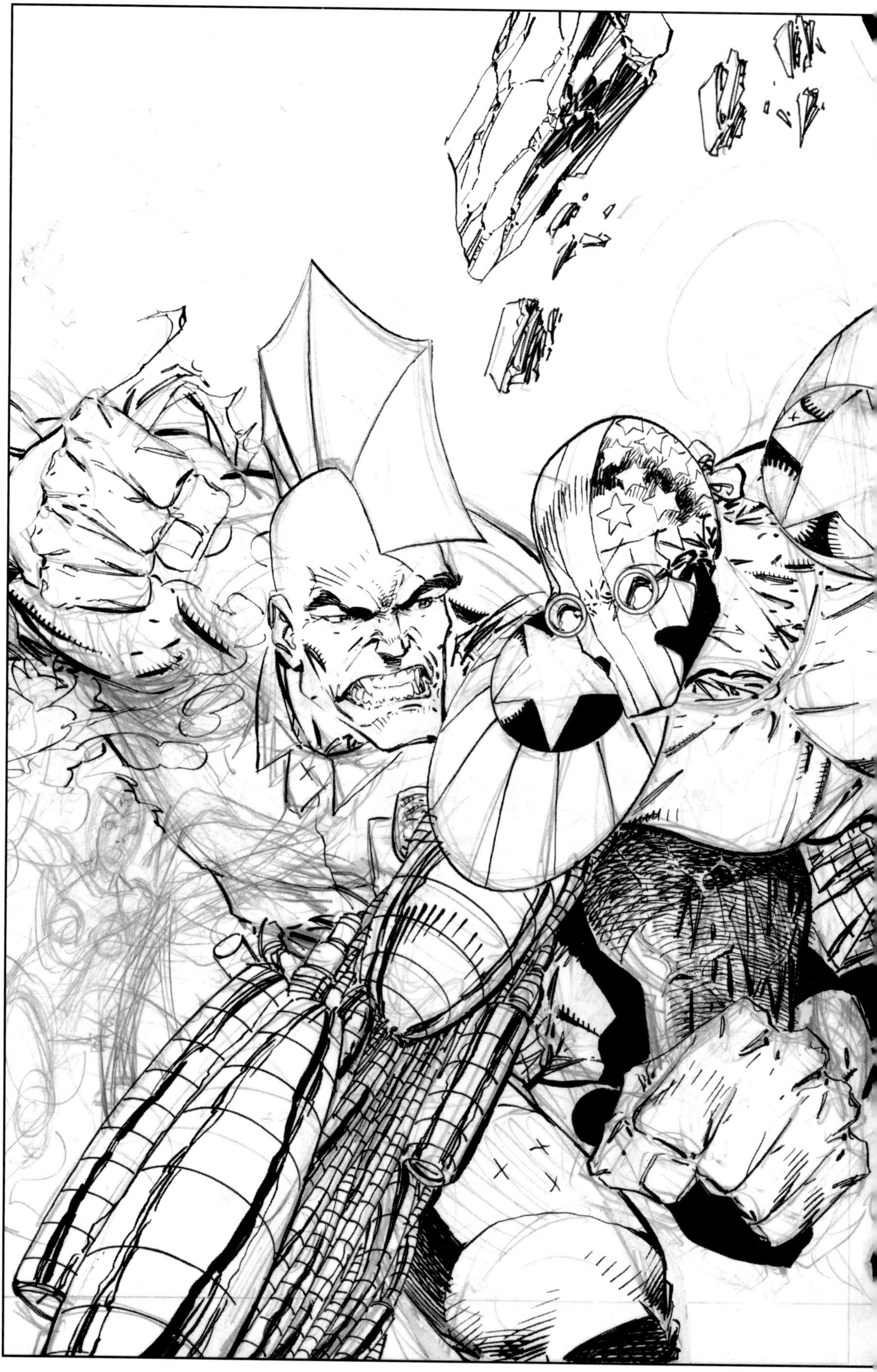

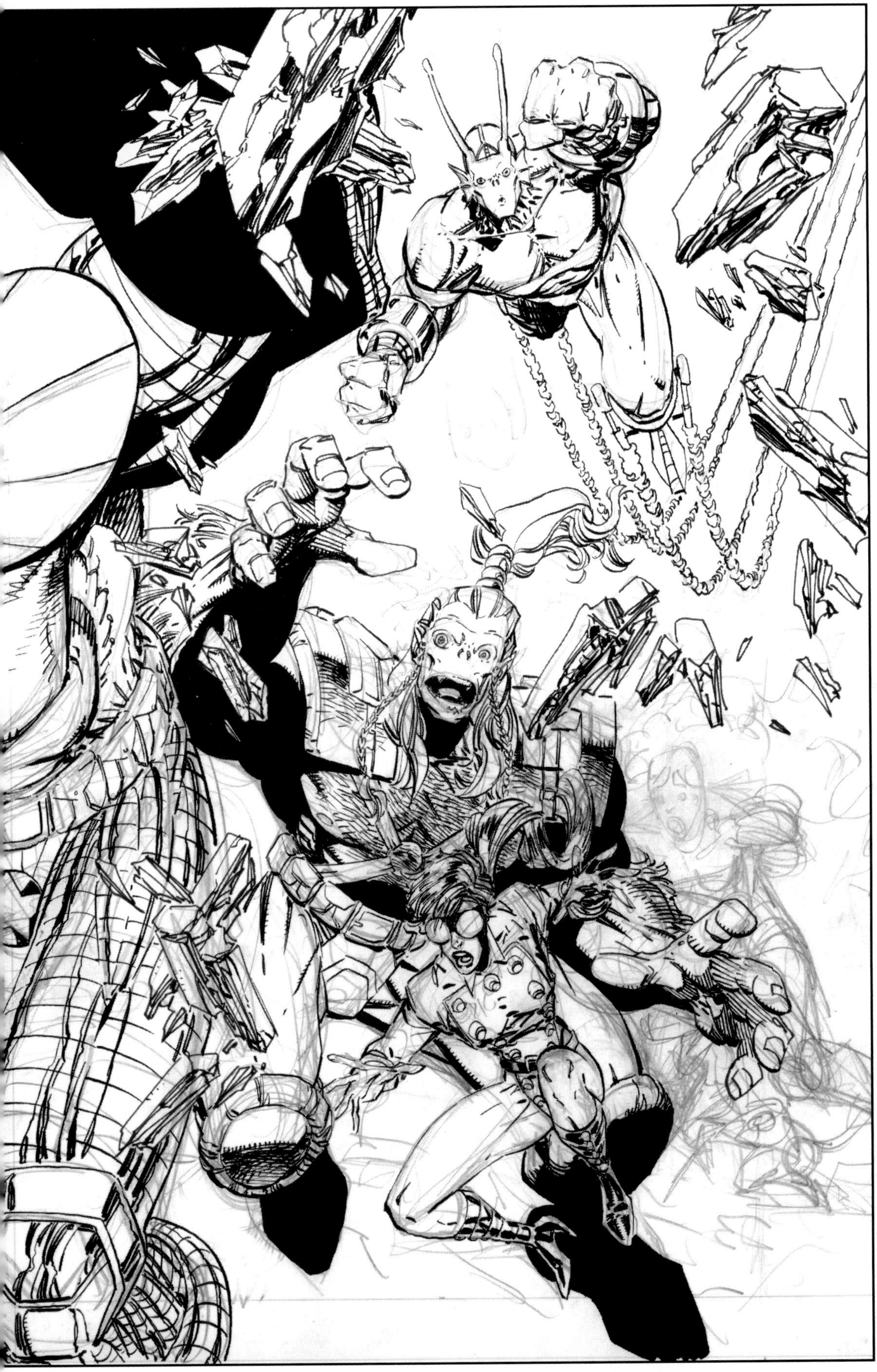

At some point, I sat down and drew covers for a number of Savage Dragon trade paperbacks. This was intended to be the one for Gang War. I got this far and ran out of characters. By now I could have filled it easily but since the idea was to use characters that had actually appeared in the Gang War story it couldn't be completed. After using the right hand side of the drawing as both a trading card and a poster, I decided to do an entirely different drawing for the cover of this book.

-Erik Larsen

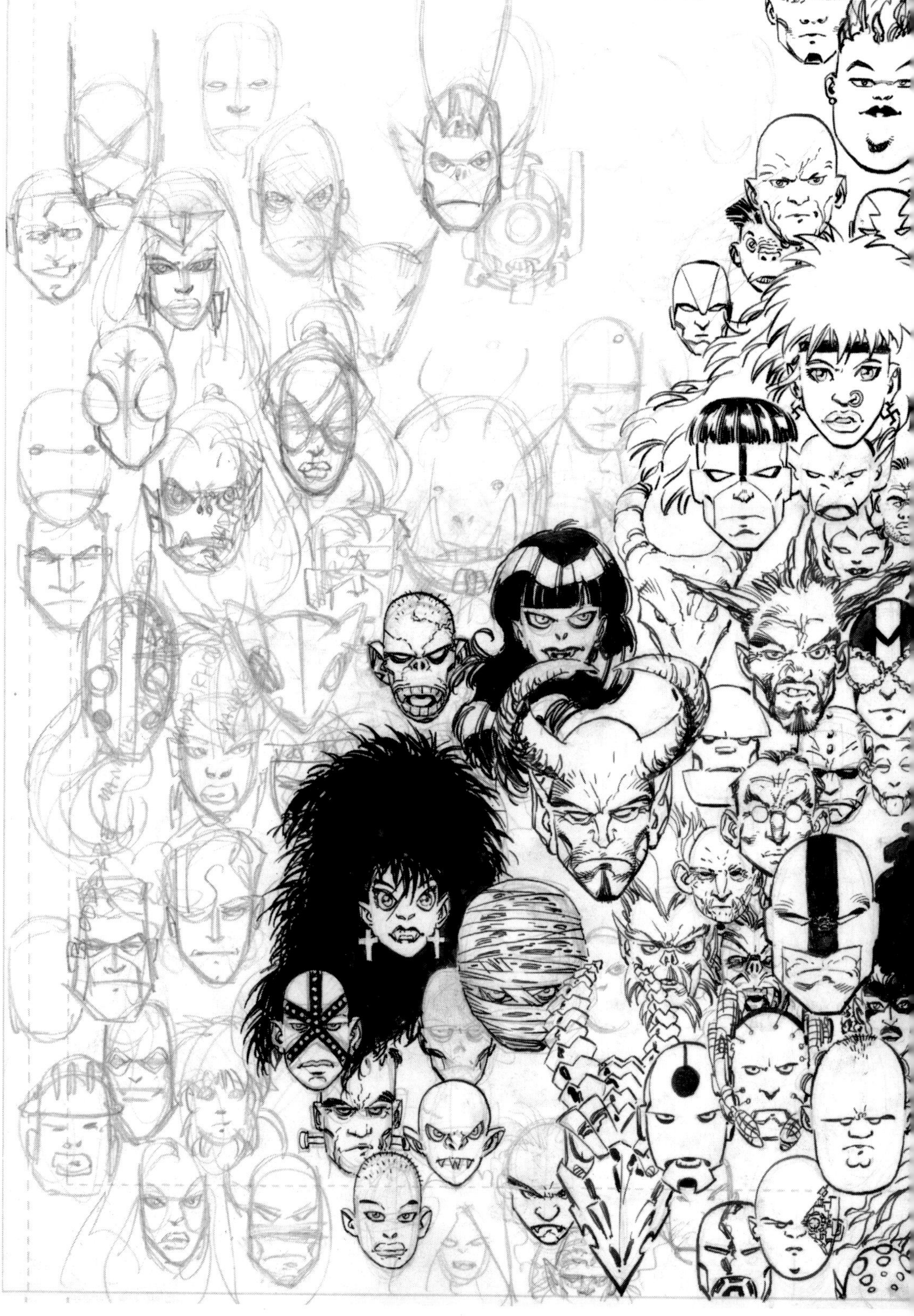

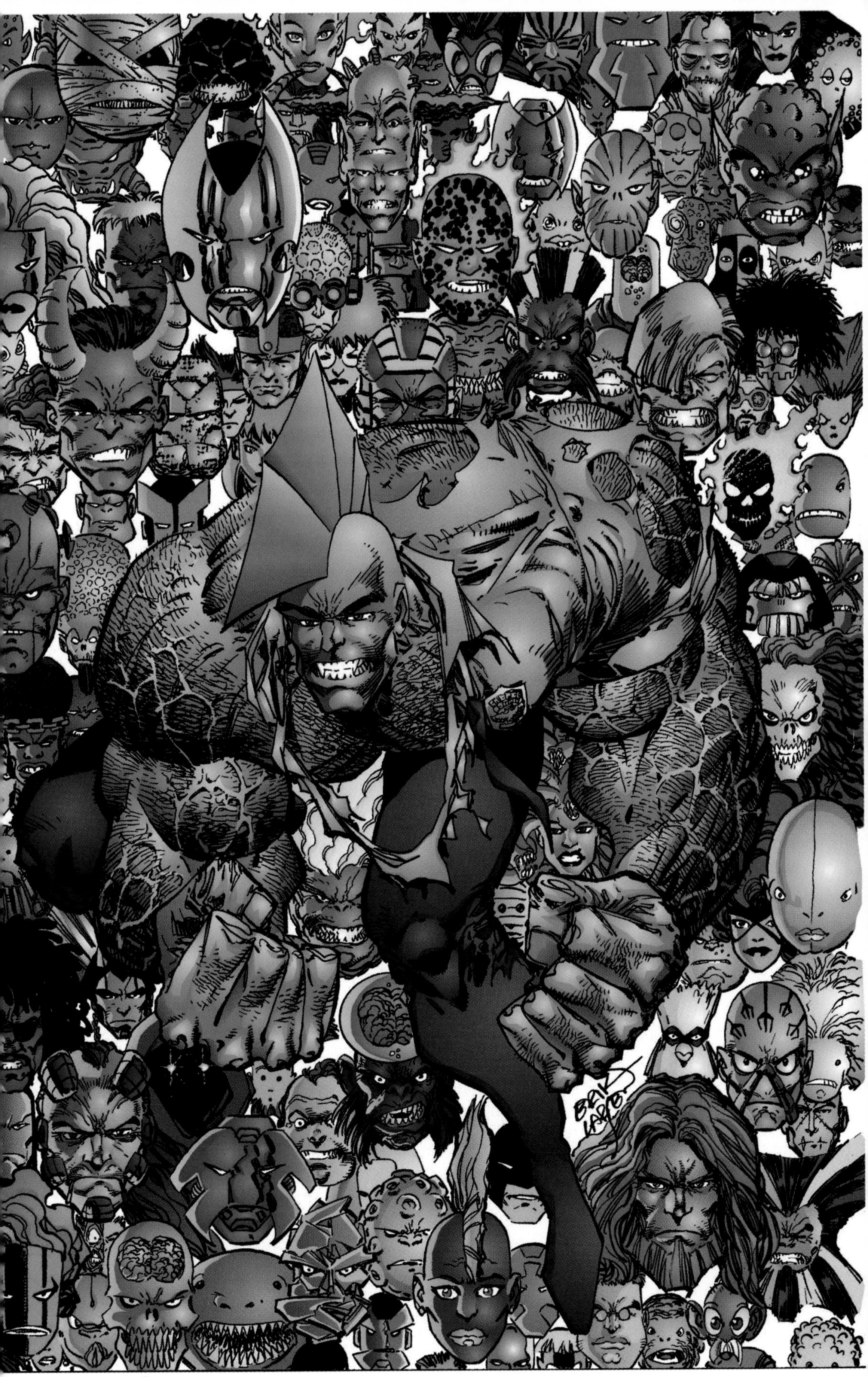

WHO'S WHO IN THE SAVAGE DRAGON.

1 DRAGON
2 SEA KING
3 RAZZ
4 BRUTE
5 CHAOS
6 CONTROL
7 ARACHNID
8 SUREFIRE
9 VOLCANIC
10 OVERLORD
11 CLIMAX
12 DOUBLEHEADER
13 CARCASS
14 MAMMOTH
15 DEMOLISHER
16 TORMENT
17 WRECKAGE
18 BODY COUNT
19 TOASTMASTER
20 RAVISH
21 GATEWAY
22 ABNER CADAVER
23 VIRAGO
24 SUDDS
25 ANARCHY
26 MEGATECH
27 STIGMA
28 RAW DOG
29 TOXIC
30 BUD UGLY
31 BASHER
32 VEIN
33 NEUTRON BOB
34 SUPER-X
35 NEGATE
36 HARDASS
37 BULLDOZER
38 INFERNO
39 BABY FACE
40 BRAIN-0
41 EVIL EYE
42 BANDIT
43 MANEATER
44 MOREGORE
45 JOLT
46 RAPIDFIRE
47 RAGING WOODY
48 ANIMAL
49 FURIOUS GEORGE
50 GATOR
51 ULTIMATUM
52 FADE
53 LIGHTNING BUG
54 SUB-HUMAN
55 ROADBLOCK
56 IMPOSTER
57 CHICAGO BULL
58 INTRUDER
59 WAR HAWK
60 FISH FACE
61 BRAINWAVE
62 ROUGHNECK
63 PHATHEAD
64 NUKE RAGE
65 SLAB
66 WAR GOD
67 BABYFACE
68 CUTTHROAT
69 HELLRAZOR
70 ASSASSIN
71 CYBERFACE
72 HORDE
73 MISFIT
74 VANDAL
75 SHAGGYMANE
76 SEDUCTRESS
77 REDNECK
78 HALFBAD
79 MINDWARP
80 MAKO
81 DOWNLOAD
82 DUNG
83 BRAINIAPE
84 THE FIEND
85 FEVER
86 HAZARD
87 ORACLE
88 SHARD
89 CESSPOOL
90 BRAWN
91 MACE
92 ARTILLERY
93 SHE-DRAGON
94 BLOOP
95 WARFARE
96 STRONGARM
97 OCTOPUS
98 SCRAG
99 MELVIN MOUSE
100 JOHNNY REDBEARD
101 LOWBLOW
102 HARDWARE
103 POWERHOUSE
104 UNDERMIND
105 TECH
106 PLAGUE
107 WILDHAIR
108 OPENFACE
109 SKULLFACE
110 BLUDGEON
111 WASHOUT
112 WEED
113 DEATHMASK
114 KILLER WHALE
115 BUBBLE BOY

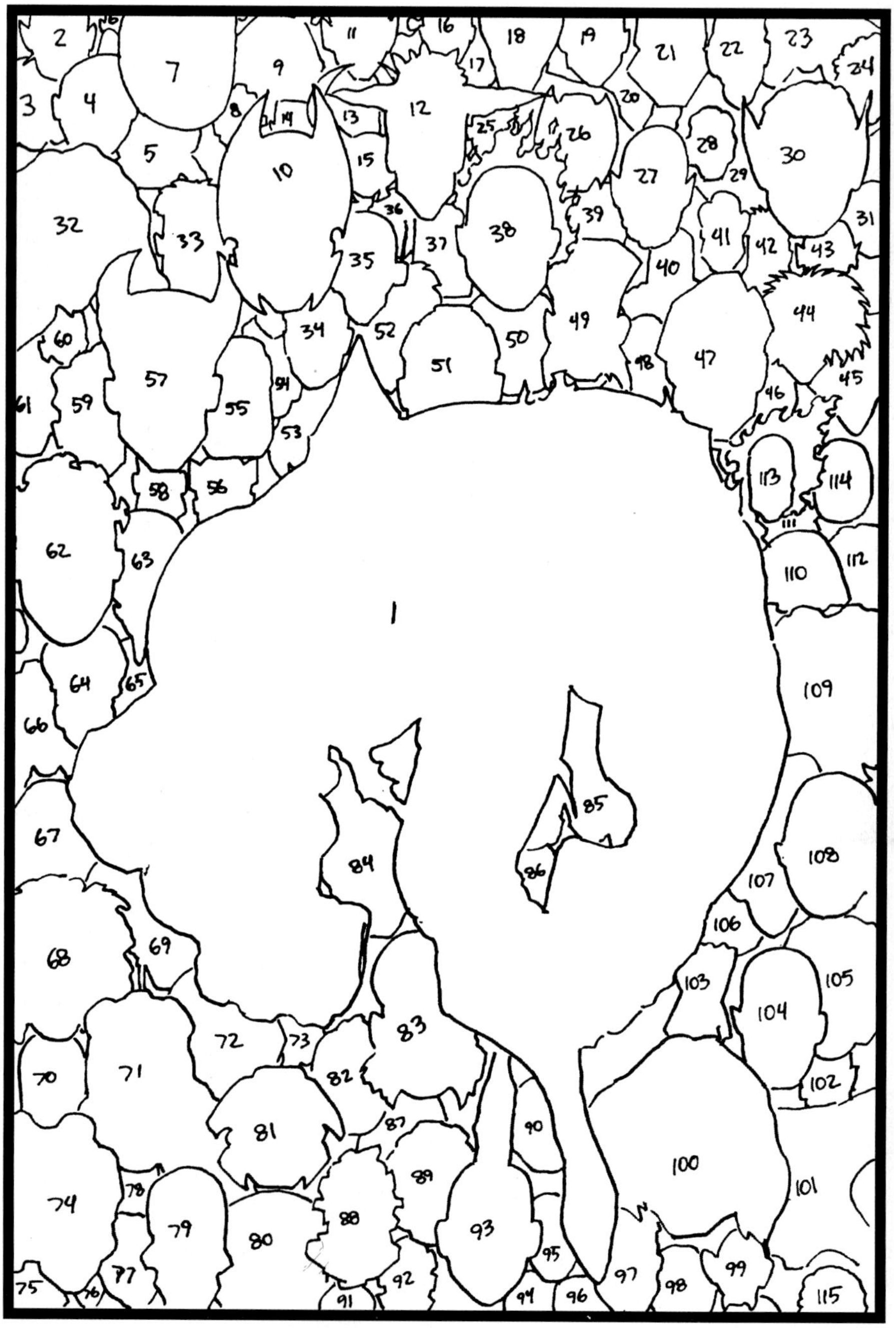